A GUIDE TO ARCHIGRAM 1961-74

建築電訊 指南 1961-74

GARDEN CITY

ARCHIGRAM
建築電訊

六○年代建築次團體
Experimental Architecture 1961-74
2003.03.15 - 06.08

策展人／Curated by   丹尼斯・克藍普頓／Dennis Crompton

主辦／Organized by   臺北市立美術館 TAIPEI FINE ARTS MUSEUM ／ARCHIGRAM ARCHIVES

協助／Supported by   BRITISH COUNCIL 英國文化協會

贊助／Sponsored by   台北市建築師公會 Association of Architects, Taipei

葉榮嘉建築師事務所 GLORY YEH ARCHITECTS & ASSOCIATES

agnès b.

A Guide to Archigram   1961-74

ISBN：957-0406-96-8
Organizer：Taipei Fine Arts Museum ARCHIGRAM ARCHIVES
Commissioner：Tsai-Lang Huang ARCHIGRAM ARCHIVES
Curator：Dennis Crompton
Chief Curator：Fang-wei Chang
Assistant Curators：Tsun-ling Liao, June Chu
Exhibition Display：Chien-hua Feng, Chiung-yu Chen, Tai-shen Chia, Hsiu-ying Lu, Pao-nan Pai
International Relations：Hui-ru Hu, Li-wei Lu
Information Technology Department：Chaoy-ing Wu, Chien-nan Liao
Exhibition Assistant：Eric Chang
Photographer：Dubby Tu, Chung-hsin Lin
Video and Lighting：Chung-chang Ho, Monkey Fan, Chen Chang-ping, Yu-cheng Chang, Yen-shan Chen, Tsai Feng-huang
General Affairs：Chien-jin Su, Tang-lien Cheng
Accountants：Ching-zau Hsu, Hsiu-chen Wu
Translators：Chaur-Shiahn Yeh, Yi-Ting Wu, Brent Heinrich

Art Editor：Lynne Lin, Janet Hsiao
Copy Editor：Sophie Hsi
Publisher：Kevin Chen, Garden City Publishing Ltd.
Address：9F No.5, Alley 2, Lane 14, Sec.1, Hangjou S. Rd., Taipei, Taiwan, R.O.C.
Tel：(02)23972551, (02)23972719
Fax：(02)23971843
Http：//www.gardencity.com.tw
E-mail：gardenct@ms14.hinet.net

建築電訊 指南　1961－74

ISBN	957-0406-96-8
策劃單位	台北市立美術館、ARCHIGRAM ARCHIVES
總 召 集	黃才郎
策 展 人	丹尼斯・克藍普頓
展覽督導	張芳薇
執行策劃	廖春鈴 朱紀蓉
展覽佈置	馮健華 陳瓊瑜 賈台生 盧秀英 白寶南
公 　關	胡慧如 盧立偉
資訊小組	吳昭瑩 廖健男
展務協助	張至維
攝 　影	杜宗尚 林宗興
錄影及燈光	何仲昌 范文芳 陳昌平 張裕政 陳燕山 蔡鳳凰
總 　務	蘇乾金 鄭鏗聯
會 　計	許金兆 吳秀珍
翻 　譯	葉朝憲 吳伊婷 韓伯龍
藝術編輯	林銀玲 蕭瑾儀
執行編輯	席 芬
發 行 人	陳炳檥
發 行 所	田園城市文化事業有限公司
地 　址	100 台北市中正區杭州南路一段14巷2弄5號9樓
電 　話	(02)23972551, (02)23972719
傳 　真	(02)23971843
製 　版	象傑製版有限公司 (02)22268661
印 　刷	廣鑫印刷有限公司
定 　價	300元
登 記 證	新聞局局版台業字第6314號
郵政劃撥	19091744
戶 　名	田園城市文化事業有限公司
初版一刷	中華民國 92 年 3 月
網 　址	www.gardencity.com.tw
電子信箱	gardenct@ms14.hinet.net

First published in Great Britain in 1994 by
ACADEMY EDITIONS
An imprint of Academy Group Ltd.

©Archigram Archives

Chinese edition ©Garden City Publishing Ltd., 2003,
arranged with Archigram Archive through Shelley Power
Literary Agency Ltd., France

國家圖書館出版品預行編目資料

建築電訊指南 1961-74／Warren Chalk等作；
葉朝憲、吳依婷譯，——初版，——臺北市：
田園城市文化，民92
　　面；　　公分
譯自：A guide to Archigram, 1961-74
ISBN：957-0406-96-8（平裝）

1. 建築——西洋——20世紀

923.408　　　　　　　　　　　92002847

A GUIDE TO ARCHIGRAM 1961-74

建築電訊 指南 1961-74

A GUIDE TO ARCHIGRAM 1961-74

建築電訊 指南 1961-74

CONTENTS

目錄

1970

ARCHIGRAM
THE TRUE STORY TOLD BY PETER COOK
AROUND THE END OF THE 1950'S THERE WERE SOME FANTASTIC STUFF GOING ON... SUCH AS MIKE WEBB'S FURNITURE FACTORY WHICH WAS CALLED 'BOWEL-ISM' BY REYNER BANHAM
FOR OBVIOUS REASONS!
DAVID GREENE AND I GOT TO KNOW MIKE AND USED TO MEET UP PRETTY REGULARLY IN A 'GREASY SPOON' CAFF AT Swiss Cottage
WHY DON'T WE PUBLISH THE CHECKAN STUFF
WOT'S BEING BUILT NOW'S BORING

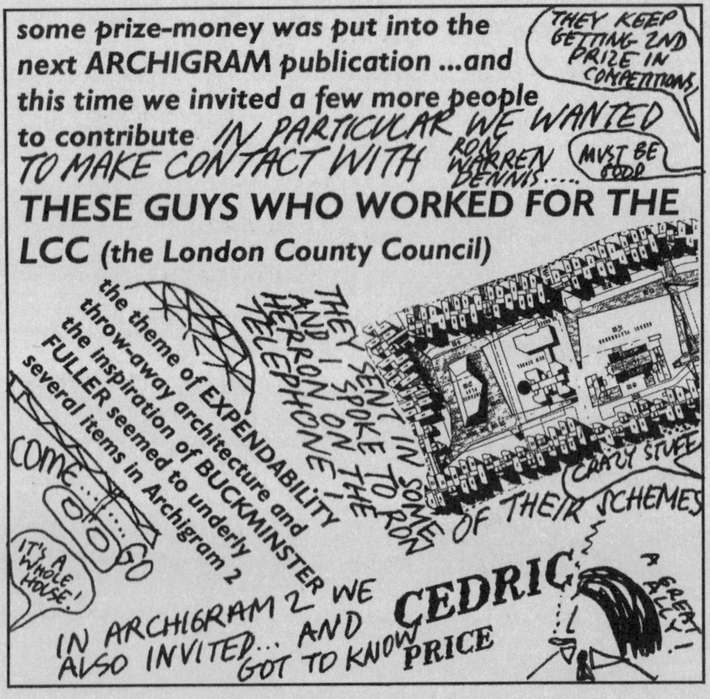

some prize-money was put into the next ARCHIGRAM publication ...and this time we invited a few more people to contribute *IN PARTICULAR WE WANTED TO MAKE CONTACT WITH* RON WARREN DENNIS..... THESE GUYS WHO WORKED FOR THE LCC (the London County Council)

THEY KEEP GETTING 2ND PRIZE IN COMPETITIONS

MUST BE GOOD

the theme of EXPENDABILITY throw-away architecture and the inspiration of BUCKMINSTER FULLER seemed to underly several items in Archigram 2

THEY SENT IN SOME AND I SPOKE TO RON HERRON ON THE TELEPHONE

CRAZY STUFF OF THEIR SCHEMES

COME...

IT'S A WHOLE HOUSE!

IN ARCHIGRAM 2 WE ALSO INVITED... AND GOT TO KNOW **CEDRIC** PRICE

A PRETTY...!

14

THEN I GOT THIS PHONE CALL ... "DO YOU WANT TO COME AND WORK ON THIS SCHEME FOR EUSTON?" IT WAS THED CROSBY (THEN AT TAYLOR WOODROW)

RON Herron
WARREN Chalk
and **DENNIS** Crompton
were already there.........
DAVID Greene,
Mike Webb and I joined

THED MOVED AROUND US SLIGHTLY BEMUSED

AND THE THREE OF US WHO WERE STILL ONLY A COUPLE OF YEARS OUT OF SCHOOL WERE STILL A BIT IN AWE OF RON WARREN AND DENNIS WHO HAD BUILT STUFF!

The Euston office became a good place for the two groups to get to know each other and.....

Mike would make these old space cities under his drawing board...

15

Theo Crosby suggested that we could do an exhibition about cities at the Institute of Contemporary Arts AND THAT IS HOW WE CAME TO DO THE EXHIBITION

LIVING CITY

WE LEARNED TO WELD
WE LEARNED TO GLUE
WE LEARNED TO FIX SWITCHES

THE LCC GROUP AND THE SWISS COTTAGE EATERS EFFECTIVELY BECAME ONE GROUP

IMPERCEPTIBLE LINKS WERE MADE AS WE WORKED ON THE EXHIBITION AND WE TALKED AND WE TALKED AND TALKED

ABOUT ART
ABOUT CITIES
ABOUT CYBERNETICS
ABOUT INVENTIONS
ABOUT ROBOTS
ABOUT AMERICANA

DENNIS WAS THE ONE WHO KNEW HOW TO MAKE THE RUBBER GROMMETS AND SWITCHES AND WE ALL DID BITS OF THE 'GLOOPS' WITHIN THE ENVELOPE

REYNER BANHAM WAS THE FIRST SERIOUS PERSON TO NOTICE US AND TALKED ABOUT THE WORK OF THE ARCHIGRAM GROUP

Funnily enough , we ourselves didn't call ouselves that name but more and mored other people did...so one day we said 'what the hell'...and made a letterhead with "ARCHIGRAM GROUP" on it...and there we were....

ARCHIGRAM 4 WAS THE FLAG FOR WHAT BECAME

AMAZING ARCHIGRAM 4

A HIGH PERIOD OF... NOT ONLY SLOGANS BUT.........

SOMETIMES INDIVIDUAL

SOMETIMES DONE BY THE WHOLE GANG

SCHEMES

ALWAYS DISCUSSED

THAT'S WHAT ARCHIGRAM HAS ALWAYS BEEN ABOUT

館長序

去年(2002)本館所舉辦的「科比意」展,對於國內已隱然成形的「建築展」話題,起了推波助瀾之效,也呼應了現下建築與當代藝術緊密互動的趨勢。當此風潮,「建築電訊」的推出,除再次凸顯出建築與視覺藝術之間交錯的關係之外,「建築電訊」獨特的建築理念,勢必將為本地對於建築文化的討論注入新意,掀起另一波「建築」熱潮。

「建築電訊」此一建築團體崛起於六○年代初期,他們以倫敦為據點,主要活躍的舞台是與團體同名的雜誌《建築電訊》。《建築電訊》發行期間從 1961 至 1974年,前衛性的建築設計與都市計畫結合實驗性的編輯風格,迥異於當時主流的建築雜誌,自樹一格。雖然他們大膽的、烏托邦式的建築提案,在當時並未實現,然而他們倡議的建築理念,大大擴展了建築的視野,直接或間接地影響了日後建築的觀點與空間的概念。

本展即是要以「建築電訊」在六○年代至七○年代初所提各種預言式提案,引領觀眾領略「建築電訊」建築理念所具有的前瞻性。在當時「大眾消費時代」、「太空時代」與「資訊時代」降臨的衝擊之下,「建築電訊」力陳以新的思維方式加以回應,因為既有建築的「金科玉律」已不足因應新時代的需求。面對不斷推陳出新的科學技術,主張應加以整合運用於未來都市與都會生活的設計當中。

「建築電訊」提案中所蘊含的多重意涵,尤其是在時代脈絡的對照之下,更加彰顯。無論是從政治經濟、科技、藝術的,乃至次文化領域的電影、時尚、流行音樂的角度,其表現充分展露出他們敏銳的時代感受力與洞察力。他們所發展的充滿趣味、奇想的建築風貌,至今仍令人津津樂道。

本展要特別感謝英國倫敦「建築電訊檔案中心」(Archigram Archives)提供三百餘件素描作品與十二件建築模型,呈現「建築電訊」所標榜的觀念與視覺化的案例。此外,也要感謝策展人丹尼斯‧克蘭普頓先生重新結合「建築電訊」重要的設計元素,精心規劃展場。最後,對於贊助展覽經費的英國文化協會、台北建築師公會、葉榮嘉建築師事務所,以及參與推廣教育活動的建築界朋友,在此致上最誠摯的謝忱,他們的熱誠付出使本展得以順利推出。

台北市立美術館館長

黃才郎

18

FOREWORD

Last year the exhibition "Le Corbusier" held by the Taipei Fine Arts Museum fanned the fires of enthusiasm for exhibitions on architecture that was already quietly taking shape in Taiwan, echoing the trend of close interaction between current architecture and contemporary art. With this on-going wave of interest, the presentation of "Archigram" once again underscores the interlocking relationship between architecture and the visual arts. Furthermore, the unique ideas of Archigram are bound to infuse new insights into local reflections on architectural culture, stirring up a new wave of fascination with architecture.

The architectural group "Archigram" rose in the early 1960s. They were based in London, and the main stage for their activities was the magazine that shared their name, *Archigram*. Published from 1961 to 1974, its avant-garde architectural designs and urban plans, combined with an experimental editing style, ran counter to the mainstream architectural magazines of the era, a unique phenomenon. Although their bold, utopian proposals were rarely brought to fruition at the time, the ideas they championed greatly expanded the vision of architecture, directly or indirectly influencing the architectural perspectives and spatial concepts that were to follow.

By presenting the many prophetic plans proposed by Archigram during the 1960s and early 1970s, this exhibition attempts to give visitors a taste of the forward-looking nature of Archigram's ideas. Impacted by the arrival of the "mass consumer age," the "space age" and the "information age," Archigram advocated responding with new thought, because the "immutable laws" of existing architecture were already insufficient to respond to the demands of the new age. With the constant introduction of new science and technology, they advocated applying it in an integrated fashion to the future design of cities and urban life.

The great meaningfulness of Archigram's proposals, particularly shown in the light of passing time, is most evident. Whether it be from the perspective of politics, economics, technology, art, or even the realms of underground film, fashion and pop music, Archigram's achievements fully reveal their acute sensitivity and insight into their times. The highly intriguing and imaginative style of architecture they developed remains a topic discussed with relish to this day.

The Taipei Fine Arts Museum wishes to extend special thanks to the Archigram Archives for providing more than 300 sketches and 14 architectural models, depicting the viewpoints upheld by Archigram, and their many visual examples. In addition, we also wish to thank exhibition curator Mr. Dennis Crompton for bringing together the major design elements of Archigram in a fresh way, and meticulously planning this exhibition. Finally, we would like to give our most sincere thanks to British Council, Glory Yeh Architects & Associate and Association of Architects Taipei, for financial support for this exhibition, and our many friends from the architectural community who participated in related educational activities. Their enthusiastic contributions helped to make this exhibition a splendid success.

Huang Tsai-lang
Director, Taipei Fine Arts Museum

SOME NOTES ON THE ARCHIGRAM SYNDROME

Peter Cook   *PERSPECTA*, Supplement no. 11, Yale 1967

ARCHITECTURE

THE NAME AND THE MAGAZINE

Why Archigram? It comes from the original desire not to put out a regularised and predictable 'magazine' with lots of pages and a cover, but to push out, excrete (almost) a thing that would explode upon the oppressed assistants in London offices and the students in the shape of a large piece of

彼得・庫克 《觀點》，第11期增刊，耶魯大學，1967年

...TELE GRAM

名稱與雜誌

為何稱為「建築電訊」？此想法的原始希求是不希望出版一本具有眾多篇幅頁數與封面之規範化且可預期的「雜誌」；而是以一張海報、影像拼貼或小冊子……等任何當時所需之形式，

poster, collage of images, or booklet . . . whatever was necessary at the time. Hence the need for a name that was more analogous to a thing like a message or some abstract communication, telegram, aerogramme, etc.

The first *Archigram* was a sheet, with some D. Greene poems. After this utterance, brushed off by the few senior architects who saw it as a student joke, and only selling (at the time) 300 copies, everybody thought it would die a natural death. The next *Archigram* came a year (and three competitions) later. Much more formal, with pages, typesetting and the convenience of stapled ends, it had a project and a statement from several different young architects, not all similar, but presenting an otherwise unheard viewpoint. The AA's 'Christian Weirdies' (a medievalist group), Cedric Price and ourselves were included together.

The beginnings of the instinct towards a consideration of expendability as a serious motive for a way of building came at this point. Half the schemes in the magazine were concerned in some way with throwaway, though there had not been any collusion or discussion. This came later. Certainly by the time of the third *Archigram* it was a central issue.

The fourth *Archigram* had become the mouthpiece of the larger, combined group and the issue was largely the work of Warren Chalk. Like the first *Archigram*, it upset a lot of people who still felt that architecture was some-how a sacred discipline that should not be played with and certainly not placed at the same level as comics or

擠出、排泄（幾乎是）出某種可打破倫敦建築師事務所裡遭受壓制的助理與學生之迷思的東西。因此便需要一個更類似於某種信息或抽象通訊，諸如電報、航空郵簡……等的名稱。

第1期《建築電訊》只是一張紙，上面寫著一些大衛・葛林的詩。這次發聲之後，一些資深建築師們只視它為一個學生的玩笑而不當一回事，而且只賣出300份，大家都認為它會自然地陣亡。第2期《建築電訊》（及3個競圖）於一年之後出現。更正式些、更多的篇幅頁數、打字排版、舒適的裝訂……這期雜誌有個設計案與一篇來自幾位不盡相同年輕建築師的聲明，代表著另類未被聽見的觀點。建築聯盟建築學院的「基督怪徒」（一個研究中古世紀者的團體）、賽卓克・普萊斯與我們自己都是成員之一。

一開始即本能地朝向視消費性為建造方式之嚴肅動機這個主題上。雖然沒有任何的事先串通或討論，但雜誌中半數的方案就某方面而言都是與用後即丟棄的概念有關。它出版地稍遲一些。無疑地在第3本《建築電訊》出版之前，它是相當重要的一期。

第4期《建築電訊》變成了規模更大之結盟團體的傳聲筒，大部份內容以華倫・裘克的作品為主。就像第1期《建築電訊》一樣，它惹惱了許多仍視建築為神聖不可侵犯之學科、不該被嬉弄且擺在與連

things like that. The fifth *Archigram* was a more widespread document, in that the group had by this time begun to seek out allies in other countries whose work was very often close in spirit and (sometimes) form. The sixth issue took a look back at the neglected 1940s which really contained the breakthrough in prefabrication in England, and at the same time had a 'current scene' section introducing some of the first batch of students taught by Archigram people.

The next stage for the magazine is going to be more complex. The group's ways of demonstrating its ideas are spreading. *Archigram* 7 (in the pipeline at the time of writing) is another 'manifesto' issue: in that the time has come to restate some fundamentals of the Archigram point of view that is now, with increased exposure, constantly being misinterpreted. The second stage has arrived. The detail of the technology and methods can now be stated. There is a growing number of younger architects who accept many of the points made in the early stages about expendability, the need to think of architecture not as a tight discipline, the need to regard the city, or whatever replaces it, not necessarily a series of 'buildings' as such, but as an infinitely intermeshed series of happenings, and the need to look at housing more as an extension of human emancipation and sustenance, rather than the provision of 'houses'.

Archigram 7 is going to be a tough hard, document. But the Archigram Group is too optimistic not to include the

環漫畫之流的東西同一層次的人。第5期《建築電訊》的銷售更為普及,於此之前團體成員已開始於其它國家中找出作品之精神及(某些時候)形式與其相當接近的同好。第6期雜誌則回顧遭忽略且事實上包含了英國組合式房屋組件之突破的1940年代,同時闢有〈即時傳真〉一章以介紹一些「建築電訊」成員的首批學生。

雜誌的下個階段將更複雜。團體表達構想的方式正廣為流傳。《建築電訊》第7期(當時正籌備中)則是另一份「宣言」版本:隨著「建築電訊」的日益曝光與持續遭受誤解,此時正是重申「建築電訊」觀點之某些原則的時候。第二階段已翩然到來。科技與方法的細節現在可以說明了。越來越多的年輕建築師接受早先提及的「消費性」觀點,無須視建築為嚴苛的學科,而須顧及城市,或任何可取代它的東西,無須是一系列的建築物,而是一連串相互無限嚙合的事件,且須視住宅為人類解放與本體的外延,而非「房舍」的提供。

《建築電訊》第 7期將會是份嚴峻無情的紀錄。可是「建築電訊」團體太過樂觀,而未將可提供一更寬廣立場以深入相關細節問題之探索的最新提案及一些「第二代」作品納入其中。

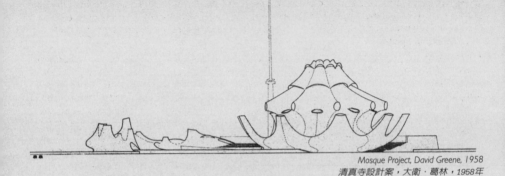

Mosque Project, David Greene, 1958
清真寺設計案，大衛·葛林，1958年

latest proposals and some of the work of the 'second' generation that is providing a wider front of investigation into the detail problems involved.

ARCHITECTURE AND THE CHANGING SCENE 1961-66

The first Archigram was an outburst against the crap going up in London, against the attitude of a continuing European tradition of well-mannered but gutless architecture that had absorbed the label 'Modern', but had betrayed most of the philosophies of the earliest 'Modern'. No one wanted to know. The middle period was a 'carry-on-laddie' stage, with Living City as a nutty object to amuse the West End art world. Its message was only heard by a few.

By bashing away at the architectural public in Archigram, but always being as concerned with the object as the idea, we became known by about 1964 as 'that lot'. Many young architects in London don't agree with us. They are often embarrassed by the fruitiness of the objects as much as by the undermining of the continuing story of architects' architecture which is implied. The fruit is really as much a basic necessity to the central idea as a list of priorities. It is easy enough to keep values abstract, to strategise without the battle being fought. Draw the object and you can discuss it: you can then change and develop it. Make it better.

We are often asked about the Pop imagery. We are not really concerned about its connection or lack of connection with the movement in painting, graphics. There must be a connection at a dynamic or historical level between us and the others.

建築與變化中的情勢 1961-66年

第1期《建築電訊》激烈地反擊倫敦甚囂塵上的一派胡言，反擊長久以來端正舉止但缺乏勇氣且貼著「現代」標籤，卻又背離大部份最早期之「現代」哲學的歐洲建築傳統。沒有人想知道。中期則是個「撐下去－年輕人！」的階段，將「生活城市」視為娛樂倫敦西區藝術界的瘋狂對象。此訊息只有少數人知曉。

藉由在《建築電訊》雜誌裡痛擊建築界，同時亦始終關切著物件與構想，我們大約自1964年起便以「那批傢伙」著稱。許多倫敦的年輕建築師並不認同我們。他們經常對我們於物件所作出的成果，以及在其中暗含了對於建築師所定義之建築的持續陳述之破壞感到侷促不安。然此結果實際上既是核心構想的基本需求，亦須列於優先名單之上。保持價值觀的抽象性與未經一番考驗的策略其實都簡單的很。畫出個物件，而後就可以討論它：然後可以改變並發展它。使它變得更好。

我們經常被問及普普意象的問題。事實上我們並不在乎它與繪畫及圖解中的情節變化是否具有關聯性。於動態或歷史的層面上，我們與他者之間必定存有某種關聯性。

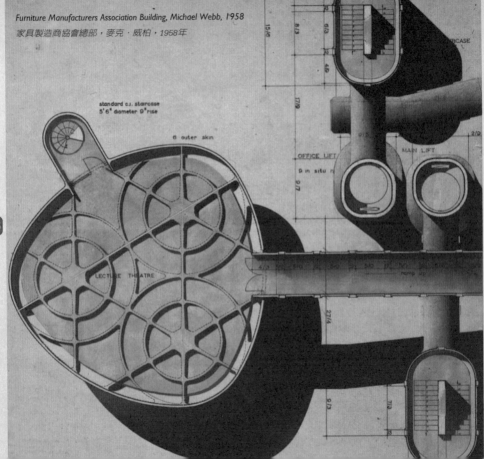

Furniture Manufacturers Association Building, Michael Webb, 1958
家具製造商協會總部，麥克·威柏，1958年

The pre-packaged frozen lunch is more important than Palladio. For one thing it is more basic. It is an expression of human requirement and the symbol of one efficient interpretation of that requirement that optimises the available technology and economy.

Similarly, the dwelling capsule reproduces the question and — technological — answer to a similar degree. The scale and complexity are larger, but the philosophical statement is the same. Does the pre-pack become a pre-ferred object? If it does, this might become merely a regeneration of the tradition of art symbolism in architecture. The Ionic column was a preferred object in its time. Tinfoil could become a preferred symbol now. In our most recent work we have become very aware of the need to jettison some of the parts (image-wise) as soon as they are no longer valid. Only then are we really interpreting the values as well as the symbols of an expend-able architecture.

There is now much more talk about 'plug-in' as an idea. Quite mainstream architects can be heard advocating changeable dwellings. We are now able to use television and other people's four-colour photogravure to describe what we are about. Some of our students (and we ourselves, I hope) are going to have to build throw-away capsules. But because we can be quoted or copied we don't want to become the playthings of a poor but sophisticated culture. We are not politically over-developed as a group, but there is a kind of central emancipato-

調理包的冷凍午餐比帕拉底歐更為重要。首先它是更基本的東西。這是人類需求的表現，亦是充分運用可利用之科技與經濟下，此需求之有效詮釋的象徵。

同樣地，某種程度上，住宅艙室再現了這個問題與——科技性的——答案。規模與複雜度更大些，但哲學性聲明卻是一致的。「預先包裝」是否變成一種偏愛的對象呢？如果是的話，這可能只不過變成建築中藝術象徵性傳統的再生罷了。愛奧尼亞柱式在當時是偏愛的對象。而錫箔紙可能已變成當下偏愛的表徵。在我們最近的作品中，我們變得十分警覺必須拋棄一些不再有效的元件（有關影像方面的）。唯有如此我們才能真正詮釋消費性建築的價值與象徵。

現在愈來愈多人論及視「插接」為一種構想。可聽到相當多的主流建築師們在鼓吹可變更住宅。現在我們可以利用電視與其他人的四色照相製版印刷來描述我們所做的事。一些我們的學生（還有我們自己，我希望）將必須建造可拋棄式艙室。但因為我們可能被引用或抄襲，我們並不想變成這貧瘠但複雜之文化的玩物。我們並非策略性地過度發展成一個團體，不過在我們大部分的方案背後都存有某種主要的解放驅策力。人類正處於真正理解自己的潛力或對於生存全然失去知覺的險境。特別是目前的英國，我們已警覺到必須運用機智來生活：人類必須自我創造以脫離他現狀中可怕的選擇，並自我

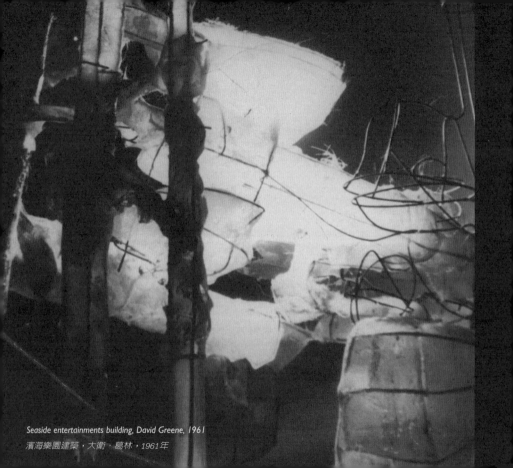

Seaside entertainments building, David Greene, 1961

濱海樂園建築，大衛．葛林，1961年

ry drive behind most of our schemes. Man is on the precipice of really realising his potential or passing out of existence completely. Especially in England at the moment, we are very aware of the need to live on our wits: man must invent himself out of the terrifying options of his situation and invent himself into a way of life that gives him real consumer choice. We are very interested in seeing our projects as consumer objects. The capsule house is very much a shop-bought object, its parts to be traded in and changed, to be juxtaposed almost infinitely. The nature of the 'place' will be transient in the definition of its parts, but the real personality of the owner will be able to come through much more easily. For 'house', read 'man'.

We sometimes use the techniques of the newspaper, the political rally or the academic. Archigram t-shirts sell very well. We are intensely involved in producing a curriculum in the AA's fifth year that reflects this broader humano-architecture and at the same time gets more work out of sophisticated but indolent students. One thrives on the discipline upon oneself to teach to the best of one's ability a student who is not interested in plug-in but wants to make nice brick houses in the European tradition. One does not attempt to convert him. The architectural tradition is a useful conversation; formal values of a kind that we ourselves do not rate are still discussible.

創造以進入能提供他真正消費者選擇的生活方式。我們非常樂於見到自己的設計案是消費性物件。艙屋正是可於商店中購得之物件,它的元件可以舊換新抵購與更換,幾乎可以無限地並置。「場所」的特質將是過渡性的,視其元件而定義,但其擁有者的個性將能更容易地展現出來。視其「人」,知其「屋」。

我們有時候會利用報紙、政治集會或學院式的技巧。「建築電訊」的運動衫賣得不錯。我們積極地參與制定建築聯盟建築學院中可反映這種更廣博之人性-建築的五年級課程,且同時由這群老練卻懶散的學生那裡獲得更多的作品。我們仍會盡最大力量去教導對於插接不感興趣而希望建造傳統歐洲漂亮磚屋的學生。我們並不想改變他們。建築傳統是有幫助的話題:某種勉強過得去的形式價值觀,我們本身評價雖不高,但仍可提出討論。

'IT'S ALL HAPPENING'

Perhaps a slightly passé phrase, but it is still all happening. Architecture is fun, and one isn't being superficial. Just take a few of the things we are involved in at the moment: the harnessing of the electric city as a controllable, clean, interchangeable, handy unit. The old battle between man, the road and the car may not ever be won; simply by-passed.

The electric car 6ft. × 4ft. 4in. can become not only a service to the front door — even if 30 storeys up — it can become a unit of the house itself. The chair can take off from the rugside and whistle down the path to the country or the drive-in downtown (or whatever takes its place). A home is not a house (Reyner Banham, 'Art in America' and he's dead right). Neither is a room a room, or a wall a wall, if we don't want it to be. The 'cage' dwelling is a recent series of schemes that plug and clip into the plug-in city, or anywhere for that matter; it has only a minimal structure from which can be hung trays, sub-capsules (the pre-pack lunch as opposed to the ice-box choice-mixture), cars or hoverchairs. It is a series of 'zones' rather than parts. It suggests certain situation coordinates rather than lines where hard objects have to remain. These coordinates suggest a series of options: hence the need to design series of tracks for screens, points in the floor from which we can get air to inflate the floor or screen sides. Furniture will disappear, like architecture. It is a categorisation that has become a preventa-

「一切都正在發生」

也許聽起來有點兒陳腔濫調了，但一切仍在發生中。建築是有趣的，而且我們並不膚淺。就拿此刻我們參與的一些事情為例：利用電力城市當作可控制、乾淨、可替換且近便的單元體。人類、道路與汽車間的舊戰役也許永無定論；只能略過。

6呎 ×4呎4吋的電動車不只是宅前──即使有30層樓高──的交通運輸設施而已，它本身也可以成為一個房屋單元體。椅子可從地毯邊出發並呼嘯前往鄉間小道或免下車式鬧區（或任何其它地方）。家不是房子（萊納・班漢，〈美國的藝術〉，他說得一點兒也沒錯）。房間也不再是房間，牆也不再是牆，如果我們不希望它們是的話。「籠式」住宅是最近一系列可以插或夾在插接城市或任何其它這類地方的方案；它只有最少的結構可以懸吊台架、次要艙室（相對於冷凍庫中各類選擇的調理包午餐）、汽車或氣墊椅。它是一系列的「區域」而非元件。它建議了某種情境座標而非硬體物件所必須維持之輪廓外型。這些座標建議了一系列的選擇：因此必須設計一系列的隔板軌道，以及我們可以取得空氣以充氣樓板或隔板的場所。家具將會消失，如同建築一般。這是一種已成了我們思想上預防性

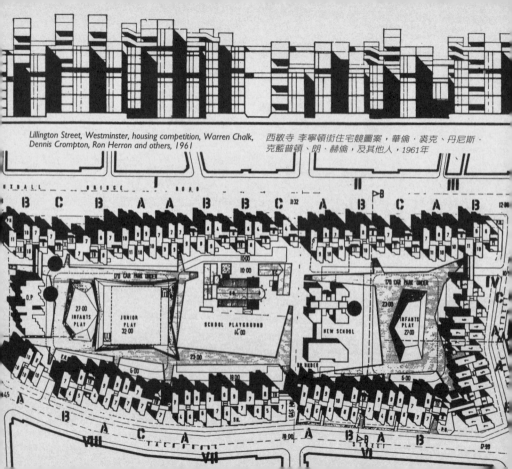

Lillington Street, Westminster, housing competition, Warren Chalk, Dennis Crompton, Ron Herron and others, 1961

西敏寺 李寧頓街住宅競圖案，華倫・裘克、丹尼斯・克藍普頓、朗・赫倫，及其他人，1961年

tive limit on our thinking, and has prevented people from really being given what they wanted or needed in the interests of some abstract tidiness.

The building can now really become an animal, with inflatables and hydraulics and the cheap, localised electric motor. It can grow: not only larger, but now smaller, different, better. The city is not only a series of incidents but a network of incidence. Christopher Alexander's 'City is not a Tree', in his cool mathematician's logical way, said what we had all been trying to think. Is it a coincidence that Plug-in City, Friedman's scheme and the Japanese helicoidal scheme were all concerned with the potential of the multilayer cage and the diagonal to respond to situations rather than to incarcerate events in flat, defined, boxes?

And now McLuhan . . . cries of 'It's what we've been saying' from the Archigram Group . . . No, Professor, we didn't say it first or anything, but it's more than coincidental. We are subject to the same pressures as the rest, after all.

IT'S ALL HAPPENING

的限制的類屬,並為了某種難言明的嚴整目的而阻止人們真正被賦予他們所想要的或所需要的。

建築物如今真正可以變成一隻擁有充氣式、油壓式與廉價、局部性電動馬達的動物了。它可以成長:不只可以更大,也可以更小、更不同且更好。城市不只是一連串的事件,也是事件的網狀系統。克里斯多夫·亞歷山大於他所著的《城市不是一棵樹》中,以冷靜的數學邏輯方式,提到了我們大家都一直在思索的事情。插接城市、費里得曼的計劃案以及日本的螺旋形計劃案全都專注於回應情境,而非將事件囚禁於乏味、限定的盒子裡之多層式龍艦與對角線的潛力,這些並非出於巧合。

而現在麥克魯漢……高喊著,「從『建築電訊』團體中所聽到的「是我們一直提到的」……」您搞錯了,教授,並非我們先提到的,但它並不僅止於是巧合而已。畢竟,我們與其他人承受了相同的壓力。

一切都正在發生

At the start of the new decade — Two dogs sent into orbit in a Soviet spaceship — First laser action developed in USA — 'Tiros', the world's first weather satellite, launched from Cape Canaveral — John F. Kennedy inaugurated as US President — East Germany builds Berlin wall — Soviet Cosmonaut Yuri Gargarin is the first man in space — US – failed invasion of Cuba at the 'Bay of Pigs' — The 'Pill' launched on the market — Tristan De Cunha volcano erupts, island evacuated — Russian ballet star Rudolf Nureyev defects to the West — France: Trouble with Algeria. General de Gaulle puts tanks on Paris streets — Last journey of Paris–Bucharest Orient Express train — UN General Secretary Dag Hammerskjöld is killed in aircrash — Ban the Bomb demonstrations increase — The Kennedys make popular visit to Paris — Adolf Eichman found guilty of war crimes to humanity — Sony launch first transistorised video recorder — The twist craze hits Britain — Fashionable fashion photographer David Bailey becomes prominent trend-setter — American writer Ernest Hemingway dies — Dag Hammerskjöld awarded Nobel Peace Prize posthumously — MUSIC — 'Let's Twist Again' — 'Moon River' — 'Calendar Girl' — PLAYS (THEATRE) — 'Beyond the Fringe' — 'Becket' — 'Oliver the Musical' — CINEMA — 'A Taste of Honey' — 'Westside Story' — 'Breakfast at Tiffanys' — BOOKS — 'Catch 22' — 'Burnt Out Case' — 'Rabbit Run' — 'Tropic of Cancer' — FASHION — Photographers and designers become one of the most emulated social groups.

新的十年開始－蘇聯太空船載兩隻狗環繞地球－雷射技術首度在美國發展運用－世界第一枚氣象衛星「新手」自卡納維爾角發射－約翰‧甘迺迪就任美國總統－東德築起柏林圍牆－蘇聯太空人尤利‧加加林首次進入太空－美國－入侵古巴失敗，是為「豬玀灣事件」－口服避孕藥上市－崔斯坦島火山爆發，全島人民疏散－蘇聯芭蕾明星魯道夫‧紐瑞耶夫投奔西方－法國：與阿爾及利亞紛爭中。戴高樂於巴黎街頭部署坦克－巴黎‧布加勒斯特東方快車開出最後一班車－聯合國秘書長道格‧漢默史寇德墜機身亡－大量取締炸彈示威－甘迺迪訪問巴黎造成轟動－納粹戰犯阿道夫‧艾希曼被判有罪－新力發表首款電晶體錄影機－妞妞舞狂熱席捲英國－時尚攝影師大衛‧貝利成為炙手可熱的流行先趨－美國作家厄涅斯特‧海明威辭世－達‧哈馬紹獲頒諾貝爾和平獎－**音樂**－《讓我們再扭扭》－《月河》－《日曆女郎》－**戲劇**－《超越邊緣》－《貝克特》－《奧立佛歌舞劇》－**電影**－《蜜糖的滋味》－《西城故事》－《第凡內早餐》－**出版**－《第22條軍規》－《懷抱中子》－《兔子快跑》－《北回歸

1961

The love is gone

The poetry in bricks is lost.

We want to drag into building some of the poetry of countdown,

orbital helmets, discord of mechanical body transportation methods

and leg walking

Love gone.

Lost

our fascinating intricate movings are

trapped in soggen brown packets all hidden all

art and front, no bone no love.

A new generation of architecture must arise with forms and spaces
which seems to reject the precepts of 'Modern' yet in fact
retains these precepts.

**WE HAVE CHOSEN TO BY PASS THE DECAYING BAUHAUS IMAGE
WHICH IS AN INSULT TO FUNCTIONALISM.**

you can roll out steel   any length

you can blow up a balloon   any size

you can mould plastic   any shape

blokes that built the Forth Bridge

THEY DIDN'T WORRY

you can roll out paper   any length

take Chamber's dictionary   THAT'S LONG

You can build concrete   any height

FLOW ?   water flows or doesn't or does

flow or not flows

YOU CAN WEAVE STRING   any mesh

TAKE THIS TABLE you've got a top there

top and four legs

you can sit IN it   you sit ON it,   UNDER it   or half under

David Greene, Archigram Issue One, 1961

愛已逝去。

　　　磚造的詩情已逝。

　　　我們想把一些倒數與環繞軌道之盃狀物的詩情勉強地插入建築物，

　　　機械軀體運輸方式與徒步不合

　　　　愛已逝。

　　　　　　失落

　　　　我們迷人的錯綜複雜感動

　　　　陷入了褐色包裹全都藏起來

　　　　　　藝術與立場，無骨無愛。

新一代的建築必須利用

似乎否決了「現代」的告誡然而事實上

仍保有這些告誡的形式與空間而甦醒。

我們選擇忽視有辱實用主義的

腐朽包浩斯影像

你可以將鋼延展至　　任何長度

你可以將汽球充氣至　　任何大小

你可以將塑膠鑄造成　　任何形狀

　　建造佛斯河橋的傢伙

　　　　　　他們並不擔心

你可以將紙延展至　任何長度

拿「騫柏司」字典來試　**那可長得很哩**

　　　　　　你可以將混凝土建造至　　任何高度

　　　　　　　流動？水流動或不流動或流動

　　　　　　　流動或不流動

　　　你可以將線織成　　任何網子

　　　　　取這張桌子你會有個桌面

　　　　　　桌面和四隻腳

　　　　　　你可以坐在裡面坐在上面，坐在下面或下面一半

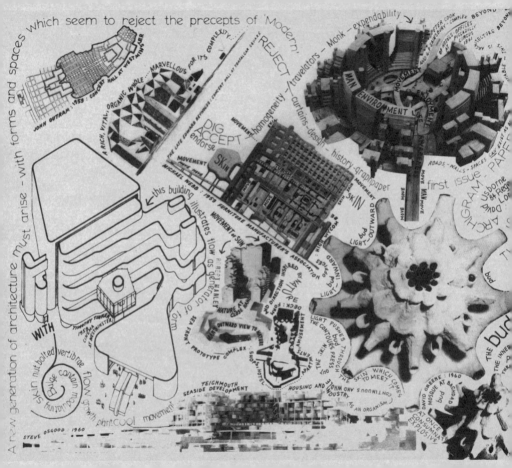

A new generation of architecture must arise - with forms and spaces which seem to reject the precepts of 'Modern'

JOHN OUTRAM : 1953 : CONCERT HALL AT WESTMINSTER

A RICH, VITAL, ORGANIC WHOLE ... MARVELLOUS FOR ITS COMPLEXITY ...

THE LATE EDWARDS BEYOND ... CONCERT HALL AT TRAFALGAR SQUARE

MICHAEL NEBB : 1953 FURNITURE MANUFACTURER'S ASSOCIATION

DIG ACCEPT endorse

MOVEMENT ... homogeneity ... REJECT ... travelators - Monk - expendability ...

curtains - design - history - graph paper

MOVEMENT

SKIN

MOVEMENT

HIGHWAY.COM

SKIN

PETER COOK ... complex beyond

OF HOTELS - OFFICES AND A SHOPPING COMPLEX BEYOND AT PICCADILLY

1961

ITCHITECTURE BEYOND

IS TO...

MAN ENVIRONMENT LIFE

MOVEMENT AND LIFE MOVEMENT

ROADS - WALLS - SPACES

MOVE M&N MOVE

first issue ...

Usborne & Regen DAVID

ARCHIGRAM PAPER

this building illustrates flow as generator of form

MOVEMENT of SUN

TIMOTHY TINKER 1958 AT WESTMINSTER

WITH

WE contain movement

skin nutbolted vertibrae flow containing growth plant cool movement

STEVE OSGOOD 1960

FIRST MANNER OF MAN

NO DIRECTION INSPIRED

DECK: POWER

NATURE AT MOVEMENT

SEA FRONT PROTOTYPE COMPLEX

OUTWARD VIEW TO

SHOPS - HOTEL

AMUSEMENT

TEIGNMOUTH SEASIDE DEVELOPMENT

HOUSING AND INDUSTRY

AS AN ORGANISM

bud LIGHT - OUTWARD

bud INWARD

LIGHT

LIGHT PUSHES THROUGH THE CONTOURS bud PRESS OUT THE SKIN WHICH COMES TO MEET IT

CONTINUOUS AND WHOLE AS AN ORGANISM

DAVID GREENE 1960 MOSQUE AT BAGDAD bud

ART ONCE CONSUMMATE CONSUMMATE EXPLOSIVE

THE INNER

THE bud

THE FUTURE OF ARCHITECTURE LIES IN THE BRAIN*
*ARCHIGRAM GROUP

Pascal Schöning

建築的未來取決於大腦*
*「建築電訊」團體

帕斯卡・休寧

Le Corbusier spent the last two years of his life mainly in the smaller of his two huts in Cap Martin. This small cabin stood on unspoilt natural ground, close to the other cabin and about 50 metres from the shore of the Mediterranean. This was his favoured place. It was just big enough to hold a drawing table under its window. From there, in good weather conditions, one could see as far as Corsica over the mirror of the sea, where the sky joined the water. Outside, the space one could embrace was endless; inside, it was reduced to what was absolutely essential.

A few years after Le Corbusier drowned in the wide sea, a small capsule landed on the moon and man set foot there for the first time. The dimensions of the capsule were reduced to the absolute essential. From the window of its cabin one could see, in clear weather conditions, the planet Earth. The space one could embrace was endless. All possible horizons were joined.

Some years before these events a small group of young architects in London came together and started to formulate their visions of space and time on a universal scale. They postulated: 'The future of architecture lies in the brain.' This was the kind of complex thinking that Buckminster Fuller had called for when he questioned why no architect had been involved in the American space programme (whereas he, as an engineer, had for years been developing complex architectonic visions at all scales). Fuller also introduced the idea that architecture should be flexible, making use of advanced technology and reacting to the changing needs of its users. The Archigram group set out to find possible means to join space and time, to combine the ideas of living and housing with the changing needs of different societies.

Corb's cabin was made out of plywood and Eternit; it stayed where it was built. The lunar capsule was the epitome of High-Tech; it was designed to move and to respond flexibly to extremely unpredictable conditions. Fuller's visions were a kind of space programme for the planet Earth. Archigram combined all of these aspects in their vision of an architecture of the mind.

For Archigram, it was the human brain – a collection of cells with an extraordinarily high concentration of absolutely essential functions and energy – that allowed the most far-reaching imagining of dimensions. This idea was confirmed by the insights of astrophysics in other spheres. Micro- and macro-space were mutually dependent – as demonstrated by the fact that mankind needed a small concentrated cell in order to reach out into the universe.

A complex thought may be bigger than the universe. The design of a computer's circuitry is as complex as the ideal network of a city or a global communications system, and it should be as flexible as the brain. The realisation that there were as many dimensions as could be imagined was one of the main creative achievements of Archigram. Besides the three classical dimensions of architecture, they took into account the dimension of time.

No other movement had so uncompromisingly incorporated hitherto unseen, unrealised values, images and thoughts. Archigram produced structures that changed like a change of mind, like the development of an idea, a thought. Their architecture was a direct output of what you could think, what you wished to think, do, feel, imagine – a motor activity of the psyche, the mind, the senses, ideas acted out, reacted to, changed, and then done again. There was an immense *acceleration* in process from Le Corbusier to Buckminster Fuller to the space programme to Archigram. This meant that the group had to install a language of its own, with no references to the classical ideals of traditional architecture; a language of acceleration of geometry, structure and function; a language which used the known ingredients – image, thought, function – in a mind-blowing way; a language misread by most architects (then and since).

While the architects of the Modern Movement also tried to discover new dimensions of space and time, they

柯比意在過世的前2年，主要待在他位於馬汀山頂的2棟小屋中較小的一棟。這棟小屋矗立於未遭破壞的自然環境中，鄰近另一棟小屋且距離地中海岸約55米遠。這是他最喜歡的地方。空間大到足以容納一張圖桌於窗口下。天氣好的話，可以從窗口看到海平面那頭的科西嘉島，海天連成一線。外部可擁抱的空間無限，內部則將空間精減至最基本。

柯比意溺斃於寬闊的海洋數年後，小型太空艙首度登陸月球且人類也踏出了第一步。太空艙的大小精減至最基本。天氣好的話，可以從艙室的窗口看到地球。人們可擁抱的空間無限。所有可能的水平線全部結合在一起。

這些事件發生之前，有一小群倫敦的年輕建築師們聚在一起，並自宇宙的尺度開始有系統地闡述他們對於空間與時間的觀點。他們提出假設：「建築的未來取決於大腦。」此即為當布克敏斯特‧富勒詰問為何沒有建築師參與美國的太空計畫時（身為工程師的他，數年來已持續地發展了各種尺度的複雜建築術的觀點），所要求的複雜思考。富勒也引薦了建築必須具備彈性，且利用先進科技並回應使用者之變化需求的觀念。「建築電訊」團體著手尋找結合空間與時間的可能方式，將生活與住宅及不同社會的變化需求的構想連結在一起。

柯比意的小屋是以三夾板及「艾特尼特」屋瓦所築成；它停留於被建造之處。登月太空艙是高科技的縮影；它被設計為可根據極不可預知的狀況而彈性地移動與反應。傅勒的觀點為某種地球的太空計畫。「建築電訊」心目中的建築想像兼具了所有這些面貌。

對「建築電訊」而言，人腦才能——具備絕對必要之機能與能量的極高度集中的細胞聚合——允許最深遠的次元想像。這種觀念已由其它領域中的天體物理學洞察所證實。巨－微空間相互依存——正如人類需要小型集中的細胞以延伸至宇宙的事實所示。

複雜的思緒或許遠大於浩瀚宇宙。電腦的電路設計就像城市的典型聯絡網或全球通訊系統般複雜，而且它應該像大腦一樣具有彈性。瞭解到存在任何想像得到的次元是「建築電訊」的主要創造性成就之一。除了建築的三個典型次元外，他們亦考慮到時間的次元。

迄今尚無其它運動如此不妥協地結合不可見及未意識到的價值觀、影像與構想。「建築電訊」創造了如同意見的改變及觀念或構想的發展般變化的結構。他們的建築是您所能想到與所希望想到、做到、感受到及想像到的直接產品——某種精神、心智、感覺的驅動活動，及構想的行動表現、反應、變化與重複。自柯比意至布克敏斯特‧富勒至太空計畫至「建築電訊」的過程中，存有極劇的加速。這意味著該團體必須設置自己的語彙，而不參照傳統建築的典型語彙；某種促進幾何學、結構與機能的語

limited themselves to static solutions. Only Archigram viewed the process itself as a motor capable of giving developments their own accelerating dynamic. This was the only way to overthrow previous states of definition, to exchange pure Newtonian physics for modern multi-dimensional relationships. In this Archigram was at the forefront of the avant-garde, preparing the way for the appearance of High-Tech. Subsequent movements returned to relatively static solutions and slowed the acceleration down (to a dead stop, in the case of Post-Modernism).

'When you are looking for a solution to what you are told is an architectural problem – remember, it may not be a building.'

Any evaluation of an architectonic work must not stop at its visible dimensions, because architecture is a complex of space and time dimensions, which extend beyond the purely physical functional or visual qualities.

You can test the quality of a restaurant by ordering a glass of water and seeing how it is served. Are you asked if you would like it cooled, heated up, kept at a certain temperature? Are you offered ice and lemon separately? Do you get an extra napkin, is the glass itself absolutely clean, without a speck of dirt? What kind of glass is it – does it come on its own, or on a saucer and a little tray, and so on. You can gauge the quality of everything, from the water itself, to the process of serving, to the ambience of the place. Nothing can be falsified, each thing adds to the next, and the result is an accumulation, a process of acceleration rather like an avalanche. This is not just a summary, but a multiplication of one thing with every other thing – a process, more than a state.

Here, the choice of *sujet* is also interesting. Water is a basic material. To drink is an essential matter. In addition, the restaurant is a place of communication, of common activity. If one can describe the qualities of a *sujet* like a glass of water (instead of wine, for example, which may be rated more highly), one may conclude that the choice of *sujet* doesn't matter, so long as it is a choice. More important is what it can generate under specific circumstances. Pop Art showed that a can of Campbell's soup (Warhol) was as valid a *sujet* as a portrait (Dürer). Coming back to the glass of water, the restaurateur has also to know what water is good, and where to get it. The quality of the water itself depends on the source conditions and the means of processing. We may think of a glass of water as a minor thing – something we just go to the tap and take without even registering what we are doing – but we can see also how it can be part of an extensive chain of relations.

What then is architecture? Was the description of the restaurant scene already a description of aspects of architecture? How physical has it to be? Archigram proved that the *sujet* of architecture could be something other than the established norm, and in this, it was also part of the Pop culture experience.

Archigram's Space-Time-Communication: Family Outings into the Universe

Archigram's journeys through time and space were journeys through their own history of development. They were exploring, in search of understanding. Because everything was new, it had to be experienced anew. Only

彙，某種以令人興奮的方式，利用已知構成要素——影像、構想、機能——的語彙；某種遭受大部分建築師所誤解（當時與其後）的語彙。

當現代運動的建築師們亦試圖發現空間與時間的新次元時，他們自我設限於靜態的解決方法。唯有「建築電訊」將過程的本身視為足以提供其促進動態發展的發動機。此為顛覆過去定義的狀態，並以現代多次元關係交換純粹的牛頓物理學的唯一方法。就此方面而言，「建築電訊」可算是為高科技的登場暖身的前衛派先鋒。繼起的運動再度回歸至靜態的解決方法並減緩了加速。（直至完全停滯，就後現代主義的例子而言）。

「當您正尋求一個大家所謂之建築問題的答案時——必須牢記——答案也許不是一棟建築物。」

任何建築術作品的評估都不該只停留於其視覺次元，因為建築是空間與時間次元的複合體，可延伸超越純粹的實體機能性或視覺性特質。

您可以藉由點杯水並觀察其服務情況以鑑定一家餐廳的品質。他們是否問過您需要冷的、熱的或是溫的水嗎？他們是否將冰塊與檸檬片分開呢？您是否拿到額外的餐巾呢？玻璃非常乾淨嗎？是否一塵不染呢？哪種玻璃呢？它單獨或是伴著托碟與托盤之類的器皿供應給您呢？您可以評價每個細節的品質，自水的本身至服務的過程及場所的氛圍。任何事都無法造假，每件事都累加至下件事，其結果是一種累積，頗類似於雪崩的加速過程。這不只是摘要，也是一件事物與其它所有事物的加乘——是一種過程，而非狀態。

於此，主題的選擇亦十分有趣。水是基本的物質。喝水是必要的事。除此之外，餐廳是交流與公共活動的場所。若人們可以如形容一杯水般地形容一個主題的話（而非如酒這類可能高度評價之物），人們或可下結論說主體的選擇並不重要，只要是選擇即可。更重要的是某些特定情況下它所能引發的。普普藝術證明了金寶湯罐頭（安迪‧沃荷）與肖像（篤黑）是同樣有效的主體。回到那杯水的話題，餐廳老闆也必須知道何謂好水，且可由何處取得。水本身的品質視水源狀況與處理方式而定。我們可能視一杯水為日常生活中的瑣細——某種我們只需到水龍頭下取用，且甚至毫無察覺自己動作的東西——但我們也可以察看它如何能夠成為廣泛的關係鍊中的一部份。

那麼建築又是什麼呢？餐廳景致的描述已算是建築外貌的描述了嗎？它必須多麼實體性呢？「建築電訊」證明了建築的主體可以是某種既定規範以外的東西，且就此方面而言，它亦是普普文化經驗中的一部分。

「建築電訊」的空間－時間－通訊：進入宇宙的「家庭之旅」。

this was naive, and not their point of departure. They had all done their bit already: Warren, Ron and Dennis had worked as architects on several buildings of some size; Peter, David and Mike had developed their own distinct conception of the Modern Movement, starting the *Archi*(tecture-tele)*gram* magazine when relatively fresh out of school. They met when they all worked together for Taylor Woodrow Construction (thanks to Theo Crosby, on projects like Euston Station). They would stay late after work and escape into a free world of unlimited possibilities, driven by a romantic dream of a universal structure and means of expression, of a distinct society made up of distinct individuals. The way was prepared for them by Buckminster Fuller and the Independent Group. There was also a new sense of liberation in all sorts of fields: Pop Art, pop music, fashion, film, literature and relationships, space craft and computer technology – and London was the dynamic cultural centre of Europe.

The group seldom worked all together. Instead, each member would tend to develop his own proposals, which were then taken up by the others, with the addition of the Archigram *acceleration* effect. This was a natural way of working, given the fact that they were extreme individuals sharing similar interests. The effectiveness of their work came out of the high regard they had for each other, and the full acceptance of each member's input as part of the process of an Archigram project.

The group members themselves played different roles.

44

Warren Chalk, the oldest, was a kind of father figure: articulate, earnest and highly critical – so much so that he gave up designing in the end.

Ron Herron: impeccably practical, an outstanding designer and practitioner who based his work on very diverse interests.

Dennis Crompton: very much the man who transformed systems into practice, interested in all aspects of communication and production.

Peter Cook was the continuous formulator, designer and producer – and probably the main motor of the group.

David Greene was the sensitive artist – a painter, poet and thinker who maintained a critical distance from design.

Mike Webb was the genial outsider, continuously designing and thinking about the process of design.

Warren Chalk died in 1987. At the end of this text is a poem he gave to me in 1984 when we were teaching together at the AA. It is the last work I know by him.

All the other members are still teaching and working in their various fields (and sometimes collaborating on projects with each other).

「建築電訊」的穿越時空之旅亦即穿越他們自己的發展史之旅。他們探索以尋求理解。因為所有事都是新的，因此必須被重新體驗。只有這點是天真的，而絕非他們的出發點。華倫、朗與丹尼斯曾擔任建築師，完成過一些不同規模的建築物；而彼得、大衛與麥克則發展出他們自己獨特的現代運動概念，剛自學校畢業不久即創辦《建築電訊》雜誌。他們相遇於一起工作於泰勒•伍德洛營建公司時（歸功於西奧•克羅斯比，類似倫敦優仕頓車站的設計案）。他們下班後一起留在公司，遁入一個充滿無限可能性的自由國度，由宇宙結構與表達工具，以及獨特個體所組成的獨特社會，如此浪漫的夢想所驅動。布克敏斯特•富勒與「獨立團體」（由史密斯森、保羅濟、漢米爾頓……等人組成）已為他們備妥坦途。在各種領域裡也存有一股新的解放感：普普藝術、流行音樂、時尚、電影、文學、太空船及電腦科技——且倫敦是充滿活力的歐洲文化中心。

團體成員們並不常一起工作，而是由每位成員發展自己的提案，這些提案將由其他成員同時著手進行，但總帶著「建築電訊」特有的加速效應。對該團體而言這是極為自然的工作方式，因為他們都極度的個人主義且具有類似的興趣。他們作品令人印象深刻之處在於他們對彼此的高度尊重，並全然接受每位成員的意見為「建築電訊」設計案發展過程中的一部分。

團體成員分別扮演了不同的角色。

華倫•裘克，最年長，類似父執輩角色，表達清晰、嚴肅且具高度批判性——因此最後他放棄了設計。

朗•赫倫：絕對的實際，出色的設計師與從業者，其作品以多樣性興趣為基礎。

丹尼斯•克藍普頓：將系統轉為實行的能手，對所有通訊與製造方面的事物均感興趣。

彼得•庫克是位持續的表述者、設計師與製作者——且或許為團體的主要原動力。

大衛•葛林是位敏感的藝術家——與設計維持著某種批判性距離的畫家、詩人及思想家。

麥克•威柏是位溫和的局外人，持續地從事設計並對設計過程進行思考。

華倫•裘克於1987年辭世。本文的最後是一首他於1984年交給我的詩，當時我們一同任教於建築聯盟建築學院。此為據我所知他的遺作。

所有其他成員至今仍執教或工作於不同的領域（有時候也與彼此共同合作設計案）。

在相當短暫的期間裡，他們曾以團體的形式存在過（這包括當他們已分散於世界各地從事教職的那段

During the relatively short time they existed as a group (which includes the time when they were already spread out, teaching all over the world, but mainly in the USA, and they communicated by telegram, telecopy and telephone), the development of the different strands of their work was a process like that of growing up, as can be seen in four of their main project types.

The *megastructures* were social and psychological nets which allowed one to live in wider dimensions while secured by relatively defined roles, rules and signs (integrated within family and society). *Nomadic* architecture represented adventures in experiencing and testing social and psychological roles, rules and behaviour, and was related to personal definition (loosening the ties to family and society and growing to maturity). *Fun* architecture, was to make dreams come true, to help one find a niche in regulated, clearly defined fields (a release function, both private and public). *Metamorphosis* was to balance and integrate all the above aspects into a process system, which dissolved through interference at the same time as it stabilised the network (selected integration and division of roles within the family, with a responsibility towards society).

The group determined its relation to society as a family of independent members, the smallest form of society. Their micro-society was thus expanded to a macro-society.

時間，但主要是在美國，並以電報、傳真及電話彼此聯繫），他們作品的不同時期發展類似於成長的過程，可自其四種主要的設計案類型中察覺出。

超大型結構是社會與心理的網路，允許人們生活在一個更寬闊的次元，藉由相當明確的角色、法則及符號（統合於家庭與社會中）所保護。「游牧式建築」意味著體驗及試驗社會與心理的角色、法則與行為的歷險，並與個人的定義有關（鬆動家庭與社會的概念並發展至成熟）。「趣味式建築」，試圖使夢想成真，並於規範且明確定義的領域中找出適當的位置。（兼具私密與公共的放鬆功能）「變形」平衡並整合上述的各種觀點至一種過程系統之中，此觀點為穩定網絡之時，透過干擾所分解而成的（家庭中角色的選擇性整合與區分，兼具社會責任）。

該團體決定自己與社會的關係為具有獨立成員的族群，最小形式的社會。他們的「微社會」如此地被擴展成為「巨社會」。

INSIDE OUT UPSIDE DOWN
Warren Chalk, 1984

由裡而外倒轉過來
華倫·裘克，1984年

VERTICAL PARK URBAN UNDERGROWTH GARDENSCRAPER　　垂直公園都市矮樹叢花園刮刀

GROWING GLAZING LOOK OUT　　生長上釉往外看

CHOPPED CONCRETE CONSPIRATORIAL SPACE　　劈砍混凝土陰謀空間

NOOK & CRANNY LOOK IN CELLULAR THERAPY　　角落與裂縫往內看細胞療法

TRELLISES VERANDAHS BAY WINDOWS BOWED　　格架陽台弧形凸窗

RANDOM SPAGHETTI STRANDS PHOTOGRAPH　　隨意的義大利麵串照片

THE UPS & DOWNS OF VOLUMES ERODE　　書卷侵蝕的高低起伏

FREEZE FRAME PROGRESSION VIEW BY VIEW　　一景接一景的凝結畫面

TUCKING FOLDING PLEATING　　摺摺摺

DEMATERIALISATION OF SPACE CAMOUFLAGE　　空間偽裝的非物質化

VIOLENT VENETIAN BLINDS　　粗暴的活動百葉

WALLS HAVE EARS APPLIED EYES CLAMPED ON　　隔牆有耳運用眼睛箝制

THE UNDERGROUND OVERGROUND CONNECTION　　地下地上連結

SPIDER MAN & WEBS OF GOSSAMER DISINTEGRATION　　蜘蛛人與蜘蛛網瓦解

LONDON NIGHT & DAY FLOODLIGHT HEADLIGHT SPOT　　倫敦日夜的探照燈前照燈聚光燈

REAR VIEW GLANCE SEARCHLIGHT　　後方見探照燈

ANIMAL SKIN SOCKS & STOCKINGS CENTREPOINT　　皮革短襪與長襪中心

SOFT CROSS & DOWNDRAUGHT WINDS OBSCURE　　柔和的側吹與下吹風搞亂了

CUCKOO CLOCK PATTERNS SPIRAL OVERLAYS　　布穀鳥鐘圖案螺旋覆蓋物

DISSOLVE DECOMPOSE VANISH. FACING THE SUN　　溶解分解消失。面向朝陽

SPRAY PLASTIC HOUSE

David Greene, 1961

Why don't rabbits burrow rectangular burrows? Why didn't early man make rectangular caves?
Supposition: Architect . . . Client wanting single-storey house in the landscape

Phase 1, Burrows . . . Purchase foamed polystyrene block 40ft. by 40ft. by 15ft. and suitable burrowing tools, e.g. electric hedge-cutter, blowlamp. Block placed on site, burrowing commences, kids carving out playroom, etc., parents carving rest. Architects advising.

Phase 2, Dissolve . . . House burrow completed. Enter burrow with plastic and fibreglass spray machinery, (with client) spray burrow under supervision of plastics engineer. Client chooses regions of surfaces to be transparent or translucent, the spray mixture alters accordingly.

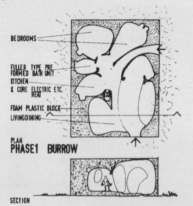

BEDROOMS

FULLER TYPE PRE
FORMED BATH UNIT
KITCHEN
K CORE ELECTRIC ETC.
HEAT
FOAM PLASTIC BLOCK
LIVING DINING

PLAN
PHASE1 BURROW

SECTION

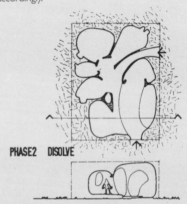

PHASE2 DISSOLVE

第1階段，挖洞……買一塊40呎乘40呎乘15呎的海綿狀聚苯乙烯，及適當的挖穴工具，例如，電動樹籬剪、吹熖管。將其置於基地上，開始挖洞，小朋友負責鑿刻遊戲間……等，而父母親則負責鑿刻其它的部分。由建築師負責提供建議。

第2階段，溶解……房屋洞穴施工完成。帶著塑膠與玻璃纖維噴灑機械裝置進入洞穴，（與業主）在塑膠工程師的監督下噴灑洞穴。業主選擇希望呈現透明或半透明的表面區域，噴灑混合將依情況而改變。

噴式塑膠屋

大衛‧葛林，1961年

為何兔子不挖矩形的洞穴呢？為何早期的人類不挖矩形的洞穴呢？
假設：建築師……業主想要一棟景觀中的單層住宅

Phase 3, Completion . . . Shell entered by architect and service consultants and client. Client decides upon regions of lighting, wall, floor, heating, sinks, power points.

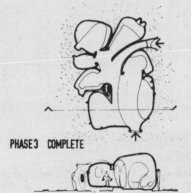

PHASE 3 COMPLETE

Also decided are finishes, e.g. sprayed rubber, flooring, carpet, etc. Services and equipment fixed, insulation sprayed on ready to receive finishes. (Spray outside of burrowed block with acetate, dissolving the polystyrene, leaving plastic cocoon which is wired to the ground. Structural correction made.)
Flats utilising spray plastic system:
Total environment by planners and architects and sociologists, etc. Anticipation.... Serviced decks, i.e. stairs, ramps, heat, electrics, fire escape, total traffic organisation on to which each person puts their own living cell, giving complete control over immediate surroundings. No art strait-jacket.

第3階段，完成……建築師、設備顧問與業主一同進入此殼架中。業主決定燈光、牆面、樓板、暖氣、水槽與電源的位置。

同時需要決定的尚有裝修，例如，噴上橡膠、舖設地板與地毯……等。安置水電配送設施，噴灑隔絕材料以備裝修。（洞穴體外部噴上醋酸鹽，溶解聚苯乙烯，留下塑膠繭殼固定於地面上。結構正確地安置。）
公寓式住宅利用噴式系統：
整體環境由規劃師、建築師與社會學家……等進行規劃。期盼……服務設施層，亦即包括樓梯、坡道、暖氣、電力、消防逃生及動線系統……等，每個人可將他們自己的生活小屋置於其上，提供對於即時環境的完全操控。毫無藝術上的束縛。

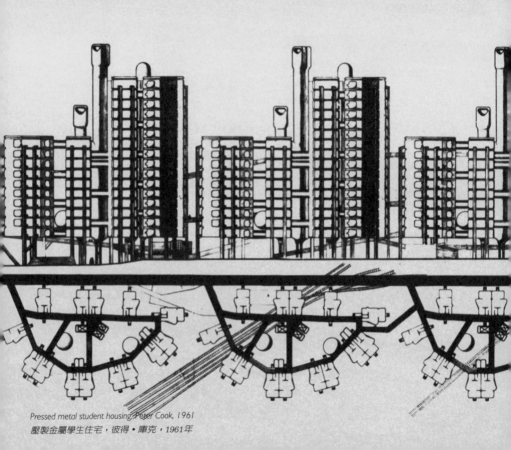

Pressed metal student housing, Peter Cook, 1961
壓製金屬學生住宅，彼得・庫克，1961年

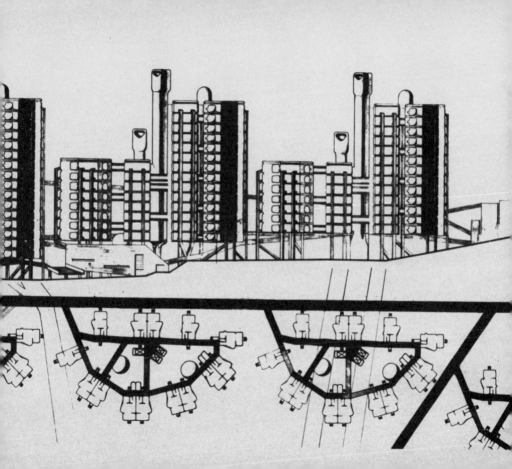

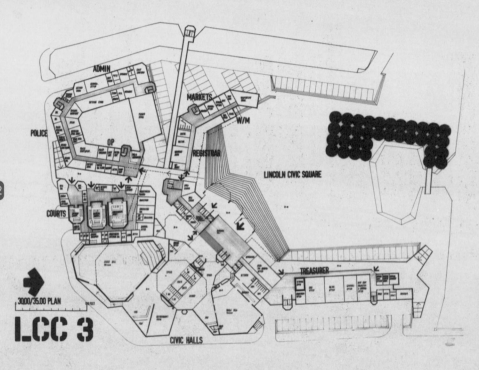

Lincoln Civic Centre competition, Warren Chalk, Dennis Crompton and Ron Herron, 1961
林肯市政中心競圖，華倫・裘克、丹尼斯・克藍普頓與朗・赫倫，1961年

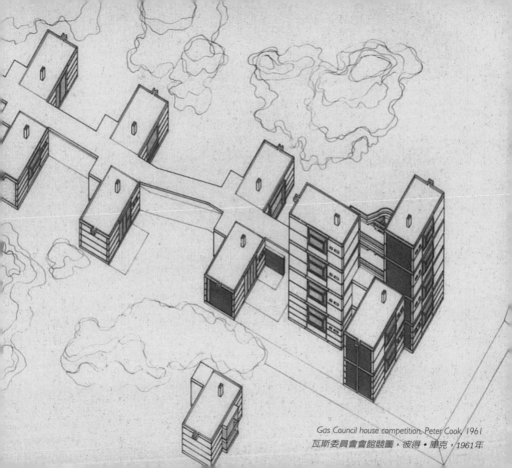

Gas Council house competition, Peter Cook, 1961
瓦斯委員會會館競圖，彼得・庫克，1961年

John Glenn is first American astronaut to orbit earth — Cuban crisis – the world comes close to Global war as Russia stations missiles in Cuba — U. Thant appointed UN Secretary General — Sony develop 5-inch micro television — Nazi war criminal Adolf Eichman hanged in Israel — 'Telstar' communications satellite launched at Cape Canaveral; transmits television pictures between America and Europe — Coventry Cathedral consecrated — Battles between Blacks and Whites in Mississippi over integration of schools — Two Britons, Chris Bonnington and Ian Clough, climb North Face of the Eiger — Assassination attempt on President de Gaulle of France — World's first Hovercraft service starts in Britain — Britons Crick and Watson win Nobel Prize for Medicine for their DNA research — John Steinbeck wins Nobel Prize for Literature — Dag Hammerkjöld's posthumous Nobel Prize is returned and money donated towards promoting international understanding — Marylin Monroe dies — MUSIC — The Twist explosion — The Beatles emerge in the Cavern Club, Liverpool — 'Love Me Do' — 'If I had a Hammer' — 'Return to Sender' — 'Locomotion' — THEATRE — 'Who's Afraid of Virginia Woolf?' — 'Chips with Everything' — CINEMA — The first James Bond film, 'Dr No' — 'Lawrence of Arabia' — 'A Kind of Loving' — BOOKS — 'Ipcress File' — 'The Drum' — 'One Flew Over the Cuckoo's Nest' — 'Another Country — One Day in the Life of Ivan Denisovitch' — FASHION — Jean Shrimpton becomes THE female image.

約翰‧葛蘭為首位進入地球軌道的美國太空人－古巴危機－蘇聯於古巴部署飛彈，世界大戰一觸即發－吳丹被任命為聯合國秘書長－新力發展5吋迷你電視－納粹戰犯阿道夫‧艾希曼於以色列被處以絞刑－「天王星」通訊衛星於卡納維爾角發射；自此美歐間可傳輸電視畫面－科芬特里大教堂奉獻禮－美國密西西比州黑人與白人因學校種族平等問題起衝突－兩名英國人，克里斯‧波寧頓及伊安‧克勞福攀登艾格北峰－法國總統戴高樂險遭暗殺－英國開始世界首次氣墊船飛行服務－英國人克里克與華生因去氧核醣核酸研究獲頒諾貝爾醫學獎－約翰‧史坦貝克獲頒諾貝爾文學獎－達‧哈馬紹死後獲頒之諾貝爾獎被歸還且獎金捐作促進國際間彼此瞭解之用－瑪麗蓮夢露辭世－音樂－妞妞舞引爆狂熱－披頭四發跡於利物浦的洞穴俱樂部－《愛我所為》－《倘若我有把斧頭》－《還給發信人》－《運動》－戲劇－《靈慾春宵》－《chips with everything》－電影007系列第一集《第七號情報員》上演－《阿拉伯的勞倫斯》－《一夜風流恨事多》－出版－《機密檔案》－《鼓》－《飛越杜鵑窩》－《它鄉異國》－《伊凡的一天》－時尚－名模珍‧史林普頓成了女性代表形象。

1962

Archigram
Archigram

1s 6d

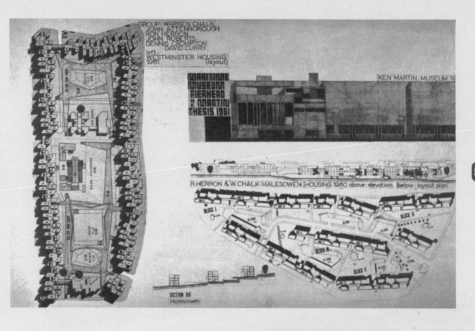

GROUP: WARREN CHALK
JOHN ATTENBOROUGH
RON HERRON
JOHN ROBERTS
DENNIS CROMPTON
DAVID CURRY
left
WESTMINSTER HOUSING
(layout)
1961

MARITIME
MUSEUM
PIERHEAD
K E MARTIN
THESIS 1961

KEN MARTIN : MUSEUM 19

R.HERRON & W.CHALK: HALESOWEN HOUSING 1960 above: elevation below: layout plan

SECTION BB
Halesowen

ARCHIGRAM 2

Editorial, *Peter Cook*

As with *Archigram 1*, this magazine is a statement of the mood of our generation of architects – more or less recently emergent from the schools of architecture. Our situation may be referred back to five years ago, with its feeling of the insufficiency of General Motors architecture, and disillusionment with the output of the postwar English architects. Enclosure and form were due for a comeback into (if nothing else) the mainstream of architectural theory.

In student circles, work of exceptional talent suddenly crystallised this mood. Edward Reynolds' Concert Hall at Trafalgar Square (*Archigram 1*) led to at least two years of riotous free-forming and plasticity at the AA. A year later, 'Bowellism' appeared at the Polytechnic in the shape of a handful of Furniture Factories at High Wycombe. The joint impact established the fact that the straight line of modern architecture was in for some twisting. Comment on this work has been consistent in its misrepresentation and misunderstanding. One's mind naturally associates the forms of Bowellism with Gaudí and Mendelsohn, and the blame does lie, to some extent, with the inability of the designers to discover an aesthetic original to the mood. The similarity occurred partially because the first gestures were of a similar expressionism to that of Mendelsohn or Art Nouveau. But the 40 years between had given the new work infinitely more to build with. Technology was ready. The 'Dan Dare' quality these buildings have springs from their common involvement with Dan Dare's psychology – with that of Superman, Lunar architecture and shred-

《建築電訊》第2期

社論　彼得・庫克

就像《建築電訊》第1期一樣，本期雜誌是我們這一代──或多或少最近才剛自建築學院畢業──建築師心境的宣言。我們的狀況或可歸因於5年前，對於通用汽車建築的不足與對於戰後英國建築師作品失望的感受。當時的構築方式與形式已準備好重回建築理論的主流。在學生圈裡，格外傑出的作品突然具體化了這種氛圍。愛德華・雷納德的特拉法爾加廣場音樂廳（《建築電訊》第1期）的設計在建築聯盟建築學院中引發了至少兩年的自由型態與可塑性的騷亂。一年後，「腸形派」以某些家具工廠型態出現於亥威昆的綜合技術學校。所有這些發展清楚地指出現代建築的明確方向必須仰賴某些創新。對此努力的評論一直包含了誤解與誤會。一般人自然地將「腸形派」的形式與高第及孟德爾松聯想在一起，並於某種程度上，歸咎於設計師無能發現氛圍的美學原創性。相似性的存在，部份是因為其最初的姿態是與孟德爾松或新藝術作品中的姿態類似的表現派。但這40年間已提供無限的新素材可供人們用以建造。科技已臻成熟。這些建築物所散發出來的「丹・戴爾」特質，是來自對於丹・戴爾心理學的專注──對於超人、月球建築及碎麥的熱中，以及以實體的角度而言，對於放熱格柵及發射台的投入。畫家類似的姿態此時已較為人熟知，然而其存在並非純然巧合。若少了這些事件

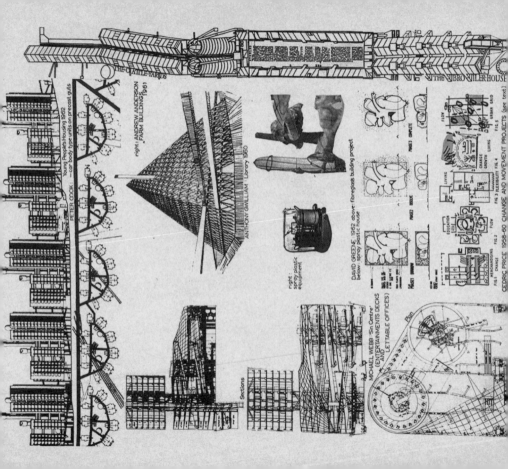

THE CATTLE YARDS

THE VIBRO-BILER HOUSE

Young People's Housing 1962
'car' body type units on precast guts

PETER COOK

right: ANDREW ANDERSON
'FARM BUILDING' 1961

ANTHONY GWILLIAM 'Library' 1960

DAVID GREENE 1962 above: fibreglass building project
below: spray plastic house

right:
spray plastic
equipment

Sections

MICHAEL WEBB 'Sin Centre'
(ENTERTAINMENTS DECKS
AND
LETTABLE OFFICES)

Plan

CEDRIC PRICE 1958-60 CHANGE AND MOVEMENT PROJECTS (see text.)

ded wheat, and in physical terms, with that of the radiator grille and the launching pad. Similar gestures by painters are at the moment better known, but their existence is far from just coincidence.

The situation today, this year, could not be the same without these occurrences. Form, space, enclosure, and complete involvement with our packaged environment is already ceasing to be self-conscious. Modern architecture is coming to include these things. If we are involved in all this, the public image of modern architecture seems terribly irrelevant. Flat roofs, a lot of glass and blank walls. The distinction between Highpoint flats and Bucklersbury House becomes hard to make in these terms.

The statement in *Archigram 1* was that the architecture of our generation can be closer in basics to the first modern architecture than most of the postwar building – which is supposed to be a continuance of it.

Our statement this time is a sum of the implications of what is shown and said; in recreating a set of values we can give equal value to the 'roots' quality of Andrew Anderson's farm buildings and the spatial dynamic of Michael Webb's Sin Centre. The emergence of 'expendability' as a topic in several schemes is coincidental but significant. It is a symptom that may well grow into the basis of a zeitgeist.

的發生，則今日的情勢將不可能會相同。形式、空間、構築方式以及與我們包裹好的環境的完全融合，已逐漸丟棄忸怩羞怯。現代建築將更專注於思索這些問題。若我們專注於所有這一切的話，則現代建築的公眾形像將顯得絲毫不具重要性。平坦的屋頂，大量的玻璃與單調的牆面。就此觀點下，「高點公寓」與「巴克勒斯伯利住宅」之間的差異性將變得難以辨認。

《建築電訊》第1期的聲明認為，我們這一代的建築，其基礎應可更接近第一代的現代建築，而非可視為其延續的大多數戰後建築物。

我們這次的聲明是那些已展示過且表達過之事物其含意的摘要；在重造一套價值標準時，我們可以給予安德魯·安德森「農場建築物」的「根」特質與麥克·威柏「罪惡中心」的「空間動力」特質等齊的評價。一些計劃案中所浮現的「消費性」議題雖是巧合但卻意義深長。這是可適切地發展成為一種新時代精神的基礎的徵兆。

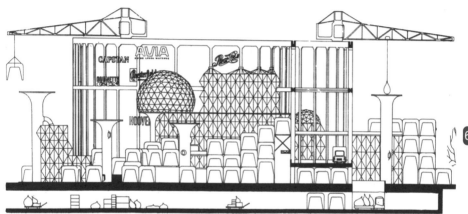

Nottingham shopping centre, Peter Cook and David Greene, 1962
諾丁罕購物中心，彼得・庫克與大衛・葛林，1962年

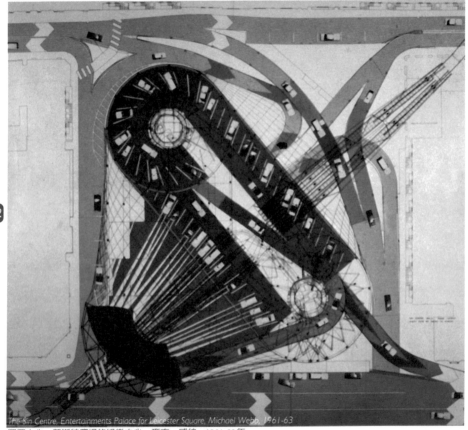

The Sin Centre, Entertainments Palace for Leicester Square, Michael Webb, 1961-63
罪惡中心，萊斯特廣場的娛樂中心，麥克‧威柏，1961-63年

62

President Kennedy assassinated — Suspected assassin Lee Harvey Oswald in turn shot dead — Soviet cosmonaut Valentina Tereshkova is first woman in space — Black Civil Rights campaign begins in US — riots in Birmingham, Alabama — Martin Luther King makes his 'I have a dream' speech — UK — Great Train Robbery — Winston Churchill given honorary US citizenship — The 'Profumo Affair' becomes public — Pope John XXIII dies — Pope Paul VI elected — Volcano erupts in Bali, killing 11,000 — Linus Pauling wins Nobel Peace Prize — French singer Edith Piaf dies — MUSIC — Vast boom in sale of records, especially singles — Beatlemania begins — 'She Loves You' — 'I Wanna Hold Your Hand' — 'From Me to You' — 'Twist and Shout' — 'Glad All Over' — The Mersey beat booms — Liverpool groups dominate — Rolling Stones emerge — THEATRE — National Theatre opens — CINEMA — 'The L-Shapes Room' — 'Tom Jones' — 'Cleopatra' — 'The Birds' — 'From Russia with Love' — FASHION — Trousers for women become popular — Mary Quant starts Knickerbocker craze — BOOKS — 'The Spy Who Came in from the Cold' — 'Another Country' —

甘迺迪總統遇刺身亡－暗殺嫌犯李・哈維・奧斯華隨即遭槍殺身亡－第一位女太空人蘇聯倫堤娜・泰拉史柯娃登陸太空－黑人民權運動於美國展開－阿拉巴馬州伯明罕市暴動－美國黑人人權運動領袖馬丁・路德・金恩發表「我有個夢想」演講－英國－火車搶劫－溫士頓・邱吉爾獲頒美國榮譽市民－「普羅福摩醜聞」爆發－教宗若望23世辭世－教宗保羅6世繼任－峇里島火山爆發，1萬1000人喪生－萊納斯・鮑林獲頒諾貝爾和平獎－法國歌手伊迪絲・琵雅芙辭世－**音樂**－唱片空前熱賣，尤以單曲為甚－披頭四旋風－《她愛你》－《我想握你的手》－《自我至你》－《扭曲與尖叫》－《高興一切結束》－默西節奏風行－利物浦團體聲名大噪－滾石樂團出現－**戲劇**－英國國家劇院開幕－**電影**－《陋室紅顏》－《湯姆・瓊斯》－《埃及豔后》－《鳥》－007系列《第七號情報員續集》－**時尚**－女性褲裝大受歡迎－瑪莉・關掀起了女性內褲狂熱－**出版**－《來自冷戰的間諜》－《它鄉異國》。

1963

ARCHIGRAM 3
Editorial, Peter Cook

MORE AND MORE

Almost without realising it, we have absorbed into our lives the first generation of expendables . . . foodbags, paper tissues, polythene wrappers, ballpens, EPs . . . so many things about which we don't have to think. We throw them away almost as soon as we acquire them.

Also with us are the items that are bigger and last longer, but are nevertheless planned for obsolescence . . . the motor car . . . and its unit-built garage.

Now the second generation is upon us – paper furniture is a reality in the States, paper sheets are a reality in British hospital beds, the Greater London Council is putting up limited life-span houses.

THROUGH AND THROUGH

With every level of society and with every level of commodity, the unchanging scene is being replaced by the increase in change of our user-habits – and thereby, eventually, our user-habitats.

We are becoming much more used to the idea of changing a piece of clothing year by year, rather than expecting to hang on to it for several years. Similarly, the idea of keeping a piece of furniture long enough to be able to hand it on to our children is becoming increasingly ridiculous. In this situation we should not be surprised if such articles wear out within their 'welcome' lifespan, rather than their traditional lifespan.

The attitude of mind that accepts such a sit-

《建築電訊》第3期

社論，彼得‧庫克

愈來愈多地

幾乎在從未瞭解的情況之下，我們已將第一代的消費品併入了我們的生活之中……購物袋、衛生紙、聚乙烯包裝套、原子筆、唱片……等，這麼多我們無須考慮的東西。我們丟棄它們的速度幾乎和我們得到它們的速度一樣快。

我們身邊也有一些更大更持久，但仍是設計為丟棄式的東西……汽車……以及它的單元體式構造車庫。

現在第二代正影響著我們——紙家具已經出現在美國，紙被單已經出現在英國醫院的病床，倫敦議會正提出有限壽命房屋的建議。

徹頭徹尾地

社會各階層與商品各個層面裡不變的情勢，正由我們的使用者／習慣以及有關的使用者／居所之不斷改變而遭取代。

我們正變得更習慣於每年更換一件衣物的觀念，而非期待穿戴著它好幾年。類似地，長久保存一件家具以傳給我們子孫的觀念正變得愈來愈荒謬。在這種情況之下，若這些物品在它們的使用「蜜月期」

THERE IS A GAP
BETWEEN IDEA AND IMAGE

left: EXPANDING HOUSE
by CESARE PEA
below: BATHROOM
(patent drawing) by
BUCKMINSTER FULLER

SOME PROBLEM

THE NEAREST THE BRITISH PUBLIC IS ALLOWED TO GET TO HAVING EXPENDABLE BUILDINGS
THAT ARE WHAT THEY ARE - UNASHAMEDLY - CHALETS, HUTS, CARAVANS - ALL HAVE FAILED

PROBLEM IS THIS EXPENDABLE ARCHITECTURE?

SOME THINGS BRIDGE THE GAP

uation is creeping into our society at about the rate that expendable goods become available. We must recognise this as a healthy and altogether positive sign. It is the product of a sophisticated consumer society, rather than a stagnant (and in the end, declining) society.

Our collective mental blockage occurs between the land of the small-scale consumer-products and the objects which make up our environment. Perhaps it will not be until such things as housing, amenity place and work place become recognised as consumer products that can be 'bought off the peg' – with all that this implies in terms of expendability (foremost), industrialisation, up-to-date-ness, consumer choice, and basic product-design – that we can begin to make an environment that is really part of a developing human culture.

Why is there an indefinable resistance to planned obsolescence for a kitchen, which in 12 years will be highly inefficient (by the standards of the day) and in 20 years will be intolerable, yet there are no qualms about four-year obsolescence for cars? The idea of an expendable environment is still somehow regarded as akin to anarchy . . . as if, in order to make it work, we would bulldoze Westminster Abbey . . .

We shall not bulldoze Westminster Abbey

Added to this, the idea of a non-permanent building has overtones of economy, austerity, economy. Architects are the first to deny the great potential of expendability as the built reflection of the second half of the 20th century. Most of the buildings that exist that are technically expendable have the fact skilfully hidden . . . they masquerade as permanent buildings – monuments to the past.

而非傳統壽命期時損壞的話，我們不應該覺得太過驚訝。

接受這種情況的心理狀態大約正以消費品出產的速度蔓延至我們的社會。我們必須看待此為有益且完全正面的徵候。這是錯綜複雜的消費型社會，而非停滯（且終將變得衰微）社會的結果。

我們在小型的消費品市場與構成我們環境的物件之間產生了集體的心理封鎖。也許直到有一天像住宅、休閒場所與工作場所……等都被認定為消費品且都可以「現成購買」的時候——這一切都暗示著就消費性（最主要的）、工業化、最時髦的、消費選擇以及基本的產品設計……等觀點而言——我們就可以開始創造一個真正成為發展中人類文化一部份的環境。

為何我們對於12年後將變得非常無效率（以今天的標準來看）且20年後將變得令人無法忍受的廚房被設計為丟棄式存有一種無法言喻的抗拒，卻對於汽車用過4年之後即廢棄毫無疑慮不安呢？

消費性環境之概念不知何故仍被視為類似於無政府狀態……就彷彿像是，為了達到目的，我們會劑平西敏寺似的……

我們不會劑平西敏寺

除此之外，非永久性建築物的概念具有經濟上的含意，簡樸而精省。建築師是第一個否定了消費性成為20世紀下半建築內省的無窮潛力。大部份現存之技術上具消費性的建築物具有一巧妙隱藏的事實……它們喬裝成永久性建築物——過往的紀念性遺跡。

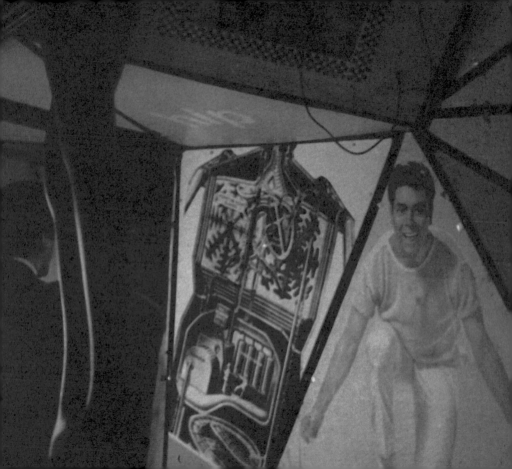

our belief in the city as a unique organism underlies the whole pro-ject

72

In the Living City man is the ultimate subject and principal conditioner.
the theme is interpreted by presenting evocations, accentuations and simula-tions of city life, not a display of suggest-ed forms.
the image is a total image of
it all like a film.

INTRODUCTION
Peter Cook

There are two main types of exhibition made by architects and designers. The first is the reaction to a need; something has to be said at that moment, something is wrong on the scene and there is no time or opportunity to build the statement. Similar ideas may have crossed several minds and these wish to postulate something which perhaps has no means of being realised. The outcome is the exhibition – a demonstration. Suitable gestation periods for such exhi-bitions occur at the point where architects enter upon a new creative wave. Such periods as the 1910s in Germany, 1920s in France and Italy, 1930s in Sweden and so on. Sometimes the parallel spadework has been done by other creative artists, and the architecture is a reflection of a sin-gle movement embracing them all. England has not

我們視城市為獨特有機體的信念是整體計劃案的基礎

在「生活城市」中，人是根本的主體與主要的調節者。其主題的詮釋是藉由呈現城市生活的喚起、強調與刺激，而非建議形式的展現。其影像所呈現的是一種整體，宛如電影一般。

概論

彼得‧庫克

建築師與設計師的展覽有兩種主要的類型。第一種是需求的反應：某些事必須立即明確地表達，場景中某些東西不對勁，而且沒有時間或機會真正將聲明建造出來。可能很多人都曾有過類似的想法，而且他們希望假定某些或許沒有辦法實現的事情。其結果是一個展覽—— 一個證明。適合這類展覽的醞釀期，會出現在建築師們開始著手一股新的創造浪潮的時候。諸如1910年代的德國、1920年代的法國與義大利、1930年代的瑞典……等。有時候，類似的籌備工作已由其他的創作藝術家們先行完成，而建築師則是接納它們全部的某種單一運動的反射。英國並未經歷過許多這類的過程，而且發現吸收

seen many such demonstrations, and has found it easier to absorb exhibitions of another kind. These are the 'reviews' which come to be held under the auspices of some established body, or mark an event or conference. In these the professionals allow their work to form a summary of the idioms of the moment. The 'informed' public indulges in the role of critic and prophet. The tragedy of so many of these well-intentioned shows is the lack of effect that they have on their public; confronted with some of the best ideas (thrown up by an odd contributor who is the precursor of something really great, but often beyond the scope of the exhibition or even in contradiction to it) the thing is misinterpreted and another decade is lost. Nevertheless, these reviews have had a solid value and are very necessary to our national self-respect in architecture.

Three exhibitions of recent years have been of more lasting importance to the mainstream of architectural thought in this country. In 1938 the *Mars Group* showed the new modern architecture in the New Burlington Gallery, a distinct gesture from a small group of pioneers directly stimulated by European émigrés who had been in the forefront in the 1920s. *Mars* was an inspiration for the first years after the war. Then came the *Festival of Britain*, which involved several of the same people and certainly did more to design in Britain than anything a decade before or since. It was a tragedy that the *Mars* influence withered away, and we are left now with an image of 'post Festival' – Victoriana, yachtsman's picturesque – and a shudder. Another tragedy of the same period was the negative payoff (in purely visual terms) of the sociological aspirations of the immediate postwar generation of architects.

There is a clear break, both in socio-political motive and age, between all this and the majority of the designers of *This is Tomorrow* at the Whitechapel Gallery in 1956. By definition a diverse collection of talents, with each exhibit designed by architect, painter and sculptor, it was clear that the architects had not only moved well away from the white-walled classic-modern of *Mars,* but had also rid themselves of the morality of 'people's architecture' and were free to enjoy indulging in an art show. Here too were the signs of the positive influences upon the hip architecture-culture of the 1950s; Brutalism and Americana.

In all cases the demonstration was in answer to the situation of the moment. *Mars* was the Coming-out Ball for modern architecture in England. The Festival, a more serious affair (from every point of view) had to employ an enforced gaiety as a contrast to years of austerity, and this may very well have been its downfall. The situation for *This is Tomorrow* was altogether healthier, and the impression it gave was of a healthy exuberance and, despite its unevenness, a positive gesture. What is needed again is a positive gesture, but of a different type, for it has become increasingly difficult to discern the path by which the environment around us can go forward and maintain its vitality, with at the same time an identifiable aesthetic that must be part of architecture-as-culture. The architects of *This is Tomorrow* have proved more versatile and able than those before them, and the exhibition included at least two who have become of international importance, and have had great influence on the generation of the organisers of *Living City*.

其它類型的展覽似乎更容易些。這些展覽是由某些已創立機構的贊助所舉行的「回顧」，或紀錄某個事件或研討會。在這些展覽中，專家們顧慮到讓自己的作品形成當時風格的摘要。「熟知內情的」觀眾耽溺於批評與預言的角色。這麼多立意良好的展覽的悲劇，主要在於缺乏對大眾的影響；面對著一些（被某位卓越先驅的古怪捐助者放棄，但往往已超越或甚至與展覽的範疇互相矛盾的）最好的構想，所有事都被誤解，而另一個十年也迷失了。然而，這些回顧已具有穩固的價值，並對於我們建築上的國家自尊十分必要。

英國近年來有3個展覽對於主流的建築思想具有較長久的重要性。1938年的時候，「現代建築研究團體」在新伯靈頓美術館展示了新的現代建築，這是來自一個小型先驅者團體的不同姿態，他們直接受到代表1920年代先鋒的歐洲移民的影響。「現代建築研究團體」在戰後的第一年是一種啟發。隨之而來的是「英國節」，參與的是一些相同的人士，而且比起前後10年的其它事件，的確對於英國的設計界貢獻更大。「現代建築研究團體」影響的衰微是件不幸的事，而如今遺留給我們的是「節慶展覽後」的影像——維多利亞式遊艇愛好者的景象——與一股顫慄。同一時期的另一椿悲劇是戰後一代的建築師在社會學上的努力的（純粹視覺領域中的）負面結果。

在社會與政治的動機與時代上，前面所提及的與1956年懷特查互美術館的「這是明日」展覽中的大部分設計師之間，存有一道明顯的裂痕。藉由釐清才華洋溢的各式各樣建築家、畫家與雕刻家所設計的每件展覽品，很明顯地建築師不僅順利地擺脫了「現代建築研究團體」的白色圍牆的古典現代性，同時也去除了「人民的建築」的道德枷鎖，並可以自由地享受縱情於藝術的展覽之中。這也是對於1950年代時髦建築文化之正面影響的跡象：野獸主義與美國主義。

在所有情況中，展覽都是對於當時情境的回應。「現代建築研究團體」是英國現代建築的初試啼聲。自各種觀點而言，「英國節」都算是更嚴肅的事情，必須運用強迫的歡樂作為多年嚴峻的對比，而這可能正是它沒落的原因。「這是明日」的整體情況更健全，它所呈現的印象是健康的豐富性與積極的姿態，儘管有些不規則性。我們再度需要的是一種積極的姿態，不過是不同的類型，因為想要辨識出我們周遭環境所能前進並維持其活力之道，同時具備一種必須為「視建築為文化」之一部份的可資識別的美學，已變得越來越困難了。「這是明日」的建築師們被證明為更多才多藝，且比前人更有能力，而至少有兩個展覽已變得具有國際性重要地位，並對「生活城市」創辦者的那一代有著深遠的影響。

目前的展覽不能說是一種回顧，因為它的計畫是進化式的，並且唯有關係到展覽本身中的實際經驗，

The present exhibition cannot be said to be a review, for its programme is evolutionary and it can only be definitive in relation to the actual experience within the exhibition itself. Can we predict the balance of evocations of the 'city' until we see them for the first time? Whether the present exhibition is a valuable gesture depends upon whether one demands a single line of argument, whether one states that black is black and white is white, and moreover, that they are diametrically opposite. There are several lines of argument implicit in our collection of exhibits, but like a jigsaw, the picture is amassed from the whole, and it is a coloured jigsaw with many shades of grey, also.

Certainly, *Living City* has come about as the reply to the situation as it appears to us, who are involved in the creation and evaluation of environment. We are in a European city, of long-established precedents, but with no clear way ahead for us to build upon them. The re-creation of environment is too often a jaded process, having to do only with densities, allocations of space, fulfilment of regulations: the spirit of cities is lost in the process. It is from America that the real warning has come. William H. Whyte in the *Exploding Metropolis* and more recently Jane Jacobs in *Death and Life of Great American Cities* treat the threat of the dénouement of city centres with a concern that is at the same time intelligent and frightening. They search hard for any signs of a reversal of the general trend, or a way out, or some path back to the situation when 'city' meant something vibrating with life. The Atlantic time-lag is about to catch up with us. The problem facing our cities is not just that of their regeneration, but of their right to an existence.

There is no comfort from the dusts of Brasilia or Chandigarh, the two opportunities in recent years for a city to be created *in toto*, unhampered by limitations of location or taste. Whether we have a liking for their aesthetics or not, neither is a living city. Perhaps in 50 years, or a 100? But it will be almost despite the architecture rather than because of it.

The real terror for us is that the cities we have will be sacrificed for an overall conformity covering the whole of this piece of Europe, for endless suburban communities, providing, it is admitted, a high standard of material comfort, but devoid of the quality of the city, because in the process this will have died.

In this exhibition above everything else we are being positive. The enemy is the negation of something of unique value. We are defending, moreover, a quality which is almost undefinable. The life-blood of cities runs through all that goes on in them. Some of these things are in themselves bad – vice, corruption of the young, overcrowding, exposure to risks; some are tedious, timewasting, or just banal; but overriding all these are the positives. So far in our creation of a way of life we have enriched experience by rule-of-thumb where environment is concerned. The living city is a unique experience, but the experience is not complete without the dark greys as well as the light.

The total impression of a collection of phenomena of city life will vary between spectators. It is, however, the privilege of the exhibitor to load the emphasis and guide their conclusions. The reaction of visitors to the *Mars*

它才是明確的。在首次看見它們之前，我們能夠預測「城市」所喚起的平衡嗎？目前的展覽是否為有價值的姿態，端視是否要求單一的論點，是否聲言黑即是黑且白即是白，且除此之外，它們是否正相反呢？我們的展覽品中隱含了不同的論點，但就像拼圖一樣，整體圖像來自於單獨碎片的累積，同時它也是具有許多灰色調的彩色拼圖。

無疑地，「生活城市」回應了我們周遭出現的情境，而我們則是環境的創造者與評估者。我們身處於一座具有悠久既定先例，但卻無明確方向可循，且無法以其為基礎的歐洲城市之中。環境的重新創造經常是一個令人疲倦的過程，只與密度、空間配置與達成法規要求有關而已：城市的精神於過程之中迷失了。在美國，威廉·懷特與珍·賈德斯分別於《爆裂的大都會》與《美國大城市的生與死》之中已經提出警告，抱著智性與驚駭的憂心，論述著城市市中心結果的威脅。它們努力尋找一般趨勢的逆轉跡象，或出路，或路途，可以回到當城市仍意味著某種充滿活力且令人悸動的東西的狀況。大西洋的時差就快趕上我們了。我們城市所面臨的問題並不只是更新的問題，而是它們的生存權利問題。

從巴西利亞或香地葛的沙塵中得不到任何慰藉，這是近年來一座城市可以完全重建的兩次機會，而無地點或品味的限制阻礙。不管我們是否喜歡它們的美學，或是「生活城市」的。或許在50年裡，或者100年？若情況真是如此的話，這將幾乎無關乎建築且非因其之故。

我們真正畏懼的是，我們城市中涵蓋整個歐洲的全面一致性將被犧牲，無數的市郊社區也將被犧牲，因為儘管提供了高水準的物質舒適性，但卻缺乏城市的品質，因為它將葬身於變遷過程之中。首先我們在這個展覽中的態度是積極的。對某些價值獨特事物的否定是我們的敵人。除此之外，我們正為某些幾乎難以下定義的特質進行辯護。城市的活力泉源穿越了所有城市裡進行中的事物。這些事物中有些本身是不好的——罪惡、年輕人的墮落、過度擁擠、暴露於危險之中；有些冗長乏味、曠日費時，或僅僅平庸無趣；但超越所有這一切的是正面性。截至目前，在創造某種生活方式時，我們藉由有關環境的基本原則以豐富經驗。「生活城市」是某種獨特的經驗，但此經驗若缺乏深灰及光亮就不算完整。

對城市生活現象的整體印象，將視觀者不同而有所差異。然而，支配強調焦點並左右其結論是展出者的特權。就算沒有展出品的名單，「現代建築研究團體」展覽中參觀者的反應也是可預期的：有教養者將深感有趣，而一般人則將懷疑植入這污穢但卻親切之地點的冷峻姿態模樣。節慶展覽的整體是較為通俗性的。「這是明日」以其獨特的方式呈現，就像直接由個人而非計劃所完成的產品一樣。

我們自己的裝備並無於任何特定方向提供太深入的證據。因為城市是多向性的，且對所有人而言意義

exhibition would have been predictable, without a listing of the exhibits: the sophisticated would be amused and the unsophisticated distrustful of the arid shapes implanted on grubby but friendly localities. The *Festival* was an altogether more popular affair. *This is Tomorrow* was loaded in its own peculiar way, as things are when they are directly the product of personalities rather than programmes.

Our own paraphernalia do not load the evidence too far in any one direction. Just as the city is multi-directional and all things to all men, so must this be. The people who have made the exhibition are similarly elastic in their outlook towards assembling it. Six of us are normally involved in architecture, one in furniture design and one in graphics, but we all overlap. To some extent we are the opposite of professional in doing so. This is a group effort, in which the assemblage has been made by all, the selection is with the consent and stimulus of us all, and the motives are shared by us all.

In the living city all are important: the triviality of lighting a cigarette, or the hard fact of moving two million commuters a day. In fact they are equal – as facets of the shared experience of the city. So far, no other form of environment has been devised that produces the same quality of experience shared by so many minds and interests. When it is raining in Oxford Street the architecture is no more important than the rain; in fact the weather has probably more to do with the pulsation of the living city at that given moment. Similarly all moments of time are equally valid in the shared experience. The city lives equally in its past and its future, and in the present where we are.

Most of the pieces of the exhibition are of today, but there must also be phenomena of the past and predictable items, which in this context must not be taken as architectural statements so much as the continuance of the spirit of the city in its physical image. Perhaps the key to the evasiveness of city spirit is the spirit of people themselves. In the first place they came together, for one reason or another, to make cities. They continue to interact upon each other in the shared experience. The image of the city may well be the image of people themselves, and we have devoted much of the exhibition to the life-cycle and survival kit of people within cities. Man is the ultimate subject around which we are exhibiting, and he conditions any space into which he comes. The *Living City* exhibition is a series of small spaces, and they alone will be fantastically affected by the number of people walking around them.

The items used to show all this will vary from trivia to valued drawings, and monster versions to miniscule versions of everyday things. This again is a reflection of how the city is seen by different people in different moods. And again they are all equally valid. Typography, sound, colour, feelies, they are all in a way facets of experience in themselves. Disparate as the total effect may well be, as is the intention, we have used two devices, and only two, which act as a control to the form of the exhibition. The first is the decision to use a system of triangles as the structural and formal basis. This has come about through the ability of this figure to twist itself around spaces, a freedom very necessary in our presentation. The triangles are nevertheless a structurally sensible unit

均不相同，此處的情況必定也是如此。策展者對於安排展覽的看法具有類似的彈性。我們六個人通常都專注於建築領域的工作，其中一位從事家具設計，另一位從事平面藝術設計，但我們的領域全都部分重疊。就某種程度而言，我們這種做法與時下的專業者正好相反。這是群體的努力，由眾人之力所結集而成，我們大家秉持著相同的動機，在彼此激勵與一致贊同下選擇展出內容。

在「生活城市」中，一切都是重要的：在生活城市中一切都很重要。點燃一根煙的瑣細或是一天移動兩百萬通勤者的辛苦事實。事實上，它們都同樣是城市中分享經驗的不同面貌。至今尚未設想出可創造如此眾多意見與利益均能共享相同經驗品質的其它環境形式。當牛津街正在下雨的時候，建築並不比雨水更重要，事實上氣候在某些時刻或許與生活城市的脈動更有關係。同樣地，分享經驗中的所有時刻都具有相同的效力。城市平等地存在於過去、未來與我們身處的現在。大部分的展覽作品來自於現在，但其中必定也有過去的現象與可預知的作品，在此整體關聯性中，它們不該被視為建築的聲明，而是城市精神之形體化的延續。或許城市精神不可捉摸的關鍵在於人們自己的精神。當初他們為了某種原因而聚在一起，共同建造城市。他們持續地在分享的經驗上彼此互相影響。城市的影像或許正是人類自身的影像，而我們將許多展覽致力於城市中的生命循環與人類的生存裝備。在我們的展覽中，人是最終的主體，他支配了任何他所至之空間。「生活城市」的展覽是一系列小型的空間，而它將被許多圍繞周圍的人們巧妙地影響著。

用以表現這一切的事物，將包含自瑣細至有價值的圖畫，以及自日常事物中的怪異變體至細微變體。再者，這是城市如何由不同人於不同情緒下所領會的反映。另一方面，它們全都同等地有效。活版印刷術、聲音、色彩及多感覺藝術品……等，就某種意義而言，全都是它們本身經驗的各個層面。因為整體效果與意圖的不同，我們運用了兩種裝置，唯一的兩種，於某種程度上控制展覽的形式。第一種決定利用了三角形系統作為結構與形式的基礎。這是藉由這種圖形在空間中扭轉自己的能力而實現的；而此能力為我們表現法中必要的自由。儘管如此，三角形是一種結構性明顯且可以預製的單元。並不需要加油添醋我們運用三角形的這項事實，我們再無其它意圖了！另一項裝置是主要空間或「凹室」的劃分（我們彼此稱之為「構浪棚」：一個或許創造自「環圈」，或「緊密空間的圍繞」的字）；每個「構浪棚」有一個主題內容，並且就某種意義而言，代表了城市的某些地區與我們心中的某些角落裡的這些主題的強度。它們分別是：人、生存、群眾、溝通、運動、場所與情境。然而，它們並不緊密，而且他們部分重疊，正如它們在現實中的情況一般。

在接下來的幾篇文章裡，您將會逐一地讀到多位作者的看法。這些代表了我們個人的興趣與我們個別

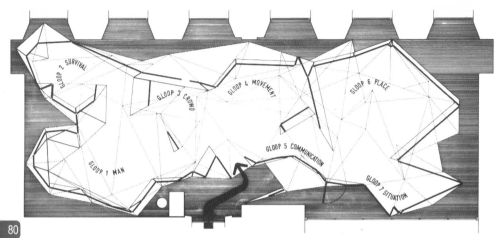

GLOOP 2 SURVIVAL

GLOOP 3 CROWD

GLOOP 4 MOVEMENT

GLOOP 6 PLACE

GLOOP 1 MAN

GLOOP 5 COMMUNICATION

GLOOP 7 SITUATION

that can be prefabricated. Nothing more should be read into the fact that we have used triangles, nothing more was intended. The other device has been the division of the major spaces or 'alcoves' (we have called them 'gloops', amongst ourselves; a word probably coined out of loop, or encompassment of a tight space); each gloop has a division of subject-matter and in a way represents the intensity of these subjects in certain parts of city and certain corners of our mind. They are as follows: Man, Survival, Community, Communications, Movement, Place and Situation. They are, however, not tight, and they overlap, just as they do in reality.

In the following pages you will read and view the outlooks, one by one, of the various contributors. These represent our personal interests and the angle from which we have individually approached the problem of the Living City. As we overlap, so too have we come to overlap much more until the whole exhibition is there, and our personalities are hidden somewhere far beneath. It will be asked: 'Why have you not stated an answer to the problem, why have you not an image of the city of the future'? We feel that it has been primarily necessary to define the problem. We have set the scene. We have attempted to capture that indefinable something: the *Living City*.

We shall not hesitate to postulate concrete ideas – but that is for another exhibition. Let this be said, if nothing else, that **our belief in the city as a unique organism underlies the whole project**.

探索「生活城市」問題的觀點。當我們的想法開始交會重疊時，我們會儘可能地持續重疊，直到完成了整個展覽的作品，而我們的個性則潛藏於深處。有人會問道：「為何你們不提出一個問題的答案呢？為何你們沒有一個未來城市的影像呢？」我們覺得首先必須先定義這個問題。我們已經安置好場景。我們企圖捕捉某種難以定義的東西：「生活城市」。我們不該猶豫假設具體的構想──不過那是為了另一場展覽。這麼說好了，若無其它想法，則**「我們視城市為獨特有機體的信念是整體計劃案的基礎」**。

CITY INTERCHANGE

Warren Chalk and Ron Herron

Communication interchange – first step to Living City.

The knot – node point for static and motivated communication complex.

Rail – public transit interchange – long distance and inter-regional rapid transit using linear induction motor-propelled trains.

Inter-city electric underground ring.

Sub-underground inter-centre links and outer metropolis commuter services.

Road – north/south east/west communication crossover and interchange for feeder roads off express trunk routes skirting metropolis.

Mass transit express bus turn-about.

Car and bus long- and short-term underground parking.

Air – heliport and hovercar station connecting to supersonic air travelport on perimeter of outer metropolis.

Services – service line control station for inter-regional distribution.

Pedestrian – high speed vertical lift interchange links within interchange station amenity arena.

Horizontal low-speed travelator and escalator arteries radiate out to periphery.

Static communications control centre.

Towers – suspended from central masts containing services.

Tower groups contain electronic data transmission, traffic control and administration, radio-telephone tower, communication and news service relay station, inter-commercial closed circuit television hook-ups, public television and telstar rediffusion centre.

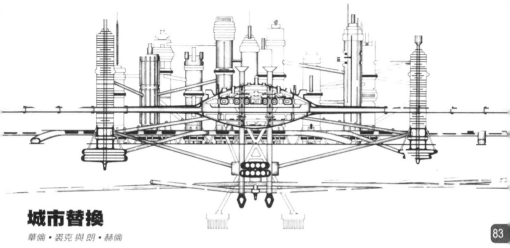

城市替換

華倫・裘克 與 朗・赫倫

通訊交換－邁向生活城市的第一步。

結點－靜態與誘導式通訊複合體的結點。

鐵路－公共運輸交換 — 利用線性誘導電動機驅動火車的長途與區域間快速運輸。

城市間電動環形地鐵。

地鐵中心間的連結與都會外通勤者的服務設施。

道路－東西向及南北向交通轉線軌，以及支線道路離開環繞都市之高速幹道的交流道。

大眾運輸高速公車終點站。

汽車與公車之長期與短期的地下停車場。

航空－連結至都會外緣的超音速航空港的直升機機場與氣墊車車站。

服務設施－區域間配電與配水的設施管線控制站。

行人－換車站休息區內的高速垂直升降梯交換連結。

水平低速自動人行道與電扶梯幹線放射至周邊地區。

靜態通訊系統控制中心。

塔樓－自包含服務設施的中央桅桿懸出。

塔樓群包含了電子資料傳輸、交通控制與管理、無線電話塔樓、通訊社轉播站、商業有線電視轉播，以及公共電視與通訊衛星有線轉播中心。

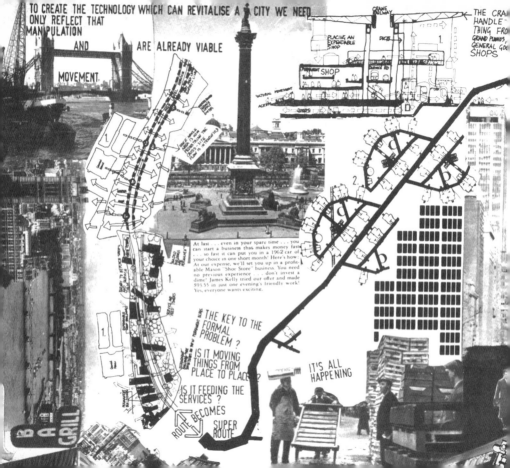

TO CREATE THE TECHNOLOGY WHICH CAN REVITALISE A CITY WE NEED ONLY REFLECT THAT MANIPULATION AND MOVEMENT ARE ALREADY VIABLE

MOVEMENT.

THE CRANE HANDLES THING FROM GRAND PIANOS, GENERAL GOODS SHOPS

PLACING AN EXPENDABLE SHOP

CRANE RAILWAY

SHOP

At last . . . even in your spare time . . . you can start a business that makes money faster . . . so fast it can put you in a 1962 car of your choice in one short month! Here's how. At our expense, we'll set you up in a profitable Mason "Shoe Store" business. You need no previous experience . . . don't invest a dime! James Kelly tried our offer and made $93.55 in just one evening's friendly work! Yes, everyone wants exciting.

THE KEY TO THE FORMAL PROBLEM ?

IS IT MOVING THINGS FROM PLACE TO PLACE ?

IS IT FEEDING THE SERVICES ?

ROUTE BECOMES SUPER ROUTE

IT'S ALL HAPPENING

B A GRILL

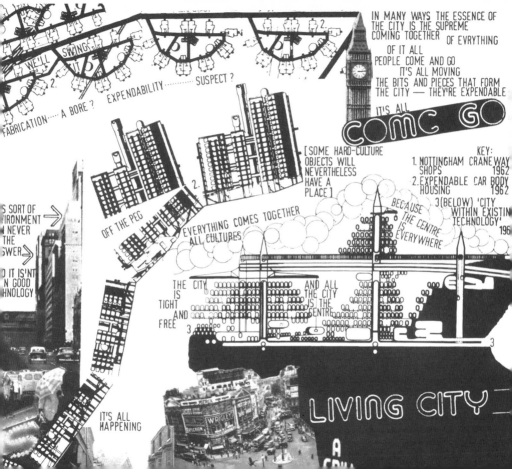

IN MANY WAYS THE ESSENCE OF
THE CITY IS THE SUPREME
COMING TOGETHER OF EVRYTHING

OF IT ALL
PEOPLE COME AND GO
IT'S ALL MOVING
THE BITS AND PIECES THAT FORM
THE CITY — THEY'RE EXPENDABLE

IT'S ALL

COME GO

WE'LL SWING IT

FABRICATION.....A BORE ? EXPENDABILITY..........SUSPECT ?

[SOME HARD-CULTURE
OBJECTS WILL
NEVERTHELESS
HAVE A
PLACE]

KEY:
1. NOTTINGHAM CRANEWAY
SHOPS   1962
2. EXPENDABLE CAR BODY
HOUSING   1962
3 (BELOW) 'CITY
WITHIN EXISTIN
TECHNOLOGY'   196

S SORT OF
IRONMENT
NEVER
THE
SWER

D IT IS'NT
N GOOD
HNOLOGY

OFF THE PEG

EVERYTHING COMES TOGETHER
ALL CULTURES

BECAUSE
THE CENTRE
IS
EVERYWHERE

THE CITY
IS
TIGHT
AND
FREE

AND ALL
THE CITY
IS THE
CENTRE

3

3

IT'S ALL
HAPPENING

LIVING CITY

CITY SYNTHESIS

Dennis Crompton

The city is a living organism – pulsating – expanding and contracting, dividing and multiplying.

The complex functioning of the city is integrated by its natural computer mechanism. This mechanism is at once digital and biological, producing rational and random actions, reactions and counter-reactions. The computer programme is a conglomeration of logical reasoning, intuitive assumption, personal preference, chance, sentiment and bloody-mindedness which is assimilated and interpreted. The solutions follow automatically.

The trigger to the computer programme is social man. He creates the City Scene at conscious and subconscious reaction levels by his own complexity. He is identified with the natural computer and is an integral part of its dataprocessing operation – but they are NOT ONE – each has an individual nature which functions independently. At its logical (or illogical?) limit this division of nature causes the DEATH of both. The city is ascendant when they are in unison, in decay when they divide.

The feed-in for city synthesis has three stages:

1. Primary information about population: birth rate, death rate, age, unit size and habits. Also city site data: location, topography, geological and geographical conditions, the inter-relation with other urban complexes.

The overall network is formed from this information and then absorbs it, processes it, and throws out the subsequent stages.

2. Secondary information: health, housing, marriages, fertility rate, crime rate, journey to work, wages and salaries. Rates of development and obsolescence, density, communications, and land values. At this stage the network is modified and amplified, and the substance of the city created.

3. Trends, conditioning of the city and population caused by the problems and solutions resulting from stages 1 and 2. Movement within the complex; personal action, shopping, entertainment (personal and mass), recreation, market survey, bus timetables, etc.

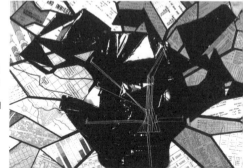

The last stage is a continuing feed-back in which every facet of city life is relevant to the whole, values are relative to the observer. The absolute ceases to exist after stage 1. The expansion and contraction of centres and suburbs, the dead ends, the exciting and the mundane – all are now an integral part of the city scene, enveloped in a net of inter-relationships ultimately controlled by the Natural Computer.

城市綜合體

丹尼斯・克藍普頓

城市是生活的有機體 — 悸動 — 擴張與緊縮,劃分與增殖。

城市的複雜機能藉由其自然的電腦結構而整合。此結構同時兼具數位式與生物性,產生理性與偶發性作用、反作用與反反作用。電腦程式為邏輯性推理的複合體、直覺性假設及個人的偏好、機遇、感情與固執的吸收與詮釋。解決方法自動接踵而至。

電腦程式是由社群中的人所觸發。他藉由自己的複雜性於意識及潛意識反應層面創造了「城市場景」。他與自然的電腦融為一體,且為其資料處理操作的絕對必要部分——但他們並非一體——彼此均具備可單獨運作的個別特質。於其邏輯性(非邏輯性?)限制上,這種特質的劃分導致了兩者的滅亡。當他們處於和諧時,城市即提昇;劃分時,城市即衰微。

城市綜合體的開始包括三個階段:

1. 關於人口的主要資訊:出生率、死亡率、年齡、單元尺寸與習慣。以及城市敷地資料:地點、地形、地質與地理狀況,及與其它都市複合體的相互關係。

整體網絡由此資訊所構成,而後吸收它、處理它,並暗示了繼起的階段。

2. 次要資訊:健康、住宅、婚姻、生育率、犯罪率、工作路程、工資與薪水。發展與萎縮率、密度、通訊與土地價值。於此階段,網絡將被修正與擴充,而城市的實質內容將產生。

3. 趨勢,由產生自第1與第2階段的問題與解決方法所引發的城市與人口調整。複合體內的活動:個人活動、購物、娛樂(個人與大眾)、休閒、市場調查、公車時刻表……等。

最後階段為持續的回饋,於此,城市生活的各面向與整體息息相關,而價值觀則與觀察者有關。第一階段後不再存有絕對性。市區與市郊的擴張與緊縮、死胡同、刺激與平淡——現在全是城市場景中的絕對必要部分,圍繞在最終由自然的電腦所控制的相互關係網裡。

SITUATION

THE PASSING PRESENCE

This thing we call Living City contains many associative ideas and emotions and can mean many things to many people: liking it or not liking it, understanding it or not understanding it, depends on these personal associations. There is no desire to communicate with everybody, only with those whose thoughts and feelings are related to our own. What we feel and think about the city is not new in the sense that it was unthought of before, but only in that the idea of the Living City has not been acted upon before by our generation.

In this second half of the 20th century, the old idols are crumbling, the old precepts strangely irrelevant, the old dogmas no longer valid. We are in pursuit of an idea, a new vernacular, something to stand alongside the space capsules, computers. and throw-away packages of an atomic/electronic age. The point of departure for Gloop 7 is *Situation*. Situation concerns the state of change within the city environment caused by the fluctuating come/go of people and things over a time scale. All of us find Living City in Situation. An awareness of the city is necessary before we can move forward.

Situation is concerned with environmental changes and activity within the Living City context, giving characteristics to defined areas. Important in this is the precept of Situation as an ideas-generator in creating the Living City. Cities should generate, reflect and activate life, their environment organised to precipitate life and movement. Situation — the happenings within spaces in city, the transient throw-away objects, the passing presence of cars and people — is as important, possibly more important, than the built demarcation of space. Situation can be caused by a single individual, by groups or a crowd. Situation can be traffic, its speed, direction, classification. Situation may occur with a change of weather, the time of day or night. As the spectator changes, the moving eye sees. Situation is related to individual perception, and the place of the individual in the environment. This time/movement/situation thing is important in determining our whole future attitude to the visualisation and realisation of city; it can give a clue, a key, in our effort to escape the brittle ingratiating world of the architect/aesthete, to break away into the real world and take in the scene.

情境

這個我們稱之為「生活城市」的東西包含了許多構想與情感的結合,且對許多人而言具有不同的意義:不論您喜歡與否、瞭解與否,都視這些個人的結合而定。並無意與所有人溝通,而只與那些於想法與情感上與我們同類者交流。就過去未思及的方面而言,我們對於城市的感覺與想法並不新穎,除了「生活城市」的構想尚未對我們這一代產生作用之外。自從20世紀後半開始,舊有的成見逐漸地瓦解,舊式的戒律疏遠而無時代感,古老的教條不再有效。我們追求一種觀念,一種新的時代性,某種足以匹配原子/電子時代的太空艙、電腦與丟棄式組件的東西。「構浪棚 7」的起點是情境。情境與一段時間之內,人事物不安定的變動所引起之城市環境中的變化狀態有關。我們都認為「生活城市」是處於「情境」中的。在我們可以繼續前進之前,必須先對城市有所察覺。

「情境」關係到環境的變化與「生活城市」背景中的活動,賦予特質以定義領域。其中重要的是「情境」被視為創造一個「生活城市」的構想發生器的教訓。城市應該引發、反映與活化生活,其結構應組織以促進生活與發展。「情境」——城市裡空間內部的事件、人類瞬間無常丟棄式的世界、汽車短暫的存在——與構築環境及空間構築界限一樣,且甚至更為重要。「情境」可能由單一個體、團體或群眾所引起。「情境」可能是交通與其速度、方向及類別。「情境」可能因為氣候與日夜時間的變化而產生。當觀者變換環境時,游移的目光覺察著。「情境」與個體的知覺,以及環境中個體所在的場所有關。這類時間/運動/情境之類的事在決定我們對於城市的具像化與現實化的整體未來看法時十分重要;它可以在我們致力於逃避唯美主義建築師對於世界的脆弱迎合討好,並強迫自己進入真實世界以理解實際情勢之時,提供一個線索與解鑰。

STORY OF

THE THING
for boys at heart

this things come a long way since we
started this exhibition

wasn't it a great floating city to
begin with—a Europe city that spanned
the channel

why did we give that idea up?

perhaps because of the purely

visionary nature of the idea it'll be
years before there's a political set-up

sufficient for this to come into being and

as liberators of ideas they are

but their technology can on

anyway with communications, closed circuit TV

we may not want to live in cities any more

yeah, I think thats where Keisler and

Schulze Fielitz with his space frame city fall down

A SYSTEM OF TENSION IN FREE SPACE A CHANGE OF SPACE INTO
URBANISM   NO FOUNDATIONS   NO WALLS   DETACHMENT FROM
THE EARTH   SUPPRESSION   OF THE STATIC AXIS IN CREATING
NEW POSSIBILITIES FOR LIVING IT CREATES A NEW SOCIETY

Keisler

FINAL NOTES ON THE LIVING CITY

As an exhibition it has been thought of throughout not as a display of data but as an experience – the condensation of phenomena in order to create a mood.

Architecture as such will be less evident than might be expected of a group predominantly architectural – but it must be remembered that the aim of the exhibition is a mood rather than a physical statement.

The time and place – 1963 in London, England – must have an influence upon what is presented. Try, as we have tried, to see beyond this. The crisis facing the Living City here is equally facing Tokyo or Los Angeles.

The exhibition revolves around people, for cities are their creation, and people have created the problems of the city. People's habits and reactions to city situations reflect this basic premise.

The exhibition does not exist in a vacuum and certainly in the minds of its inceptors the situation will have begun to change further by the time the exhibition closes. We all have a positive belief, however, that despite the questionings and challenges implicit in the situation as shown, we can work towards a solution which is of the Living City.

Warren Chalk, Peter Cook, Dennis Crompton, Ben Fether, David Greene, Ron Herron, Peter Taylor, Michael Webb.
London 1963.

生活城市的最後注解

就一個展覽而言，它全然未被視為一種資料的展示，而是某種經驗——某種為了創造一種情緒的現象凝縮。

像這樣的建築將比預期中所謂的主要建築團體更不明確——但必須牢記展覽的目標在於情緒而非實體的陳述。

那個時空——1963年的英國倫敦——必定影響了當時的呈現。試試看，如我們曾嘗試過的那般，超越這些仔細端詳。此處面對「生活城市」的危機與面對東京或洛杉磯的危機是一樣的。

此展覽以人為主題，因為城市是他們的創造物，且人們製造了城市的問題。人們對於城市情境的習慣與反應，反映了這種基本的前提。

此展覽並非存於真空之中，且無疑地於其創始者的心裡，於展覽結束之前，情境將早已展開進一步的改變。然而，我們全都有明確的信念，儘管遭遇情境中所固有的質疑與挑戰，我們仍能朝向「生活城市」的解決之道而努力。

華倫・裘克、彼得・庫克、丹尼斯・克藍普頓、班・費瑟、大衛・葛林、朗・赫倫、彼得・泰勒、麥克・威柏。
倫敦1963年。

HOUSING AS A CONSUMER PRODUCT

Warren Chalk

One of the most flagrant misconceptions held about us is that we are not ultimately concerned with people. This probably arises directly from the type of imagery we use. A section through, say, something like City Interchange, appears to predict some automated wasteland inhabited only by computers and robots. How much this is justified is difficult to assess, but if our work is studied closely there will be found traces of a very real concern for people and the way in which they might be liberated from the restrictions imposed on them by the existing chaotic situation, in the home, at work and in the total built environment.

Human situations are as concerned with environmental changes and activity within the city, as with the definition of places. Important in this is the precept of Situation as an ideas generator in creating a truly living city. Cities should generate, reflect and activate life, their structure organised to precipitate life and movement. Situation, the happenings within spaces in the city, the transient throwaway world of people, the passing presence of cars, etc., are as important, possibly more important than the built environment, the built demarcation of space.

This is in fact a follow-on from thinking related to the South Bank scheme where the original basic concept was to produce an anonymous pile, subservient to a series of pedestrian walkways, a sort of Mappin Terrace for people instead of goats.

So once again the pedestrian, the gregarious nature of people and their movement is uppermost in our minds and the built demarcation of space used to channel and direct pedestrian patterns of movement.

In an attempt to get closer to the general public, to study their attitudes and behaviour, we have extended ourselves beyond the narrow boundaries of conventional architectural thought, causing the misconceptions about what we are trying to do. We must extend the conventional barriers and find people without any formal architectural training, producing concepts showing a marked intuitive grasp of current attitudes related to city images and the rest. In the world of science fiction we dig out prophetic information regarding geodesic nets, pneumatic tubes and plastic domes and bubbles.

If we turn to the back pages of the popular press we find ads for do-it-yourself living room extensions, or instant garage kits. Let's face it, we can no longer turn away from the hard fact that everyone in the community has latent creative instincts and that our role will eventually be to direct these into some tangible and acceptable form. The present gulf between people, between the community and the designer may well be eventually bridged by the do-it-yourself interchangeable kit of parts.

In a technological society more people will play an active part in determining their own individual environment, in self-determining a way of life. We cannot expect to take this fundamental right out of their hands and go on treating them as cultural and creative morons. We must tackle it from the other end in a positive way. The inherent qualities of mass production for a consumer-orientated society are those of repetition and standardisation, but parts can be changeable or interchangeable depending on individual needs and preferences, and, given a world market, could also be economically feasible.

In the States one can select a car consisting of a whole series of interchangeable options: as Reyner Banham has pointed out (in his article on Clip-on Architecture), Chevrolet produce a choice of seventeen bodies and five different engines.

The current success of pop music is to an extent due to the importance of audience participation; the 'Frug' and the 'Jerk' are self-expressive and free-forming. The pop groups themselves are closer in dress and habits, including musical dexterity, to the audience. Despite pop music becoming a vast industry its success depends on its ability to keep up with the pace of its consumer taste.

Of course the idea of mass-produced expendable component dwellings is not new. We are all familiar with Le Corbusier's efforts in collaboration with Prouvé and with Prouvé's own bits and pieces, with Buckminster Fuller's Dymaxion house, the Phelps Dodge Dymaxion bathroom and the Dymaxion deployment unit, Alison and Peter Smithson's House of the Future at the Ideal Home Exhibition of 1955, Ionel Schein's prefabricated hotel units and the Monsanto Plastic House in Disneyland; there has also been work done by the Metabolist Group in Japan and Arthur Quarmby in England.

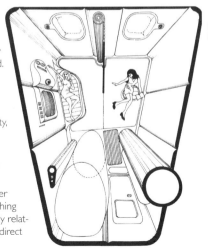

The Plug-in Capsule Home is an attempt to sustain the idea in the hope that some brave soul might eventually be persuaded to finance research and development.

The techniques of mass-production and automation are a reality, yet we see the research that goes into, and the products that come out of, today's building and are dismayed.

The Plug-in Capsule attempts to set new standards and find an appropriate image for an assembly-line product.

The order of its design criteria are in correct order to consumer requirements. First, a better consumer product, offering something better than, and different from, traditional housing, more closely related to the design of cars and refrigerators, than placing itself in direct competition with tradition.

住宅即消費品

華倫・裘克

有關我們最聲名狼藉的誤解之一就是我們終究並不在乎人。這或許直接與我們所使用的意象類型有關。就好比,「城市替換」這類構想的某些部份,似乎預示了某種只存在電腦與遙控機械裝置的自動化不毛之地。這到底具有多少道理是很難評斷的,但若仔細地研究我們的作品,將會發現一些對於人的真切關懷的足跡與人們如何自居家、工作及整體構築環境中之既有混亂加諸於他們身上的限制中得到解放的方式。

我們同樣地關切人類處境中的環境改變與城市中活動及場所的定義。其中重要的是場所被視為創造一個真實有生氣城市的構想發生器的教訓。城市應該引發、反映與活化生活,其結構應組織以促進生活與發展。情境、城市裡空間內部的事件、人類瞬間無常丟棄式的世界、汽車短暫的存在⋯⋯等,與構築環境及空間構築界限一樣,且甚至更為重要。

事實上,這是與南岸設計案有關之構想的延續,其原始的基本構想為創造一群附屬於連續的人行步道之無特徵建築物,某種為了人類而非山羊之考量的「麥朋梯丘」(譯註)。

因此就行人而言,我們心裡最關心的事情是人類的群居天性與他們的運動,以及用以引導行人之運動模式的空間構築界限。

我們延伸自己超越傳統建築思想的狹隘界限,試圖更接近一般社會大眾,研究他們的看法與行為,也造成了外界對於我們企圖做的事情的誤解。我們必須延伸超越傳統的阻礙並尋找不具任何正式建築訓練的人,為其創造能呈現出與城市影像以及其它事物有關之對於目前看法之明顯的直覺領會的概念。從科幻小說的世界裡,我們挖掘出與測地學通訊網、充氣管以及塑膠圓頂和塑膠泡⋯⋯等有關的預言性資訊。

如果我們翻到一般通俗出版品的底頁我們會發現「自己動手做」的客廳擴建,或是立即可用的車庫裝備的廣告。面對現實吧,我們不再能夠漠視社區內的每個人都具有潛在的創作本能而我們的角色終將變成只是指導他們一些確實與可接受的形式的事實。人之間和社區與設計師之間現存的鴻溝或許終將可以藉由「自己動手做」的可替換式元件裝備所克服。

在科技社會裡,愈來愈多人將於自己個人環境的決定與生活方式的自決中扮演主動積極的角色。我

們不能自他們的手中剝奪這種基本的權利並繼續視他們為文化與創作的白癡。我們必須從另一個角度以肯定的方式來處理這個問題。消費者導向社會的大量生產本質為重複與標準化，但是元件可以依據個人的需求與喜好而改變或替換，而且，若是全球市場的話，從經濟學的觀點而言也是可行的。

在美國人們可以挑選一部含有全系列可替換式選擇配備的汽車，正如萊納·班漢所指出的（在他有關夾式建築的文章裡），雪佛蘭汽車公司生產了17種車身與5種不同引擎的選擇性。

目前流行音樂的成功某種程度上是因為聽眾參與的重要性的緣故；「佛魯格舞」與「健身操」是自我表達與自由形成的。流行音樂團體本身在穿著與習慣上，包括音樂上的靈巧性方面，都比較貼近聽眾。儘管流行音樂變成了龐大的工業，它的成功與否仍視它是否跟得上消費者口味之步調的能力而定。

當然大量生產之消費性成分住宅的觀念如今已不算新。我們都熟悉柯比意與普魯威共同的努力及普魯威自己的小東西，還有布克敏斯特·富勒的「至高機能住宅」、菲爾普斯·道奇之「至高機能浴室」與「至高機能部署單元體」、艾麗森與彼得·史密斯森於「理想之家」博覽會的未來住宅、位於迪士尼樂園的伊恩耐爾·史艾的組合式旅館單元體與蒙山托塑膠屋；此外尚有代謝主義團體在日本以及阿瑟·庫安比在英國所完成的作品。

插接艙形住宅企圖延續這些想法，希望某些勇敢之士最終能夠被說服願意資助這項研究與發展。

大量生產與自動化的科技是事實，我們還看見了投入今日建築物的研究與產生的結果，但同時也是令人不安的。

插接艙室試圖為量產裝配生產線立下新的準則並找出適當的形象。

它的設計準則順序是消費者需求的適合順序。首先，是一個提供迥異且優於傳統住宅的消費產品，更貼近於汽車與冰箱之設計的想法，而非與傳統的正面較勁。

譯註：「麥朋梯丘」(Mappin Terrace) 是彼得·卻爾莫思·米契爾爵士與約翰·詹姆斯·裘司為英國倫敦動物園所設計之提供動物一處自然化棲息地的山形景觀獸欄區。

MONTREAL TOWER

Peter Cook

The Montreal Tower was a project commissioned by Taylor Woodrow and executed in the Euston office. It was presented to the authorities of the (then) forthcoming Montreal Expo as a 'central feature'. It had to incorporate a central concrete tower and provide a wide variety of public entertainment functions. This brief was extended to form a 'skin' and 'guts' proposition: a vertical tree with enormous roots on to which could be hung temporary exhibition elements that would be removed and replaced after the Expo.

In many ways, the project served as a trial run for notions of structural and component replacement that were developed in the Plug-in City. By comparison, the structure of the tower is closer, and the lift tubes – though diagonal – still form a separate structure. A skin wraps around the whole of the temporary infill.

蒙特婁塔

彼得・庫克

蒙特婁塔是由泰勒・伍德洛委任且由優仕頓事務所執行的設計案。它將提交給(當時)即將舉行的蒙特婁博覽會的有關單位作為「主要象徵」。它必須結合一座主要的具體塔形建築物並提供各式各樣的大眾娛樂功能。主要任務為延伸構成一個「外部皮殼」與「內部機構」的提案:一棵具有能夠暫時將展覽元件懸掛於其上且展覽後可以移除與替換之巨型根部的高聳樹木。

在許多方面,這個設計案是「插接城市」中所發展的結構與組件替換概念的試航。相較之下,塔形建築物的結構更接近這種概念,而升降梯管道——雖然是對角線的——仍舊構成一個獨立的結構。一層覆蓋著整個臨

Lyndon Baines Johnson wins Presidential election — Civil Rights Act bans much discrimination in US — Martin Luther King awarded Nobel Peace Prize — South Vietnam launches big attack on North — American involvement in Vietnam increases — Olympic Games held in Tokyo — Nelson Mandela is sentenced to life imprisonment — General MacArthur dies in US — UK – Forth Bridge opens — Cole Porter dies — Fighting in Cyprus between Greeks and Turks — Constantine II succeeds Paul I as King of Greece — MUSIC — Beatles first US tour — Rise of the Rolling Stones and Dave Clark 5 — Radio Caroline, first pirate radio, goes on the air — 'It's All Over Now' — 'Baby Love' — CINEMA — Beatles' first film, 'A Hard Day's Night' — 'Dr Strangelove' — 'Charade' — 'Goldfinger' — THEATRE — Stratford upon Avon celebrates 400th anniversary of Shakespeare's birth — FASHION — The Youth revolution changes the face of fashion — London boutiques become the new moving force in fashion — BIBA boutique opens — Andre Courrèges designs trouser suits for women — Little flat square-toed boots (Courrèges boots) become the rage — BOOKS — 'The Spire' — 'A Moveable Feast' — 'Herzog'

林頓・班納斯・詹森贏得總統大選－美國通過公民法案禁制各色歧視－馬丁・路德・金恩獲頒諾貝爾和平獎－南越大舉進攻北越－美國積極介入越戰－東京奧運－奈爾森・曼德拉遭判終身監禁－麥克阿瑟將軍於美國辭世－英國－福斯鐵路跨海大橋啓用－百老匯巨擘柯爾．波特辭世－希臘與土耳其爭奪塞浦路斯主權－康士坦丁2世繼任希臘國王－**音樂**－披頭四首度美國巡演－滾石樂團與戴夫・克拉克5崛起－首座地下電台「卡洛林電台」開播－《一切都結束了》－《稚愛》－**電影**－披頭四電影處女作《一夜狂歡》－《奇愛博士》－《謎中謎》－《007情報員－金手指》－**戲劇**－史特拉福市慶祝莎翁400週年誕辰－**時尚**－年輕革命改變了時尚面貌－倫敦精品店成為時尚新浪潮－畢巴精品店開幕－安德勒・古黑居為女性設計褲裝式套裝－小而平的方頭靴（古黑居靴）風靡一時－**出版**－《尖塔》－《慶典》－《公爵》。

1964

SPACE PROBE !

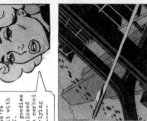

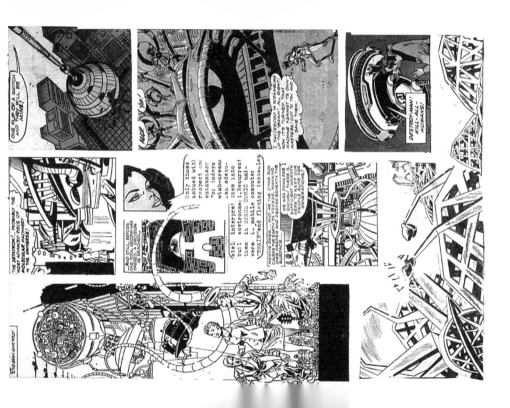

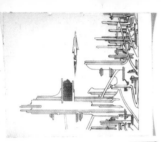

These SPACE COMIC cities reflect without conscious intention certain overtones of meaning---illuminate an area of opinion that seems the breakdown of conventional attitudes, the disruption of the "straight-up-and-down" formal vacuum----necessary to create a more dynamic environment.

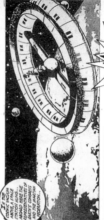

4

ZOOM AND REAL ARCHITECTURE

Archigram 4. Editorial, *Peter Cook*

We return to the preoccupation of the first Archigram – a search for ways out from the stagnation of the architectural scene, where the continuing malaise is not just with the mediocrity of the object, but, more seriously, with the self-satisfaction of the profession backing up such architecture. The line that 'Modern Architecture has arrived' seems more than ever inappropriate.

Certainly it has never been more possible to produce buildings that are at once well mannered . . . and quite gutless. Great British architecture now has more to do, organically, with the 'line-of-least-resistance' tradition from Queen Anne's Mansions to the Hilton, through Dolphin Square – than with the New Architecture of the twenties and thirties. Though it would be ridiculous to force an 'heroic' phase in the present decade, the cycle has too quickly reached the 'tragic'.

Mainstream fanciers can currently report further unashamed use by everybody of the 45° corner, stepped section, 3-D precast panel, and the rest – a cosmetic borrowed from the originals' beauty-box to tart up the latest 'least-line-tradition' scheme.

It would have been too easy to look over one's shoulder and fill Archigram with three dozen of the respected goodies of the last fifty years (interesting that so many would be pre-1930), and the comment, 'What have we lost? What are we missing?' Yet set against such a feeling of loss is the continuance of something that has not yet disappeared into historical perspective – a tradition that is still developing, and is still original to many of the basic gestures of modern architecture. It shares much of its expression with those dim, neurotic, enthusiastic days of the Ring, Der Sturm, and the Futurist Manifesto – the architectural weirdies of the time feeding the infant Modern Movement. Our document is the Space-Comic:

its reality is in the gesture, design and natural styling of hardware new to our decade – the capsule, the rocket, the bathyscope, the Zidpark, the handy-pak.

Is it possible for the space-comic's future to relate once again with buildings-as-built? Can the near-reality of the rocket-object and hovercraft-object, which are virtually ceasing to be cartoons, carry the dynamic (but also non-cartoon) building with them into life as it is? Or shall we be riding in these craft amongst an environment made of CLASP? The ridiculousness of such a situation can be compared with the world of Schinkel seen by the Futurists.

《建築電訊》第4期社論，彼得．庫克

變賣與變賣建築

我們回到第一份《建築電訊》所專注的——尋求脫離建築的停滯現實之道、現況中持續的沉滯並非只與物件的平庸有關，而是更嚴重地與專業的自我滿足於支持這樣的建築有關。然而「現代建築所找出」的方向似乎更不適當。

當然絕不可能再創造出同樣止得體的……卻又有點兒膽怯的建築物。英國現在的建築、根本上、從「希爾頓」至「安文王宅邸」「最少阻力路線」的傳統——而非20年代與30年代的新建築。雖然在近十年裡勉強進行「大膽冒險」的階段段有些荒唐，然而整個循環就快讓成「悲劇」了。

主流玩家可以毫不費勁地說出大家對於45度角、階梯式地形、立體預鑄讓板以及其它部分會更來而毫無顧忌的利用方式「（傳統）的設計。是從創意人的「最少阻力路線」（傳統）的設計。

若只是回顧歷史並在《建築電訊》雜誌裡面塞滿三、四十件近50年來受重視的作品（有趣的是大多數會是1930年之前的）並下註腳，「我用錯失了什麼？我們正失去什麼？」那就未免太輕鬆了。話雖如此，對照這種錯失

的感受是延續某種尚未消失變成歷史觀點的東西——一種仍發展中、目對於近代建築的許多基本表現而言仍是原創的傳統。它於狂飆運動與來派當時的那些模祖、神經自能症狂熱的日子裡有富諸多的表現——當時的建築怪傑孕育了初期的現代運動。我們的文藝檔案是「太空連環圖畫」：

其真實性在於我們對此物件代的意象為全新之硬體設備的表現、設計與自然風格——太空艙、火箭、雷達觀測器——遊樂場與遊樂器。

「太空連環圖畫」未來可能再次與「真實的建築物」有關嗎？最終已不再像漫畫式的火箭與氣墊船之類電式物件的近似實物，是否可能讓其充滿活力的（但亦非漫畫式的）建造物原原本本地進入現實生活之中？或者我們應該乘坐這些船艇美飛艇於扣環所構成的環境之中呢？這種情況的荒謬性可與未來派者所見之平宇爾的世界相比擬。

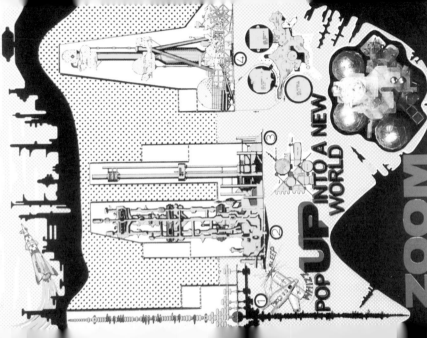

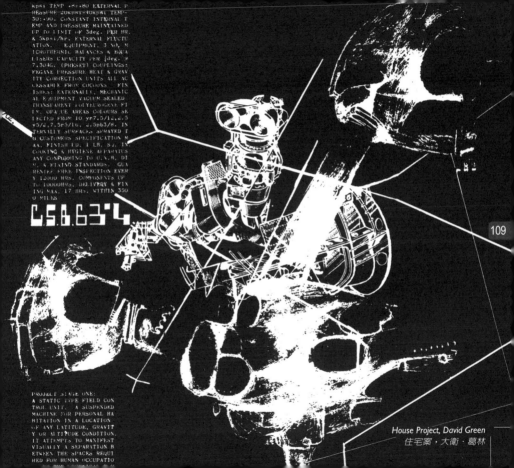

House Project, David Green
住宅案，大衛·葛林

PLUG-IN CITY

Peter Cook

The Plug-in City as a total project was the combination of a series of ideas that were worked upon between 1962 and 1964. The metal cabin housing was a prototype in the sense that it placed removable house elements into a 'megastructure' of concrete. The discussions of *Archigram 2* and *3* built up a pressure of argument in favour of expendable buildings: and it was then inevitable that we should investigate what happens if the whole urban environment can be programmed and structured for change.

The *Living City* exhibition paralleled these material notions with equally explosive ones regarding the quality of city life: its symbolism, its dynamic, its gregariousness, its dependence upon situation as much as established form. As a final preliminary, the Montreal Tower was useful as a model for the structuring of a large 'plug-in' conglomeration, with its large, regular structure and its movement-tubes (which were to be combined in the 'city' megastructure), and its proof that such a conglomeration does not need to have the dreariness that is normally associated with regularised systems.

It is difficult to state which phase of the work on Plug-in City forms the definitive project. During the whole period 1962-66 elements were being looked at, and notions amended or extended as necessary: so the drawings inevitably contain many inconsistencies. The term 'city' is used as a collective, the project being a portmanteau for several ideas, and does not necessarily imply a replacement of known cities.

My axonometric drawing is usually assumed to be the definitive image, for obviously classical reasons. It is

插接城市

彼得 · 庫克

整個「插接城市」設計案是一系列1962年與1964年間所進行之構想的組合。「金屬艙住宅」是將可移動住宅單元置入具體的「超大型結構」中的典型。《建築電訊》第2期與第3期裡的討論逐漸建立了有利於消費性建築物的辯論壓力：在當時我們無可避免地必須探究若可以規劃與組織整體都市環境以獲得改變的話情況將會如何。

「生活城市」展覽與這些在城市生活品質上──其象徵性、其原動力、其群居性，及其對於情境與既有形式之依賴──同樣具有爭議性的材料觀念是一致的。身為最後的暖身實驗，且因其巨大之系統性結構與運動管道（這些都將被併入「城市」的超大型結構中）之故，視「蒙特婁塔」作為一個大型「插接」的複合體構造典範極有助益，同時證明了這樣的複合體並不一定存在組織化系統中常見的乏味性。

很難說出是「插接城市」中的哪個階段構成了最終明確的設計案。在整個1962-66年期間，各個元素被檢視，各種觀念被修正與延伸──若有必要的話──因此圖書必然包含了許多前後不一致之處。「城市」一詞被用為集合名詞，設計案變成種種構想的混成語，且不一定表示取代了既有的城市。

我的透視圖通常被認為是最終明確的形象，因為

... 114

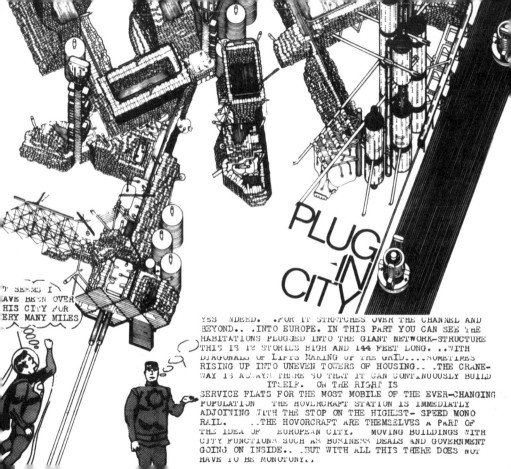

PLUG IN CITY

IT SEEMS I HAVE BEEN OVER THIS CITY FOR VERY MANY MILES

YES INDEED. .FOR IT STRETCHES OVER THE CHANNEL AND
BEYOND.. .INTO EUROPE. IN THIS PART YOU CAN SEE THE
HABITATIONS PLUGGED INTO THE GIANT NETWORK-STRUCTURE
THIS IS 12 STORIES HIGH AND 144 FEET LONG. ..WITH
DIAGONALS OF LIFTS MAKING UP THE GRID....SOMETIMES
RISING UP INTO UNEVEN TOWERS OF HOUSING.. .THE CRANE-
WAY IS ALWAYS THERE SO THAT IT CAN CONTINUOUSLY BUILD
                    ITSELF.   ON THE RIGHT IS
SERVICE FLATS FOR THE MOST MOBILE OF THE EVER-CHANGING
POPULATION   THE HOVERCRAFT STATION IS IMMEDIATLY
ADJOINING WITH THE STOP ON THE HIGHEST- SPEED MONO
RAIL.   ..THE HOVORCRAFT ARE THEMSELVES A PART OF
THE IDEA OF   EUROPEAN CITY.   MOVING BUILDINGS WITH
CITY FUNCTIONS SUCH AS BUSINESS DEALS AND GOVERNMENT
GOING ON INSIDE.. .BUT WITH ALL THIS THERE DOES NOT
HAVE TO BE MONOTONY..

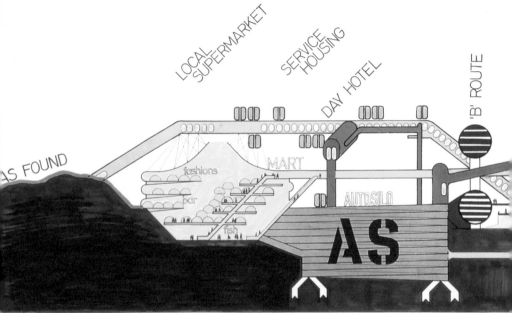

Europa, Perer Cook, 1963-64
歐洲，彼得，庫克，1963-64年

LOCAL SUPERMARKET

SERVICE HOUSING

DAY HOTEL

'B' ROUTE

AS FOUND

fashions

MART

bar

AUTOSILO

fish

AS

EUROPA LOCATION LON-S 50

DATE +20   NAME: KENT BUSINESSTOWN

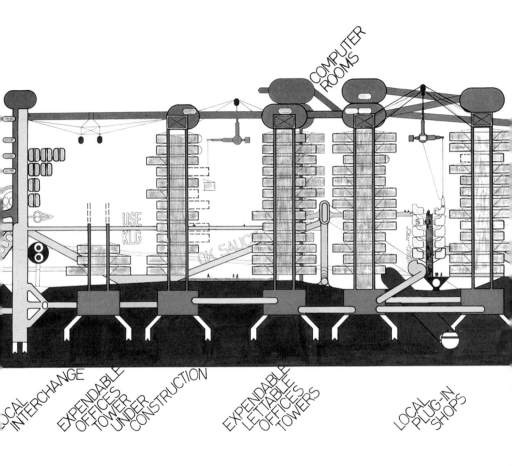

COMPUTER ROOMS

USE KLG

OK SAUCE

LOCAL INTERCHANGE

EXPENDABLE OFFICES TOWER UNDER CONSTRUCTION

EXPENDABLE LETTABLE OFFICES TOWERS

LOCAL PLUG-IN SHOPS

'heroic', apparently an alternative to the known city form, containing 'futurist' but recognisable hierarchies and elements. Craggy but directional. Mechanistic but scaleable. It was based upon a drawn plan, which placed a structural grid on a square plan at 45° to a monorail route that was to connect existing cities. Alongside ran a giant routeway for hovercraft (the ultimate in mobile buildings), the notion being that some major functions of the several linked parts could travel between them. The essential physical operations are stressed: the craneways and the bad weather balloons, and the lift overruns are deliberately exaggerated. But overriding all this was the deliberate varietousness of each major building outcrop: whatever else it was to be, this city was not going to be a deadly piece of built mathematics.

In the various studies that built up the total project, one can trace the succession of priorities that are gradually overlaid, and one can see how the sections evolved. The Nottingham project was a proposal for shopping, but the problems of frequent servicing and the breakdown of normal 'department store' or 'lockup' boundaries triggered a notion of a viaduct-like structure against which the shops could lean. The goods servicing and the unit replacement were complementary: and already a major part of the Plug-in proposition existed. With the craneway running along the viaduct and a service tunnel system, it is only a short step to the incorporation of housing elements.

We then turned towards a specific application of 'Plug-in' thinking: the rentable office floor. We created a pylon to contain lifts and services with a 'tray' hanging off each side. One tray is the 'front' office, the other the 'backroom' office. Each part would be

其顯而易見的典型理由。它是「極端誇張」的，很明顯地與既有城市不同，包含了「未來派」但卻仍可分辨的體系與元素；形如峭壁但具方向性，機械化作用但具尺度性。它是根據一份完成的平面圖，將45度方陣的結構座標方格置於連結既有城市的單軌鐵道路線上。沿途有一條巨大的氣墊車路線（移動式建築物的最終結果），其概念是某些連繫元件的某些主要機能可於其間移動。強調重要的實體管制中心：諸如起重機道與惡劣天候氣球，以及被刻意誇大的升降梯。但最為重要的是每棟主要建築物的顯現皆是深思熟慮後的變體：不管它會成為什麼，這座城市就是不會變成一件工程數學運算下的無聊產物。

從逐漸建立整體計畫案的各種研究裡，我們可以回溯逐漸被掩蓋的先後序列，並可看出各組成部份是如何被發展的。諾丁罕設計案是購物區的提案，但是經常性使用的服務性設施以及一般「百貨公司」或「上鎖區」之邊界瓦解的問題，引發了商店可以依靠的高架橋式結構的概念。商品服務與單元體更換具有互補性；此外「插接」計畫的主要部份已經存在了。有了沿著高架橋設置的起重機道與服務性隧道系統後，距離住宅元件的整合只剩下一小步而已。

然後我們轉向「插接」想法的特殊應用上：出租辦公室樓層。我們創造了一個塔形建築物，設有升降梯及於每側均退縮的「台架」式服務

exchangeable. Various ideas about automated shopping and diagonalised movement combine with the Plug-in Office tower in a hypothetical 'business-town' along an international route.

The **Plug-in City** is set up by applying a large scale network-structure, containing access ways and essential services, to any terrain. Into this network are placed units which cater for all needs. These units are planned for obsolescence. The units are served and manoeuvred by means of cranes operating from a railway at the apex of the structure. The interior contains several electronic and machine installations intended to replace present-day work operations. Typical permanence ratings would be:
Bathroom, kitchen, living room floor: 3-years.
Living rooms, bedrooms: 5-8-years.
Location of house unit: 15 years' duration
Immediate-use sales space in shop: 6 months
Shopping location: 3-6 years
Workplaces, computers, etc.: 4 years
Car silos and roads: 20 years
Main megastructure:
40 years

設施。一個台架是位於「正面」的辦公室，另一個則是「密室」形辦公室。每個元件均可更換。「插接」辦公塔樓兼具各種自動化商店與對角線運動的構想—— 一個堅持國際性路線的假設性「商業城」。

「插接城市」 藉由應用大規模的網路結構而組成，包含通往任何地區的出入通道與重要設施，可滿足所有需求的單元被置入此網路中；這些單元體藉由結構頂點上的鐵路運作起重機巧妙地操控與執行任務。其內部包含一些電子與機械裝置，試圖取代目前的工作管制中心。一些具代表性的耐久性評估如下：

浴室、廚房、起居室樓層：3年即廢棄；
客廳、臥室：5-8年即廢棄；
住宅單元體場所：15年的使用時間；
商店中即刻使用的銷售空間：3-6年；
購物場所：3-6年；
工作場所、電腦……等：4年；
汽車塔形支柱構造與道路：20年；
主要超大型結構：40年。

Plug-in City, Maximum Pressure Area, Peter Cook, 1964 →
插接城市，最繁忙區域，彼得．庫克，1964年→

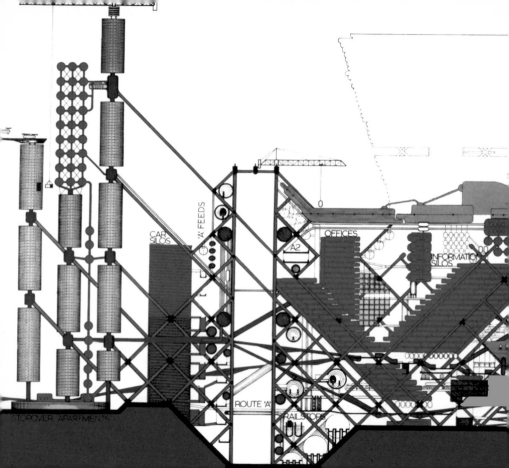

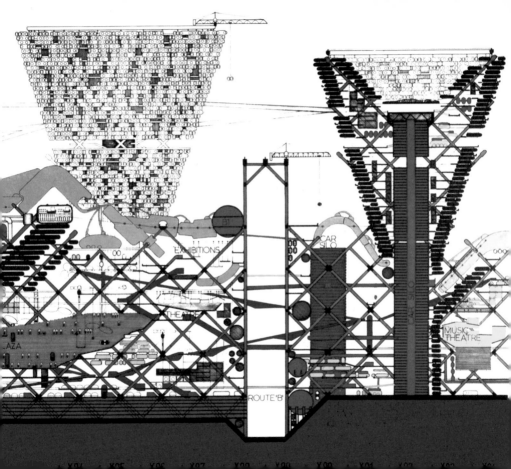

METROPOLIS

archigram 5   metropolis archigram 5

ARCHIGRAM
Magazine for new ideas in architecture

Editorial / Production Panel:
Peter Cook .. Editor
Warren Chalk
Dennis Crompton

Cover designed by Rae & Ben Fether

METROPOLIS ISSUE

EDITORIAL,

Peter Cook

Outside architecture, the intensity of metropolitan life has been sought and cherished as being somehow more conducive to all the great positives: to creativeness, emancipation, involvement, enlightenment and the rest. Metropolitan architecture has overtones and undertones beyond the satisfaction of a brief by the adaption of a style: a breakaway gesture can be contained within a four-walled context which itself is in quite a normal urban organisation. Random situations have also from time to time generated ingenuity that has directly fed the development of architecture. The intellectual wing has always been fond of solving the problem of 'The City', as a vehicle for connecting style with sociology. By establishing a complete environmental context they justify their preconceptions in toto.

Suddenly all this has been called into question. Are cities still necessary? Do we still need the paraphernalia of a metropolis to house the executive function of a capital city? Do we need the agglomeration of five, ten or twenty million people in order to learn, be entertained, enjoy good food or take part in higher productivity? The idea of cluster, and then of grouping

社論

彼得・庫克

除了建築之外，都會生活的強度一直被追求且珍視為更有助於所有重要的正面性：對於創造性、解放、參與、啓迪以及其它。都會建築並不滿足於風格改造的提示而具有其它的意涵；一個獨立的行為可被容納於本身即為相當普通之都市組織的四道牆文本中。隨機的情境有時也會產生直接孕育建築發展的創意。知識份子總是樂於解決「城市」的問題，作為連結風格與社會學的媒介。藉由建立一個複雜環境的文本，他們為自己所有的先入之見做辯護。

突然間所有這一切都受到了質疑。城市還是必要的嗎？我們還需要大都會的裝備來安置首都城市的執行功能嗎？我們需要5百萬人、1千萬人或2千萬人的居民點以獲得學習、娛樂、美食或達到更高的生產力嗎？族群的觀念，與之後的元件與功能的聚合，儘管它們是如此的相異但卻又如此

... 122/123

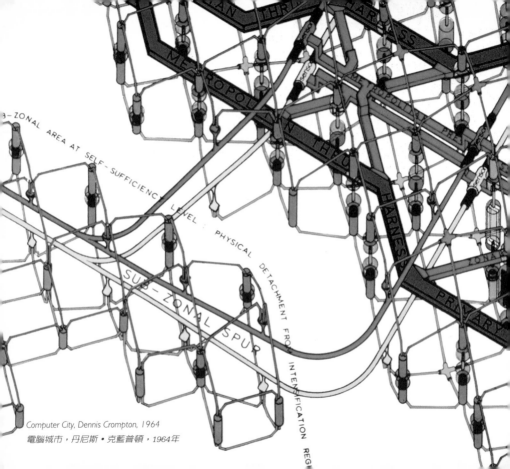

Computer City, Dennis Crompton, 1964

電腦城市，丹尼斯・克藍普頓，1964年

of parts and functions that are so different but sited so close together that elements cease to be defined, is a further sophistication of metropolitan organisation. This leads us to the proposition that the whole city might be contained in a single building. The concept of vehicular/pedestrian segre-gation is now an accepted part of planning theory. But once one accepts this and the idea of multi-level single buildings, it is only logical to conceive of multi-level cities. The organisation of, say, New York, which tolerates multi-level components connected by only two horizontal levels (street and subway), and both of those at the base, is archaic. However, a truly multi-level city will demand a connection system and an environment-penetration that is not just vertical or horizontal but also takes advantage of the diagonal.

THE CRUST OF THE CITY The dictionary definition of crust is a 'hard outer layer'. This outer layer is, in our definition, the zone where activity hits the air. In present-day cities this consists of a relatively unsophisticated series of chunks of building riddled by roads. The relationship to the sun, air, sky and distance rarely takes advantage of the potential of different and scattered elements congealing together in a random way.

THE MOLEHILL With the molehill (or 'heaped-up') section the crust surface can take maximum advantage of the air against its balconies as well as against its roof surfaces. It is a natural environment 'heap', with perhaps biological and psychological overtones as well.

STRUCTURE, DIAGONALS AND CONNECTIONS Any discussion of the connection between the significant diagonal and a multi-level city eventually separates into those diagonals that occur by necessity (the road filter from Tange's Tokyo Bay plan), those that emerge from the implications of a basic (or heroic) idea, and those that come about through sheer contrivance.

The implications of space-use in a complex organisation have been realised by degrees over many years. Piranesi obviously foresaw today's city situation. Much later, in the early 1920s, Neutra devised a first-stage multi-level connection, only involving, for the moment, two connecting levels above ground. Tony Garnier's Cité Industrielle had certainly used connecting fingers at high level but the derivation was strongly associated with real industrial situations, which was a justification of a heroic device. In a direct 'working-part' situation, there is the need to communicate with any part of the machine for maintenance purposes, and the further need for the fluids and solids being processed to flow from one zone to another.

A major problem of the organisation (and the imagery-control) of large areas of city is the achievement of a consistency running through parts with widely differing functions and sizes: add to this the problems of absorbing growth and avoiding the piecemeal one-offness of block-to-block relationship. The answer may be found in a large-scale structural idea, which is anyhow a necessity of a product of current engineering experimental consistent building.

'METABOLISM GROUP' (Japan) plan for part of Tokyo

The emergence of the diagonal is not only a product of current engineering experimental preference, it also implies a purpose of the structure that is new to buildings: to provide an umbrella within which growth and change (of the smaller, functioning parts) can take place. Nor, despite the prominence of the controlling structure in all these schemes, do they ever become boring.

緊扣，以致人們不再定義各元件，而事實上這是一個都會組織裡更為精密複雜之處。這引發了我們提出整個城市或許可以安置於一幢獨立的建築物裡的構想。車輛／行人的隔離概念在目前的設計規劃理論中廣受採納，但是一旦接受了這個概念與多層獨立建築物的構想之後，唯一符合邏輯的做法就是繼續構思多層城市了。採用水平的兩層（街道與地鐵）來連結多層組件，且此二者均位於底層的組織作法，例如紐約，已不再適用了。無論如何，真正的多層城市將需要一個連結系統與一個非僅垂直或水平且同時利用對角線的環境－穿透性。

城市之殼　字典上「殼」的定義是「硬的外部皮層」。在我們的定義裡，這個外部皮層是活動觸及空氣的區域。在目前的城市裡，這是由一系列量大且不複雜之道路貫穿的建築物所構成。與陽光、空氣、天空、距離的關係極少利用到差異與零星元素隨意凝固在一起的潛力。

鼴鼠丘　藉由鼴鼠丘式（或是「堆積式」）的劃分，殼面可以充分地利用到陽台與屋頂上的空氣。這是一個自然環境的「堆積」，或許也兼具生物學與心理學的含意。

結構、對角線與連結　任何關於重要的對角線與多層城市之間連結的討論，最後將區分為來自必要性的對角線（丹下健三的東京灣規劃案）、來自基本（或雄偉式）概念含意的對角線，與來自全然設計性的對角線。

複雜組織中的空間使用含意多年來逐漸地被理解。皮拉奈西顯然早已預見了今日的城市情況。稍晚於1920年代初期時，紐特拉設計出初步的多層連結，當時只專注於地面層以上的兩個連結層。東尼‧葛赫尼耶的工業新城於其高層部位必定運用了連結指狀物，但其由來則令人強烈地聯想到現實的工業情況，並可作為雄偉式設計的明證。在可直接正常運作的情況裡，為了維持運作必須能與機器的每個元件溝通，而為了更進一步的需求，流體與固體也有必要被加工處理並由一區流至另一區。

城市廣大區域之組織（與意象控制）的主要問題就是，如何達到機能與尺度差異性極大的各個元件之間的一致性；除此之外，尚有吸納成長與避免街廓間零碎的「僅此一次」關係等問題。答案或可於大尺度的結構構想中找到，不論如何，此一構想都是目前工程實驗之具有一貫性的建築物產品中所不可或缺的。

對角線的出現不只是當前的工程實驗偏好，它也暗示了某種結構上的目的（這對建築是新的構想）：提供一個成長與（較小的機能元件的）改變可以發生於其中的庇護傘。儘管在所有體系中都具有明顯的控制結構，但它們仍不至於變得無趣。

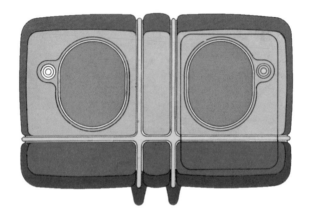

Capsule Homes, Warren Chalk, 1964
艙屋，華倫‧裘克，1964年

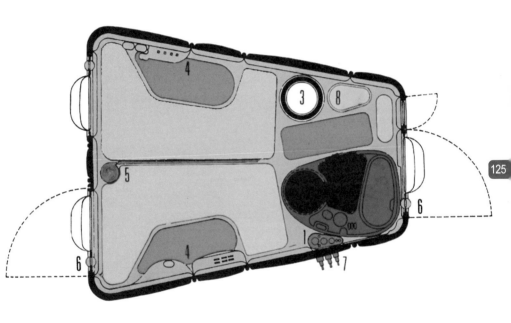

An unaccustomed dream

Warren Chalk

No magic is so strong that it may not be overtaken by a newer brand; images and iconography are disposable and extravagant homage inevitably arouses suspicion.

Initially associated with the iconography of the space programme and its underwater equivalents (and possibly the only architect member of the British Interplanetary Society), the urgent appeal of the 1960s has now cooled for me. Man has leapt up and down on the moon, played a golf stroke even, and we are not much better for it.

We have plumbed the depths of the ocean and anti-gravitated to another planet, but it is belligerently simple – clearly a military defence operation – and the spin-off back on earth in the final analysis is minimal.

Nevertheless, Archigram in 1964 and long before that, seeking new directions, embraced this technology wholeheartedly and produced underwater cities, living capsules and the rest.

David Greene, Spider Webb and I clamoured ecstatically over the rocket support structures at Cape Kennedy. I visited the NASA control centre at Houston and later witnessed the second Surveyor (manless) moon landing on the monitors at the Jet Propulsion Laboratories in Los Angeles, collecting small fragments of the moon surface. But there was an omen. The technician assigned to me, sitting in front of a bank of 39 close-circuit TV monitors of the lunar operation, was in fact watching the Johnnie Carson Show on the 40th.

But it remains an enigma. Transient urges, buried instances of a personal past, still stir the blood: because still no single architect or designer can hold a candle to the particular iconography that happened then.

Not to worry, the artist, designer, architect, may have no relevant role in society in any accepted form, but leaping about stimulates hide-bound mentalities. Cartoons and clowns are more meaningful than the Nixons, Heaths, Germaine Greers or Frosts of this world – hollow pretentiousness for humane humility.

Only more sophisticated humanity, only more sophisticated technology, working together in harmony, will help our children's children's children.

一個不尋常的夢

華倫・裘克

沒有任何魔法可以強到無法被更新的後繼者所超越。形象與肖像都是用後即可丟棄且過度臣服而終將引發質疑。

最初是將太空計劃與海底設備的圖像結合在一起（可能是英國行星協會中唯一的建築師會員），60年代時的迫切吸引力對我而言已經冷卻了。人類已經可以在月球上跳躍，甚至可以打高爾夫球，但我們並未因此而更好。

我們已經量測出了海洋的深度與另一個星球的抗引力，但它只是單純作戰上的——無疑地是一種軍事防禦作用，而最終的分析提供給地球的應用寥寥可數。

儘管如此，《建築電訊》在1964年或甚至更早，便開始尋求新的方向，全心全意地採納這種新科技並創造出「海底城」、「生活艙」以及其它的構想。

大衛・葛林、史派德・威派德與我對於甘迺迪角（譯註：即卡納維爾角）的火箭太空船支撐結構忘形地叫囂。我參觀了位於休斯頓的美國國家航空太空總署的控制中心，之後又在位於洛杉磯的噴射推進實驗室裡的監控器中目睹了第二次的探勘號（無人）月球登陸，收集了月球表面的小碎片。但這是一種前兆。我分配到的技術人員，坐在一排共39台月球運作的閉路電視監控器前，事實上正看著第40台的強尼・卡森秀呢！

但這也是一個謎、一個瞬間的衝動，雖是個人過往的遺忘實例，依舊令人激動；因為仍未有任何建築師或設計師擁有比得上當時發生的獨特圖像。

無須擔心藝術家、設計師與建築師可能在社會中找不到任何可接受形式的適切角色，而只能四處地刺激躲藏受困的心態。連環圖畫與小丑都要比這個世界上的尼克森、海斯、裘門・葛麗爾絲或佛洛斯特——合乎慈悲謙卑的虛偽矯飾——更有意義。

唯有更複雜精巧的人性與更複雜精巧的科技一起和諧地運作，才能夠幫助我們一代又一代……。

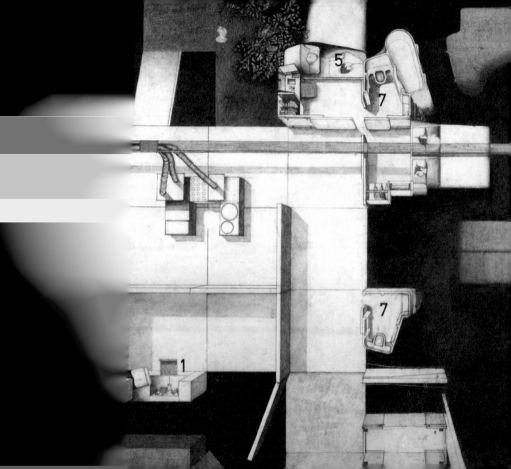

Drive-in housing

Mike Webb

The project is a preliminary study in the design of automated constructional, servicing and dismantling techniques applied to a large building development.

The building has been designed large enough to include its own component production units. These manufacture moulded reinforced plastic panels, which are conveyed, folded up, to their position in the structure and then open out to form usable floor space.

Plastics have been chosen in preference to steel as a constructional medium because the full advantages of on-site component production can be taken. In the case of plastics, transport consists of raw materials arriving at one of the ports and being, ideally, pumped through pipelines to the site production units.

This diagram shows the automatic casting plant on the left, with the finished units being conveyed to their position.

免下車式住宅

麥克・威柏

這個設計案是自動化建造、服務設施與拆解技術廣泛地應用於建築發展的初步研究。

建築物被設計成夠大到足可容納它本身的組合生產單元。它們鑄造出強化塑膠面板，而後輸送、摺疊、放置於結構中的所屬位置，然後再攤開形成可使用之樓板空間。

在構造材料方面，塑膠比鋼更適於使用，因前者具有充分的現場組合生產之優勢。若選用了塑膠，其運輸過程為：原料抵達港口之後，依照理想再經由輸送管道抽送至基地生產單元體。

本圖顯示自動化鑄造工廠位於左側，且完成之單元體正被輸送至它們的位置。

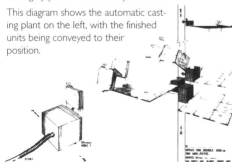

WALKING CITY

Ron Herron, 1964

步行城市

朗・赫倫，1964年

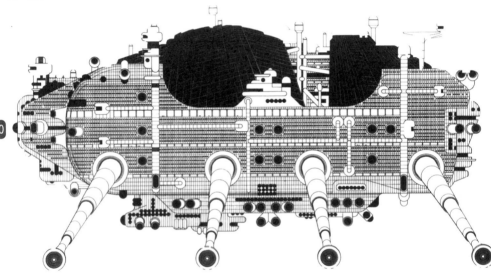

It is unlikely that the engineers who designed the various movable structures at Cape Kennedy ever heard of the Archigram Group. Indeed, the idea of a walking city would probably horrify them. Yet these engineers have designed and constructed a couple of dozen structures, some the height of 40 storey office buildings, that move serenely across the flat landscape. Yet in visionary architecture such concepts as prefabbed apartments hoisted into position on a skeletal frame, to be plugged into prepared utilities, are still considered impractical by most designers and builders.

Yet there are important urban problems – like intra and interurban transportation, for example – which could be attacked immediately, effectively, and speedily if there were a similar degree of courage and commitment – especially financial. The proud achievements of Cape Kennedy are proof of our ability to tackle the most staggering problems; and, by implication, they are an indictment of those who would not expend the same kind of effort on our urban ills.

在甘迺迪角設計各式各樣可移動結構的工程師們不可能曾經聽說過「建築電訊」這個團體。事實上,「步行城市」的構想可能會嚇壞他們。然而這些工程師們曾經設計建造過數十種結構,有些高達40層辦公大樓的高度的構造,沉穩地移動於平坦的景緻中。然而在紙上建築裡,這種將預製公寓吊於骨架中並插接上預先準備之設施的概念,依舊被大多數設計師與建造商視為不切實際。

迄今為止仍然有一些重要的都市問題——像是都市內部與各都市彼此間的交通運輸——可能立即、快速且強烈地遭到攻擊,但願他們也能有類似程度的勇氣與投入——特別是財務上。甘迺迪角上令人驕傲的成就證明我們有能力可以處理最棘手的問題;此外,它們也隱含了對於那些不願在我們的都市弊病上花費相同努力者的控訴。

彼得・布雷克,《建築論壇》,1968年

EACH WALKING UNIT HOUSES NOT ONLY A KEY
ELEMENT OF THE CAPITAL , BUT ALSO A LARGE
POPULATION OF WORLD TRAVELLER-WORKERS.

A WALKII

RowHenson. 1966

CITY

Lyndon B. Johnson inaugurated as 35th President of US — Winston Churchill dies and is given a State Funeral — Soviet cosmonaut Alexei Leonov makes first ever space walk — Vietnam War escalates — Malcolm X shot dead in New York — Edward H. White becomes first American astronaut to walk in space — Anti Vietnam War demonstrations in US and UK — Humanitarian Albert Schweitzer dies — Ferdinand Marcos becomes President of the Philippines — Swiss architect Le Corbusier drowns — Britain abolishes Death Penalty — Nat 'King' Cole dies — MBE for Beatles in Queen's Birthday Honours — Race riots in Watts, Los Angeles — 'Early Bird', first communications satellite, launched by US — MUSIC — Strobe lights used for the first time at a concert — Beatles and Rolling Stones are still prominent — Folk/protest boom starts — 'The Times They Are A-Changing' — 'Satisfaction' — 'Help' — 'Ticket to Ride' — 'I Got You Babe' — CINEMA — 'Darling' — 'Help!' — 'The Knack' — 'Sound of Music' — BOOKS — 'The Making of the President' — 'The Looking Glass War' — Russian writer Mikhail Sholokov awarded Nobel Prize for Literature — FASHION — London 'swings' — Mini skirts — Shoulder-length hair for men — Op Art inspired fashion accessories — Pop Art Union Jack jackets — Carnaby Street is mecca for 'switched on' people

林頓・班納斯・詹森就任美國第35任總統－溫士頓・邱吉爾逝世並予國葬－蘇聯太空人阿雷克西・里歐諾夫成為第一位太空漫步的太空人－越戰情勢升高－麥爾坎X於紐約遇刺身亡－愛德華・懷特成為美國首位太空漫步的太空人－美國及英國反越戰遊行示威－人道主義者艾柏特・史懷哲逝世－斐迪南・馬可仕成為菲律賓總統－瑞士建築師柯比意溺水身亡－英國廢除死刑－爵士巨匠納京高過世－披頭四接受女王贈勳－洛杉磯華茲種族暴動－美國發射「早鳥」通訊衛星－**音樂**－電子閃光燈首度使用於音樂會－披頭四與滾石樂團仍廣受歡迎－反戰民謠風起－巴布・狄倫的《時代在變》－《滿意》－《幫幫忙》－《乘車券》－《抓到你了寶貝》－**電影**－《親愛的》－《救命》－《竅門》－《真善美》－**出版**－《總統的誕生》－《鐵蹄少壯魂》－蘇聯作家米樹以・修羅科夫獲頒諾貝爾文學獎－**時尚**－倫敦「搖擺風」－迷你裙－男士蓄留及肩長髮－歐普藝術啟發時尚配件靈感－普普藝術聯盟傑克外套－卡納比街成為流行時尚聖地。

1965

ARCHI GRAM N06°

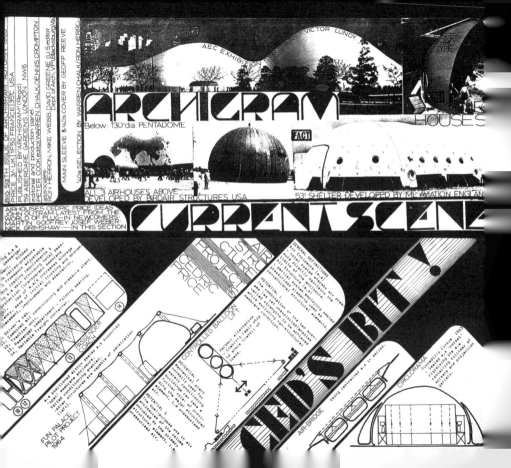

BIG SIXTH ISSUE OF ARCHIGRAM. AUTUMN 1964

PRICE 3/- UK 1F50 FRANCE 135¢ USA

PUBLISHED BY ARCHIGRAM (Regd)
99 ABERDARE GARDENS, LONDON NW6

editorial and production panel:
PETER COOK editor WARREN CHALK DENNIS CROMPTON
associates
PETER HERRON, MIKE WEBB, DAVID GREENE (US editor)
40s SELECTION BY WARREN CHALK/RON HERRY
MAIN SLEEVE & 40s COVER BY GEOFF REEVE

AEC EXHIBITION STRUCTURE VICTOR LUNDY

ARCHIGRAM

HOUSES

Below: 130' dia. PENTADOME

FACT

ALL 3 AIRHOUSES ABOVE
DEVELOPED BY BIRDAIR STRUCTURES USA

53' SHELTER DEVELOPED BY ML AVIATION ENGLAND

AIR-HOUSES CEDRIC PRICE: IDEAS
JOHN OUTRAM: LATEST FROM THE
WORLD OF PLUG-IN: NEWCOMERS
MARTIN GODFREY: JOSEF WEBER:
NICK GRIMSHAW— IN THIS SECTION

CURRENT SCENE

AIR
CURRENT
PROJECTS
CEDRIC PRICE

GENERAL DEFINITIONS

CONTROLLED BALLOON LIFT

FUN PALACE
PILOT PROJECT
1964

PASSENGER
COACH

AIR-BRIDGE

CIRCLORAMA

NED'S BIT!

phenomena for how

A NEW ARHITECTU IS THE HARNESSIN OF ENERGY

NOW FLYING

crane-way / lift-slab-structure-itself / pylon,as feed & support

NOW FLYING helicopter that carries and discharges trailer unit

DO WE STILL NEED HOUSES

COMPARATIVE ERECTION SUSTAINANTS

IMPLIES — INFLATABLE or CONCERTINA ENVELOPE — 2-MAN CAPACITY

BUFFER OPERATES BRAKE AT WALKABOUT SPEEDS

VEHICLE CAN BE COLLAPSED & TAKEN INDOORS

UP LIFTS ETC.

THE NEXT VEHICLE: WHICH ELIMINATES THE CAR

O WE. STILL **PANELS?**

WHEN WE HAVE THE ABILITY TO EVOLVE THE COMPLETE ENVIRONMENT: COMPLETELY SUSTAINED: AND INFINITE VARIETY WITHIN ?

RANGE
FULLY COMPUTERISED
INDUCTION PATH 30mph
PEEL-OFF EVERY 1m.
UNDER 30mph STILL
INDUCTION CONTROLLED
BUT PEEL-OFF EVERY
300yds.
SEGREGATED ROUTES TO REALLY
DRIVER 4mph AND PLUG-IN
DRIVER CONTROLLED USED
AMONGST PEDESTRIANS

WITH A GRAM-MER OF EVER-CHANGING PHENOME

THE EXISTENCE OF THE POCK TAPE RECORDER HAS T SAME MEANING FOR AS THE TOWER CRANE.

living occupat·n control

COTTAGE	FIELD	CASTLE
VILLA	FACTORY	BANK
UNIT	TEAM	GOVT POLICY

ZONE of most frequented identity — LEISURE occasional motivat'n — SYNTH LESSER net·work

Q: DOES 'HOME' REMAIN VALD
WHEN ANY ATMOSPHERE OF LIVING CAN BE CONJURED AT A MOMENT'S NOTICE - BY THE PRESS OF A SWITCH — 2000-

COMPARABLE SPACE-ENCLOSURE METHODS (EMMERICH'S CHART)

| PLAQUE | VOILES | COQUES | TUBES | | |

ONOMY OF MEANS
SONY TV now available in

1. equipment 2. operations(kitchen)
3. anti-gravity pad 4. soft floor
5. zip-out screen
6. door wall
7. service sockets
8. wc

PLUG-IN CAPSULE HOMES DISSECTED

Warren Chalk
Ron Herron

QUICK SCENE
USA

TRANSPORT NODE
Terry Stuart

ceiling unit

ZOOM rave hits Bristol
by ARCHIGRAM editor on Plug-in scene & world of Zoom

Students made ZOOM T-shirts for lecture visit

CARDIFF AIRHOUSE

ceiling unit / screen / wall etc / floor tray

LONDON

orange/white stripes — pink — blue translucent

orange — white — **EXHIBITION STRUCTURE**

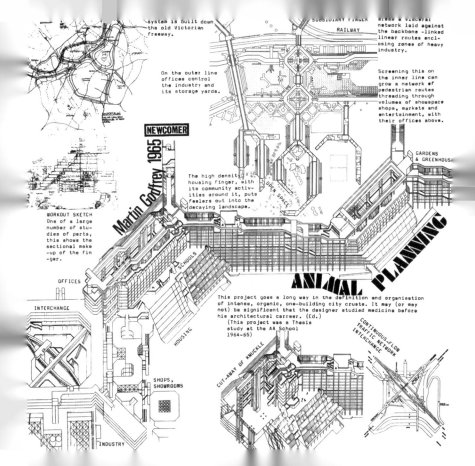

system is built down
the old Victorian
freeway.

On the outer line
offices control
the industry and
its storage yards.

SUBSIDIARY FINGER
RAILWAY

areas a visceral
network laid against
the backbone -linked
linear routes encl-
osing zones of heavy
industry.

Screening this on
the inner line can
grow a network of
pedestrian routes
threading through
volumes of showspace
shops, markets and
entertainment, with
their offices above.

NEWCOMER

Martin Godfrey 1965

The high density
housing finger, with
its community activ-
ities around it, puts
feelers out into the
decaying landscape.

OPEN SPACE

GARDENS
& GREENHOUSE

WORKOUT SKETCH
One of a large
number of stu-
dies of parts,
this shows the
sectional make
-up of the fin
-ger.

OFFICES

INTERCHANGE

SCHOOLS

HOUSING

ANIMAL PLANNING

This project goes a long way in the definition and organisation
of intense, organic, one-building city crusts. It may (or may
not) be significant that the designer studied medicine before
his architectural carreer. (Ed.)
    (This project was a Thesis
    study at the AA School
    1964-65)

CONTINUOUS-FLOW
TRAFFIC NETWORK
INTERCHANGE

CUT-AWAY OF KNUCKLE

SHOPS,
SHOWROOMS

INDUSTRY

peter cook **UNIVERS**

peter cook UNIVERS

1 FIRST GROUP OF PYLON-FEEDS

2 SILO DECKS HAULED UP

3 SILO ESTABLISHED

4 LIFT TUBES ESTABLISHED

5 TEACHING ROOMS PLUGGED IN

BRAIN SILO FEEDS INFO. DOWN.

FIRST GROUP STARTS OPERATING

6 SECOND GROUP GETS UNDER WAY

7 BOTH GROUPS OPERATING AND UNIV. NODE IS ESTAB.D

8

NODE WILL INTER-ACT WITH OTHER UNIVERSITY UNITS & STUDENT HOMES VIA PATHS ——→

NODE IS ALSO CENTRE FROM WHICH INFORMATION IS PIPED

9 MORE TEACHING ROOMS PLUGGED IN

10 MAX. TEACHING ROOMS +SILO OUTCROPS

11 SILO EXPANDS

12

BY THIS TIME TREND IS TOWARDS DISPERSAL OF STUDY INTO HOME,WORKPOINT, FUN CENTRE, ETC.

BRAIN SILO IS NOW 'BROADCASTING' CENTRE

13 SILO EXPANDS MORE TEACHING ROOMS DECREASE

14 SILO DEVELOPS,HOUSING REPLACES TEACHING RMS.

15 SILO & INFLATABLE-ASSEMBLY SPACE NOW FORM UNIV. NODE

?

IDEA OF THE 'UNIVERSITY' AS SUCH MAY GO BUT PLUG-IN SYSTEM ALLOWS FOR PHYSICAL CHANGE

PLUG-IN UNIVERSITY NODE

Peter Cook, 1965

The University Node was an exercise to discover what happened to the various notions of gradual infill, replacement and regeneration of parts on to a Plug-in City megastructure: but with a specific kind of activity.

Peter Cook was at this time working with a group of students who were also looking at the future of universities as institutions – and at new ways of teaching. The sequence below anticipates the loosening-up of parts. The 'always-complete-but-never-finished' nature of Archigram projects continues from now (1965) onwards.

The main enclosures are simply tensioned skins slung on trays which collectively create the 'node'. Each student can have a standard metal box and can choose to have it located anywhere on the decking. In a sense, this anticipates the 'nomad' nature of subsequent projects.

The nature of Plug-in City, involving the replacement of one function by another (though occupying the same location), could be demonstrated and a more intense glimpse of the likely detail of rooms, lift-tubes, skins and even hand-rails disclosed.

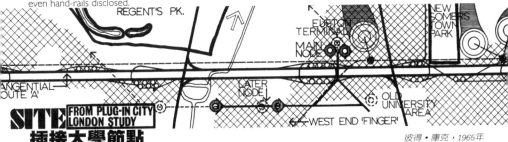

彼得・庫克，1965年

「大學節點」是為了發掘在「插接城市」此一超大型結構中逐步填實以及組件的更換與更新之多樣化概念的訓練，但仍具有其特殊的活動內容。

彼得・庫克這回是與一群身為制度設施之同樣檢視大學的前途——並檢視新的教學方式——的學生一起合作。下方的連續圖期盼各元件能夠融為一體。「建築電訊」設計案中「永遠－完整－但－從未－完成」的特質自此（1965年）開始。

主要的外殼單純地只是懸吊於集體塑造出「節點」之台架的張力構造皮殼上。每位學生擁有一個標準的金屬盒子，並可選擇設置於樓層板上的任何位置。就某種意義而言，這點預期了隨後設計案中的「游牧」特質。

「插接城市」的特質：明白呈現出功能彼此間的取代性（雖然處於相同位置上），並且可以更清楚地瞥見房間、升降梯管道、皮殼、甚至扶手的模樣。

THE 40's

STIRRUP PUMPS

Made to M.O.W. Specification with improved stirrup. Supplied complete with 20ft of best quality 1 1-braided hose and straight jet The barrel is protected by a heavy rubber sleeve. 8' standard

40年代

……除此之外，40年代前半期在維在維必需品，科技進步與大量生產技術等方面，歷經了發明大躍進，證明了人類在戰爭壓力下的才智，勇氣，努力與投資。這個時期所產生了一種奇怪的理想主義。這種理想主義遲早會歸零，但科技却不盆：飛行器的合成夾板或測地線架構，橋樑的焊接式管狀構造，以反阻隢低空飛行敵機的障礙氣球的凌空結構。除此之外，還賠色了我們的看法與學門。

在第二次世界大觀的最後階段期間，一些預鑄房屋類型承接了「夾上」／「插接」的特質。若有邱吉爾貴為官方的批准，它們就可以為臨時住宅計劃大量生產了。

145

THE 1940s

......apart from all that, the first half of the 1940s saw a great inventive leap made out of necessity for survival, advancing technology and mass production techniques and demonstrating man's ingenuity, courage, effort and investment under the stress and pressure of war. Out of this period came too a strange social idealism. The idealism was to fade but the technology, the laminated timber or geodesic framework of an aircraft, the welded tubular construction of a bridge, the airstructure of a barrage balloon, and much more, filtered through to colour our attitudes and disciplines today.

During the final stages of World War II several prefabricated house types emerged as part of the 'clip-on' / 'plug-in' heritage. They were given the official blessing of Winston Churchill, and produced in quantity for the temporary housing programme.

Of all the systems the ARCON MARK V. (45,000) and the AIROH (54,000) are probably the most significant – it's all there, the 'heat unit', 'package kitchen' and other 'plug-in' goodies that appear so with-it 25 years later. However, soon the market was flooded with prefabricated systems.

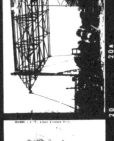

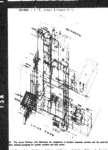

所有系統的「阿蘭孔馬克思5號(45000)與艾格(54000)於25年後看來或許是最重要的——全都在那兒了，「核心單元」「套裝廚房」及其它的「插接」的基本理念。然而，很快地市場便記錄著組合式預製系統，摧毀了大量生產的基本理念。再加上大眾偏見與「預製」這個字的社會污名，再再都成了最大的致命傷。

相較於今天，大眾流行文化對於40年代所言而言依舊是晦澀難解的，但人人均可打扮成珍·羅素與正宗「海報」女郎一貝蒂·葛雷柏的模樣。「情歌王子」依舊正當紅，目辛那屈正當紅。流行音樂是棘手的——安布羅斯的〈他們無法逃離月球〉但是爵士樂迷們會在他門隙米勒與肯頓作品的同時，也調整頻率至美軍無線電通訊網收聽「烏」或泰德·戴莫隆的一小段音樂。

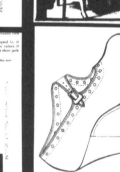

148

destroying the very basis of mass production, and this, together with public prejudice and the social stigma attached to the word 'Prefab' proved fatal.

Compared with today, in the 1940s pop-culture remained obscure, but it was there to be had in the shape of Jane Russell, and the original 'pin-up' girl, Betty Grable. 'Crooners' were still 'in' and Sinatra was King. Pop music was sticky – 'They Can't Black Out the Moon' by Ambrose, but Be-bop addicts tuned into A.F.N. [the American Forces Network] to hear snatches of Bird or Tadd Dameron in between Miller and Kenton.

On the fine art scene there was little true pop. The romantic literary Englishness of John Piper and Edward Bawden held sway, and there was Trog. The Ad-man was still the art man, and commercial art smacked of the 1930s, all collage and Constructivist typography. For pop reading there was the Tropics by Henry Miller, the original beat, and of course Lilliput and Picture Post. Meanwhile the straight-up-and-down architectural situation had seen an end to the 'white boxes' of the 1930s and the Modern Movement had become acceptable to all but the most reactionary. The standard of architecture was poor and little of it was worth recording here; only Lubetkin struggled

FRANK SINATRA
IN "STEP LIVELY"
(RKO)

CENTRAL LINE
WESTERN EXTENSION
OPEN JUNE 30

see for yourself

Such a nice

Lilliput

GLENN MILLER

BRITAIN
GOES AHEAD
EXHIBITION

在藝文界裡很少有真正的通俗作品，派普與愛德華·鮑普的浪漫派文學「英國風」大行其道，此外尚有楚若戈等人，廣告人仍是藝術人，大眾文學作品則有亨利·米勒的《北回歸線》。原創性十足的披頭族，當然還有《小人國》與《卡片》。

此時，劇烈起伏狀的建築情勢中已可見到30年代時「白色盒子」的終局，而現代主義運動已變成除了最保守復古者外均可接受的。建築師的標準十分廉之，並沒有什麼值得於此起記錄下來的；在諸多明證皆顯示了佩特里新城的天歐之前，只有當員將金緊緻地持續奮鬥下去。社會理想主義者蹣跚轉往瑞典，鍍銅屋頂誕生，日塞斯坦的工廠（法韻區）悄悄成立於威尼斯。陣營轉往瑞典，鍍銅屋頂誕生，日塞斯坦的工廠（法韻區）悄悄成立於威尼斯。那些炸彈摧毀過的城鎮具雜亂無章的提案局或許只有赫特福特福過的希望化了40年代的希望。

manfully on, until the Peterlea New Town fiasco proved too much. The social idealist camp looked towards Sweden and the copper clad mono-pitch was born, and a Mies type factory (Frankel) went up quietly in Wales.

Possibly only the Hertfordshire achievement shaped up to the promise of the 1940s; the welter of proposals for the bomb-battered towns and cities certainly did not.

During the war fashion design played a double game: on the one hand the squared shoulders, military-looking hats, shoulder strap handbags and clumpy shoes got close to the Services uniforms, while the other provided the absolute antithesis, with silly little hats, silk stockings and 'frocks'. In the austerity peace that followed the most shattering events were the 'wasp-waist' and the 'New Look' skirts dropping their hemlines to the ankles. Paradoxically, the atom bomb inspired another fashion revolution in the form of the 'Bikini'. War surplus found its way onto the consumer market and everything, from jeeps to duffle coats, has influenced us since.

During the allied invasion of Europe at the end of the War, the Americans captured over 200 V2s from the Germans and shipped them back to the States. Later, the warheads were removed and

9

8 8A

7A

9A

12A 12

11 11A

CRYSTAL PALACE COMPETITION

13 13A

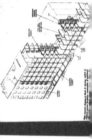

PRESTIGE
pressure cookers

PRESSURE COOKING IS
QUICK AND EASY

定是沒有辦法的。

戰爭期間，服裝設計受了口是心非的技倆的影響，一方面是方肩、軍用帽、肩帶式手提包與類似軍靴的鞋款，而另一方面則是全然的對比，小呆帽、絲質長襪與洋裝，緊接著軍裝員毀滅性戰事的到

古太平運當然是「柳腰」與長及足踝長裙的「新風貌」。很多情地，原子彈啟發了它的剩餘價值──從吉普車到厚毛粗呢

革命──「切事物」自此影響我們至今。戰爭在消費市場找到了一波另一波的時尚

上衣的一切事物，自此影響我們至今。

戰爭末期間，美國由德國擄取了超過200枚的V2火箭彈，並將其運返美國。

之後，彈頭被轉換成電子設備並發射進入太空，預示了太空計劃的濫觴。諸如此類不勝枚舉地

151

replaced with electronic equipment and fired off into space, heralding the beginning of the space programme. Events such as this – too many to enumerate here – occurring in the 1940s, have shaped the patterns and attitudes that we subscribe to today. The contributions made in so many disparate disciplines should be important to us in our search for a way out from the current stagnation and misdirection.

Also included here are the more satisfactory contributions to the Festival of Britain which, though not strictly 1940s acted as a watershed for opinions about design and ways of life in the same way as the MARS group exhibition in 1937.

The 1951 exhibition, an expensive piece of pseudo-social scientific naval gazing designed to boost the wilting popularity of the Labour government, sold 'Contemporary' architecture to the public and we have suffered and tried to escape its devastating influence ever since.

This then is a highly personal view of the 1940s, trying to evoke some of the look and feel of the period which, if not architecturally great, is certainly worth recording.

Warren Chalk, October 1965

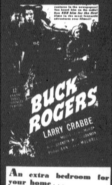

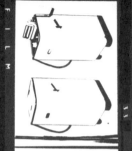

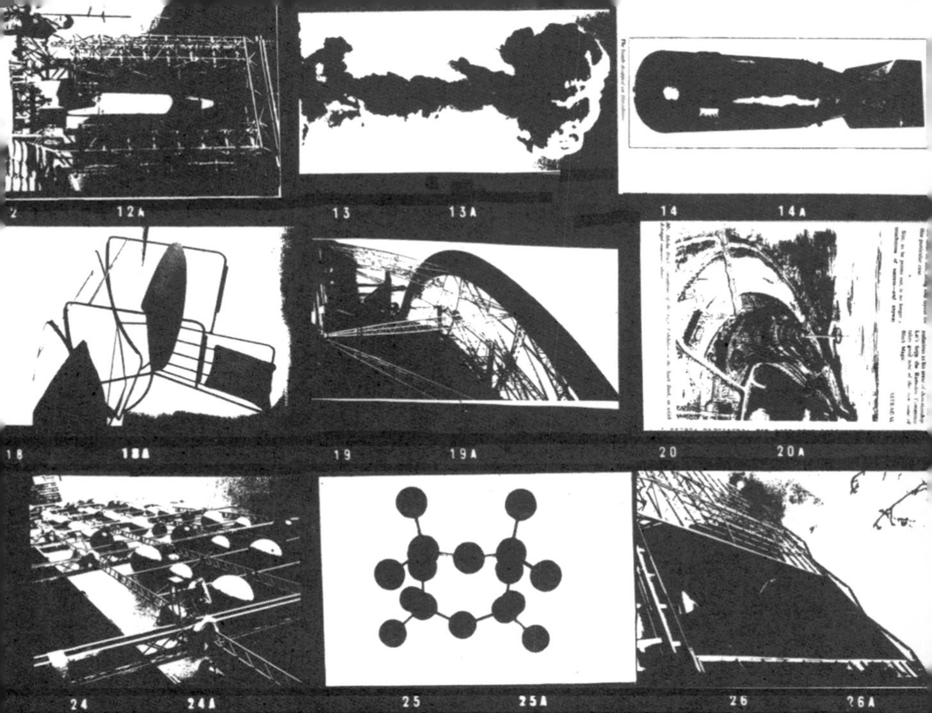

発生於1940年代的事件形成了今日我們所認同的典範與看法。如此衆多異類科學貢獻對於我

們尋求自停滯與錯誤方向中脫困的方法而言十分重要。

這些貢獻當中尚包括令人更為滿意的「英國園」。儘管1940年代中並不全然如同1937年的「現代建築

研究」團體展覽脫胎成為有關設計與生活方式之看法的轉捩點。

1951年的展覽──被規劃為提高工業及其真實並試圖逃離它破壞性的影響。

「當代」建築給予民衆，由此我們身受其害對凋零絕望的一次召喚為社會昌貴的破綻。 眅賣者

這目然是個有關1940年代非常個人的觀點，試圖喚起那時代的面貌與氛圍，即使建築學方面並

無耀眼的建樹，但整體而言仍値得回憶。

華倫·裘克·1965年10月

153

THE CAPSULE

Warren Chalk started to use the word 'capsule' in 1964. The Archigram Group at that time formed a part of the Taylor Woodrow Design Group, under Theo Crosby, and it was the habit of the company to feed the Group with experimental projects. The notion of a completely new prefabricated dwelling was one of these: the only constraint was that it should stack up into a tower structure.

From every point of view the space capsule was an inspiration: how different in concept and in efficiency from the tradition of buildings! The statement was a capsule dwelling, with the ergonomy and the sophistication of a space capsule. The parts would be tailored and able to be updated as technology moved forward, and as the dweller changed his needs. Simultaneously, the Plug-in City was being developed, and whilst both projects remained quite separate it soon became obvious that the capsule dwelling would be a preferred type within a Plug-in City. It also became obvious that the wedge-shaped unit sitting into a tower was a limitation of the concept.

The capsule dwelling was a set of components: whilst snugly and efficiently locked together they were capable of total inter-changeability. To use the automobile as an analogy: the Ford floor tray could be traded in for a Chrysler floor tray. There would be a continual exchange taking place, with constantly changing and evolving parts. Perhaps a dream-machine as well as a mere 'house'? The whole tower would be organised to allow the larger elements to be replaced by crane and the smaller elements to be manoeuvred from within: as a result all parts would be capable of being opened-out or clipped-in. The main parts were conceived as pressed – metal or GRP, though later the possibility of pressed paper started to interest the Group.

Conceptually, the 'capsule' serves to describe an approach to housing by presenting a series of very sophisticated and highly designed elements locked together within a 'box' which is itself highly tailored. It is an industrial design approach. It implies a deliberate – even a preferred – lifestyle. It suggests that the city might contain a defined conglomeration of such a lifestyle, rather like a hotel. At the same time it is definitive, and would by-pass many of the myths of urban design which depend upon hierarchies of incident and the treatment of housing as a folk art.

艙室

華倫・裘克於1964年開始使用「艙室」這個字。「建築電訊」當時與泰勒・伍德洛設計團隊結盟，由西奧・克羅斯比領軍，而公司的慣例則是提供該團隊實驗性的設計案。全新的預製住宅概念即為其中之一：唯一的限制是它必須被堆疊成一個塔形結構。

從各種觀點來看「太空艙」都是一種靈感：它與建物傳統在概念上與效能上有多麼大的差異啊！其宣言是一棟兼具人體工學與太空艙精密複雜性的「艙室住宅」。元件裁製而成，並可於科技再發展與居民需求改變時更新。在此同時，「插接城市」仍繼續發展，雖然兩個設計案各自獨立，但明顯地「艙室住宅」很快就成為「插接城市」裏偏好的類型，同時很明顯地位於塔中的楔形單元體成了概念上的限制。

「艙室住宅」是一系列的組件：雖然適切有效地固定在一起，但它們全都是可替換的。若以汽車作為類比的話：福特汽車底盤可以抵購作為克萊斯勒汽車底盤。利用不斷演變與進化的元件，更換將持續地進行下去。也許是部夢幻機器，同時又不過是棟「房子」？整座塔形構造將被編制為允許較大元件可以起重機替換，而較小元件則可由內部操作：因此所有元件均可以被攤開或夾入。主要元件被構思為壓製的──金屬或強化玻璃纖維塑料，不過後來壓製紙的發展潛力也開始吸引團體成員的興趣。

概念上，「艙室」適合於描述一種藉由提供一系列非常複雜精巧且高度設計性的元件，一起固定於一個本身即為精細裁製的「盒子」裡的住宅方式。這是一種工業設計的探討。它暗示著一種審慎的──甚至偏好的──生活方式。它暗示著城市或許可以容納一座像這樣生活方式的界定化複合體，甚至類似於一座旅館。同時它是完整界定的，且無須顧及許多依賴事件的階級體系與將住宅處理成民俗技藝的都市設計神話。

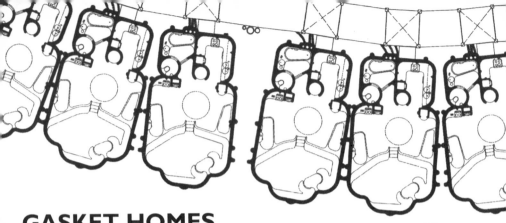

GASKET HOMES

Ron Herron, Warren Chalk

The capsule concept stimulated another experiment. The *Gasket* house, which, as its name suggests, uses a series of plastic strip profiles of different patterns that can be built up into an almost infinite series of enclosures. Without the restriction of the tower layout these units show a more relaxed attitude towards servicing and enclosure. They are suspended from a megastructure, and are independent of one another. In many ways this project anticipated the Living Pod of 1966. It too is a *capsule*, but the number of elements that are peripheral to the *industrial design* part begin to multiply out. We have by this time the instance of the capsule as only one of a series of environmental elements that are only sometimes interdependent. The Pod and the Auto Environment, and in fact all of Archigram's later housing experiments, move away from the *preferred relationship* concept. But without it, they would have been impossible. There have been several built examples of capsule-like units (particularly in Japan and Germany), but they nearly all miss the point of the essential hybrid quality of the capsule dwelling, the tautness – even a delightful artificiality of its intended lifestyle?

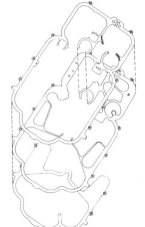

接合住宅

朗・赫倫、華倫・裘克

「艙屋」的概念一年後激發了另一項實驗：「接合住宅」，顧名思義，它運用了一系列不同樣式的連環圖重組案，稻果成幾乎可以一連串無限繁衍下去的圍蔽物。除去了塔形構造配置的限制，這些單元在維護性與圍蔽性上表現出更為輕鬆的姿態。它們懸吊於一個超大型結構之上，並且彼此獨立。就許多方面而言，這個設計案加速了1966年的「生活莢」設計。「接合住宅」也是一個艙室，但「工業設計」的周邊設備元件數目開始增加。在此之前我們的「艙室」案例只是偶爾才相互依賴之一連串的環境元素之一。「生活莢」與「汽車環境」，以及事實上所有「建築電訊」晚期的住宅實驗，都已經自「偏好關聯性」的概念轉向了。但若無此概念，其它的構想也不可能產生。目前已出現過一些類似艙室單元體的建築實例（特別是在日本與德國），但它們幾乎全都遺漏了一點「艙室住宅」最為重要的混雜特質：嚴謹性——甚至連其意欲達成的生活方式應具有的舒適人工性都沒有？

PLUG'N CLIP

Peter Cook

插／夾

彼得・庫克

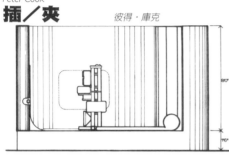

ELEVATION

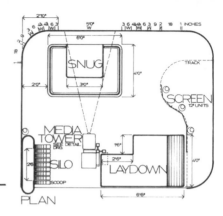

PLAN

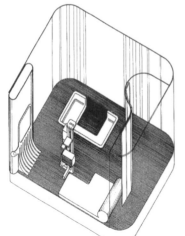

Room set at Woolands for the Sunday Times
為《週日時報》設計的「吾爾藍茲」房間組件

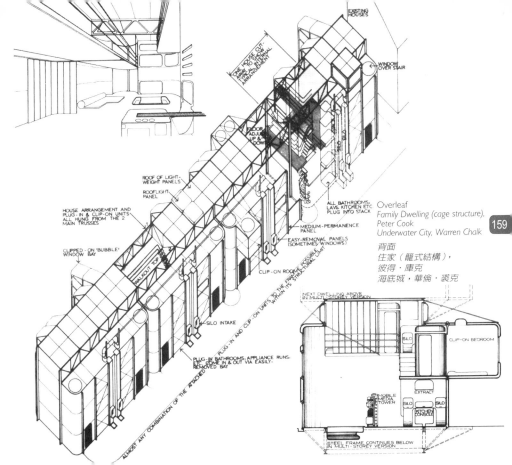

ONE HOUSE OUT· AWAY· NO STRUCTURAL CHANGE· INTERNAL ARRANGEMENT

EXISTING HOUSES

WINDOW OVER STAIR

FLOOR ADJUST· UP & DOWN

ROOF OF LIGHT-WEIGHT PANELS

ROOFLIGHT PANEL

HOUSE ARRANGEMENT AND PLUG-IN & CLIP-ON UNITS ALL HUNG FROM THE 2 MAIN TRUSSES

CLIPPED-ON 'BUBBLE' WINDOW BAY

ALL BATHROOMS: LAVS· KITCHEN ETC PLUG INTO STACK

MEDIUM-PERMANENCE PANEL

EASY-REMOVAL PANELS (SOMETIMES WINDOWS)

CLIP-ON ROOF

WALKOUT TOP HAT

SILO INTAKE

PLUG·IN AND CLIP·ON UNITS IN THE FRAME· HOUSES WITHIN ITS STRUCTURAL LIMIT

PLUG-IN BATHROOMS· APPLIANCE RUNS· ETC· COME IN & OUT VIA EASILY-REMOVED BAY

ALMOST ANY COMBINATION OF THE ATTACHED

Overleaf
*Family Dwelling (cage structure),
Peter Cook
Underwater City, Warren Chalk*

159

背面
住家（籠式結構），
彼得・庫克
海底城，華倫・裘克

NEXT DWELLING ABOVE IN MULTI-STOREY VERSION

SILO

CLIP-ON BEDROOM

EXTRACT

MOBILE MEDIA TOWER

SILO

KITCHEN CONSOLE

SILO

STEEL FRAME CONTINUES BELOW IN MULTI-STOREY VERSION

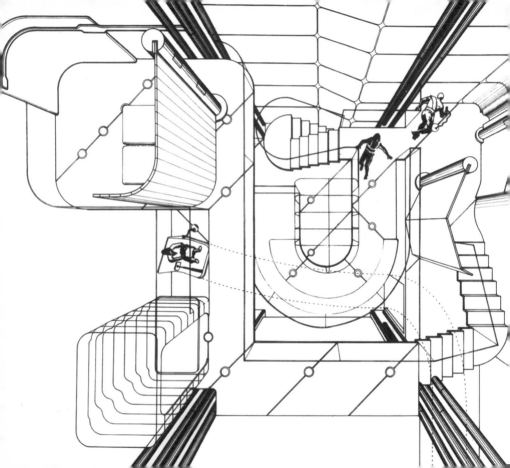

US astronauts dock in space — First regular English Channel Hovercraft service begins — Cultural Revolution begins in China — Francis Chichester embarks on round-world yacht voyage — UK – Abefan disaster as coal slagheap slides — Soviet spaceship orbits moon — Vietnam War protests at American Embassy, London — Race riots in Chicago, New York and Cleveland — Freddie Laker forms cut-price transatlantic airline — Unmanned US spacecraft lands on moon — Floods in Florence and Venice ruin many art treasures — England football team win World Cup — Walt Disney dies — MUSIC — Drug-orientated songs make the charts — Light and Sound shows appear — 'The Who' is the first band to put out singles in stereo — Last ever Beatles concert in San Francisco — Bob Dylan and Joan Baez become cult figures — 'Yellow Submarine' — 'Eleanor Rigby' — 'I'll Be There' — 'Good Vibrations' — 'Paperback Writer' — BOOKS — 'The Comedians' — 'Wide Sargasso Sea' — 'Valley of the Dolls' — FASHION — Era of the 'Dolly Bird' — Twiggy replaces Jean Shrimpton as the female image — Mary Quant receives OBE — Geometric shapes, Mondrian dresses, giant zips — Boom in production of synthetic fibres such as PVC and Terylene gives rise to new concept of throwaway clothes — — CINEMA — 'Alfie' — 'Morgan: A Suitable Case for Treatment' — 'Modesty Blaise' — 'Thunderball' — 'Dr Zhivago'

美國太空人進駐太空－第1架英吉利海峽氣墊船正式服役－中國文化大革命－法蘭西斯・契卻斯特爵士單人駕艇環遊世界－英國－煤山災變－蘇聯太空船環繞月球軌道飛行－倫敦美國大使館前反越戰示威－芝加哥、紐約與克里夫蘭種族暴動－佛雷迪．雷克公司販售歐美大西洋航線平價機票－美國無人太空船登陸月球－佛羅倫斯與威尼斯因水患破壞諸多藝術珍品－英格蘭足球隊贏得世界杯－華德・迪士尼辭世－**音樂**－以毒品為題的曲風大為流行－聲光秀登場－「誰」樂團首次推出立體聲單曲－披頭四於舊金山舉辦告別演場會－巴布・狄倫與瓊・拜亞成為偶像－《黃色潛水艇》－《艾琳諾・瑞比》－《我將在此》－《良好感觸》－《平裝書作者》－**出版**－《喜劇演員》－《寬闊藻海》－《娃娃谷》－**時尚**－「俏妞」時代－名模崔姬取代珍・史林普頓成為女性形象－瑪莉・關收到大英帝國勳章－幾何造型，蒙德里安式洋裝，大拉鍊－聚氯乙烯與特利林……等之人造合成纖維的大量生產引發丟棄式衣物的新概念－**電影**－《風流奇男子》－《摩根》－《女諜玉嬌龍》－007系列《霹靂彈》－《齊瓦哥醫生》。

1966

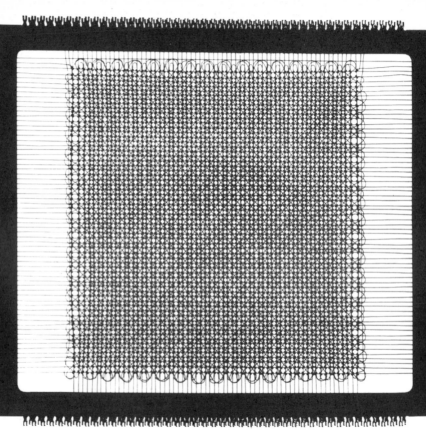

ARCHIGRAM SEVEN   BEYOND ARCHITECTURE

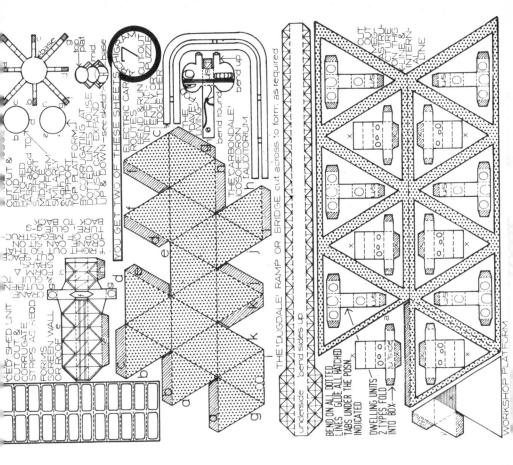

LETTER TO DAVID GREENE:
'GHOSTS' (with reference to Albert Ayler)

Warren Chalk

Architecture is probably a hoax, a fantasy world brought about through a desire to locate, absorb and integrate into an overall obsession a self-interpretation of the everyday world around us. An impossible attempt to rationalise the irrational. It is difficult to be exact about influences, but those influences that enter our unconscious consciousness are what I call 'ghosts'.

Our lives exist within a complex web of these influences; which we either accept or reject; those we find acceptable are turned to advantage; they become our preoccupations, prejudices or preconceptions. Systematic analysis is such a preconception.

Ghosts help to reinforce and establish attitudes, to build a very personal language, a complex labyrinth of ideals, constraints, theories, half-remembered rules, symbols and words that, ultimately digested, affect our concepts. It is unpopular, but essential, that existing attitudes come in for constant and rigorous renewal or reappraisal. We are confronted with a dynamic shifting pattern of events at both popular and intellectual levels, both simulating and confusing. In this ever-changing climate, old ghosts may be cast out and replaced by new: it is right that influences should last only as long as they are useful to us, and our architecture should reflect this. At a general level it is becoming increasingly apparent that due to historical circumstances the more tangible ghosts of the past – those grim, humourless, static, literary or visual images – will succumb to the onslaught of the invisible media, the psychedelic vision; the insight accompanying a joke; the phantoms of the future.

HELP!

OUCH!

OOOH!

OWW!

PHANTOMS

ARCHIGRAM
7
W. CHALK

鬼魅」（關於亞伯特‧艾勒）

華倫‧裘克

建築也許是一場惡作劇，一個藉由探出、同化與融入某種對於我們周遭日常世界的自我詮釋之全然迷戀的慾望所引起的狂想世界。一種合理化不合理的不可能企圖。想要精準地描繪出影響是很困難的，但那些進入我們未察覺意識裡的影響正是我所謂的鬼魅。

我們的生活存在於這些影響的複雜網路裡：我們對其不是接受就是拒絕；我們覺得可接受的被轉變成為優點；它們變成我們的專注、偏見或是先入為主的看法。系統性的分析就是一種先入之見。

鬼魅有助於強化與建立看法，建立一種非常個人化的語彙，一種理想、約束、理論、局部遺忘規則、象徵與言語的複雜迷宮，其最終將被整理分類，進而影響我們的概念。它不受歡迎，但又不可或缺，現存的看法進入以進行持續且嚴密的更新與重新評估。我們面臨了通俗與知性兩種層面上事件的動態轉變模式，既具模仿性又令人困惑。在這種不斷改變的氛圍裡，舊鬼魅可被驅逐且被新鬼魅所取代；影響應該只維持至它們對我們仍有用處之時是對的，而我們的建築應該能夠反映這點。整體而言，情況變得愈來愈明顯，由於歷史情勢之故，過去較可觸知的鬼魅——那些沉悶的、無幽默感的、乏味的、文學性的或視覺性的影像——將屈服於不可見之媒材與引起幻覺之視覺的猛烈震撼；洞察力隨著玩笑而

First published in *FORUM* October 1966

HARDWARE OF A NEW WORLD

Warren Chalk

'Pirate' Radio City in
the Thames Estuary

泰晤士河口的「地
下廣播」無線電城

Two apparently unconnected news items hit the headlines in Great Britain this summer: the first concerned a strong-arm bid to take over Radio City, a 'pirate station' broadcasting non-stop pop music from a wartime anti-aircraft fort, outside territorial waters in the Thames Estuary; the second item concerned some oil rigs out in the North Sea, which had made natural gas strikes large enough to change the face of Britain. Although of no apparent connection, together these news items contributed a fresh flush of enthusiasm to a small band of young British architectural hopefuls concerned with predicting patterns of the future.

The ack-ack forts in the Thames Estuary are relics of World War II; they bristled with anti-aircraft guns and radar equipment, as early-warning stations against hostile aircraft or invasion fleets. One of the stations, the 'Shivering Sands Fort' off Whitstable, Kent, is now occupied by pirate Radio City, a commercial station that pipes round-the-clock pop music and commercials to an estimated 25 million regular listeners. This June saw an attempted commando-style raid, the fort invaded and its transmitters silenced for several days. Then followed news that the pirate pop-radio chief had been shot, and that a full-scale inquiry had been launched by Scotland Yard. Questions in Parliament led to a new Government anti-pirate bill being published which may silence the transmitters for good.

The natural gas finds in the North Sea, which could help substantially to make the British economy more stable, might at the same time produce a visual disaster area similar to the US coastline along the Gulf of Mexico. The oil rigs used in these gas strikes, however, such as the ICI's and Burma Oil's 'Ocean Prince' or the monster 'Sea Quest', British Petroleum's semisubmersible drilling barge, have a close hybrid structural and visual affinity with the Thames forts and with certain architectural projects for cities of the future.

Symbolism and reality are in a sense interconnected, the bridge between them serves to support a new visionary understanding of what architecture might become. A view from this bridge provides a glimpse of a physical world of architecture subservient to the media

it supports, and refocuses the work and doctrines of the Modern Movement in terms of the transient nature of life in this century.

As in the instance of the Thames forts, where one medium gave place to another, where apparatus of war at one moment in time was later thrown out and replaced by pop-music transmitters – so, in the fabric of future cities, the 'architecture' can be conceived as an adaptable megasystem cradling a continually changing range of media. And suddenly the medium is seen to be more important. Architecture will no longer be concerned with individual buildings or groups of buildings, but with forming a permissive environment that is capable of any configuration according to circumstances.

Just as important is the realisation that with the culture explosion brought about by mass production, advertising, throwaway packaging, etc., as well as the widening of horizons due to space and underwater explorations, architects and designers themselves will change. They will eventually have to reorient themselves, ease out from under their traditional role, and accept the new phenomena in order to survive.

Unforeseen by the founders of modern architecture, ignored or feared by the large mainstream of contemporary architectural thought, but recognised by those outside that mainstream – these space-age commodities will be instantly absorbed and understood, taken for granted even, by younger generations. The world of architecture will eventually move away from the idea of buildings as something fixed, monumental, great and edifying, into a situation where buildings take their rightful place among the hardware of the

Thames Fort　泰晤士堡壘
Sea Quest　海洋搜索

首度發表於1966年10月《論壇》

新世界的硬體設備

華倫・裘克

今年夏天在英國出現了兩則表面上毫無關聯的頭條新聞：第一則是有關強制投標接管「無線電城」，一座位於泰晤士河口領海之外的戰時防空堡壘，全天候播送流行音樂的「地下電台」；第二則是有關北海上的石油裝備，發現大量足以改變英國面貌的天然氣。雖然表面上並無關聯，但這兩則新聞的結合卻燃起了一小群專注於未來型態預測的年輕英國建築新秀的熱情。

泰晤士河口的高射砲堡壘是二次世界大戰的遺跡：林立著防空槍砲與雷達裝置，為對抗敵機或入侵機群的初期警告站。其中一站，位於肯特的懷特斯特保的「顫慄砂堡」，目前正被地下「無線電城」——一座全天候有線播送流行音樂與廣告給大約二千五百萬名聽眾的商業電台——所佔據。今年六月經歷了一場意圖未遂的突襲，堡壘遭到入侵，其發射器也因此沉寂了數日。接踵而至的是地下流行樂電台首腦遭刺的消息，倫敦警察廳已全面展開調查。國會的質詢引發新政府頒布了可使發射器永不再發聲的反無照廣播法案。

北海發現了天然氣，實質上可助於更穩定英國的經濟，同時亦可能製造類似於美國沿灣西哥灣海岸線的視覺災難區。然而發現這些天然氣的石油鑽探設備，諸如ICI與布爾瑪石油的「海王子」或怪物般的「尋海」——「英國石油公司」的半潛式鑽探駁船，都與泰晤士河的堡壘及某種未來城市的建築計劃有著緊密混雜的結構與視覺類似性。

就某方面而言，象徵主義與現實是相互連結的，二者間的橋樑為了建築可能變成什麼，提供了一種新的視覺性理解所需的支持。來自這座橋樑的觀點，傳達出有助於它所支持之媒介的建築實體世界的驚鴻一瞥，並自本世紀生活的過渡性特質的角度，重新對焦於現代運動的作品與學說中。

正如泰晤士河堡壘的例子，一種媒介被另一種所取代，某個時期的戰爭裝備稍後被丟棄且被流行樂發射器所取代——因此，在未來城市的結構中，「建築」可被視為一種彈性的巨大體系，容納著媒介持續的各式各樣變化。突然間，媒介被視為更重要。建築將不再僅與單棟建築物或成群建築物有關，而是與可容許根據環境而產生任何構形之寬容環境的形成有關。

同樣重要的，是對於伴隨著因大量生產、廣告、丟棄式包裝……等所引起的文化爆炸的理解，以及因

world. Then architects as presently known will cease to exist, and a very different kind of animal will emerge, embracing science, art and technology in a complex overview. Established disciplinary boundaries will be removed and we will come closer to the all-at-once world of Marshall McLuhan.

This far-out research is happening now and must be studied and understood if we are, eventually, to produce an architecture that recognises the technological implications of our time. Young architects in Britain, who have no first-hand experience of space or underwater programmes, look to whatever hardware is available to them for indications of a future. If the Thames forts and oil rigs are seen, not as isolated facts, but as a confirmation of our attitudes, then our analogies become less suspect. These sea structures

have a deep significance to us, as pointers to the shifting nature of architecture and environment: at a purely visual level, this marine hardware parallels the Archigram Group's work on projects such as 'Plug-In City', 'Walking City' and 'Underwater City'. The same tube connectors, the use of the diagonal, the linking of nodal points, an understanding of the language of mobility, making sense of technological know-how without destroying the characteristics of sea and sky, land and space – all these are evident here. The unselfconscious process of marine engineering and its attendant economy of conception are similar in spirit to the plug-in concept.

When you trace the implications further afield, a comparison can also be drawn with the work of the Metabolists of Japan, Kenzo Tange's Tokyo Plan, Kiyonori, Kikutake's Marine Civilisation and the spatial

太空與海底探險所拓寬的視野，建築師與設計師本身將有所改變。他們終將必須重新適應，逐漸地擺脫其傳統的角色，並接受新現象以求生存。

未被現代建築的創始者所預知，遭受大量主流之當代建築思潮的忽視與畏懼，但卻為主流外的思想所認同——這些太空時代的產品將迅速地被吸收與理解，甚至被年輕的一代視為理所當然。建築的世界，終將自視建築物為某種固定、紀念性、偉大且深具啟發性的東西的想法，轉移至某種建築物可置身於全世界硬體設備中之適當位置的情境。然後目前所熟知的建築師將不再存在，而將出現某種非常異類的東西，包含科學、藝術與科技於一個複合體之中。既定的學科界線將被移除，而我們將更接近馬歇爾‧麥克魯漢的「同時」世界。

這種嶄新的研究正在發生，而且若我們終將創造出一種能夠明白我們這個時代的科技含意的建築的話，就必須細究瞭解。英國的年輕建築師們，並無直接的太空或海底計劃經驗，於是依賴任何近便的硬體設備以擷取未來的暗示。若泰晤士河堡壘與石油鑽探設備不是被視為孤立的事實，而是我們態度的確認，則我們的類比就變得較不可疑。就身為建築與環境的移動特性的指標而言，這些海洋結構物對我們深具意義；就純粹的視覺層次而言，這種海中硬體設備類似於「建築電訊」的設計案作品，諸如「插接城市」、「步行城市」及「水底城市」；同樣的管狀連結構件、斜桿的應用、節點的連接、移動性語彙的領會，使科技技術合理化卻不至於破壞海洋、天空、陸地與太空的特質——於此這些都是顯而易見的。海洋工程的非自覺性變遷與其概念的附加經濟價值，在精神上是與「插接」概念類似的。

當您更進一步地追溯這種科技含意時，亦可比較日本代謝派的作品，諸如丹下健三的「東京規劃案」、菊竹清訓的「海洋文明」與磯崎新的「太空工程」。許多代謝派設計案都是有關視海洋城市為陸地的延伸，或海上漂浮的孤島。也許丹下健三的「東京灣」提案最為人所熟知：它是近海海上拓地中最傑出的嘗試之一。

然而，丹下的設計案並無充分地開發海上拓地的潛力，而依舊是極度仰賴機械裝置系統且奠基於陸上的組織體。海洋學家長久以來便瞭解海中與海床之下蘊藏著豐富的資源有待開發。海底資源顯得令人著迷，一處採集石油、天然氣、礦產及硫酸鹽的寶庫；甚至可發現黃金與鑽石，且商業漁場理論上是可行的。

這些活動終將致使水面上與海底的海上拓地淪為普通的群落。這種載人的海底群落構想直接來自於約翰‧史考特‧荷丹教授於1906年所進行的研究，其後並有諸如奧古斯特‧皮卡德、羅伯特‧戴維斯爵

constructions of Arata Isozaki. A number of the Metabolist projects are concerned with ocean cities as extension of land or as floating offshore islands. Possibly, Tange's Tokyo Bay proposal is the most familiar: it is one of the finest essays in offshore marine settlements.

This said, Tange's project none the less fails to exploit the full potential of a marine settlement, and is still very much a land-based organisation with movement systems. Oceanographers have long realised the untapped sources of wealth to be found in the sea and under the sea bed. Underwater resources appear fantastic, a storehouse for harvesting petroleum, natural gas, minerals and sulphates; even gold and diamonds are to be found, and commercial fish-farming is a theoretical possibility.

These activities will give rise, eventually, to on-surface and undersea marine settlements as unexceptional communities. The notion of manned undersea communities arises directly from research carried out by Professor John Scott Haldane in 1906, and the continuing experiments by such men as Auguste Piccard, Sir Robert H. Davis, Edwin A. Link (the inventor of the Link Trainer for simulated flight conditions), George F. Bond and Commander Jacques-Yves Cousteau.

These men and others have been responsible for the development of numerous underwater inventions and hardware including the aqualung, the SPID (submerged portable inflatable dwelling) various deep-submergence research craft, underwater houses and laboratories.

Buckminster Fuller's observation that the space capsule is the first completely designed human environment may finally apply also to undersea conditioned environments. Environmental control in a sea settlement could be designed to the ultimate, with televisual communications links and 'artificial gill' air supply. Recent developments in undersea and surface craft, such as the Westinghouse Deepstar deep-submergence craft and the SRN1 Hovercraft (or similar Ground Effect Machine), could form transportation links with land.

A recent issue of Esquire magazine showed an aquarium for people, designed as an underwater house by Corning Glass Works: a glass bubble capable of travelling six miles down into the sea attached to a surface saucer-home with solar batteries embedded in its roof to provide electricity. This suggests that besides the great commercial implications of marine cities there also may be an equal leisure potential – a potential that may make the line, 'We all live in a yellow submarine', more prophetic than even the Beatles might have imagined.

士、愛德恩・林克（林克飛行模擬訓練裝置的發明者）、喬治・龐得以及賈克－伊夫・庫司多指揮官等人接續實驗。

這些人與其他人負責發展了許多水底發明與硬體設備，包括有水肺、攜帶式潛水充氣居所、各式各樣的深潛式研究船艇、水底屋與實驗室。

布克敏斯特・富勒觀察到，太空艙可能是第一個終可應用於海底條件環境之完整設計的人類環境。有了電視通訊連結與「人造腮」空氣補給的輔助之後，海上拓地的環境控制終究是可以設計實現的。最近的水面上與海底船艇的發展，諸如「西屋深星深潛艇」與SRNI氣墊船（或類似的「海底效果機器」），可構成與陸地的交通連結。

最近一期的《君子》雜誌，展示了一個供人使用的水族箱，由康寧玻璃工藝坊設計為海底屋：一個可以6英哩時速潛入海中的玻璃泡泡，附著於以太陽能蓄電池嵌入其屋頂上以提供電力之碟形屋的表面。這暗示了在海上城市的巨大商業含意之外，也可能存有同樣的休閒潛力——這種潛力或可寫成如下歌詞，「我們全都住在黃色潛水艇裡」，或許比披頭四所能想像到的更具預言性哩！

THE FLYING HOUSE

Warren Chalk

From ARCHITECTURAL DESIGN June 1966
摘錄自1966年6月《建築設計》雜誌

In the current preoccupational climate of mass-produced capsule dwellings, one of the principal constraints has been the bulk restriction discipline imposed by existing road, rail and shipping transportation regulations governing the size of objects in transit from factory to site. This inevitably swung opinion in favour of on-site assembly kit ideals as opposed to a complete factory-assembled product. However recent developments in Russia and the United States with helicopter transporters could well lead to increased development in the other direction. The Buckminster Fuller helilift, so long with us, may soon be due for revision.

飛行屋

華倫・裘克

在現今專注於大量生產艙室住宅的風潮裡，主要約束的其中之一就是，既有道路、鐵路與航運法規所強制規定的大量紀律限制，支配了自工廠搬運至基地的物件尺寸。此無可避免之轉變觀點有利於現場裝配組件的理想，而不利於全然的工廠組裝產品。然而，最近俄國與美國在直升機運輸裝置上的發展，可能引領其它方面發展的增加。長久以來對我們極具價值的布克敏斯特・富勒的直升機運輸，或許很快就將被修正了。

Leasure Study: Seaside Bubbles. Ron Herron
休閒研究：海濱泡泡，朗•赫倫

Free Time Node: Trailer Cage, Ron Herron
休閒節點：拖車籠屋，朗・赫倫

PLUG IN YOUR HOME NODE

LIVING-POD

David Greene

Paradigms: Trailer homes, 'Prefabs', etc. Development: The 'house' is regarded here as consisting of two major components: a living-pod and attached machines.

Description: Part one, a pod (type KR2) 2-level GRP BS P91304. Colour; bonded white. Twelve support nodes (6 tension, 6 compression). Four apertures (25 per cent surface), I access aperture, all with vacuum fixing seals, inner bonded sandwich of insulation and/or finish. Multi-purpose inflating floor 45 per cent area.

Part two: Machinery, 4 automatic self-levelling compression legs for maximum five feet water or 40° slope. Two transparent sectionalised sliding aperture seals with motors. Transparent entry seal with ramp and hydraulics. Two wash capsules with electrostatic disposal, air entry, and total automatic body cleaning equipment. One only with total body water immersion possibility. Two rotating silos for non-disposable clothing, sundry dispensers and silos for disposable toilet and clothing objects, etc. Vertical body hoist. Climate machinery for temperate zone (with connections to inflating sleep mats and warm section of inflating floor). Non-static food dispenser with self-cook modifications. Non-static media, teach and work machine with instant transparent cocoon ring. Inflating screens to sleep mats.

Appraisal: Although this capsule can be hung within a plug-in urban structure or can sit in the open landscape it is still a 'house'. Really one is left with a zoom-land trailer home. Probably a dead end. A basic assumption that must be reassessed in terms of the possibility of increasing personal mobility and technological advance. Anything is probable. The outcome of rejecting permanence and security in a house brief and adding instead curiosity and search could result in a mobile world – like early nomad societies. In relation to the Michael Webb design, the Suit and Cushicle would be the tent and camel equivalent; the node cores an oasis equivalent: the node cluster communities conditioned by varying rates of change. It is likely that under the impact of the second machine age the need for a house (in the form of permanent static container) as part of man's psychological make-up will disappear.

With apologies to the master, the house is an appliance for carrying with you, the city is a machine for plugging into.

Teaching machine plan
教學機器平面圖

生活莢

大衛・葛林

範例：拖車屋、「組合屋」……等。
發展：「住宅」在此被視為包含兩種主要的組件：一個生活莢與一些附屬機械裝置。

描述：第一部份，一個莢體（KR2類型）、雙層GRP BS P91304、彩色、白色接合。12個支撐節點（6個張力、6個壓力）。4個開口（25%的表面積）、一個出入口、全都具有真空固定密封裝置、隔絕與／或加工修飾的內部黏合夾層。多功能充氣樓板佔45%的面積。

第二部份：機械裝置、4個水深最多5呎或呈40度斜坡的自動化自行平穩壓縮支腳。兩個透明區分的移動開口銜接馬達。透明入口銜接坡道與油壓設施。兩個具有靜電處理、空氣入口與全自動身體清洗設備的洗滌艙。只有一個可以全身浸入水中。兩個供非丟棄式衣物的旋轉式筒倉、雜貨販賣機與供丟棄式浴廁與衣物用品之筒倉……等。垂直式機體起重機。溫帶區之氣候調節機械裝置（與充氣式床墊及充氣式樓板的溫室區相連結）。具自炊設計之非靜電式食物販賣機。非靜電式媒體，具有即時透明防護罩圈之教學與工作機器。將隔板充氣為床墊。

評估：雖然這座艙室可以被懸吊於插接的都市結構中或是座落於戶外，但它仍舊是一棟「房屋」。實際上留給人們的是變焦世界的拖車屋。或許並無發展前途。基本前提是必須以增加個人機動性與科技進步之可能性的角度再評估。任何事都是可能的。丟棄房屋中的耐久性與安全性而加入好奇心與探索，可能會產生某種移動式的世界——就像早期的游牧社會。有關麥克・威柏的設計，「衣服」與「氣墊車」就像與帳篷與潛水箱；節點核心類似於綠洲；節點簇群社區由替換之變化率所決定。可能在第二次機械時代的影響之下，房屋（以永久靜態容器的形式）成為人類心理學之構成的一部份之需求將會消失。

先向大師們致表歉意，房屋是可以攜帶的裝備，城市是可以插接的機器。

Food machine plan
食物處理機平面圖

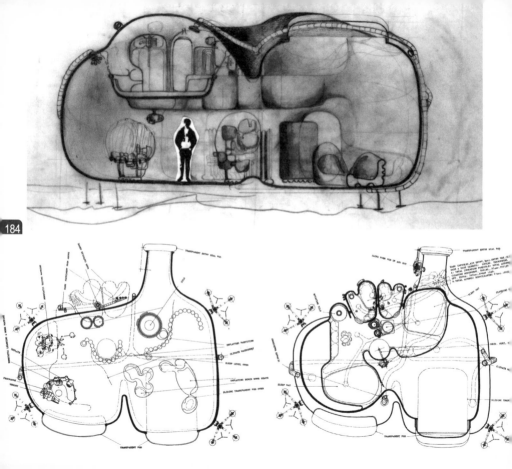

184

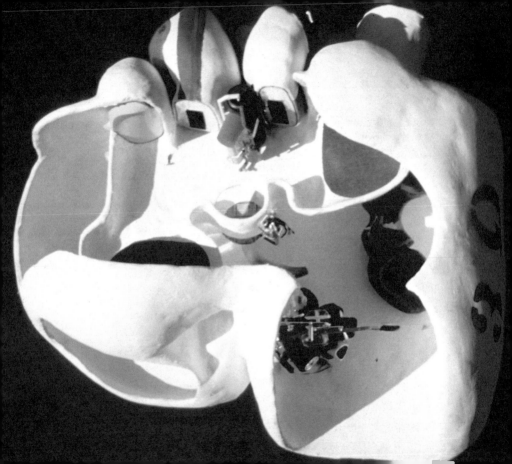

THE CUSHICLE

Mike Webb

The Cushicle is an invention that enables a man to carry a complete environment on his back. It inflates-out when needed. It is a complete nomadic unit – and it is fully serviced.

It enables an explorer, wanderer or other itinerant to have a high standard of comfort with a minimum effort.

The illustrations show the two main parts of the Cushicle unit as they expand out from their unpacked state to the domestic condition. One constituent part is the 'armature' or 'spinal' system. This forms the chassis and support for the appliances and other apparatus. The other major element is the enclosure part which is basically an inflated envelope with extra skins as viewing screens. Both systems open out consecutively or can be used independently.

The Cushicle carries food, water supply, radio, miniature projection television and heating apparatus. The radio, TV, etc., are contained in the helmet and the food and water supply are carried in pod attachments.

With the establishment of service nodes and additional optional apparatus, the autonomous Cushicle unit could develop to become part of a more widespread urban system of personalised enclosures.

Chassis unopened
未開啓之底盤結構

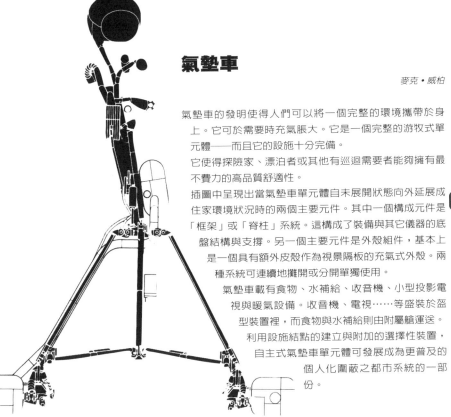

氣墊車

麥克‧威柏

氣墊車的發明使得人們可以將一個完整的環境攜帶於身上。它可於需要時充氣脹大。它是一個完整的游牧式單元體——而且它的設施十分完備。

它使得探險家、漂泊者或其他有巡迴需要者能夠擁有最不費力的高品質舒適性。

插圖中呈現出當氣墊車單元體自未展開狀態向外延展成住家環境狀況時的兩個主要元件。其中一個構成元件是「框架」或「脊柱」系統。這構成了裝備與其它儀器的底盤結構與支撐。另一個主要元件是外殼組件，基本上是一個具有額外皮殼作為視景隔板的充氣式外殼。兩種系統可連續地攤開或分開單獨使用。

氣墊車載有食物、水補給、收音機、小型投影電視與暖氣設備。收音機、電視……等盛裝於盔型裝置裡，而食物與水補給則由附屬艙運送。利用設施結點的建立與附加的選擇性裝置，自主式氣墊車單元體可發展成為更普及的個人化圍蔽之都市系統的一部份。

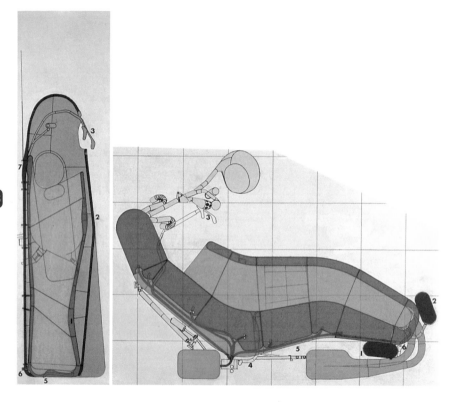

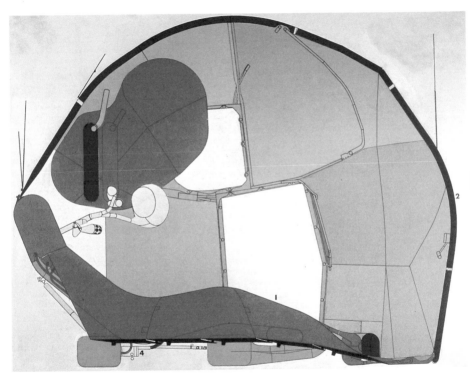

BLOW-OUT VILLAGE

Peter Cook

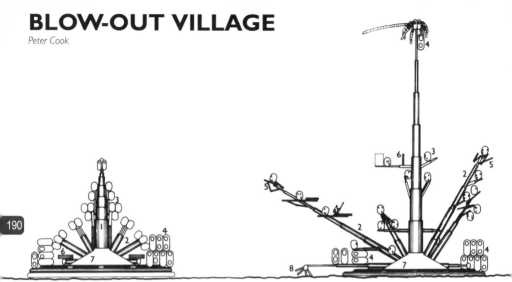

Stage 1: The hovercraft is in motion
階段 1：運轉中的氣墊車

Stage 2: The village is beginning to blow-out
階段 2：村落開始爆裂開來

Mobile villages can be used everywhere to rehouse people hit by disaster, for workmen in remote areas, and as fun resorts sited permanently or seasonally at the seaside and near festivals. When not in use the village is quarter size. This is done by drawing off the hydraulic fluid from the main mast and the arms: the village then contracts. It is moved on to a site by a hovercraft motor and anchored by the two feet seen in the diagram. The main mast is raised hydraulically to the chosen height. Air-inflated ribs fall from the top of the main mast supporting a weather-proof transparent plastic cover over the whole village.

Items:
1. Main mast, 2. Sub masts
3. Appliance units, 4. Machine and control cabins, 5. Dwelling units, 6. Home screens, 7. Main engine room and hydraulics unit, 8. Ground spread locators, 9. Access ways, 10. Air inflated rib to control dome, 11. Entry point, 12. Movie projection on to dome, 13. Free-standing dance floor.

爆裂村落

彼得・庫克

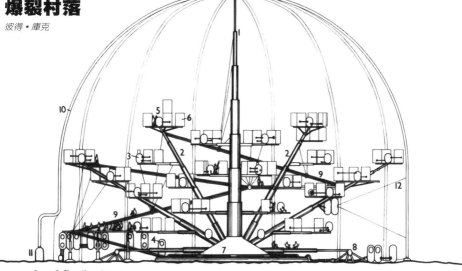

Stage 3: The village in use
階段 3：使用中的村落

「移動式村落」可運用於任何地方以安頓災民，供偏遠地區工人之用，並可永久性或季節性地設置於海邊與節慶表演附近的渡假區。當非使用期時，村落只有四分之一的大小。這是藉由自主要桅竿與臂竿抽出油壓液而達成；而後村落即可縮小。它可藉由氣墊車引擎繼續移往下個基地並依靠圖中所見的兩個基腳固定。主要桅竿藉由油壓升至預定高度。充氣式骨架自支撐整體村落之氣候防護的透明塑膠遮蓋的主要桅竿頂端落下。

品目：

1.主桅竿 2.副桅竿 3.裝備單元體
4.機械與控制艙 5.住宅單元體 6.
住宅隔板 7.主引擎室與油壓單元
體 8.地面展開定位器 9.出入通道
10.操控式半球型建築物的充氣
式骨架 11.入口點 12.電影投射於
圓屋頂

Six-Day War between Israel and Arab countries — Stalin's daughter Svetlana defects to US — Dr Christiaan Barnard carries out first ever human heart transplant in Cape Town — Disaster aboard first manned Apollo spacecraft: three astronauts are killed by fire in launch pad rehearsal — Hollywood actor Ronald Reagan becomes Governor of California — Ché Guevara shot dead in Bolivian jungle — Concorde makes first public appearance in Toulouse — Donald Campbell crashes 'Bluebird' speedboat on Coniston Water — Greek King Constantine flees Greece after coup — Liner QE2 launched by Queen Elizabeth II on Clydeside — Death of Jack Ruby, Lee Harvey Oswald's killer — Red Army takes over Peking, China — MUSIC — Psychedelic sound — Pink Floyd, Procul Harum and others tour with light shows — Use of LSD and cannabis becomes widespread — Duke of Bedford holds first pop festival — 'All You Need is Love' — 'Whiter Shade of Pale' — 'Penny Lane' — 'Strawberry Fields' — 'San Francisco' — 'Sgt Pepper's Lonely Hearts Club Band' — CINEMA — 'Blow up' — 'Bonnie and Clyde' — 'A Man for all Seasons' — 'Far from the Madding Crowd' — FASHION — 'Hippy' look takes over — T-Shirts — Leather waist-coats — Capes for men and women — Flower Power — Flower People.

以色列與阿拉伯國家發生「六日戰爭」－史達林的女兒思薇特拉娜向美國投誠－克利斯帝安‧巴納德於南非開普敦首度進行人類心臟移植手術－首度載人太空船阿波羅號發生災難：3名太空人於模擬演練時座艙起火喪生－好萊塢演員羅納德‧雷根當選加州州長－切‧格瓦拉於波利維亞叢林中遭射殺身亡－協和客機首度於土魯斯亮相－唐納德‧坎培爾於寇尼斯頓湖駕駛「藍鳥」快艇失事－希臘國王康士坦丁於政變後逃離希臘－女王伊莉莎白2世於克萊德河港口主持遠洋客輪「伊莉莎白2世」下水儀式－謀殺李‧哈維‧奧斯華的兇手傑克‧魯比死亡－紅軍接管中國北京－**音樂**－迷幻樂風－平克佛洛伊德、普羅酷兒‧哈藍等巡演團體於演唱會結合燈光秀－迷幻藥與大麻蔚為風潮－貝德福公爵首度舉辦流行音樂節－《你所需要的只是愛》－《蒼白的慘白陰影》－《潘尼‧連》－《草莓田》－《三藩市》－《花椒軍曹寂寞芳心俱樂部》－**電影**－《春光乍現》－《我倆沒有明天》－《良相佐國》－《瘋狂佳人》－**時尚**－嬉痞風盛行－T恤－皮背心－印第安斗蓬－嬉痞風－嬉痞。

1967

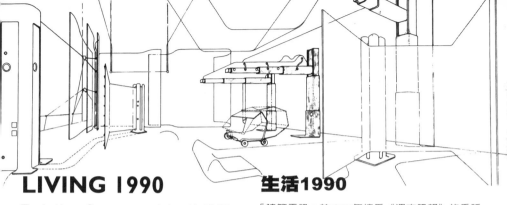

LIVING 1990

The Archigram Group was commissioned in 1967 by the Weekend Telegraph to design a 'house for the year 1990'. Naturally the definitions of function imply a fixed and permanent location. In essence the exhibited area illustrates the main part of the lower floor of a dwelling cage. The 'Robots' are a development in the direct lineage of the media trolley (in the Plug'n Clip house, p. 158) and the movable services, walls and machines that serve the occupants in Mike Webb's projects.

Walls, ceilings, floors – in this living area – are wall, ceiling and floor conditions, which adjust according to your needs. The enclosures of the living area are no longer rigid, but adjustable, programmed to move up and down, in and out. The floor state, too, is variable. At particular points the floor can be made hard enough to dance on or soft enough to sit on.

Seating and sleeping arrangements are inflatable, and

生活1990

「建築電訊」於1967年接受《週末訊報》的委託設計了一棟「1990年之屋」。機能的定義自然地暗示了一個固定且永久性的座落位置。展示區根本上即說明了住宅籠艙較低樓層的主要部份，而其狀態與結構類似於第158頁的例子。其中「自動裝置」是中型電車（「插／夾住宅」，頁158）與麥克•威柏的設計案中供居住者使用的移動式服務設施、牆面與機器等相繼發展的成果。

牆、天花板、樓板──在這個起居區裡──全都成了根據您的需求而調整的牆、天花板與樓板。起居區的外殼不再呆板而無法通融，而是設計為可調整並上下、內外移動的。樓板狀況亦如此。在某些特殊點上，樓板硬得足以跳舞或軟得足以坐下歇息。

座椅與睡眠裝置是充氣式的，而如床罩重量、坐

details such as weight of bed covers and number of cushioned elements are controlled by the user. The old concept of a movable chair has become a travelling chair-car. The model in the living area is designed on the hovercraft principle, and can also be used outside for driving around the megastructure city. The robots can shoot out screens which enclose a required area of space. The ceiling lowers at this point, and whoever requires it has a private area. The robots are movable. Refreshments can be drawn from them. The robots also incorporate radio and television – including favourite movies and education programmes, which can be switched on when you want them. The television is, at the present stage of development, seen on wide screens, and can be programmed so that viewers are surrounded by realistic sound, colour and scent effects. The service wall connects with a vast service stack, shared with the megastructure city, which is one of the key facilities of the structure.

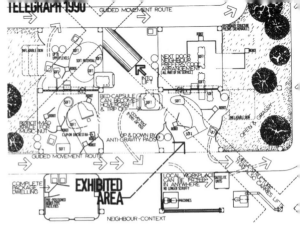

The design of the living area goes some way towards allaying the widely-held fears that the future points inevitably to standardisation and conformity of living accommodation.

James . . . . and . . . .

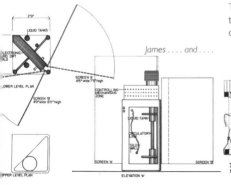

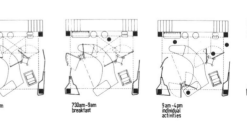

墊物件的數目……等細目
都由使用者控制。移動式
座椅此一陳舊概念已經轉
變為旅遊座椅車。起居區
的模型依照氣墊車原則設
計,亦可於超大結構城市
中四處行駛作為戶外之
用。「自動裝置」可伸出
圍蔽所需之空間領域的隔
板。天花板可調降以使需
要者可以擁有一個私密的

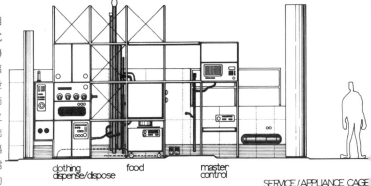

clothing dispense/dispose　food　master control

領域。「自動裝置」可以移動,也可由此取出茶點,同時配備有可充氣家具的壓氣機。它們亦具備一
個為起居區吸塵的元件,以及備有收音機與電視機──播放最受歡迎的電影與教學節目,可於您希望
時打開收聽或收看。目前階段正在開發讓電視機播放於寬闊的隔板上,並依程式設計使觀眾能身歷其
境地為音響、色彩與味覺效果所環繞。設施牆面連結了一大群與超大結構城市共用的設施管線,為此
結構中最具關鍵性的設備之一。

每個起居區均備有超音波烹調設備以提供最衛生、最快速的炊煮,並根據烹調喜好可另有其它裝設。
起居區的設計朝向緩和對於起居住宿設備的標準化與一致性
之無可避免的未來問題所普遍懷有的恐懼感上。

... Fred

6:30pm-8pm
teens/adults
activities

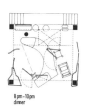

8 pm-10pm
dinner

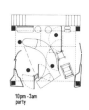

10pm-3am
party

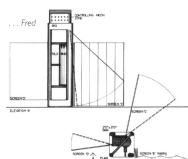

CONTROLLING MECH.
ZONE

ELEVATION 'B'

SCREEN 'D'　SCREEN 'E'

SCREEN 'C'

PLAN

20' x 20'
RABS

SCREEN 'D'　SCREEN 'E' RAISING

CONTROL AND CHOICE

The determination of your environment need no longer be left in the hands of the designer of the building: it can be turned over to you yourself. You turn the switches and choose the conditions to sustain you at that point in time. The 'building' is reduced to the role of carcass – or less.

Paradoxes were obvious and the first 'Control or Choice' conversation took the form of a deliberately hybrid document. Fixed diagrams of an architectural organisation seemed increasingly inadequate, yet this could also be said of the verbal dissertation about something that was after all, about response to space and objects.

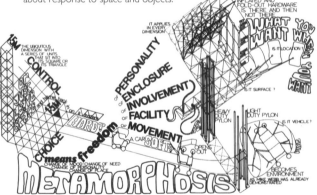

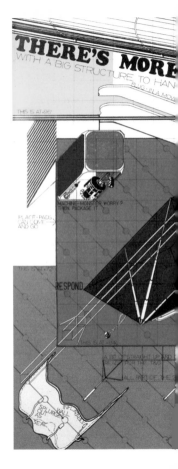

控制與選擇

您環境的決定不再需要置於建築物的設計師之手：它可以轉交至您自己的手中了。您打開開關並選擇當時您所需要的環境條件。「建築物」被簡約為扮演骨架的任務——或甚至更不如。

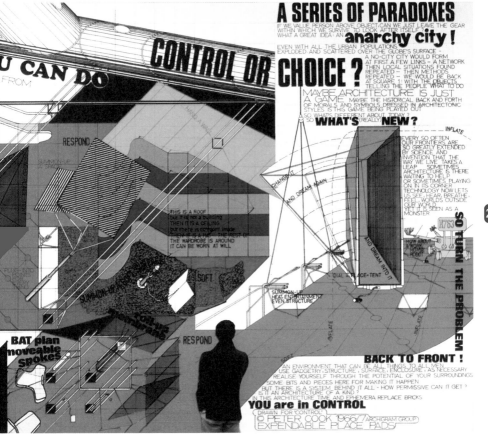

A SERIES OF PARADOXES

IF WE VALUE PERSON ABOVE OBJECT CAN WE JUST LEAVE THE GEAR
WITHIN WHICH WE SURVIVE TO LOOK AFTER ITSELF
WHAT A GREAT IDEA: AN **anarchy city !**

EVEN WITH ALL THE URBAN POPULATIONS
EXPLODED AND SCATTERED OVER THE GLOBE'S SURFACE –
A NO-CITY CITY WOULD FORM
AT FIRST A FEW LINKS – A NETWORK
THEN LOCAL SITUATIONS FOUND
REPEATED – THEN METHODS
REPEATED – WE WOULD BE BACK
AT SQUARE 1 – WITH THE OBJECTS
TELLING THE PEOPLE WHAT TO DO

MAYBE ARCHITECTURE IS JUST
A GAME   MAYBE THE HISTORICAL BACK AND FORTH
OF MORALS AND SYMBOLS – EXPRESSED IN ARCHITECTONIC
STYLES   IS THIS GAME BEING PLAYED OUT
ALSO WHAT'S DIFFERENT ABOUT TODAY ?
WHAT'S   NEW ?

EVERY SO OFTEN
OUR FRONTIERS ARE
SO GREATLY EXTENDED
BY SCIENCE AND
INVENTION THAT THE
WAY WE LIVE TAKES A
LEAP   SOMETIMES
ARCHITECTURE IS THERE
WAITING TO HELP
OR SOMETIMES PLAYING
ON IN ITS CORNER
TECHNOLOGY NOW LETS
US SEE, HEAR, BREATHE
REALITIES OUTSIDE
OUR WORLD
YET IT IS SEEN AS A
MONSTER

CONTROL OR CHOICE ?

U CAN DO
FROM

RESPOND

SUMMON-UP A SPACE

THIS IS A ROOF
but it is not a building
THEN IT IS A CEILING
but there is nothing inside
THEN IT IS A HAT – THE REST OF
THE WARDROBE IS AROUND
IT CAN BE WORN AT WILL.

CHANGE IT

AND DREAM AGAIN

INFLATE

AND DREAM INTO IT

DIAL-SPACE-TENT

WHAT ABOUT
A WHOLE
ROBOT

SOFT

SUMMON-UP
HEAT ENVIRONMENT
EVEN STRUCTURE

INFLATE

SO TURN THE PROBLEM

BACK TO FRONT !

**BAT plan
moveable
spokes**

RESPOND

AN ENVIRONMENT THAT CAN BE ALL THINGS TO ALL MEN
USE GADGETRY, STRUCTURE, SURFACE, ENCLOSURE; AS NECESSARY
REALISE YOURSELF THROUGH THE POTENTIAL OF YOUR SURROUNDINGS
SOME BITS AND PIECES HERE FOR MAKING IT HAPPEN
BUT THERE IS A SYSTEM BEHIND IT ALL – HOW PERMISSIVE CAN IT GET ?
IS IT AN ARCHITECTURE OF A KIND ?
IN THIS ARCHITECTURE TIME AND EPHEMERA REPLACE BRICKS

YOU are in CONTROL

(DRAWN FOR 'CONTROL')
© PETER COOK 1966 / ARCHIGRAM GROUP
EXPENDABLE PLACE PADS

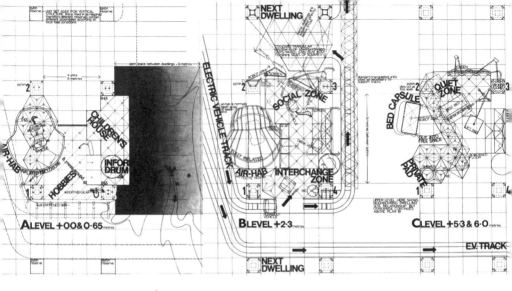

When Archigram was asked to send an exhibit to the 1967 Paris Biennale des Jeunesses the 'Control or Choice' conversation was extended very naturally into a project which was given the same name. In the cartoon on page 200 the word 'metamorphosis' is a summary of the whole discussion and the new set of parts that might make the project physically possible.

There is a natural fear in most of us that suspects the power of the machine and its takeover of human responsibility. This familiar bogey of the first machine age becomes even more terrifying with the dependence upon the unseen potential of electronic systems (they have even greater power of control than the obvious, symbolic and almost humanoid presence of a machine). The dependence upon such things for an emancipatory life is one of our paradoxes. The problem of exploitation of systems and machines and the continued recognition of 'friendly' and even 'passive' objects at the same time naturally leads to a hybrid assembly of parts.

Much of the project is still concerned with structure, mechanics and is of a defined mathematical order. It is necessary to postulate a system that can integrate with existing cities or imperfect sub-countryside.

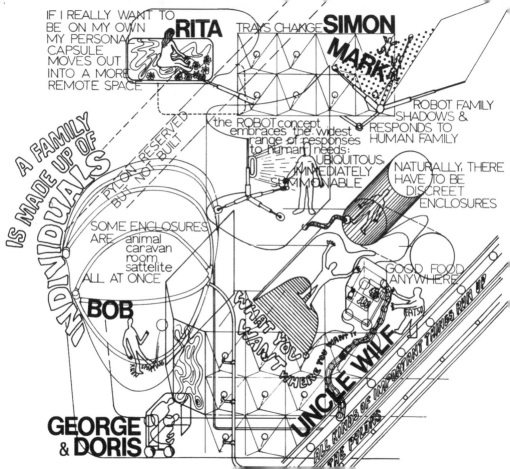

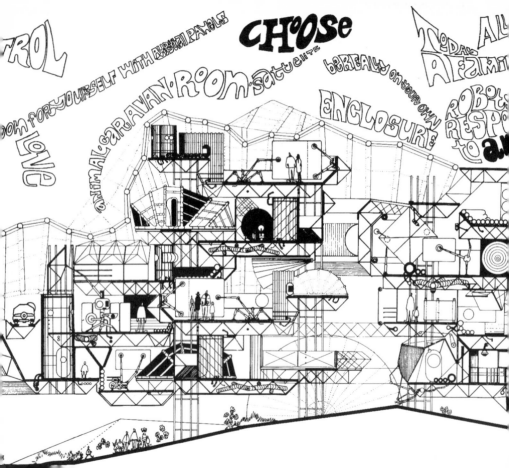

矛盾顯而易見，且第一次「控制與選擇」的對話刻意採取混和資料的形式。建築中空間組織之僵固圖示對我們而言愈來愈不適用，相關之言辭論過亦如此，因其畢竟與空間和物件之回應有關。當「建築電訊」受邀送交一份展覽作品參加1967年「巴黎青年藝術家雙年展」時，「控制與選擇」的對話於是很自然地被延伸成為一份同名的設計案。在此連環圖畫中，「變形」一字可算是整體討論以及可能使設計案實現之新元件的總結。

我們大多數人的心理都無可避免地存有一股恐懼，質疑機械的力量與它可能接手人類職責的能力。第一次機械時代裡一些大家都熟悉的駭人東西，因其對於電子系統尚未被覺察之潛力（它們甚至比一目了然、具象徵性的、且近乎人型的機器更有威力）的依賴而變得更加嚇人。對於解放生活所需的這些東西的依賴是我們的矛盾之一。系統與機械之開發利用問題，及對於兼具「親切性」甚至「被動性」之物件的持續認同，自然地促成了混合式裝配元件的出現。

此設計案的大部份仍舊與結構、機械有關，並具有明確的數學秩序。先決條件是必須先有一個足以整合目前的城市或不完善之附屬鄉間地帶的系統。

205

k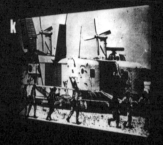

l

m

n

o

ARCHIGRAM GROU
BEYOND
ARCHITECTURE

p

PROJECTION OF 640 IMAGES commences 22 February 1967 MUSEUM OF MODERN ART OXFO

SUITALOON

Michael Webb

Clothing for living in – or if it wasn't for my Suitaloon I would have to buy a house.

The space suit could be identified as a minimal house. In the previous Cushicle, the environment for the rider was provided by the Cushicle – a mechanism like a car. In this project the suit itself provides all the necessary services, the Cushicle being the source of (a) movement, (b) a larger envelope than the suit can provide, (c) power. Each suit has a plug serving a similar function to the key to your front door. You can plug into your friend and you will both be in one envelope, or you can plug into any envelope, stepping out of your suit which is left clipped on to the outside ready to step into when you leave. The plug also serves as a means of connecting envelopes together to form larger spaces.

Various models of Cushicle envelope and suit would of course be available ranging from super sports to family models.

家衣

麥克・威柏

可居住的衣服──倘若沒有我的「家衣」的話,我只好買棟房子了。

這個空間衣服可定義為一種極簡的房子。在先前的「氣墊車」裡,駕駛者的環境由氣墊車所提供──一種如同汽車般的機械裝置。而在這個設計案裡,衣服本身提供了所有的必要設施,「氣墊車」變成 (a) 運動、(b) 提供比衣著更大的外殼、(c) 動力的來源。每件衣服都具有一個類似於您家大門鑰匙功能的插座。您可以插接於您的朋友,然後您們都將處於同一殼中;或者您也可以插接至任何其他外殼上,步出您的衣服,而您的衣服當您離開時會被夾在殼外待您回來。插頭也可以當做是將不同外殼連結在一起以形成更大空間的工具。

各式各樣的「氣墊車」外殼與衣服,從運動型到家用型,當然都有供應。

AIR HAB Ron Herron
充氣式住所 朗·赫倫

ST KATHERINE'S DOCK

Peter Cook, Dennis Crompton, Ron Herron

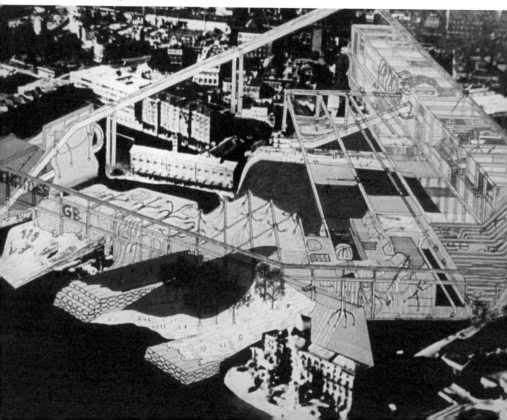

聖凱薩琳船塢

彼得・庫克、丹尼斯・克藍普頓、朗・赫倫

Alexander Dubçek becomes Czech leader — Cecil Day Lewis made British poet Laureate — Soviet cosmonaut Yuri Gargarin killed in air crash — Olympic Games held in Mexico City — Martin Luther King assassinated in Memphis — Violent clashes between students and police in Paris; Sorbonne closed — Robert Kennedy assassinated in Los Angeles — Student riots in Berkeley, California — Peace talks begin in Paris on Vietnam War — Dr Spock jailed for anti- war activities in US — Race riots in Watts, Los Angeles — Richard Nixon elected US President — Soviet tanks invade Czechoslovakia — Crowds clash with police in Londonderry during Civil Rights march — Demonstrations against Vietnam War in front of US Embassy in London — Three-man US spaceship Apollo 8 orbits the Moon ten times — John Steinbeck dies — MUSIC — 500,000 people attend Woodstock Festival in New York State — Beatles discover Maharishi Yogi — 'Magical Mystery Tour' — CINEMA — 'Barbarella' — 'Camelot' — 'Up the Junction' — '2001: A Space Odyssey' — 'Yellow Submarine' — 'A Lion in Winter' — THEATRE — Rock musical 'Hair' shocks the nation — BOOKS — 'Myra Breckinridge' — 'First Circle' — 'Cancer Ward' — Crick and Watson's 'Double Helix' — FASHION — Hippies — Indian influences — Thong tie belts — Cotton kurta shirts — Beads galore — 'Micro' skirts.

亞歷山大・杜貝克成為捷克領導人－瑟希・戴・路易斯受封英國桂冠詩人－蘇聯太空人尤利・加加林於空難中喪生－墨西哥奧運－馬丁・路德・金恩於曼菲斯市遭暗殺－巴黎學生與警察暴力衝突，巴黎索邦大學關閉－羅伯特・甘迺迪於洛杉磯遭到暗殺－加州柏克萊大學學生暴動－越戰和平談判於巴黎舉行－史波克博士在美因反戰被捕－洛杉磯華茲種族暴動－李察・尼克森競選美國總統－蘇聯坦克入侵捷克－北愛爾蘭倫敦德里民權遊行中群眾與警察激烈衝突－倫敦美國大使館前反越戰示威－美國3人-太空船阿波羅8號環繞月球軌道10次－約翰・史坦貝克過世－**音樂**－50萬人參與紐約州胡士托音樂節－披頭四發掘並跟隨瑪哈禮師超覺靜坐－《不可思議的神秘之旅》－**電影**－《上空英雄》－《鳳宮劫美錄》－《交叉線上》－《2001太空漫遊》－《黃色潛水艇》－《冬之獅》－**戲劇**－歌舞劇《毛髮》震驚全國－**出版**－《蜜拉・布雷金莉姬》－《第一輪》－《癌症病房》－克里克與華森的《雙螺旋》

1968

OPEN ENDS

Editorial from Archigram 8

The notions that have been running through our heads since the phase of the 1990 House and other experiments are much less easily frozen. As it is more irrelevant to contain an experiment in a single 'idea' such as a capsule house – where the image of capsule can replace the earlier image of cottage – or even a complex assembly like the Plug-in City can be read against a walled city of ancient times – it is now less a question of replacement ideas. It is less a question of total idea and total consistency. Yet there is a consistency somewhere: perhaps in the generics of the work now being done by Archigram which all, in some way, springs from the earlier outbreaks. Without setting up too introspective a discussion, it is interesting for any one of the Archigram group to trace the step-by-step-ness of the new work.

There then emerges a stage where the notions themselves can be taken outside the description of a single design or proposition, and read against several. They can be detected in some ideas, and come through fiercely in others. We have eight notions that are still unanswered by any complete set of experiments though we have begun the series. They are dreams because we keep returning to them. They are dreams because they may never be completely satisfied by what a designer or a strategist or any operator can do. They are open-ended, and whatever we are doing by the time that you are reading this may in some way have sprung out of a dream or two.

METAMORPHOSIS

Oxford Dictionary definition:
'Change of form (by natural development, etc.). Changed form, change of character, condition, etc.'
Archigram usage:
Continuous evolution from one state (or arrangement of forms, values, incidences or whatever) to another. Always alive but never the same. Always complete but always in metamorphic transience.

Most cultured designers have been bred to regard one state of organisation against another in terms of preference. Even non-formally, there are arrangements that are 'good' and 'bad'. Religion, formula, ideal, thesis, antithesis – all force one towards stating a fixed preference: a stated state. If we really believe in change, it will be a change in what we believe in, rather than a change in the means towards a different ideal. Growth itself has a dynamic and becomes a useful objective because it is the natural analogue of change. Now the analogy must be widened so that all parts are in an evolutionary state.

This business of widening range has taken us through some weird territory. It means that most of the projects we make are hybrid in content as well as notion, they themselves are in a constant change of state, assembly, and value. This last is the most difficult: and may be what metamorphosis is all about. Therefore there seem to be two levels of metamorphosis: the simple one by which an object has

開放式結局

《建築電訊》第8期社論

自從「1990住宅」與其它實驗作品之後，持續盤繞於我們腦海中的概念變得更加難以凝聚固定。因為於一個單一「構想」包含一個實驗的方式已經更不具意義了，譬如一棟艙屋——在這裡艙室的形像可以取代早期的別墅小屋形像——或甚至像「插接城市」這般的複雜機件裝配組合亦可解讀為反早期的城牆環繞式城市——現在比較不是取代性構想的問題了。也比較不是整體構想與整體一致性的問題。然而某些地方還是存有一致性：或許，就某方面而言，「建築電訊」目前所完成的一般作品是湧現自早期的開端。不提出太多內省式的討論，而讓「建築電訊」團體的每位成員去探溯新作品中的逐步發展階段是十分有趣的。

而後於是出現一個概念本身可採用單一設計或提案以外之方式的階段，並可同時有數種解釋。它們可由某些構想中察覺出，並猛烈地順利穿越過其它的構想。我們仍有8個至今尚未能藉由任何一組完整的實驗而獲得解答的構想，雖然我們已經開始進行這一系列的工作了。它們是夢想，因為我們不斷地回頭思索它們。它們是夢想，因為它們絕不可能藉由一位設計師或一位策士或任何執行者所能做到的而全然達成。它們是開放式結局的，而且，不管當您讀到這段文字之前我們做了什麼，就某方面而言可能又已經湧現出1或2個夢想了。

變形

牛津字典的定義：
「（藉由自然發展等方式所產生之）形式的變化。改變的形式、特性與狀態的變化，諸如此類。」

「建築電訊」的用法：
從一種狀態（或形式的安排、價值範圍或任何其它事物）至另一種狀態的持續演變。始終存在但絕不雷同。始終整體但總是變化無常。

大部份具涵養的設計師們都被調教成必須依照偏好的觀點，將組織中的某種狀態視為與另一種狀態互相衝突。甚至就非形式而言，解決方式也有「好」、「壞」之別。信仰、公式、理想、命題、反命題——全都迫使人們朝向定出一個固定的偏好：一個指定的身分地位。如果我們真的相信改變這件事的話，這將會是我們信仰的一大改變，而非邁向一種不同理想之方式的改變。成長的本身具有一種原動力並變成一種有用的目標，因為它是改變的自然類比物。現在類比必須被拓展，如此才得以令所有要素處於演進的狀態。

拓展範圍這個任務已經引領我們穿越過一些怪異的領域：意思是我們所完成的大部份設計案在內容與概念上都是混合的。它們本身就處於一種狀態、組合與價值的持續改變。後者是其中最困難的：或許正是變形的最佳詮釋。因此變形似乎具有兩種程度：較簡單的變形是一個物件必須改變以保持運行（F-III戰鬥機必須搖擺其雙翼以保持正常運作），而較複雜的變形則是我們自己對於現象

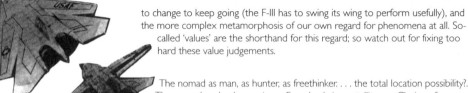

NOMAD

Oxford Dictionary definition:
*'Roaming from place to place.
. . wandering'.*

Archigram usage:
*includes the related notions of
the satellite and the complete
operation not necessarily tied
to a locative system.*

to change to keep going (the F-III has to swing its wing to perform usefully), and the more complex metamorphosis of our own regard for phenomena at all. So-called 'values' are the shorthand for this regard; so watch out for fixing too hard these value judgements.

The nomad as man, as hunter, as freethinker. . . . the total location possibility?. . . The nomad on land, sea, air. . . . Everybody is a satellite. . . . Choice of unseen or seen attachment to an organisation or system. . . . Trailers. . . . Hovercraft. . . . Tents. . . . Pack-on-back. . . . Underwater. . . . Moon probe. . . . Suit environment. . . . Disappearing off for a smoke. . . . 'Don't bug me, Mac'. . . . 'See you'. . . .

This could be the most upsetting idea since it is close to the instincts of many people who like to be thought of as steady guys: those who rely upon being able to plug into a known network, who demand of life a continuity. It is these guys who are nearest the edge of escaping from it all. The car is useful for the game of freedom. The implication that the whole surface of the world can give equal service is possibly pointing to the time when we can all be nomads if we wish. At the same time the network of support (even if 'soft' like radio) is still there to be escaped from.

At the moment the situation is open-ended. This is the attraction of the car-as-satellite-of-the-pad. Next the car becomes its own pad. Next the pad itself takes on the role of car. It divides and regroups. So too could larger combinations of environment. The status of the family and its direct connotation with a preferred, static house, cannot last. What about the evidence of the Teenybopper family-within-the-family? Multiplication and proliferation (and a dynamic use of mass availables) could lead to breakaway and regroup as naturally as the traditional strict hierarchies. Time is a factor. Coming together and independence are compatible if we use time.

The effect of hybrid assemblies that are at once mass-produced and private world already exist. If developed, the extension of personality might become the central reason for environment. The interface of one man with one enclosure is a raw example. The moment-village is a project suggested by this development out of Nomadism. Its group-regroup-shift implication suggests that its ultimate might be an anarchy-city or that the concept of 'place' exists only in the mind.

的關心。所謂的「價值」即是這種關心的簡略表達方式；因此得當心勿將這些價值判斷定得太僵。

遊牧

牛津字典的定義：
「自一個場所流浪至另一個場所……四處徘徊。」

「建築電訊」的用法：包含與衛星及不一定受定位系統束縛之完整運轉有關的概念。

遊牧者如人類、獵人、自由思想者……全然定位的可能性？……遊牧者在陸上、海上、空中……每個人都是一座衛星……一個組織或系統之不可見附屬物或可見附屬物的選擇……拖車屋……氣墊車……帳篷……攜帶式容器……海底潛水……月球探測……衣服環境……偷溜掉去吸口煙……「別煩我，老兄」……「再見」……

這可能是最令人煩惱的構想，因為它與許多喜歡被視為穩定的人——那些相信能夠插接上一個已知網路的人，那些要求生活是一種連續性的人——的本能十分地接近。正是這些人最瀕臨逃離所有這一切的邊緣。汽車對於自由的計劃是有幫助的。可能唯有當我們所有人願意時便可以成為遊牧者的那一刻到來時，全世界各個角落才可能有辦法提供同等的服務。話雖如此，我們仍舊必須避開支援網路（即使是「軟體的」，例如收音機）。

這時候便是開放式結局的情況。這正是「汽車身為房屋衛星」的吸引力所在。之後汽車變成了房屋。之後房屋本身承擔了汽車的任務。它分離又重組。因此更為龐大的環境組合也可以如此。家庭的現狀以及它直接的言外之意所指的偏好與靜態的房屋，已經無法存續。青少年的「家中之家」正是一個實例，不是嗎？增殖與分裂增殖（以及大量可用品的充分利用）就像傳統的嚴格階級體系一樣，也可能引起分離與重組。時間是一大因素。如果我們善用時間的話，結合與獨立是可以相容的。

立即大量生產的混合性組合之影響與私人的世界早已存在。若進一步開發的話，獨特氣氛的延伸可能變成環境的主要動機。人與外殼的介面是個粗略的例子。「即時村落」是由遊牧生活所得出之發展所聯想到的設計案。它的聚集－重組－改變的含意暗示了它的最終結果可能是座無政府狀態的城市，或者暗示了「場所」的概念只存在於腦海裡。

COMFORT

Oxford Dictionary definition:
'relief in affliction . . . cause of satisfaction, conscious well-being . . . possession of things that make life easy'.

Archigram usage:
the broad instinct for well-being. Perhaps the greatest justification for environment – or any man-made effort – is well-being. Or is this moralising?

'Comfort' in its current English usage is an old, rather 'hairy' (and therefore suspect) word, but it is interesting that the most impressive modern architecture is most often accused (by lay people) of being 'uncomfortable'. This is at the level of the most literal interpretation of the word, but it serves as a warning that if we are not careful we shall end up by providing a commodity that by its inhumanity is just aesthetic fetish.

Returning to the fundamental comfort-instinct, it is reasonable to check designed situations against their probable 'plus' or 'minus' in terms of whether they make people feel safe or unsafe, propped-up or isolated, happy or unhappy.

Goodies. Enjoyment. Security. 'System' of structure, facilities, service, etc. is a comfort-giving thing as much as ice-cream is a comfort-giving goody.

舒適

牛津字典的定義：
「苦難中的釋然……由於滿足、自覺的幸福……擁有令生活安逸的事物。」
「建築電訊」的用法：
幸福廣義的本性。也許環境最重要的理由──或是任何人為的努力──就是幸福。或者這不過是泛道德化而已？

「舒適」在現今英文的用法裡是個老舊且稍微「嚇人」（因而令人可疑）的字眼，但有趣的是最令人印象深刻的現代建築卻最常被指控為「不符合舒適性」。此為這個字之最表面上的字面解釋，但它足以構成一種預警，亦即若我們不夠謹慎的話，下場將是我們提供了一些非人性化之美學崇拜下的產品。

回到根本的舒適本性上，就設計的情境是否使人感到安全或不安全、受支持或被孤立、快樂或不快樂的角度，而將其與它們可能的「優點」或「缺點」相互核對是極為合理的。

美食。享受。安全感。結構、設備、公共設施……等「系統」是令人舒適的好東西，而冰淇淋是令人舒適的美食。

COMFORT········

FRANCOIS DALLEGRET ESTHETICIEN ACID

DALLEGRET & CO   4825 SAINTE CATHERINE OUEST   MONTREAL CANADA   935 47 50

positive cloud for exposed trip

McGraw Hill Lost Visuals

a miniature farm de Clavie ri l'a née

HARD-SOFT

This refers to the 'hardware-software' relationship found in systems analysis, cybernetics, and the terms come from computer jargon. They are not yet in the Oxford Dictionary.

'Hard', e.g. monument, New York, wall, machine, hard architecture, metal, plastic, etc. Against 'soft', e.g. programme, wire, message, instruction, graphic synopsis, equation, mood, abstract, informed machine, electronic music, light show, computers, information feedback, information motivators.

In systems planning we are reaching a point where the 'software' – the unseen relationship – is sufficient to determine the control and positioning of elements with which we live. The environment can now be determined by a systems analysis of our requirements, and the 'seen' world could become servant to the 'unseen' motivation. Now, naturally, we are all excited about this. At last we can escape from the hangup on hardware that has beset architecture throughout history; we need not bother about preference even. This over-simplification has the rhetoric that is necessary at this moment in history. In many ways it parallels the great excitement of the discovery of the machine for the Futurists 50 years ago. Hardware has limitations, and the symbolism of bits and pieces can be a bore for a rational attitude to planning or performance specification. Software is at this moment being pitched against it in order to explode this seeming irrationality.

But once again, we are falling into this black versus white trap. Systems are not a panacea. They have a necessary place in the evolution of intelligence. They will take short-cuts towards solving problems. The Plug-in City needed the Computer City as its shadow, otherwise it could not function. The Control and Choice discussion revolved around the potential of the unseen microswitches and sensors, but more than this: these devices would need the intelligence of a computed relay of information so that they came into your service at the moment when you needed them.

We shall really get somewhere when it has all cooled off a little, and hard and soft become relative to each other rather than in opposition.

硬－軟

在系統規劃上，我們正邁往「軟體」——不可見的關係——足以決定我們生活所需之元件的控制與定位的階段。如今環境可藉由對我們的需求進行系統分析而決定，而且「可見的」世界可能轉變為從屬於「不可見的」動機。現在，自然地，我們對此都感到極為興奮。終於我們可以擺脫長久以來困擾著建築的硬體障礙；我們甚至不需要煩惱偏好的問題。這種過度的簡化擁有此刻所需要的修辭。就許多方面而言，這類似於50年前未來派者發現機器時的欣喜若狂。硬體有其限度，而零件的象徵性對於規劃與執行細節的理性態度而言可能是令人厭煩的東西。軟體目前被設定為與此想法相對抗，以推翻這種貌似真實然而其實未必之不合理性。

但再一次地，我們又落入了這個黑白對抗的陷阱之中。系統並非萬靈丹。它們在智力的演化上占有必要性的位置。它們會循著捷徑解決問題。「插接城市」需要「電腦城市」當做它的庇護，否則它無法運作。「控制與選擇」的討論思索著不可見的微開關與感應器的可能性，但不只如此，這些裝置都將需要資訊的電算中繼智力，如此它們才可以在當您需要它們的時候能夠為您服務。

當一切都稍微平靜之後，我們應該能有真正的進展，並且硬與軟將變得彼此相對而非對立。

EMANCIPATION

The history of the last 100 years has been one of continued emancipation, irrevocably moving forwards despite the immense obvious setbacks of war and poverty, and the more hidden ones sustained by facets of culture and tradition that seek to preserve as much as possible in the face of social change. We are nearing the time when we can all realise our aspirations. It is too simple to see this merely as the amassing of objects, but they represent pretty accurately the directions outwards that our mental environment can reach: to the furthest imaginable limits. This is the crux of the matter: in the past the indulgence of the mind and intellect (as applied to artefacts) was the privilege of the rich.

If architecture laid claims to human sustenance, it should surely have responded as human experience expanded. For architects the question is: do buildings help towards emancipation of the people within? Or do they hinder because they solidify the way of life preferred by the architect? It is now reasonable to treat buildings as consumer products, and the real justification of consumer products is that they are the direct expression of a freedom to choose. So we are back again to the other notions of determinacy and indeterminacy and change and choice. We may reach a stage where this whole discussion seems academic because we shall all be much more relaxed about the choices we have and actually want a bit of abrasion in the way of bad buildings, but we are nowhere near that yet.

EXCHANGE AND RESPONSE
EXCHANGE

Even the broad march of history that measures the action and reaction of one movement against another – and at every scale down wards – capitalises upon interaction. At a purely functional level, the exchange of facility between one object and another is the basis of most design. It seems to us strange that architecture is expected to support a single value-system when today there is exchange between different fields of operation that can increase the possible means of our survival.

The other attractive aspect of 'exchange' as a fundamental is its implication of 'revision'. This has strong links with our concern with the necessity of building as an exchangeable commodity: extendable, expendable and under constant scrutiny. All effort is responding to something. An active architecture – and this is really what

解放

牛津字典的定義：
「使獲得自由，特別是脫離奴役……脫離思考上或道德上的桎梏。」

「建築電訊」的用法：
特別將其直接地參照於人們對於建築物的使用。

過去100年的歷史可說是持續解放的歷史，向前邁進無法回頭，不顧戰爭與貧窮強大明顯的阻礙，較為潛藏的歷史部分則藉由面對社會轉變時盡可能圖存的文化面與傳統而持續著。我們正一步步地接近我們稱之為全然瞭解我們渴求目標的時刻。若只將其視為物件的聚集那就太單純了，事實上它們相當精準地描繪出我們的精神環境所能觸及的方向：直到想像的最大極限。這是問題的關鍵所在：在過去，精神與智性的耽溺（亦適用於人造製品）是富者的特權。

若建築宣稱其為人類維持生活所需之物，則當人類的經驗擴展之時，它當然應該有所回應。對於建築師而言，問題在於：建築物是否有助於居於內者邁向解放之途呢？或者它們是否有所阻礙，因為它們結集了建築師偏愛的生活方式？現在將建築物視為消費產品是很合理的，而消費產品的實證在於它們是自由選擇的直接表現。因此我們再度回到了諸如決定性、獨立性、改變性與選擇性的其它概念上。我們可能會步向一種整體討論仍顯得十分具學術理論性的階段，因為我們對於我們所擁有的選擇性上都應該更寬鬆一點，並實際地要一些「壞建築的瑕疵性，然而我們還差得遠呢！

交流與回應
交流

牛津字典的定義：
「施與，領受，代替它者，被它者取代；可被接受為同等。」

「建築電訊」的用法：
事件彼此之間的交互作用，直接類比於兩種設備間的交互作用（與不確定性，於許多情況中）。

即使是評斷一項運動對於另一項運動的作用與反作用之廣泛歷程發展中的每個等級都運用了交互作用。就純粹的機能方面而言，物件之間設備的交流是大多數設計的基礎。我們覺得很奇怪的是，今日不同領域間早已存在著可以增加我們生存的可能方式的運作交流，然而建築卻也被期待能支持單一的價值體系。視「交流」為基礎之另一引人之處在於它「修正」的暗示。這與我們對於將建築物之必需品視為可交流商品：可延續的、可消費的且持續接受細查的——之關注有著強烈的關聯性。所有的努力成果都回應著某些事。積極的建築——而

RESPONSE

Oxford Dictionary definition:
'Answer given in word or act . . . feeling elicited by stimulus or influence.'

Archigram usage:
Effective reply by situation or design or artefact to a need, stimulus or an idea.

we are about – attempts to sharpen to the maximum its power of response and ability to respond to as many reasonable potentials as possible. If only we could get to an architecture that really responded to human wish as it occurred then we would be getting somewhere.

Deliberate confrontation of forces so that one responds to the other: robot-serves-person; machine-serves-facility; machine-interacts-with-other-machine; person-'summons'-facility; appliance-serves-food, person-responds-to-scene. Objects: robots, enclosures, facility-machines. Man/machine interface. Information feedback results in environment change.

回應

牛津字典的定義：
「藉由言語或行動的回答……藉由刺激或影響而有獲得的感受。」

「建築電訊」的用法：
藉由情境、設計或人造物而對一種需求、刺激或構想所做出的有效答辯。

這正是我們目前所做的事——企圖加強它的回應能力至極點與盡可能回應最多之合理可能性的能力。但願我們可以開始著手一種真正能夠回應人類期望的建築，屆時我們才將可能有所進展。

審慎地面對各種力量以便彼此能夠相互地回應：自動裝置－服務－人；機器－服務－設備；機器－與－其它－機器－交互作用；人「召喚」設備；家電製品提供食物，人類回應現況。物件：自動裝置、外殼、設備－機器。人／機器介面。資訊的回輸造成了環境的改變。

Oasis, Ron Herron
綠洲・朗・赫倫

WE OFFER TEN PRE-SELECTED SETS

We offer ten pre-selected sets – or you can choose from 43 individual fixtures and custom-design your own set to suit your tastes. Part 4 – or in spite of the fact there is no sign of the Evinrude Aquanaut and skim-twin all-weather carpeted multipurpose boat this picture tells you how it is – which also happens to be part 2 of a consideration of the completely friendly and satisfying environment and how to recognise it.

The passing cluster of equipment.

The transient space.

The backyard that happens as three magic tail-gates lower and the twin barrel V8s stop feeding horses thru' Synchro-smooth drive trains.

Slip off the hi-way.

Cut out automatic pilot control and cruisomatic.

Select down.

Super diamond lustre finish feeding back bent images of sky and trees.

Sports tach fliskers dead and supawide ovals sink into the meadow.

Just unload the gear and live. Move on maybe. It's all different tomorrow any way. The backyard has become a party or kitchen and three days gunning down the Pan-American hi-way and you're stepping out of that feature foam-cushioned bucket and setting up your luxurious and convenient equipment in the jungle and there still isn't a crease in your shirt.

See the picture, it's all there, at least until it's all in your pocket, or embedded in your nervous system or we don't need to go because we can recreate it all in Bradford or on the Central Line.

DAVID GREENE

我們提供10組預選組件

我們提供了10組預選組件——或者您可以自己從43件個別附屬裝置中選擇，並訂製設計適合您自己的組件。第四部份——儘管沒有「艾文魯德」船外引擎製造公司的海底工作人員與不論晴雨雙蓬式多功能遊艇的標記，這張圖片會告訴您是怎麼回事——而這剛好是考量全然宜人且令人滿意之環境與如何認定它的第二部份。

成群的暫時性設備。
過渡性空間。
當3片神奇尾板降下且雙管8汽缸停止馬力運作穿越平坦馬路時即形成後院。
駛離公路。
停止自動駕駛與導航控制裝置。
選定座位就緒躺下。
回饋藍天綠樹曠野景象的特級鑽石般光澤潤飾。
轉速計疲憊地擺動，大型運動場沉入草原。

只要卸下傳動裝置並住下。也許會繼續走下去。反正明天一切都將不一樣，後院變成了一個派對或廚房，三天的持續徘徊泛美公路後步出泡沫墊圓背摺椅並於密林裡組合您的豪華舒適設備，也仍未見您的襯衫起過任何縐摺。
看看圖片，全在那兒了，至少在它變成您的東西之前，或是深烙在您的神經系統裡，或者我們根本就不需要去那兒，因為我們可以在布雷德佛或「中央線」地區將它全部重建。

大衛 • 葛林

Suburb, Ron Herron
市郊，朗・赫倫

MOMENT VILLAGE IS

FOR AN INSTANT

wide open

service

soft

soft

MOMENT-VILLAGE

service

soft

bring h

IDEAS CIRCUS

The notion of the Ideas Circus came after the experience of several Archigram lectures and seminars where common characteristics of college and exhibition facilities could be experienced.

There is little interchange of ideas between one institution and the next, and display or documentation facilities have to be erected from scratch.

SCHEME

To institute a standard package of five or six vehicles that contain all the equipment necessary to set up a seminar, conference, exhibition, teach-in or display. The package can be attached to an existing building, plugging-into such facilities as are there and using the shelter of existing rooms for Circus equipment. The Circus can also be completely autonomous: set up in a field, if necessary. The idea would be to circulate between major provincial centres, tapping local universities, bleeding-off from them personalities, documentation and such things as film of laboratory experiments: then carrying on to the next town. Weekend visits to smaller places could be made. Some vehicles could hive off for an afternoon teach-in at the local Women's Institute. The Circus would be programmed with basic film and slide material. The feedback facility is most important: verbatim documentation of seminars, documents, films, etc.. would be printed-off and left behind. Static educational facilities need topping-up. Mobile educational facilities could so easily be a nine-day wonder. The Ideas Circus is offered as a tool for the interim phase: until we have a really working all-way information network.

構想集會場

構想集會場的概念緊接於「建築電訊」的一些演說與研討會之後出現，會議中可體驗到學校與展覽會設施的共同特性。

各機構單位間極少有構想上的交流，而展示與文件利用之設施則須架設自臨時的拼湊。

架構

制定一批包含開辦一場研討會、會議、展覽、學校集會或展示所需之所有必要設備的5或6輛交通工具的標準組件。這批組件可以附著於一棟現有的建築物，插接於既有設施並利用現有的房室遮蔽作為集會場設備。集會場亦可以是完全獨立自主的：設置於一處曠野之中，如果必要的話。此構想為流通於主要的地方中心之間，開發利用當地的大學，自它們當中榨取一些名士、文獻資料與諸如實驗室之實驗影片之類的東西；然後繼續前往下一個城鎮。週末可造訪一些較小的村鎮。某些交通工具可區分為地方婦女會的下午集會之用。集會場將規劃有基本的電影與幻燈片媒材。回饋設施是最重要的：研討會逐字的文獻編集、文件資料、影片……等，將被沖印並留下。靜態教育設施需要增加。動態教育設施則極易只具有一時的吸引力而已。構想集會場被提供為臨時性階段的工具：直到我們有了一個真正能夠全天候運作的資訊網為止。

In the four weeks, the Circus is first programmed from London with tapes, filmstrips, etc., on the tour subject. These are prepared with help from the available institutions.

The centres visited are geographically fairly close so that little time is spent actually on the road. In the multi-vehicle version there can be a programmed echeloning of the constituent parts so as to make best use of time and resources. In this version a single unit (vehicle simplified programme) can be sent to small towns nearby for a one-night stand or appetiser demonstration. The instigation of a national information network such as that shown here between universities is important but not absolutely essential. Special personal

在4週裡，集會場首先自倫敦開始以錄影帶、幻燈式影片……等進行巡迴之旅。此將於近便機關設施的協助下進行準備。

造訪的中心在地理位置上都相當靠近，因此實際花費於道路交通上的時間並不多。在多元化交通工具的模式裡，可能有一構成元件之計劃性層級，以便能善加利用時間與資源。於此模式裡，單獨的單元體（交通工具簡化計劃）可被送往鄰近小鎮進行單次的表演或「開胃式」的宣傳。像這樣的各大學間之全國資訊網的煽動性固然重要，但卻非絕對必要。建議舉辦特殊之「個人自我提升」演講，這些再加上地面通訊電線資訊證

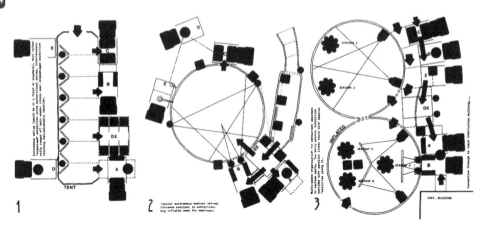

1

2 Typical autonomous seminar set-up.
Entrance corridor is exhibition.
Big inflated dome for meetings.

3

boost lectures are suggested and these plus the landlined information instance a meshing of the Circus network with any other available network.

The Circus is here shown as involved with an academic tour such as Microbiology for All, New Maths, Modern Architecture or whatever.

It could equally well cover similar territory with a commercial promotion or other non-academic tour.

明了集會場網路與任何其它可利用網路間的嚙合。

此處之集會場致力於「學院性」巡迴演講，諸如「人人可懂的微生物學」、「新數學」、「現代建築」……等。

不管是商業性促銷或是其它非學術性巡迴演出都可以相同地涵蓋到類似的領域。

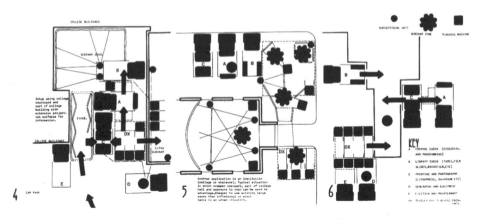

INSTANT CITY

即時城市

THE NOTION

In most civilised countries, localities and their local cultures remain slow moving, often undernourished and sometimes resentful of the more favoured metropolitan regions (such as New York, the West Coast of the United States, London and Paris). Whilst much is spoken about cultural links and about the effect of television as a window on the world (and the inevitable global village) people still feel frustrated. Younger people even have a suspicion that they are missing out on things that could widen their horizons. They would like to be involved in aspects of life where their own experiences can be seen as part of what is happening.

Against this is the reaction to the physical nature of the metropolis: and somehow there is this paradox – if only we could enjoy it but stay where we are.

The Instant City project reacts to this with the idea of a 'travelling metropolis', a package that comes to a community, giving it a taste of the metropolitan dynamic – which is temporarily grafted on to the local centre – and whilst the community is still recovering from the shock, uses this catalyst as the

概念

在最文明的國家裡,地方的外貌與它們的地方文化維持著緩慢的進展,且經常是營養不足的,有時候還會憎惡較受偏愛的都會地區(例如紐約、美國西岸、倫敦與巴黎)。當論及文化連繫與電視被視為世界之窗(與無可避免的地球村)的影響時,人們依舊覺得很沮喪。年輕人甚至懷疑他們正錯失一些能夠開拓他們視野的東西。他們希望能夠參與生活中的各個層面,在那裡他們個人的經驗可被視為正在發生中之事件的一部份。

與此衝突的是對於都會實體本質的排拒:不知何故地就是存有這種矛盾——但願我們會喜歡它並保持自己的原貌。

「即時城市」設計案以「旅行的都市」之構想回應這個現象;一整批裝備來到一個社區,讓它品嚐一下都會的活力——暫時與地方中心接合在一起——而當社區仍正由衝擊之中回過神時,利用這種

first stage of a national hook-up. A network of information education – entertainment – 'play-and-know yourself' facilities.

In England the feeling of being left out of things has for a long time affected the psychology of the provinces, so that people become either over-protective about local things, or carry in their minds a ridiculous inferiority complex about the metropolis. But we are nearing a time when the leisure period of the day is becoming really significant; and with the effect of television and better education people are realising that they could do things and know things, they could express themselves (or enjoy themselves in a freer way) and they are becoming dissatisfied with the television set, the youth club or the pub.

觸媒作為全國連結的第一個階段。一種資訊的網路—教育—娛樂—「寓教於樂」的設施。

在英國，地方長期以來有被冷落的感受，因此人們不是變得過度保護地方的文物，就是心存一種不如都市的荒謬自卑之複雜情緒。但我們正邁向白天休閒時段變得十分重要的時刻；有了電視與更好的教育影響之後，人們瞭解到他們可做與可知的事，他們可以表達自我（或更自在地好好享樂），並且變得不能滿足於電視機、年輕人俱樂部或小酒館。

URBAN ACTION - TUNE UP

PUSH
TODAY

3 5 2

TUNE UP - NOW

ACTION
VARIABLE SHELTERS
-ZEROX- INFORM
ATION SCREEN

URBAN
IMMEDIACY

SERVICING
KIT OF PARTS, SHORT LIFE,
MOBILE, ACTIVE, COMMUNITY
EDUCATIONAL SERVICING
STUD CARELS-SELF PACE
SKILL AND LEARNING
MACHINES- WORK
SHOPS- CCTV-
AUDIO VIS
UAL LIB
RARY

INSTANT CITY
RON HERRON - ARCHIGRAM
APRIL 1969   L.A.

A BACKGROUND FROM ARCHIGRAM WORK

The old Plug-in City programme of 1964 pulled together a series of seemingly disconnected notions and small projects (a throwaway unit here, an automatic shop there, or even an idea about a megastructure), reinforcing and qualifying the theme and eventually suggesting a total project – a portmanteau for the rest. Later on, the work that Archigram had done with the Hornsey Light-Sound Workshop and on several exhibitions (with the actual techniques of audience participation and control of a responsive audio-visual system) began to form a working laboratory for the techniques of Instant City.

The Instant City is both collective and coercive: by definition there is no perfect set of components. On the drawings which have been made over a period of two years there are often quotes from other pieces of work (for instance, Oslo Soft Scene Monitor as the parent of Audio-Visual Juke Box). In such a machine people tune in to their environment by choosing and making from a range of audio-visual programmes; the Oslo machine is its progenitor but it really implies something where the participant plays a completely open-ended creative game. Around 1966, at an exhibition on Brighton pier, we made an experiment of putting a man in a circular drum, spinning him round and then bombarding him (two feet from his face) with wild coloured slides, and bombarding him (one foot from his ears) with wild sounds. A typical instance of a first-stage experiment, unsubtle and without feedback, unable to provide the man inside with a button to press to say 'stop'. Later, the Oslo machine moved on from this and the limit of choice was one of cost rather than of concept.

With our notion of the robot (the symbol of the responsive machine that collects many services in one appliance), we begin to play with the notion that the environment could be conditioned not only by the set piece assembly but by infinite variables determined by your wish, and the robot reappears in the Instant City in several of the assemblies.

The planning implications of Instant City have emerged more and more strongly as the project has developed, so that by the time we are making the sequence describing the airship's effect upon the sleeping town, it is the infiltrationary dynamic of the town itself that is as fascinating as the technical dynamic of the airship. Again we have to reflect on the psychology of a country such as England, where there is a historical suggestion that vast upheaval is unlikely. We are likely to capitalise on existing institutions and existing facilities whilst complaining about their inefficiency – but a country such as England must now live by its wits or perish, and for its wits it needs its culture.

242

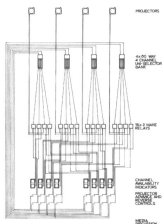

PROJECTORS

4 x 60 WAY 4 CHANNEL UNI-SELECTOR BANK

16 x 2 MAKE RELAYS

CHANNEL AVAILABILITY INDICATORS

PROJECTOR ADVANCE AND REVERSE CONTROLS

MEDIA DISCUSSION MACHINE

「建築電訊」作品的背景

1964年的舊「插接城市」計劃將一系列似乎無關的概念與小設計案拉在一起（東一個用後即丟棄的單元體，西一個自動化商店，或甚至是有關超大型結構的觀念），強化並修飾主題，並於最終提出一份完整的設計案建議—— 一個適用於其它案例的混成體。之後，「建築電訊」與「霍恩希聲光工作坊」合作所完成的作品與一些展覽（用實際的觀眾參與科技與感應式視聽系統的控制）開始形成一個「即時城市」技術的工作實驗室。

「即時城市」兼具集體性與強制性：從定義上來說，當然沒有所謂完美的組件。進行超過2年以上的設計圖上通常會引用到其它的作品（例如，「奧斯陸軟體場景顯示器」為「視聽自動點唱機」的鼻祖）。人們自這種機器裡的一些視聽程式中選擇調製出他們即將進入的環境；奧斯陸機器是它的鼻祖，但實際上這意味著參與者正在進行一場開放式結局的遊戲。大約1966年的時候，在布萊頓碼頭的展覽中，我們做了一個實驗，將一個人置於一個圓形的鼓狀容器中，將他旋轉之後以鮮豔強烈的彩色幻燈片轟擊他（大約距離他的臉2呎左右），再以強烈的音響（大約距離他的耳朵1呎左右）轟炸他。第一階段實驗的典型例子，不精細亦無回饋，無法提供內部者一個可以停止的按鈕。之後，奧斯陸機器自這種狀態繼續演變下去，而選擇的限制實際上是成本上而非概念上的。

利用我們的自動裝置概念（集合許多設施於同一器具裝備中的感應式機器的象徵），我們開始進行一種概念，亦即環境不只受到固定式機件裝配組合所支配，同時亦藉由您意願抉擇下之無限可能變化所決定，並且自動裝置也重現於「即時城市」裡的一些機件裝配組合之中。

「即時城市」具有計劃性含意，當計劃案發展之後，它的力量便愈來愈強烈地顯露出來，因此在我們一系列描述「飛船」對於癱滯城鎮之影響的作品完成之前，城鎮本身的滲透性動力與飛船的技術性動力具有同樣的吸引力。再且，我們必須考慮到一個國家的心理狀態，例如英國，那裡存有一種不可能有所浩大劇變的歷史性暗示。我們可能利用著現今的設施與設備，卻又抱怨著它們的無效率——但一個像英國這樣的國家，目前必須依靠它的智慧生存下去，否則將會滅亡，而為了擁有智慧它需要它的文化。

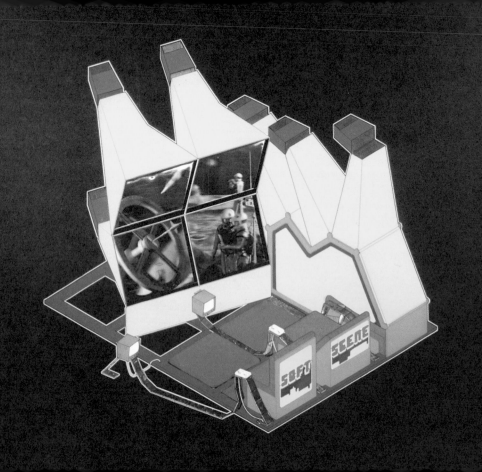

50% PERSONALISED ENVIRONMENT

A PROGRAMME BACKGROUND

The likely components are audio-visual display systems, projection television, trailered units, pneumatic and light-weight structures and entertainments facilities, exhibits, gantries and electric lights.

This involves the theoretical territory between the 'hardware' (or the design of buildings and places) and 'soft-ware' (or the effect of information and programmation of the environment). Theoretically it also involves the notions of urban dispersal and the territory between entertainment and learning. The Instant City could be made a practical reality since at every stage it is based upon existing techniques and their application to real situations. There is a combination of several different artefacts and systems which have hitherto remained as separate machines, enclosures or experiments. The programme involved gathering information about an itinerary of communities and the available utilities that exist (clubs, local radio, universities, etc.) so that the 'City' package is always complementary rather than alien. We then tested this proposition against particular samples.

The first stage programme consisted of assemblies carried by approximately 20 vehicles, operable in most weathers and carrying a complete programme. These were applied to localities in England and in the Los Angeles area of California. Later, having become interested in the versatility of the airship, we came to propose this as another means of transporting the InstantCity assembly (a great and silent bringer of the whole conglomeration).

Later we applied the method of the Instant City to proposals for servicing the Documenta exhibition at Kassel in Germany. By this time also there had developed a feedback of ideas and techniques between this project and our Monte Carlo entertainments facility.

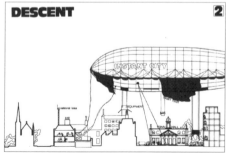

規劃背景

可能的組件是視聽展示系統、投影式電視、拖車屋單元體、充氣式與輕型結構及娛樂設施、展覽品、起重機形構架與電子燈光。

這牽涉到「硬體」（或建築物與場所的設計）與「軟體」（或環境的資訊提供與計劃制定的效應）之間的理論性分野。理論上，它也牽涉到都市散佈以及娛樂與學習之間的分野的概念。「即時城市」是有可能被實現的，因為它的每個階段中都是根據現今的科技及其於實際狀況中的應用。有一些至今依舊是各自獨立的機器、圍蔽物或實驗之不同的人造物與系統的組合。規劃牽涉到社區路線與現存可利用之公共設施的資訊蒐集（俱樂部、地方電台、大學……等），因此「城市」容器永遠是互補的，而非不相干的。然後我們以特殊的例子檢驗這個建議案。

第一階段的規劃由大約20輛汽車所載運的機件裝配成品所組成，可於任何天候之下實施，並含有一個完整的計劃。這些構想被應用至英國郊區與加州的洛杉磯地區。之後，因為開始對於飛船的多功能性產生興趣，於是我們提出這項建議作為另一種運送「即時城市」之機件裝配成品的方式（一種很棒且安靜之整個複合體的攜帶方式）。

之後，我們將「即時城市」的方法應用於德國卡塞爾文件展的提案中。在此之前，對此構想亦有了回饋性發展，以及此計劃案與我們的「蒙地卡羅娛樂設施」間的技術。

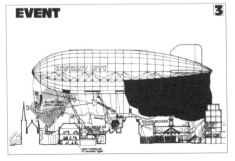

A TYPICAL SEQUENCE OF OPERATIONS (truck-borne version)

1. The components of the 'City' are loaded on to the trucks and trailers at base.

2 A series of 'tent' units are floated from balloons which are towed to the destination by aircraft.

3 Prior to the visit of the 'City' a team of surveyors, electricians, etc. have converted a disused building in the chosen community into a collection-, information- and relay-station. Landline links have been made to local schools and to one or more major (permanent) cities.

4 The 'City' arrives. It is assembled according to site and local characteristics. Not all components will necessarily be used. It may infiltrate into local buildings and streets, it may fragment.

5 Events, displays and educational programmes are partly supplied by the local community and partly by the 'City' agency. In addition major use is made of local fringe elements: fares, festivals, markets, societies, with trailers, stalls, displays and personnel accumulating often on an ad hoc basis. The event of the Instant City might be a bringing together of events that would otherwise occur separately in the district.

6 The overhead tent, inflatable windbreaks and other shelters are erected. Many units of the 'City' have their own tailored enclosure.

7 The 'City' stays for a limited period.

8 It then moves on to the next location.

9 After a number of places have been visited the local relay stations are linked together by landline. Community One is now feeding part of the programme to be enjoyed by Community Twenty.

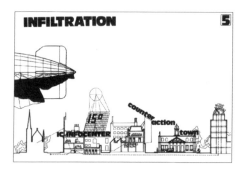

Rupert   IC2

LEARN
FRENCH
NOW

AWAY FROM WORK

B
I
C

FRENCH
3 DAYS!

THI
WE

CAB

EQUIPENT
OPTION

GRAB-
ARMS

SWINGS

INSTANT
ROUTE

HEY A
INSTANT
FRENCH

IC LEECH-TRUK

TANT CITY PROGRAM 1970 · ARCHIGRAM LONDON · SUPPORTED BY THE GRAHAM FOUNDATION CHICAGO

10 Eventually by this combination of physical and electronic, perceptual and programmatic events and the establishment of local display centres, a 'City' of communication might exist, the metropolis of the national network.

11 Almost certainly, travelling elements would modify over a period of time. It is even likely that after two to three years they would phase out and let the network take over.

As the Instant City study developed, certain items emerged in particular. First, the idea of a 'soft-scene monitor' – a combination of teaching-machine, audio-visual juke box, environmental simulator, and from a theoretical point of view, a realisation of the 'Hardware/Software' debate (which is still going on in our Monte Carlo work, as the notion of an electronically-aided responsive environment). Next, the dissolve of the original large, trucked, circus-like show into a smaller and very mobile element backed by a wonderful, magical dream descending from the skies. The model of the small unit suggests two trucks and a helicopter as the carriage, with quick folding arenas and apparatus that can quickly be fitted into the village hall. Another stimulus was the invitation to design the 'event structure' for the 1972 Kassel Documenta an elaborate art/event/theatre scene requiring a high level of servicing but a minimum of interference with the 'open-air creative act'. The 'Kassel-Kit' of apparatus can therefore be considered as a direct extension of the original IC Kit.

Are we back to heroics then, with a giant, pretty and evocative object? The Blimp: the airship: beauty, disaster and history. On the one hand we were designing a totally unseen and underground building at Monte Carlo, and on the other hand flirting with the airborne will-o-the-wisp. The Instant City as a series of trucks rushing round like ants might be practical and immediate, but we could not escape the loveliness of the idea of Instant City appearing from nowhere, and after the 'event' stage, lifting up its skirts and vanishing. In fact, the primary interest was spontaneity, and the remaining aim to knit into any locale as effectively as possible. For Archigram, the airship is a device: a giant skyhook.

Operationally, there were two possibilities. A simple airship with apparatus carried in the belly and able to drop down as required. Otherwise, a more sophisticated notion of a 'megastructure of the skies'. Ron Herron's drawings suggest that the 'ship' can fragment, and the audio/visual elements are scattered around a patch of sky. Once again, the project work of the group has picked up a dream of its own past – the 'Story of a Thing' made (almost) real.

We then built a model, which could hang out its entrails in a number of ways. This was the simpler 'ship' which reads with the scenario of a small town transformation. In the drawing with airship 'Rupert', a major shift in Instant City was first articulated: the increasing feeling for change-by-infiltration. The 'city' is creeping into half-finished buildings, using the local draper's store, gas showrooms and kerbside, as well as the more sophisticated set-up. And there is a mysterious creeping animal: the 'leech' truck, which is able to climb up any structure and service from it: with the resulting possibility of 'bugging' the whole town as necessary. Gently then, the project dissolves from the simple mechanics or hierarchies of 'structuring' and like-objects. Just as did the Plug-in City: it sowed the seeds of its own fragmentation into investigations of a gentler, more subtle environmental tuning.

運作之典型順序（卡車－運輸－版本）

1. 「城市」的組件被裝載於卡車與底部的拖車。

2. 一系列的「帳篷」單元體從氣球上漂浮起來，藉由飛船拖曳至目的地。

3. 在造訪「城市」之前，一個包含檢查員與電氣技師……等人的小組，將一棟位於選定社區內的廢棄建築物改造為一個收集、資訊與轉播的站台。地面通訊電線連接至地方學校以及一個或多個主要（永久的）城市。

4. 「城市」抵達。根據基地與地方的特性組裝起來。並不需要使用到所有的組件。它可以滲入地方的建築物與街道，它可以被打碎。

5. 事件、展示與教育的規劃部份由當地社區提供，其它部份則由當地「城市」的仲介公司安排。除此之外，主要的用途由地方的次要活動領域所構成：節目表演、節慶、市集、協會團體，以及拖車屋、攤子、展示與人的聚集，通常有一特殊根據。「即時城市」事件或許是一種於其它情況之下會個別地出現於地區裡之眾多事件的結合。

6. 架空式帳篷、充氣式防風設備與其它的遮蔽全都安裝起來。「城市」的許多單元體擁有適合它們自己的特製圍蔽。

7. 「城市」維持一段有限的時間。

8. 然後它又繼續移往下一個地點。

9. 造訪過一些地方之後，地方轉播站藉由地面通訊電線被連結在一起。「社區1」現在將部份的規劃提供給「社區20」作為娛樂之用。

10. 最後藉由這種形體的與電子的、憑知覺的與計劃制定的事件，以及地方展示中心之設立等組合，一座通訊「城市」或許因此得以產生—— 一個擁有全國聯絡網系統的大都會。

11. 幾乎可以確定地，旅行組件一段時間之後將會有所修正。甚至可能2、3年之後它們將逐漸被淘汰而由聯絡網系統全面接管。

自從「即時城市」的研究發展之後，特別出現了某些品目。首先是「軟體場景顯示器」的概念—— 一種教學機器、視聽自動點唱機與環境模擬裝置的混合體，就理論性觀點而言，算是「硬體／軟體」討論的實踐（這項討論於我們的蒙地卡羅作品中仍持續進行著，並變成一種電子輔助感應式環境的概

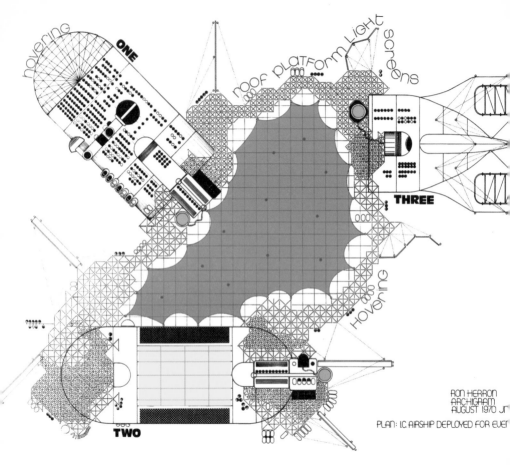

ONE

hovering

roof platform light screens

THREE

hovering

TWO

RON HERRON
ARCHIGRAM
AUGUST 1970 JN

PLAN: IC AIRSHIP DEPLOYED FOR EVENT

念）。其次，原始的龐大、卡車搬運之馬戲式的表演逐漸變成一個從天而降之絕妙神奇夢想式的較小型且十分具機動性的元件。小型單元體的模型建議由兩部卡車與一架直昇機運輸，利用可迅速安裝至市政廳之快速摺疊式圓形舞台與裝置。另一項激勵則來自於1972年受「卡塞爾文件展」之邀所設計的「事件－結構」── 一個需要大量的公共設施，但利用露天創造性行為以達到最小干擾性的精巧藝術品／事件／劇院舞台。「卡塞爾裝置組件」因此可被視為原始積體電路設備組件的直接延伸。

那麼我們是否又帶著一個碩大、漂亮且引人聯想的物件回到了大膽誇張呢？軟式小飛艇：飛船：美、災難與歷史。一方面我們在蒙地卡羅設計了一個全然不可見的地下建築物，另一方面則饒有興味地操弄著空中運輸的把戲。有如像螞蟻般四處奔竄之一連串卡車的「即時城市」可能既實際又即刻，但我們無法逃脫不知來自何處，且於「事件」階段之後一溜煙就消失了的「即時城市」構想的魅力。事實上，主要的重要性在於自發性，其次的目標則是盡可能有效地與任何地點接合在一起。對「建築電訊」而言，飛船是一種裝置：一個巨大的天鉤。

使用上有兩種可能性。一種是腹部攜有儀器裝置且於必要時可以落下的單純式飛船。另一種是更複雜的「天空超大型結構」概念。朗‧赫倫的圖中提議「船」可以碎裂，而視覺／聽覺元件則散佈於一片天空之中。再次提醒您，「建築電訊」團體的設計案作品擷取一個自己過去的夢想──「一件物體的故事」（幾乎）成真。

然後我們建造了一個可以用許多方式懸掛其內部零件的模型。這是艘依據小型城鎮變形設想情況之較單純的「船」。在「魯伯特」飛船的圖中，「即時城市」中主要的改變第一次被清楚地表達：逐漸感受到「滲透之改變」。「城市」不知不覺地變成了半成品建築物，使用地方的工場、能源中心與路邊，以及更複雜精細的佈局。此外還有一種神秘地匍匐潛行的生物：可爬升至任何結構與設施的「寄生」卡車：必要時可能會去「叨擾」整座城鎮。然後逐漸地，計劃案由單純的機械學或「結構性」與同類物件之階級體系中分解出來。正如同「插接城市」所做的一樣：它播下了自己碎裂部份的種子於一個更和緩、更敏銳之環境調頻的探究之中。

THE PIPED ENVIRONMENT

Dennis Crompton

The environment business is all tied up with the extension of man's experience, and once extended things are never quite the same again. At first it is all a struggle against adverse conditions whether it is at McMurdo Sound, Ealing or LA, but once man gets the upper hand he starts to extend into and out of his personal world, the world of the Golden Fleece and 007. This world is a product of current events and experiences and is constantly developing and progressing as aspirations become reality and new wish-dreams take their place. If we want to be something more in this environment business than a participant then we have got to become fluent dream-makers and not turn a blind eye to what is around us.

1 They are people
2 extending their experience
3 but it has very little to do with physical structures
4 although plugging-in, turning-on, dropping out demand facilities.

It seems to have all started with Bell, Baird, Faraday, and the rest, although I doubt if they thought of it in this way. What they did was to discover the facilities which have led to the Piped Environment. The immediacy of electrical response gave independence from the sun for light and heat and freed up many other situations in which the time-lag of reaction had become an embarrassing restriction. Then the transmission of sound for communication made for an infinite expansion of the available information and exchange services.

Radio gave the first real mass transmission of the Piped Environment, which started with our mums and dads transposing themselves to the Palm Court of Grand Hotel. It is curious to note that amongst the few serious environ- mentalists actually to harness this energy we see most notoriously the production lines of the factory and the boiler house, not to mention Musak, which is a world of its own. As a slight deviation there is an interesting cycle of development in the technique of audio environment. The radio and the telephone were originally highly personalised; for technical reasons playback was through headphones giving an extended individual environment which did not impose itself on others who were not plugged-in. As loudspeakers and amplifiers developed, this individual quality declined until we were all involved in the hi-fi nut's world of 100 watt Vortexions and Tannoy drive units, whether or not this was the form of extension of our experience we were after. The earphone (cans) returned with the pocket transistor radio and the astronaut cult so that the hi-fi man can now sit in oblivion extending himself in full frequency stereo sound without including the block in his experience. The drawback of the audio-induced environment is that the visual content is by implication – you have to close your eyes and think pink. In its way this works fine, you can have a highly coloured audio experience, but having had

有線播放環境

丹尼斯‧克藍普頓

環境問題全都與人類經驗的延伸緊繫在一起，且一旦延伸之後事物將不再雷同。起初全是與逆境的搏鬥，不管是在麥穆杜桑德、逸林或是洛杉磯，但是一旦人們取得了優勢之後，他們便開始延伸進出他的個人世界——希臘神話中的金羊毛或電影007的世界。這個世界是當前事件與經驗的結果並持續地發展與進步，因為願望變成了事實且新希望取代了它們。如果我們希望比過去更積極地參與環境事務的話，我們就必須變成善辯的夢想家，而非對週遭環境視若無睹。

1. 他們是延伸自己經驗
2. 的人
3. 不過這與物質結構的關聯性極少
4. 儘管插接上插頭、打開開關並掉掉需要的設備。

雖然我很懷疑他們是否曾這樣地想過這件事，但似乎一切都開始於貝耳、貝爾德、費勒戴以及其他人。他們所做的是去發現用以創造有線播放環境的設備。電子感應的即時性提供了可脫離受限於太陽光熱的獨立性，而反應時差造成阻礙的許多其它情況也獲得解放。接下來則是使可利用資訊與交流業務得以無限擴張的聲音傳輸通訊。

收音機提供了有線播放環境之首次真正大規模播送，這種環境始於我們父母親的時代，收聽時感覺宛如置身大飯店的棕櫚庭院一般。奇怪的是於一些真正利用此能源的嚴肅環境問題專家中，我們見到應用於最聲名狼藉的工廠生產線與養雞場。因為稍微的偏差而出現一種播音環境技術中有趣的發展循環。收音機與電視機原本是高度個人化的，基於技術的原因，播放是經由耳機提供一種擴大性且不會強迫其他未插接者收聽的個人環境。自從擴音器與擴大器發展之後，這種個人化特質即開始式微，直到我們全都熱中於100瓦特音響驅動裝置的高傳真音響迷的世界，無論如何這是我們當時所追求之經驗延伸的形式。覆耳式耳機因為袖珍型電晶體收音機與太空熱潮而重新受到重視，因而高傳真音響族們現在可忘情地延伸自己於全頻立體音響世界裡而不受任何阻礙。聽覺感應環境的缺點是視覺的內容必須依靠暗示，您必須閉上眼睛去想像粉紅色。以這種方式它可以運作無礙，您可以擁有一個高度彩色的聽覺經驗，但有了這種延伸的經驗之後情境將會改變，而您也得準備好繼續往前邁進。電影院、

ELEVATION

this form of extension the situation changes and you are ready to move on. Cinema and TV drop into this visual void along with more recent image projection systems and the Piped Environment takes on a higher degree of reality. The limiting factor here has been the frame which contains the image and the individual has had to move into this frame in order to become part of the transmitted experience. This was helped by the darkness of the cinema and the intimacy of the TV set at the end of the sofa, but once this has happened we are never the same again and are eager for a more sophisticated form of extension of our experience.

With multiple image technique the frame problem can be avoided and a more total, three-dimensional, situation occurs which envelops the participant. The distinctive main characteristic of this condition is that it is subject to constant and immediate change. On the face of it, this puts it out of court for the serious environmentalists because they are dedicated to the creation of static objects, but this is an accidental position. If the environmental business is concerned with the extension of man's experience then the means of achieving this is by pushing current technology.

電視,以及更新的影像投射系統都自然地陷入了視覺的虛無裡,而有線播放環境則呈現了較高程度的真實感。這裡的限制性因素是容納影像的框架,而個體則必須進入這個框架之中以變成傳輸經驗的一部份。此歸功於電影院中的一片漆黑與位於沙發末端電視機的親密性,但就另一方面而言,一旦這一切發生之後,我們將不再一如過往,而將會渴望一種更精巧複雜的經驗延伸。

利用複合影像的技術便可以避免框架的問題,並產生一種圍繞著參與者之更完全且三度空間的情境。這種條件狀況之十分獨特且成為其主要特色的因素在於它遵循著持續且即刻的改變。嚴肅的環境問題專家在面對它時抱持著蔑視的態度,因為他們致力於創造靜態的物件,但這是一種偶有的見解。如果環境問題涉及了人類經驗的延伸,那麼達成這個目標的方法就是藉由驅策目前的科技。

First published in *ARCHITECTURAL DESIGN* September 1968

UP THE DOWN RAMP

Warren Chalk

There's a little bit of VIP in all of us. All those 'only-when-you-get-to-ride-in-a-mil-lionaire's-car' things in a Plymouth. The Plymouth VIP...And The Beat Goes On...

This is Los Angeles, alluring city of the Angels. Los Angelinos, instead of spreading their wings however, are doing their thing, out there on the freeways – 'Widetracking', as the General Motors ads have it.

A strong case for LA affecting a whole generation of designers was made by Cedric Price, at a Victor Gruen lecture in 1962 at the Architectural Association. It was one of the first significant documented recognitions of Los Angeles as an alternative city proto-type; an acknowledgement of suburbia and of the significance of the automobile. There is little point in raking over the fires of old controversies; of prolonging the argument for or against centralised cities or sprawled suburbias. It may not be an either/or situation, Los Angeles being what it is, neither city nor suburbia, but megasuburbia. All one can say is that it is a categorically different environment from European and American/European city patterns of the past – an extensive network of freeways and mobility patterns that has undermined and destroyed the concept of a single-centre city, and given new value and multidirectional meaning to suburbia.

According to one observer, this is a city of illusion, 'anything may turn out to be anything else, and there is no way of knowing because nothing has a shape of its own. This is why Los Angeles has the best and the biggest signs in the world... without them, the orienta-tion of Southern Californian man would be obscure; he would have no way of knowing where he is or who he is. Most people on the planet know who they are. And, if by chance in doubt, a glance around them gives the answer. Not so the Los Angelino. If he is in a thatched Tahitian hut, he must ask himself, am I in the South Seas, Disneyland, or in a restaurant on La Cienega? Then he may discover he actually is in his chiropractor's waiting room, or at a local supermarket's pineapple sale.'

Los Angeles, in short, is an ephemeral experience of low-key or non-architectural situa-tions that have to be seen to be believed, lived in to be understood.

首度發表於1968年9月號《建築設計》雜誌

反其道而行

華倫・裘克

我們眾人的心裡都存有些許的大人物情結。所有那些在普里茅斯裡的「唯有－當您－能夠－搭乘－一部－百萬－名車」之類的事。普里茅斯的大人物……而披頭族們持續依舊……

這裡是洛杉磯，天使的迷人城市。然而，洛杉磯人並未忙著展翅，而是正在高速公路上，專注於他們自己的事——「全面追蹤」，正如通用汽車廣告上所說的。

1962年時，賽卓克・普萊克於建築聯盟建築學院的維克多格魯恩演講中，提到影響了整個世代設計師的強而有力的洛杉磯案例。這是首份認定洛杉磯為另類城市典型的重要文獻；承認郊區生活與汽車的重要性。一再地提及過時的論戰，或延續著支持或反對集中式城市或擴散式郊區的爭辯，並無太大的意義。這可能不是只能二者擇其一的情況，洛杉磯既非城市，亦非郊區，而是超大型郊區。只能說它是迥異於過去的歐洲及歐洲／美國城市之型態範疇的環境——某種摧毀與侵蝕單一市中心城市概念之基礎的高速公路與移動型態的大規模聯絡網，並賦予郊區新的價值與多方面意義。

根據某位觀察家的說法，這是一座虛幻之城，「任何事物皆有可能變成任何其它的事物，而且無法察覺，因為所有事物皆無自己的構形。這是為何洛杉磯擁有全世界最佳且最大招牌的原因……少了它們的話，南加州人的辨位將變得含糊不清，他將無從得知自己身處何處或自己是誰。地球上大部分的人都知道自己是誰。而且，倘若偶有疑慮，只要環顧四周即一目了然。但洛杉磯人則非如此，若他身處一棟茅草屋頂的大溪地小屋裡，他必須自問，我目前究竟是在南太平洋、迪士尼，還是在拉西奈葛大道上的餐廳呢？然後他可能會發現自己其實正身處脊椎推拿師的候診室，或是當地超級市場的鳳梨拍賣會上！」

簡言之，洛杉磯是個低調或非建築情境的瞬間體驗，必須眼見為憑，住過方能理解。

This is not a city for aesthetes or architects' architects, who, although they may deny it, arrive, grub around looking for Schindler houses, and pass on angry, bewildered or even hopefully feeling obsolete. This is no European black and white situation – high art and architecture on a pedestal. Here everything works, but nothing is more important than anything else, it's all the same. But if one has to single out one major coherent factor – significant city object – it would be those land piers, the freeways.

The effectiveness of the Southern Californian freeway system and its ability to handle the mounting volume of traffic is incredible. This is the most spreadeagled, and consequently car-conscious, city in the world, and its freeway system, designed to meet a very special demand, is the only system so far that fills that need. There are, of course, complaints – why with this super system should not traffic flow be more fluid and peak hour congestion overcome? What is forgotten, however, is that only 42 per cent of the projected 800-mile freeway system has so far been completed, handling 30 per cent of the weekday traffic. Between 1980 and 1985 – the target date for completion – the LA freeways will be capable of handling 60 per cent of the total traffic.

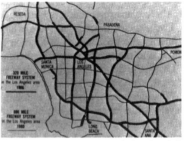

800 miles of freeway planned for Los Angeles in 1980: 1000 miles of motorway planned for the whole of Brittain

1980年洛杉磯規劃了800哩的高速公路；全英國規劃了1000哩的高速公路

One trouble seems to be that the excellence of the system heightens the LA obsession with the automobile, leading to frustrating congestion at peak hours. To alleviate this, 'Sig-Alert' broadcast warnings of obstructed routes, accidents, and pile-ups. Motorists may then select alternate routes to avoid trouble spots. Over radio station KGIL, helicopter air-watch pilots relay warnings of blockage on the freeways to drivers below. These whirly-birds, called Sky-Knights, not only control traffic, but play a large role in reducing crime and maintaining order. In fact, the chopper may be the best police tool since the LAPD radio prowl car.

Finally, however, responsibility lies in the hands of the driver. A recent Chrysler Corporation advertisement asks, 'Is your sixteen-year-old son a better driver than you?', and goes on to list ten pointers to better driving. More interesting is the fact that car dealers for the same corporation, since 1964, have loaned over 33,000 cars to more than 40,000 high schools and colleges, free of charge, for driver education courses.

Not all Angelinos are good drivers. But Americans are, by European standards, very well disciplined and obedient to the lore of the freeway. 'Dig those crazy Los Angeles freeways!' reads the postcard; and driving on them,

260

這不是一座唯美主義者或頂尖建築師的城市,雖然他們可能會否認,但他們抵達,四處尋找辛德勒之屋,然後轉為憤怒、迷惑或甚至感到絕望過時。這並非歐洲的非黑即白處境——偶像化的高級藝術與建築。這裡的所有事物均有作用,但卻沒有任何事物比其它事物更為重要,全都一樣的。但若必須遴選一個主要的一致性因素的話——重要的城市物件——將會是那些碼頭與高速公路。

This is Autopia, The mobile city. Freedom is a motor car. To hell with architecture and planning; the freeway is all

這是「汽車烏托邦」,移動之城。自由即汽車。該死的建築與規劃;高速公路就是一切了!

南加州高速公路系統的有效性與它應付與日俱增交通流量的能力令人難以置信。這是全世界延伸最廣,因而最具汽車意識的城市,而它被設計符合某種特殊目的的高速公路系統,是目前唯一滿足此需求的系統。當然會有抱怨——有了這個超級系統之後,交通流量不是應該更加順暢,而尖峰時刻的擁塞就此解決了嗎?然而被忽略的是,規劃的800哩高速公路系統目前只完成了百分之42,只解決了百分之30的平日交通流量。1980年至1985年——預定完工日期——期間,洛杉磯高速公路將可承載總交通流量的百分之60。

麻煩的似乎是,系統的優異性反而提高了洛杉磯對汽車的著迷,導致了令人失望的尖峰時刻擁塞。欲舒緩此現象,「信號警告」播送阻塞路段、意外及連環車禍的警訊。於是駕駛人得以選擇其它路線以避免不方便的地點。透過KGIL廣播電台,直升機空中警備隊飛行員轉播高速公路的堵塞警訊給地面上的汽車駕駛員。這些「迴旋鳥」,又稱「空中騎士」,不只管制了交通,也在降低犯罪與維持秩序上扮演了重要的角色。事實上,直升機或許是自洛杉磯警局的無線電警察巡邏車以來,最好的警力工具了。

然而,最終的責任仍在駕駛人身上。最近的一則克萊斯勒汽車公司的廣告問道,「您16歲的兒子是比您更稱職的駕駛嗎?」,緊接著又列出了10項優良駕駛的指標。更有趣的是,事實上,自從1964年起,克萊斯勒的汽車經銷商已經借出超過3萬3000輛汽車給超過4萬所高中與大學,免費作為駕駛訓練課程之用。

並非所有的洛杉磯人都是優良駕駛。但是就歐洲的標準而言,美國人算是十分守紀律且順從高速公路

negotiating intersections, with the essential pop music of the Charlie Tuna show, or Wolfeman Jack coming over strong on the radio, is an exhilarating, strangely enjoyable experience.

Amid the incredible press of new cars you realise that this is indeed an automobile culture. With 40 yellow pages in the phone book devoted to the automobile, Los Angeles has reached the threshold of private personal mobility. In the downtown area alone over 66 per cent of all available land space is utilised by the automobile. This is Autopia, the mobile city. Freedom is a motor car. To hell with traffic engineers, architects and planners, the car is not just a means of transportation, it is a way of life. What is required, before a positive approach to the urban transportation dilemma can be found, is an unselfconscious responsibility to society, rather than a hidebound preconception.

Consumer choice demonstrates that in spite of its inadequacies, the car is the most efficient, adaptable piece of urban transport hardware so far devised. From the standpoint of the ultimate user, it cannot be equalled in performance. It is the strongest candidate for delivering the goods and the goodies. The car is, in turn, freedom, choice, mobility, status symbol, toy, sex symbol. It is also a myth and a God. In what other city are you a second class citizen unless you own a motor car? Unfortunate people without wheels are forced to ride buses, but the system is slow and inadequate. In spite of Reyner Banham's optimism, a bus ride across town can take hours. In a city measuring, from Malibu to San Diego, Santa Monica to San Bernardino, some 70 miles by 40 miles, walking is such an absurd proposition that freeways are dreary stretches only for the car. And certain areas, such as Beverly Hills, have no sidewalks, and pedestrians run the risk of being picked up on vagrancy charges.

It Speaks Eloquently About You . . . . Yet Barely Whispers . . . .

Wherever Cadillac Goes, it makes Complimentary Remarks about its Owner . . . . peaks Softly about His Determination to Drive Performing Luxury . . . .

The car is a communications medium. Passing through the environment, it conveys a message, Regardless of how arbitrary it appears to the uncommitted observer, it exists strongly in the mind of the owner; a fetish, womblike comfort, phallic power and speed, satisfying the inherent gregarious nature of people to see and be seen. Wear your new car like a new suit of clothes. All the good things of life, instant door-to-door mobility, articulated obsolescence, mobile wardrobe, garbage can, air-conditioner, stereo and ashtray embody the car.

Customising veteran Dene Jeffries, reduced to painting white rally stripes on a 'Boss Yellow' Camero, shrugs off the whole personalised Kandy-Apple metal flake thing of the early 60s as just a passing fad. But three years after Tom Wolfe's Kandy Kolored Tangerine-Flake Streamlined Baby first hit the book stands, a visit to the custom car show at the Anaheim stadium near Disneyland dispels all doubt, closes the gap. It is still very much the same – noise, people, and a rock-and-roll band with mini-skirted teenyboppers clustered round the stand; and then there are the exhibits, the kick hot-rods and customised cars. Unlike the shockproof design-conscious paint jobs

常規的。「挖掘那些洛杉磯的高速公路！」明信片如此寫道；駛於這些公路上，穿過各個交叉口，伴著不可或缺的查理‧圖納節目的流行音樂，或是收音機裡強力播送的沃夫曼‧傑克，是種令人興奮且奇妙愉悅的經驗。

從令人不可思議的新車定期刊物中，您瞭解到這其實是一種汽車文化。高達40頁之多的電話簿汽車專頁篇幅，顯示出洛杉磯早已進入個人化移動的生活了。在鬧區裡，超過百分之66的可利用土地空間都歸汽車使用。這是個「汽車烏托邦」，一座移動之城。自由即汽車。該死的交通工程師、建築師與規劃師們，汽車不只是運輸工具而已，它是一種生活方式。在找出都市交通困境的明確處理方法之前，所需要的是非自覺性的社會責任感，而非偏狹的成見。

消費者的選擇說明了儘管仍有不足之處，但汽車仍是至今所發明的都市運輸硬體設備中最有效率且最具適應性的。自基本的使用者立場而言，它在性能上並不相同。汽車是運輸貨物與美食的最佳選擇。汽車同時也代表了自由、選擇、移動性、地位象徵、玩具與性象徵。它也是神話與上帝。在世界上某些其它城市裡，除非擁有一部汽車，否則您就會被視為二等公民呢！可憐的無車族只得勉強搭乘公車，但此系統既緩慢且不充足。儘管萊納‧班漢的看法樂觀，但一趟公車橫越市區可得花上數個鐘頭之久。在一座自馬里布至聖地牙哥，自聖塔莫尼卡至聖伯納迪諾市，面積約為70哩乘40哩的城市，步行是個荒謬的提議，而高速公路也不過是只供汽車使用的枯燥綿亙罷了。某些地區，諸如比佛利山，並無人行步道設施，行人冒著被變化無常的車流撞上的危險。

> 它生動地談著你……但僅耳語地……
> 不管凱迪拉克往哪兒走，對所有者而言它都是個恭維………輕訴著他
> 奢華駕馭的決心……

車子是溝通的工具。穿過環境，它傳達了訊息。不論對旁觀者而言有多不經意，但汽車所有者的心裡仍強烈地存在著某種崇拜，宛如身處子宮般的舒適，某種陽具般的力量與速度，滿足了人類固有之觀看與被看的群眾天性。開著一部新車就像穿上一套新衣。汽車具體化了所有生命中美好的事物：即時的挨乎移動性、清晰的暫時性、移動式衣櫥、垃圾桶、空調設備、音響與煙灰缸。

個人化汽車定製老手狄恩‧傑佛瑞斯，減少了黃色「卡馬洛」汽車上所畫的白色星線條紋，不理會60年代早期所有的個人化蘋果糖金屬鮮豔色彩只淪為一時的風尚。但三年之後，作家湯姆‧沃爾夫的《糖果圖案橘紅流線型寶貝》一書首度出現於書報攤上，造訪一趟迪士尼樂園附近的艾納海姆運動場的定製車車展即可消除所有的疑慮，並結束歧異。一切均無改變──噪音、人群，及搖滾樂團與一群

Drive-in mortuary 兎下車太平間

of Binder-Edwards and Vaughan, the Kandy Kolors are brash, belligerent, and wholly delightful; guaranteed to produce real cultural convulsions in most Europeans.

There is another side to this too. The Detroit stylists, conscious of the people's interest and involvement, have had to adjust their skirt lengths. Aware of changing trends, the swing is towards a more continental sports look. Mercury Cougar, Ford Mustang, Chevrolet Camero and Corvette, are all trend-changing, in spite of futile attempts by pressure groups to put the accent on safety. The number of imported sports cars in the show-rooms along Wilshire is another indication; high-powered swooshers . . . . The GTs like Lamborghini's Miura V12, Toyota 2000, Jaguar XKE, and the New Porsche 9IIL. The city's wealth and opulence provides, in the luxury class, a situation second to none. Where else but Beverly Hills can one see three Rolls Royces parked in a driveway? A real 'his', 'hers', and one for the maid shakedown. Conspicuous in this automobile environment are the intrinsic car-oriented structures, the immediate service satellites, garages, gas stations, body shops, automotive repair clinics, car washes, and driving schools. And the second generation drive-in parking structures, cinemas, banks, markets, stores, and even crematoria – the outward signs of a mobile society.

264

Detractors of the motor car in the Los Angeles may have a legitimate beef with smog as one of the visible signs of this Autopia. The fumes from the exhaust of four million cars, held by inversion between a layer of cooled surface air coming in from the Pacific and a layer of hot air from the desert, give air pollution control officials a headache. There is talk of gas rationing, and laws stipulate that new cars have anti-smog devices. But they are about as efficient – and ease the conscience as effectively – as a filter cigarette.

Possibly, the car technologically is a low-capability, high-performance piece of turn-on. Along with the helicopter, transistor radio and portable TV set, it is also one of the most significant urban toys. A model for the kind of instant feedback necessary to create a random responsive environment.

New symbols of new myths will have to be devised around the new modes of transportation if they are to succeed – to become acceptable and desirable in the mind of the public. Only then will the all-pervading myth of the automobile be dispelled and replaced permanently and irrevocably.

It is possible that Los Angeles was at its peak as a new city prototype in the 1950s and may have outlived its usefulness. The system of values that it represents is due for reappraisal. It is alarming the way local planners

身著迷你裙的少女樂迷簇擁台前；而後還有展示會、改造引擎汽車與訂製車。不似拜恩德、艾德華茲與佛恩具設計意識的防震繪畫作品，「糖果圖案」是輕率、好戰，且全然可愛的；保證於大多數歐洲人心中引發真正的文化撼動。

這件事尚有另一面。意識到人們的興趣及熱中的底特律設計師們，已必須調整他們的裙子長度了。由於覺察到變化的趨勢，變化更趨向歐陸式的休閒風貌。水星汽車的「美洲獅」、福特汽車的「野馬」、雪佛蘭汽車的「卡馬洛」與「寇維特」跑車，全都正趨勢改變中，儘管有來自壓力團體企圖卻徒勞的安全性強調。沿著威爾夏的汽車陳列室中的進口跑車數目是另一項指標：高性能的跑車……GT跑車，諸如藍寶堅尼的「米烏拉V12」、豐田2000、積架XKE，以及新保時捷911E。城市的富裕與豐饒為奢侈階級提供了不亞於任何人的情境。除了比佛利山之外，還有哪裡可以看到3輛勞斯萊斯同時停在汽車道上呢？一部給爸爸，一部給媽媽，一部給女傭。這個汽車環境中引人注意的是固有的汽車導向結構、衛星即時服務、車庫、加油站、美體小舖、汽車修理廠、洗車服務及駕訓班。而第二代則有免下車停車場結構、電影院、銀行、市場、商店，甚至垃圾焚化爐——移動式社會的外在徵兆。

惡意批評洛杉磯汽車的人，可能對於煙霧成為這座「汽車烏托邦」的可見標誌之一存有合理的牢騷。四百萬輛汽車所排出的煙霧廢氣，因來自太平洋的一層冷卻表面空氣與來自沙漠的一層熱空氣之間的逆轉而持續不減，令空氣污染控制官員們頭痛不已。據聞將有汽油配給措施，且法令亦將規定新車必須備有反煙霧裝置。不過它們大約只和濾嘴香煙一樣地有效——且一樣有效地使良心如釋重負——罷了。

或許，汽車技術上是低潛能、高性能，且可引人興奮之物。與直升機、電晶體收音機與攜帶式電視一樣，汽車也是最重要的都市玩具之一。它是創造一個偶發性感應式環境所必要的即時回饋模型。

若新神話的新象徵會成功的話，則它們將必須根據新的交通運輸模式而設計——變成一般社會大眾心

are trying to shape the future of the city on patterns of the past – struggling up the down ramp with archaic preconceptions for building up central areas with simulation New York, Chicago high-rises, or introducing projects for rapid transit down the Wilshire corridor. Neither of these are as revolutionary or remedial as the experts would have us believe.

We need to tear away the layers of professionalism; change the rules of the game; alter the context in such a way as to recharge the whole organisational value structure.

People have perceived the world and responded to it, usually, not through their own potentialities, but through a limited spectrum, made functional by external stimulation. Hopefully we may enter a phase where man learns to play games with the new hard- and soft-ware at his disposal.

Right now, the Angelino 'Widetracking' indicates a try-it-and-see attitude, reflecting a total rejection of any tight-up scene – heedless of the criticism accompanying any innovation. Curiosity working through self-imposed spectrums reveals the symbolic power of LA and its motor cars.

A sign on the freeway signalling an off-ramp evokes a simultaneous succession of customised responses. Similarly the car symbolises a lifestyle difficult to ignore.

Consumer excitement generated by a better alternative, characteristic of the space age, blows the mind.

Brash and delightful Kandy Kolored cars – with matching accessories – are shown at the Anaheim stadium

輕率而可愛的「糖果圖案」汽車—搭配適當的配件—於艾納海姆運動場中展出

中可接受且想望的。唯有如此，四處瀰漫的汽車神話才得以被驅散，並永久且無法改變地被取代。

或許身為1950年代新城市典型的洛杉磯當時已處於巔峰，並可能已經度過它的無效過渡期。它所代表的價值體系應該重新評估了。地方規劃者試圖根據過去的型態以塑造城市之未來的方式是一種警訊——抱持著舊有成見掙扎著反其道而行，模仿著紐約與芝加哥的摩天大樓，或順著威爾夏走廊引入捷運計劃，藉此打造市區中心。這些都不是專家希望我們相信的革命性或治本性的做法。

我們必須撕去專業主義的偽裝；更改遊戲規則，改變文本以為整體組織性價值結構重新充電。

人們已覺察到世界並有所回應，通常，並非透過他們自己的潛力，而是透過須藉外在刺激而有作用的有限範圍。但願我們可以進入人們可以自由地利用新的軟硬體以學習遊戲的階段。

目前，洛杉磯的「全面追蹤」暗示著某種「試試看會如何」的態度，反映出對於任何侷促情勢的全然回拒——完全不在意伴隨任何革新而至的批評。透過自我約束範圍而運轉的好奇心，透露出洛杉磯的象徵性力量與它的汽車。

高速公路上指示著出口的信號，引發了一連串同時的預期反應。同樣地，汽車象徵了某種生活方式的事實是難以忽視的。

由具備太空時代特徵的更佳選擇所引發的消費者興奮之情，正撼動著思緒！

US astronaut Neil Armstrong is first man on the Moon: 'That's one small step for man, one giant leap for mankind' — Moon rocks brought back to Earth by Apollo 11 astronauts are tested at Houston, Texas, and samples made available to scientists in eight other countries, including Britain — US announces troop withdrawal from Vietnam — De Gaulle resigns — Georges Pompidou becomes new President of France — Concorde makes its maiden flight in Toulouse — US Mariner 6 spacecraft launched to Mars — British troops deployed in Belfast — First colour TV transmission in Britain — Student demonstrations at London School of Economics — Arafat becomes leader of PLO — Boeing 747 Jumbo Jet makes its maiden flight — Eisenhower dies — Golda Meir becomes Israeli Premier — Jan Palach burns himself to death in Wenceslas Square, Prague, in protest at Soviet invasion — Judy Garland dies — Samuel Beckett awarded Nobel Prize for Literature — MUSIC — John Lennon returns his MBE as peace protest — CINEMA — 'Easy Rider' — 'Oh What a Lovely War' — 'Rosemary's Baby' — 'Women in Love' — 'The Prime of Miss Jean Brodie' — TELEVISION' — 'Monty Python's Flying Circus' — Live transmissions of Apollo 11 Moon Landing are watched by around 600 million viewers in 49 countries — FASHION — Flower children — Hippies — Maxi skirts — Kaftans — Patched jeans — Denim battledress — Cheesecloth dresses — Beads — Maxi coats.

美國太空人尼爾・阿姆斯壯登陸月球:「我的一小步,卻是人類的一大步」-阿波羅11號太空船帶回月球岩石於德州休士頓接受檢測,並分成數個樣本供其它包括英國在內的8個國家的科學家研究-美國宣布自越南撤軍-戴高樂辭職-喬治・龐畢度繼任法國新任總統-協和客機於土魯斯首航-太空船美國水手6號發射至火星-英軍部署於北愛爾蘭首府貝爾法斯特-彩色電視首次於英國播送-學生於倫敦政經學院舉行示威-阿拉法特成為巴勒斯坦解放軍領袖-波音747噴射客機首航-艾森豪將軍辭世-勾達・梅爾夫人就任以色列總理-強..巴拉奇於布拉格溫徹斯特廣場自焚以抗議蘇聯入侵-好萊塢明星茱蒂・迦倫辭世-山謬・貝克特獲頒諾貝爾文學獎-**音樂**-約翰・藍儂為倡議和平歸還勳章以示抗議-**電影**-《消遙騎士》-《多可愛的戰爭》-《失嬰記》-《戀愛中的女人》-《舞動人生》-**電視**-《飛翔馬戲團》-49個國家約6億名觀眾收看阿波羅11號登陸月球實況轉播-**時尚**-嬉痞風-嬉痞-長裙-「卡夫坦」-補丁牛仔褲-單寧布戰鬥裝-粗棉衣-珠飾-迷嬉外套。

1969

FEATURES:
MONTE
CARLO

ON THE VERY DAY
Peter Cook

On the very day that Archigram 9 was through the printer, a telephone call from Monte Carlo confirmed the mysterious rumours that had been filtering through to us from Milan and Vienna that we had won the competition for the 'bâtiment public' on the sea front.

The competition was in two stages, with Frei Otto and Ricardo Bofill among the final batch of 13 competitors. A jury which included Pierre Vago, Ove Arup, René Sarger and Michel Ragon met in December, with the responsibility to advise the Monaco Government. They apparently set up an 'advocacy' system, in which each scheme would be defended by a member and then attacked by the rest. The main thing that they (apparently) liked in the 'Features' was the retention of the open space and the view of the sea and the emphasis of the scheme upon the workings of the entertainments.

Between December and March the ministries and departments concerned made various recommendations that extended the original brief in several ways; but they are keen that the basic 'Features' scheme maintains its characteristics. They need more car parking, a cinema, and several public utilities. We also find that there is a hovercraft station planned at the corner of the site.

Briefed by 10 tapes of recorded negotiations and a remarkably blue sky we now embark on a building programme of three and a half years. . . . . A large hole is to be dug in the autumn of next year. . . .The mind boggles. . . . . . .

就在那天　*彼得・庫克*

就在那天《建築電訊》第9期正印刷時，一通來自蒙地卡羅的電話證實了一件自米蘭與維也納傳至我們耳中的神秘謠言，就是我們已經贏得濱海區「公共建築」的競圖案。

這個競圖案分成兩個階段，最後一批13位決賽者中包括有佛萊・奧圖與里卡多・波菲爾。由皮耶・凡果、歐孚・艾拉普、赫內・沙赫傑及米榭爾・哈貢等人所組成的評審團於12月時會面，負責對摩納哥政府提出建議。顯然他們設立了某種「辯護」的制度，即每份設計案由一位評審辯護，而由其他人攻擊。他們（顯然地）最喜歡「特色：蒙地卡羅」的部份在於開放空間與海景的保留，以及計畫中對於娛樂活動的強調。

在12月與3月期間，相關部門提出了各種可於許多方面延伸最初綱要的忠告；但他們熱切地希望基本的「特色：蒙地卡羅」計劃案能夠維持它的特質。他們需要更多的停車場、一間電影院，以及一些公共設施。我們也發現基地的角落裡規劃了一個氣墊船站。

在10卷商議及絢麗藍天的錄影帶簡要說明下，我們目前正著手一個3年半的建物計畫案……明年秋天將開挖一個大洞……簡直令人難以置信……

First published in the *ARCHITECT'S JOURNAL*, 2 September 1970

MONACO UNDERGROUND

Earlier this year the news broke on an incredulous architectural profession that the Archigram group had landed a real big fish at last. Designing toys for Expo was a harmless enough way to employ eccentric talents; winning a prestigious international competition was a different matter. **Reyner Banham** *ruminates on 'Features Monte Carlo'.*

'Come-uppance' was the word that sprang to the lips of the world's wiseacres. Said one, in my hearing, 'So it's goodbye to all that plug-in crap, now Archigram have got to design a real building like all the rest of us. 'Of course, it's people like him, who unthinkingly equate 'visionary' with 'impracticable' who get architecture a bad name, but even so, the winning of the protracted and slightly mystifying Monaco Entertainments Centre competition did look like Fate taking a small revenge. In the end, however, it may prove that those who really got their come-uppance were certain smooth international architectural operators who thought that they had the competition safely politicked and rigged, and could tolerate the inclusion of Archigram among the invited design teams as window-dressing of the 'imposing international entry-list' type. If that is so, then Archigram come-upped them by not doing what most architecture-fans would regard as an Archigram design.

Having scrutinised the site (reclaimed land-fill between the Avenue Princesse Grace and the sea) and weighed up the programme (ridiculously multi-functional at first blush) they decided to go down when everybody also was going up; instead of creating a complex architectural sculpture that would etch a stunning silhouette against the background of the blue Mediterranean, they decided to dig a hole and pull the earth back over it.

'They' in this instance (since Archigram is an elastic concept) consisted of Peter Cook, Dennis Crompton, Colin Fournier, David Greene, Ron Herron, Ken Allinson and Tony Rickaby with Frank Newby as consulting engineer. There is a lot of hard-won, deeply-lived seaside experience among them – Bournemouth, Blackpool, Santa Monica and even wilder shores than those (Hawaii, yet!). Almost, you could say, this 'heavy seaside background' gave them an unfair advantage over the rest of the competition.

The more they pondered the site, the Monte Carlo scene, the functional requirements, the more they saw that the existing municipal park on the site ought, however grotty, to be kept and not cluttered with actual three-dimensional buildings. Their first thoughts were of independent entertainment machines ('robots' in

. . . 278

272

首度發表於1970年9月2日《建築師學報》

地下摩納哥

*今年稍早，多疑的建築圈出現一則消息，談到《建築電訊》終於釣到了一條真正的大魚。為展覽會設計一些玩具是發揮古怪天份的一種無害方式；但贏得一項聲譽卓越的國際性競圖可是另外一回事！**萊納‧班漢**對於「特色：蒙地卡羅」的反思。*

「應得的懲罰」是自作聰明者嘴裡會冒出來的字眼。我聽過有人說，「終於可以結束那堆『插接』胡扯了，如今『建築電訊』得像我們大夥兒一樣乖乖地設計一棟真正的建築物了！」當然，正是像他這種不加思索地視「追求夢想」為「不能實現」的人令建築蒙羞，但即使如此，贏得這項耗時且神秘的摩納哥娛樂中心競圖，著實看來像是命運報了一次小仇。然而，結果可能證明了真正獲得應得懲罰的人，是某些國際建築界裡的長袖善舞者，安穩地自認已經暗中動過手腳打點一切，而能夠容忍「建築電訊」也包含於受邀的設計團體中，作為「風光的國際入圍名單」裡的陪榜。若真是如此的話，則

「建築電訊」懲罰他們的方式是藉由不做大多數建築迷們所認為的「建築電訊」設計。

審視基地（葛麗思王妃大道與海洋間的新生地）並權衡計劃（乍看之下為荒誕的多功能性）之後，他們決定反其道而行：他們決定挖鑿一個洞並以泥土覆蓋其上，而非創造一個蝕刻迷人剪影於碧海藍天地中海背景的複雜建築雕塑。

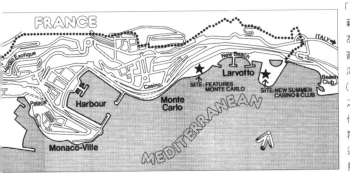

這裡所指的「他們」（因為「建築電訊」是個彈性式概念）包括彼得‧庫克、丹尼斯‧克藍普頓、柯林‧伏尼爾、大衛‧葛林、朗‧赫倫、肯‧艾利森‧湯尼‧瑞克白及身為顧問工程師的法蘭克‧紐白。他們具有許多得之不易且深刻體現的海濱經驗——波茅斯、黑潭、聖塔莫尼卡以及甚至比這些更廣闊

LAND BEACH: PARK OVER

SUSPENDED
SERVICE GRID

LAND BEACH

ACTIVITY + EVENT ZONE

LAND BEACH

ELEVATION COTE MER

的海岸（甚至夏威夷！）。您幾乎可以說，這個「沉悶的海濱背景」賦予他們一種其它競圖所沒有的不公平優勢。

他們思考越多這個基地、蒙地卡羅的景緻及功能的需求，就越清楚基地上既有的市立公園，不論有多麼令人不悅，都應該被保留下來，而非被現實的三度空間建築物弄得雜亂。他們剛開始的構想是獨立的娛樂機器（以「建築電訊」的語彙而言，即「自動裝置」）插接至灌木叢裡的隱藏式電源，或許沿著某種線型山脊，但得到啓發的常識終究獲勝，而整個基地（幾乎）也沉入了地下。

1969年5月5日的契約上寫道，「此多用途建築物應於最佳利用之情況下遮蔽體育活動、綜藝與馬戲表演、展覽會，以及舞會與宴會，最多可容納1500人至2000人。」此外「……此建築物，除了這些使用變化可能性之外，將留給設計案的設計師決定其永久性意圖。」

若您停下仔細想想，一棟足以容納如馬戲團及皇室宴會般多樣功能之具備使用變化可能性的多用途建築物，更不用說如今歸併於「展覽會」名義下之活動的無限多樣性……這樣的建築物將儲備有驚人的適應力，以及高水準的服務設施。因此，提出任何特殊「永久性意圖」的建議，將只會限制可能意圖的範圍而已。若我們的老友，開放式結局的解決之道，已經蓄勢待發的話，這正是適當時機了！

但是一旦這個論點被採納，且競圖評審委員會（歐孚・艾拉普、皮耶・凡果、米榭爾・哈貢、赫內・沙赫傑）確切採納它之後，那麼建築物類型的思考將不過是妨礙罷了。地上的洞僅為解決之道的結構部份而已，雖然構成它末端之極淺的260呎圓屋頂將必須變成一個相當均整的結構。將計劃案視為上有公共公園，下有環狀集會廳之豐富複式機械設施的皮層似乎較有意義。某些趣味性與遊戲（以

COUPE C/ TRANSVERSALE

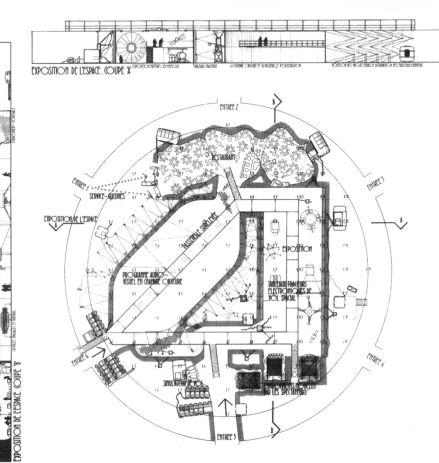

EXPOSITION DE L'ESPACE (COUPE 'A'

EXPOSITION DE L'ESPACE (COUPE 'B'

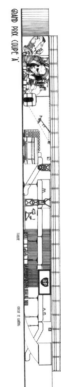

GRAND PRIX COUPE 'B'

GRAND PRIX - SPECTACLE AUDIO VISUEL   PASSERELLE SURÉLEVÉE   EXPOSITION   TRIBUNE

GRAND PRIX COUPE 'A'

ENTRÉE 2

ENTRÉE 1

ENTRÉE 3

GRAND PRIX - SPECTACLE AUDIO VISUEL

PASSERELLE SURÉLEVÉE

JEUX DE CONDUITE

EXPOSITION

FRITS

BAR - BUFFET

TRIBUNE

RESTAURANT

CIRCUIT DE KARTING

SIMULATEUR GRAVITATIONEL

ENTRÉE 6

ENTRÉE 4

ENTRÉE 5

... 272

Space exhibition 空間展覽

Archigrammar) plugged into hidden power sources among the shrubbery, perhaps along some sort of linear spine, but inspired common-sense prevailed and the whole lot (almost) went underground.

278 The 'edifice polyvalente', said the contract of 5 May 1969, should 'shelter in the best conditions of exploitation, sporting manifestations, spectacles of variety and the circus, exhibitions, balls and banquets admitting 1,500 to 2,000 persons at maximum.' Then ' . . . the edifice will have, besides these episodic utilisations, a permanent destiny which is left to the initiative of the designer of the project.'

If you stop and think, an edifice polyvalent enough for episodic utilisations as diverse as circuses and princely banquets, let alone the infinite variety of activities that now go under the heading of 'Exhibitions'. . . such an edifice is going to have remarkable reserves of adaptability, and a high level of servicing. Thus, to propose any specific 'permanent destiny' would simply restrict the range of possible destinies. If ever our old friend, the Open-ended Solution, was in order, this was the occasion.

But once this point is accepted, and the competition jury (Ove Arup, Pierre Vago, Michel Ragon, René Sarger) clearly did accept it, then edifice-type thinking is simply obstructive. The hole in the ground is merely the structural part of the solution, though the very shallow 260-foot dome that forms its end is going to have to be quite a neat structure. It makes better sense to think of the scheme as a layer of rich and complex mechanical services with a public park on top and a circular assembly hall underneath. Some fun and games ('Features', in Archigrammar) can be plugged into the ground surface of the park, as originally conceived, but many more will hang down into the assembly hall, and some more will be plugged into the floor of the hall. Not quite everything can be done with robotry, of course, and there are actually a few old-fashioned architectural-type spaces that

Sports activities 體育活動

「建築電訊」的語彙而言,即「特色」)可被插接至公園的地面上,正如原先所構思的,但有更多的元件將往下懸吊於集會廳上方,而其它元件則將被插接至廳堂的樓版上。當然,並非所有東西都可以自動裝置的方式解決,並且確實存有某些舊式建築型態的空間亦可以滿足娛樂區的需求。

但是元件組件,諸如插接的、往下懸吊的、跳躍式的、及令您瞠目結舌的,才是計劃案最終的重點所在,而此重點是否能夠被理解是十分重要的,不只希望獲得您這些溫文讀者的認可,也希望於摩納哥亦如此。「建築電訊」十分在意能否達成此目標,並堅持於制定其工程契約時,必須同時進行設備、建築及細部的研究。

將設計視為整體的話,顯然有極佳的理由堅持這種設施與建築間的契約平等性,但除此之外,仍存有比僅僅確定當圓屋頂完工時,設備不會被塞入其它事後追加物,以及上方的兒童遊樂場已重新組構設計之外的更切身問題。最重要迫切的問題在於整體設備的未來管理上,因為若無法如多變的設備般善於應變的話,整個論點將會失焦。管理一棟具有明確詳細之使用變化可能性的多用途建築物,以及您可依喜好而決定的一般性意圖,並不同於管理一棟具有任意之使用變化可能性的多用途建築物,以及僅作為全世界第一個引起幻覺的螺肉攤,或紙製比尼販賣機的一般性意圖。後者需要特殊的管理技巧,前者需要基本的想像力,以及對於每種可能組合的所有特色之潛力的徹底瞭解。在某種稍有不同的形式中,這個問題並非全新的,因為愈來愈多的現代建築物需要自覺性地操作——常言道,在相信您有能力操控吉姆•史特林位於劍橋的「歷史」建築物之前,您得先擁有一張儀器飛行許可證。但那

also service the zones of entertainment.

But the kit of parts, the plug-ins and hang-downs and leap-abouts and turn-you-rounds and blow-your-minds are what the scheme ultimately is all about, and it is very important that this is understood, not only by you gentle reader, but also in Monaco. Archigram are very concerned to get this across, and are insisting that in the elaboration of their working contract the study of the equipment must proceed in parallel with the study of the architecture and at the same level of detail.

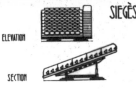

Seeing the design as a whole, there are obvious good reasons for this insistence on contractual equality between services and architecture, but there is more at stake than simply making sure that the equipment is not bunged in with other afterthoughts when the dome is complete and the children's playground on top has been re-constituted. The most critical issue at stake is the future management of the complete installation, because if this is not as resourceful as the installation the whole point will be lost. Managing a polyvalent edifice with specified episodic utilisations and a general destiny as anything you like to make it, is a different affair from managing a polyvalent edifice with episodic what-nots and a general destiny as merely the world's first psychedelic whelk-stall, say, or paper bikini dispenser. The latter cases call for specific management skills, the former calls for radical imagination and thorough knowledge of the potentialities of all the features in every possible combination. In a slightly different form, this problem is not absolutely new, because an increasing number of modern buildings need to be consciously operated – as the saying goes, you need an instrument-flying licence before you can be trusted with the controls of Jim Stirling's History building at Cambridge. But that's just to stop it leaking or over-heating, whereas Monaco in the hands of an unqualified pilot would just be a complete waste of three million quid.

And it should be emphasised that the installation needs to be understood and exploited as a whole; just being a clever mechanic will not be enough, because there are some architectural potentials to be exploited as well. For instance, there are six entrances to the underground assembly hall, and that may be two more than will ever be needed at once. But it does mean that an imaginative manager could select a pattern of access – mostly land-ward mostly seaward, or just hard to find – suited to the nature of whatever episodic utilisation is in train, or to heighten the effect of some unscheduled manifestation he just thought of in the bar.

It needs someone with a Diaghilev flair and ambition to match. The challenge and the potential would be enormous, whether the thing finished up as a continuous indoor/outdoor Woodstock nation, or (more likely in that genteel principality) the first garden party that will not have to say 'if wet, in parish hall'.

GRAND ROBOT

PLAN

ELEVATION

PLAN

CAPSULE – W. C.

ELEVATION

PLAN

TRACTEUR ELECTRIQUE

AUTOMAT

CAPSULE – TOILETTES

只是為了防止它的滲漏或過熱，有鑑於摩納哥若置於一位不合格飛行員之手的話，將會整整浪費掉3百萬英鎊。

此外應該強調必須理解與利用整體裝備；僅作為一部巧妙的機器是不夠的，因為尚有一些建築的潛力有待開發。例如，共有6個進入地下集會廳的入口，或許比將來立即所需的多出了2個。但這意味著一位富有想像力的經理人可以選出某種出入口的模式——大半是朝向陸地及面向海洋，或極難尋找的——適於任何準備就緒之使用變化可能性的特質，或加強他在酒吧裡剛剛想到的某些臨時啟示的效果。這需要某位具有迪亞吉烈夫眼光與雄心的人才適合。挑戰與潛力將是無窮的，不論結果是否會變成一個持續的室內／戶外的胡士托國度，或（也許在上流社會公國裡）首次不再需要說「若下雨的話，就改在教區大廳舉行」的庭園宴會。

First publisher in *ARCHITECTURAL DESIGN*, July 1969

THINGS THAT DO THEIR OWN THING

Warren Chalk, taking a look at the latest toys, suggests that limiting conditions are breaking down – new disciplines and directions are stimulating new interests; static, conventional ideas on urbanism are giving way to a try-it-and-see approach to planning. Things will be doing their own thing.

Long before that High Court writ, *Eye* magazine reported that John Lennon and Ringo Starr visit one another just to play with their toys. Wherever there are children there are always toys. Children today, however, are no longer content with static, inanimate playthings, or with using their own mental invention, however magical, to simulate illusion.

New toys have reflex mechanisms and are goal-directed, self-regulating or remote-controlled.

This control and communication by movement and audio-visual means stimulates interaction between child and toy and a new kind of response is set up.

Manipulating a toy, a child is caught up in that interaction we call play. It is a simplified abstraction of the real day world around us. Through play a child learns and forms concepts in his own private world that allow him to become familiar with and able to adjust to his environment – a kind of behavioural deduction.

Toys are an extension of the child; through which he plays out his own dreams through control choice and response. The remote-controlled walking talking doll offers an inclusive integral auditory pattern, giving an elementary understanding of what cybernetics imply.

Remote-controlled participation and the decentralisation of play give an increased sense of accomplishment and achievement, which dissipates feelings of frustration at not being able to manipulate the adult world.

Today the ordinary child grows up in an electronic environment, and the new toys are an extension of the integrating sense of active touch. The name of the game is fantasy, an enchanting mini-world of fun toys that really go.

For the boys the toys firms go wild.

A complete Kennedy Airport set, with taped weather reports, take-offs and landings, holding patterns and flight paths.

A 'Lost in Space' TV robot, *'follow this 12-inch robot on adventures, see how he winks and blinks his way out of dangerous situations'*. Or a TR3 solid state walkie-talkie, which gives kids their own private hotline inside and outdoors.

For son and dad appeal there is the Tyco double dipsey-doodle HO table-top raceway.

Barbarella,
Paramount Pictures

首度發表於1969年7月號《建築設計》雜誌

自己動手做的東西

華倫・裘克，瞧瞧最新型的玩具，暗示著限制性情況正瓦解中——新的學科與方向正刺激著新的興趣：都市學中的呆板、傳統的觀念正被「試試看會如何」的規劃方式所取代。可以自己動手做的東西。

早在高等法院公告之前，《鑑賞力》雜誌報導了約翰・藍儂與林哥・史達彼此會面僅為了玩自己的玩具。只要有兒童的地方就會有玩具。然而，現在的兒童已不再滿足於呆板且死氣沉沉的玩耍，或運用他們自己的思想創造力去模擬幻想，無論有多麼不可思議。

新玩具具有反射性機械裝置，並且是目標導向式、自動調節式或遙控式的。

這種藉由運動與視聽的操控與溝通，意味著刺激兒童與玩具間的交互作用，並引發一種新的反應。

操控玩具時，小朋友捲入了交互作用之中，我們稱之為遊戲。這是我們周遭真實世界的簡化抽象概念。透過遊戲，兒童學習並於他自己的私人世界，形成可以讓他熟悉且適應其環境的概念——某種行為的推論。

玩具是兒童的延伸：透過玩具，他藉由控制選擇與反應，釋放出自己的夢想。遙控式會走路說話的洋娃娃提供了一種包含完整的聽覺模式，初步瞭解人工智慧所暗示的可能性。

遙控的參與及遊戲的疏散性賦予了更多的實現感與成就感，消除無法操控成人世界的挫折感。

目前一般的兒童都成長於電子環境中，而新玩具則是主動接觸之整合感的延伸。遊戲的名稱是「幻想」，一個確實可行之令人著迷的有趣玩具迷你世界。

玩具公司為了小男生而瘋狂。

一個完整的甘迺迪機場佈景，附有錄音氣象報告、起飛與降落、等候著陸之盤旋路線與飛行路線。

一個「星際迷航」電視自動裝置，「隨著這部12吋自動裝置開始歷險，看他如何眨著眼脫離危急狀況」。或是一部TR3手提式無線電話機，提供小朋友自己的室內與戶外私人熱線。

'Race the hottest cars from HO – a Cheetah coupe and Mako Shark fastback – over the most challenging racetrack. A 60-foot course takes cars up, down, through loops, across lightning-fast straightways and through jumper and receiver track units, all complete with 1 amp electronic power pack and remote control.'

Or there is the ESR Digi-Comp, a real digital computer, both educational and entertaining – you programme it yourself.

Little girls so long deprived of stimulus and response can choose a new experience with mother. There is the Horsman Teensie baby doll, ready for adoption. A sleepy eyed 9 inch tall baby who coos, drinks and wets.

More cybernetic is the remote-controlled *walking-talking-living-love-is-a-special-way-of-feeling Tonia doll, a 12inch soft-bodied vinyl, with emerald green eyes, lashes, and dark brown rooted hair that falls softly to the shoulders.*

In a cybernetic system there is some method of monitoring the output of the system, comparing it with a desired result and then using the difference to actuate some control mechanism to adjust to the required norm.

These toys are things that do their own thing, the child acts as controller and supervisor, or as monitor to override the result. The new generation of children's toys offer deeper involvement and also more likelihood of success or reward, which is important to the child's development and ego.

Reflexive response mechanisms, homing or tracking devices, applied in the toy world, give children the freedom to make responsible decisions about their own progress and success; the need to be independent is important, basic, to a child's fulfilment.

It arises in normal human development. Through the remote-controlled toy car, plane or walkie-talkie doll, the child experiences autonomy and uniqueness, and the exercise of this unique control results in a satisfaction attainable in no other way.

Gordon Pask has stated that even in the absence of a human being, entities in the environment communicate with and learn about one another.

In the toy world mini-cyborg families are already in existence. Although not fully automated, there is a complete 'family' of Barbie dolls, including kid sister, girl friends and a boy friend, all capable of some minimal verbal communication: *I think mini-skirts are smashing,* etc. The existence of such miniature androids leaves one to postulate that it will not be long before a further development will allow them to compete with one another and cooperate in acting out pre-programmed goals. They may operate either autonomously or by remote control, and possess a trivial but nevertheless meaningful artificial intelligence. That is to say they might possess a set of human abilities such as language, simple problem-solving and pattern recognition, as elements equivalent to a human

父子同樂可以選擇「泰寇」雙筋斗總部模型賽車遊戲。「從總部出發比賽最熱門的跑車——『獵豹』跑車與『灰鯖鯊』跑車——在最具挑戰性的賽車道上。60呎的路程使汽車忍上、忍下、翻筋斗、立即閃電快速越過並通過跳越及接收跑道單元體，這一切僅需1安培電力與遙控裝置即可。」

或者還有一種ESR Digi-Comp，一部真正的數位化電腦，兼具教育性與娛樂性——您自己為它設定程式。

長久以來被剝奪刺激與反應的小女孩們，可以和媽媽一塊兒選擇一種新體驗。有一個「霍爾斯曼」小洋娃娃準備被領養。一個會咕嚕、喝奶、尿濕的睡眠惺忪9吋的小嬰兒。

具有更多人工智慧的是遙控的「走路－說話－生活－戀愛－是－一－種－特別的－感受－方式」的「托妮亞」娃娃，有著12吋高的樹脂塑膠製柔軟身軀，翡翠綠眼睛，長睫毛，及深棕色披肩長髮。

在人工智慧系統中，有一些監控系統輸出的方法，將它與希望之結果相比較，然後利用差異性來啟動某些控制機械裝置，以調整至所需的標準。

這些玩具就是可以自己動手做的東西，兒童扮演控制者與監督者，或監視員的角色，無視於結果。新一代的兒童玩具提供了更深入的參與，亦有更多成功或獎勵的可能性，對於兒童的發展與自尊心十分重要。

反射性反應的機械裝置，自動導向或追蹤裝置，應用於玩具世界裡，給予兒童自由以對於有關自己進步與成功做出負責的決定；對兒童的實踐而言，獨立的需求是很重要的。

這出現於正常的人類發展中。藉由遙控玩具汽車、飛機或手提式無線電話機娃娃，兒童體驗到自主性與獨特性，而這種獨特控制的練習，產生了其它方式所無法得到的滿足感。

戈登·帕斯克曾說過，即使人類不存在，環境中的實體仍會彼此溝通與學習。

在玩具的世界裡，迷你半機械人家族早已存在。雖然並非完全自動化，但有個完整的芭比娃娃「家族」，包括小妹、女朋友們與一位男朋友，全都具有某些極簡單的語言溝通能力：我認為迷你裙很棒，諸如此類的。這種小型機器人的存在讓人們得以

intelligence system. In this way child and toy would interact in a special dreamland, allowing the child to really do the Alice-through-the-Looking-Glass bit. Any moral worry (remember those dolls in *Barbarella*) will not be dispelled by those dreadful wooden 'educational' toys; but there is reassurance, we can always throw the switch and turn off.

In case the obvious hasn't struck yet, it looks as though an analogy can be drawn between toys and what is already happening in the environment.

Communities are not really organisms like the anthill or the beehive, but rather organisations or ad hoc mechanisms for collective living, made up from an infinite number of interacting artefacts. Urban artefacts are classifiable: television, microfilm, credit card, telephone, car-wash, drive-in movie, drive-in bank, car, aeroplane, neon sign, stop light, are but a few of the urban toys we can play with. Manzac and the Electric Tomato are toys we might have in the future.

This situation makes it imperative to understand new methods of control and the random un-regulated behaviour pattern and interaction of such artefacts. It also makes it necessary to change the rules of the game from systematic to spontaneous trial-and-error play.

Groucho Marx summed it all up to the blonde on his knee: *Read any good books lately?* But then the Marx brothers were masters at changing the rules of the game and doing their own thing, their childlike simplicity coupled with unsurpassed inventive genius.

It would be foolish to assume that the quest of man will always take the same route, or use the same vehicles. Anyone with a sense of awareness knows what the Marx brothers were saying. The option is always open to us to change the instructions on the label.

For some of us, of course, this has in part already happened; we are delighted to get our kicks and ideas from all kinds of material outside the normal range of architecture; from comic strips to fashion magazines, neon signs to movies, and collect them under one notional umbrella we call, for the sake of convenience, environment. It's all one bag so let's forget the ethics. Master planning is obsolete, a freeway network as limiting as a ghetto, and more restrictive than an airline route. The old fixed and static elements that built our cities are becoming increasingly irrelevant. New thinking and a new understanding begin to emerge, short-changing the existing rules of the game. There is a place now for re-interpretations of what is important, what really matters in the environmental complexity that surrounds us. With man's boundary conditions breaking down and new directions and disciplines providing increased stimulus of interest, the static conventional know-how we called urbanism is being edged out by the try-it-and-see rethink.

In a transient society, the mobile searchlight pinpointing an automobile sale or a movie premiere is more important than any building; a credit card system more meaningful than a high-rise bank.

Urbanism, if it is to mean anything at all, is a fluid matrix of things that do their own thing.

In William Burroughs' words, *we must keep our bags packed and ready to move all the time.*

假設，距離進一步發展使它們可以依照預先程式之目標而表現出彼此的競爭與合作，應該為期不遠了。它們可以自主地或藉由遙控而運作，並具有微不足道但卻深具意義的人工智慧。也就是說，它們可能具有一系列人類的能力，例如語言、簡易的問題解決和認知模式，以及相當於人類智力系統的元素。以這種方式，兒童與玩具將於一處特別的仙境中互動，使兒童得以真正做到「艾利絲照魔鏡」之類的事。任何道德的憂慮（記得那些「芭芭瑞拉」中的洋娃娃）將無法藉由那些糟糕的木製「教育性」玩具而消除；不過有一個保證，就是我們始終可以打開開關並關掉它。

雖然尚未十分明顯，但似乎可以自玩具與環境裡正已發生的事中找出類似性。

社區並不真的是像螞蟻窩或蜂巢般的有機組織體，反而更像為了集體生活目標的組織或特殊機械裝置，由無限的互動式人工物所構成。都市人造物可分類為：電視、顯微膠片、信用卡、電話、洗車器、免下車式電影院、免下車式銀行、汽車、飛機、霓虹燈，號誌燈……等，都只是一些我們可以耍弄的都市玩具。「寵物機器人」與「電子蕃茄」是我們未來可能擁有的玩具。

這種情況使人有必要瞭解這些人造物的新的控制方式及隨意無規範的行為模式與互動。同時亦必須自系統式至任意式的「嘗試－與－錯誤」遊戲中，改變遊戲的規則。

葛魯秋・馬克思將其總結於他膝上的金髮美人：最近看過什麼好書嗎？但後來馬克思兄弟成了改變遊戲規則與自己動手做的能手，他們天真無邪的純真結合了出色的發明天才。

假定人類的追尋將始終遵循著相同的路徑或利用相同的工具，是極為不智的。任何具有意識感的人都能理解馬克思兄弟的言下之意。我們始終可以自由選擇改變標籤上的指示。

當然，對我們一些人而言，這些事部份已經發生了：我們樂於自一般建築領域之外的各種素材中獲取刺激與構想：自連環漫畫至時裝雜誌，自霓虹燈至電影，並於我們，為了方便起見，稱之為「環境」的概念性護傘下收集它們。它不過是個收集袋而已，所以忘了道德倫理吧！整體綜合計劃早已過時了，高速公路網就像貧民窟般地具有限制性，且比航空路線的限制更多。建造我們城市所使用的舊式固定與靜態的元素將變得愈來愈不相關。新思想與新理解開始浮現，欺騙了現有的遊戲規則。目前有一個地方可以重新詮釋我們周遭環境之錯綜複雜中真正重要的部份。人類的邊界狀況正瓦解中，且新的方向與學科提供了愈來愈多的興趣刺激，我們稱之為「都市學」的呆板傳統知識已被「試試看會如何」的重新思考所取代。

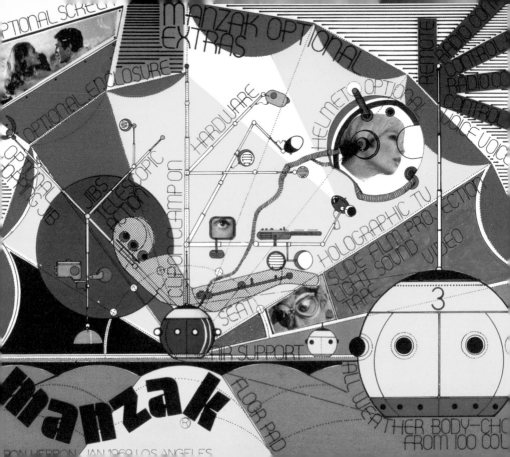

在一個稍縱即逝的社會裡，精準地照出汽車拍賣或電影首映的移動式探照燈比任何建築物都重要；信用卡系統遠比銀行大樓更有意義。都市學，如果有任何意義的話，就是身為自己動手做的東西的流動性始源。

套句威廉・布洛的話，「我們必須隨時打包，準備離開。」

ELECTRONIC TOMATO

Ron Herron, Warren Chalk, David Greene

電子蕃茄 朗・赫倫・華倫・裘克・大衛・葛林

Tired of supermarket shopping? Is it becoming a nightmare – up and down narrow aisles between high walls of brand name uniformity, with the lights glaring down and canned music boring in, as you search desperately for one can of Cream of Mushroom, where every label reads Tomato?

Then you haven't heard of MANZAK or the ELECTRIC TOMATO.

MANZAK is our latest idea for a radio-controlled, battery-powered electric automaton. It has on-board logic, optical range-finder, TV camera, and magic eye bump detectors. All the sensory equipment you need for environmental information retrieval, and for performing tasks.

Optional extras include response equipment for specific applications and subtasks to your own specification.

Direct your business operations, do the shopping, hunt or fish, or just enjoy electronic instamatic voyeurism, from the comfort of your own home.

For the great indoors, get instant vegetable therapy from the new ELECTRONIC TOMATO – a groove gizmo that connects to every nerve end to give you the wildest buzz.

厭煩了上超級市場購物嗎？它是否正變成一場夢魘——上下千篇一律的商標產品牆之間的狹窄通道，刺目的強光毫不留情地照射，預錄的音樂令人厭煩地入耳，正當您極度渴望尋找一罐蘑菇醬然而每張標籤上卻都寫著蕃茄？

那麼您一定還沒聽說過寵物機器人或者電子蕃茄吧！

寵物機器人是一部我們最近構想的無線電遙控且配備電池動力的電子自動化機器。它裝有邏輯電路、光學測距器、電視照相機與電眼碰撞偵測器。所有於環境資訊檢索與執行工作時您所需要的感應設備。

額外的選項包括為了特殊用途及您本身欢要工作細節所需之感應式設備。

指揮您的事業營運、購物逛街、打獵或釣魚、或者只是坐在您自己舒適的家裡，享受著電子全自動照相機的偷窺癖。

至於許多足不出戶者，挑個速食青菜療法吧，從最新的電子蕃茄裡—— 一個連接每條神經末梢以帶給您最強烈快感的時髦新玩意兒。

ALL WATCHED OVER BY MACHINES OF LOVING GRACE
一切「溫柔慈悲的機器」都監視著

I like to think   我喜歡想像著
    (and the sooner the better!)   （越快越好！）
        of a cybernetic meadow   一片人工智慧的草原
    where mammals and computers   那兒動物與電腦
      live together in mutually   共同生活在相互
        programming harmony   程式化的和諧中
            like pure water   就像純水
        touching the clear sky   輕觸晴空

I like to think   我喜歡想像著
    (right now, please!)   （就是現在，拜託！）
        of a cybernetic forest   一座人工智慧的森林
  filled with pines and electronics   那兒充滿了松木與電子音樂
   where deer stroll peacefully   鹿兒安詳地漫步
           past computers   與電腦擦肩而過
       as if they were flowers   宛如繁花似錦
      with spinning blossoms

I like to think   我喜歡想像著
    (it has to be!)   （不得不呀！）
       of a cybernetic ecology   一處人工智慧的生態
  where we are free of our labours   那兒我們得以免於勞苦
    and joined back to nature   回歸自然
     returning to our mammal   回到我們的動物
       brothers and sisters   兄弟姊妹的身旁
       and all watched over   而這一切
by machines of loving grace.   「溫柔慈悲的機器」都監視著

The Realist   唯實論者

First published in *ARCHITECTURAL DESIGN*, May 1969

CHILDREN'S PRIMER

devised by David Greene

Here we present a primer and sources, and some of the parts available so that you can go out now and make your own instant village. Don't hang about for all that architect-designed hardware. Also introduced here is Rokplug and Logplug, a new kit for the node-owner to supply the needs of non- or partially autonomous unit visitors that blend into the landscape and foliage, not forgetting the invitation to dream at the end. All the following pieces of living gear constitute hardware purchasable now to make instant villages, towns, etc. (camping scene not included). All right – it's still a hard network.

We all know now that a car is a self-powered mobile room, with limited support systems (air-conditioning, communications).

Wir alle wissen, daß ein Auto ein sich aus eigener Kraft bewegender, mobiler Raum ist, der ein beschränktes Versorgungssystem mit sich führt (Klimaanlage, Telephonanschluß etc.)

"I'm sorry..... but Sir Geoffrey is in his bath"

We also know that a traffic jam is a collection of rooms, so is a carpark – they are really instantly formed and constantly changing communities. A drive-in restaurant ceases to exist when the cars are gone (except for cooking hardware). A motorised environment is a collection of service points.

首度發表於1969年5月號《建築設計》雜誌

孩子的入門指南

大衛・葛林

在這裡我們要介紹一份入門指南與資料，以及一些可利用的元件，然後您便可以走出去並開始構築您的「即時村落」。不要再留戀於建築師所設計的那些硬體設備了。這裡同時要介紹的是「石插座」與「木插座」，一種由結點所有者供應「非（或部份）自主性單元體」的訪客所需的新裝備，與景觀、葉簇及最終的夢想誘惑，互相地融合在一起。所有以下的生活裝置元件都選定了目前可購得之硬體裝備以構築即時村落、城鎮……等（不包括露營情況）。好吧——它依然是個硬體的網狀組織！

我們現在都知道汽車是擁有有限支援系統的自力推動式移動房屋（空調、通訊）。

我們也知道交通阻塞是一群房屋的聚集，也是一處停車場——它們是立即形成且持續變化的社區。當汽車離開之後，免下車式餐廳即不存在（除了烹調硬體之外）。汽車化的環境是設施點的聚集。

「房屋汽車」是一個改造為可生活於其中的自力推動式容器。可引發任何生活單元體的聚集。全世界的森林都是您的市郊——只要某處有個加油站即可。

「輕便型露營用汽車」是一個容器，特地設計為可夾住小型的輕便貨車，為拖車式住宅與屋車之間的某種混合體。它的主要優勢在於分離式的牽

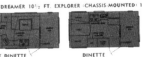

DREAMER 10½ FT. EXPLORER (CHASSIS-MOUNTED) 145

SIDE DINETTE   DINETTE

DREAMER 12 FT. ROYAL EXPLORER

DINETTE 1580 LBS.   SIDE DINETTE 1660 LB

Available: **Deluxe Hunting Lodge**

...when and where you want it.

SUPREME

Rembrandt

引擎（與屋車不同）。行駛中即排除掉所有的（拖車式住宅）拖曳問題與生活方面之習慣性用途。

「拖車屋」是一個用來長期生活的移動式容器。它需要一個高性能的牽引機。這些容器經常因為像捐血車、流動畫廊、流動銀行之類的其它目的而被改造。包羅廣泛類型之套件可輕易購得，準備做為生活之用。安裝於您所選擇的基地上。

The house-car is a self-powered container adapted for living inside. Any gathering of house-cars thus constitutes a gathering of living units. The forests of the world are your suburb – so long as there's a gas station somewhere.

The pickup camper is a container, purpose-designed to clip onto a pickup truck, a sort of hybrid between a caravan and a house-car, its main advantage being that the prime mover can be separated

LATER...

Am I glad we've got our own mobile hotel – no accommodation worries or bills – wherever we go!

SEA TRAIL CARAVANS

That's fine...you know you can choose from over 50 models here

BACK AT GALLOWS

We loved the caravan...

(unlike the house-car). All towing problems (with the caravan) and legal use of living quarters whilst underway are eliminated.

The trailer home is a movable container used for living in for extended periods. It requires a high-powered prime mover. These containers are frequently adapted for other purposes, bloodmobile, artmobile, bankmobile, etc. Extensive style ranges are available, purchasable ready for living. Hook up on the site of your choice.

Villages of trailer homes like this are relatively immobile and their major concern, usually, is to imitate straight suburbia as closely as possible. This is achieved by a comprehensive inventory of purchasable stick-on extras to make the trailer look like a 'real' house.

The main problem for mobile living support systems is, of course, the energy source. Until an effective system is devised, short-term energy will be taken from batteries or gas cylinders. For stopovers a plug will be required to draw off main power. This need will be satisfied by the ranges of Rokplug and Logplug. Read on.

This is an instant cluster of two campers next to three Rokplugs. Since it is difficult to recognise these outlets from nature's own products, they are equipped with a homing signal that locates each one within a radius of one mile. In your vehicle a dashboard visual display known as plugfind will convey this information. Location selection made by waveband selection similar to your car radio.

像這樣的拖車屋村落相對地比較難移動，而且它們通常主要關注於如何盡可能地模仿實際的郊區。這可由包羅廣泛的額外可購得貼紙達到目的，讓拖車屋看起來像一棟「真實的」房屋。

「移動式生活支援系統」的主要問題當然就是能源的來源。直到一種有效率的系統被發明之前，短期的能源將取自電池與瓦斯筒。對於中途停留者而言，將需要一個如照片所示的插頭以退除主動力。這種需求將可藉由「石插座」與「木插座」的套件得到滿足。繼續往下讀。

這是一群即時緊鄰3個「石插座」的兩部大型露營車。因為難以由大自然的環境中辨認出這些插座，因此它們於每一哩半徑之內就裝備有一個自動導向信號器。而您的汽車裡則備有一個作為插座供應的儀表板顯示器，可以傳輸資訊。地點的選擇藉由類似您的汽車收音機的波段選擇而完成。

「石插座」與「木插座」的地點將以一般的方式標示於硬體道路系統上。這些標誌也將告知所在插座裝置的正確區域號碼設定。

以下是一些典型社區的圖片。您可以認出「石插座」與「木插座」嗎？注意構成草地上戶外房間的摺疊式硬體設備。插座將增加這些社區的配送設施，使它們成為工作場所、學校、大學、圖書館與劇院，建築物可於需要之時不受阻礙地被輕易建造起來。整個倫敦或紐約，將可於全世界的枝葉茂密樹洞裡、不毛之地中，以及花開片的草地上發現它們的足跡。

目前我們必須等待，直到我們的城市、村落、城鎮的鋼筋混凝土陵墓腐敗，且郊區繁茂興隆的那一刻為止。它們將相繼地消失，這個世界也許將再度變成一座花園。而這或許是個夢想，我們都該忙著說服自己不再建造，而該著手準備空中那不可見的聯絡網。

Logplug and Rokplug concentrations will be indicated in the usual way on hard routing systems. These signs will also inform the correct dial setting for plugfind devices.

The following pictures are of typical communities. Can you spot the rokplugs and logplugs? Notice the collapsible hardware that make outdoor rooms in the grass. Plugs will increase the service to these communities and they will be workplaces, schools, universities, libraries, theatres unencumbered by buildings forming themselves conveniently when they are wished for. The whole of London or New York will be available in the world's leafy hollows, deserts and flowered meadows.

For the present we will have to wait until the steel and concrete mausoleums of our cities, villages, towns, etc., decay and the suburbs bloom and flourish. They in turn will die and the world will perhaps again be a garden. And that perhaps is the dream, and we should all be busy persuading not to build but to prepare for the invisible networks in the air there.

LOGPLUG & ROKPLUG

The ranges of Logplug and Rokplug shown here are selected GRP simulations of real logs and rocks. They serve to conceal service outlets for semi- or non-autonomous mobile living containers. They would be unrecognisable from the real thing and would thus bring into any setting a high degree of support without detracting from natural beauty (this means that when no hardware is plugged in, the village ceases to exist). All ranges are supplied with an embedded spore finish, to suit any locality, which will promote rapid moss, lichen or fungi covering.

This diagram explains the workings of a typical simulation log. The fixing gasket for both roks and logs is standard and interchangeable.

1. Access lid, 2..Cold water service
3. Cable line delivering: A/C and D/C current, Telephone, International information hook-up, Educational hook-up, 4. Operating credit and slot, 5. Plug connection, 6. Service metering and control, 7. Removable cover, 8. Plug find original source, 9. Supply cable

OPERATIONAL PROCEDURE to use Logplug and Rokplug – Raise access lid
1. Insert standard plug from mobile unit into female connection 5. Secure locking device. Place credit card in slot 4. Select service required on dial next to slot. Throw opening switch. All charges will be made onto your own credit number; these charges are displayed on your log-find device by pressing the yellow button.

It is assumed all waste is handled electrostatically and the ash either thrown to the wind or deposited in bags inside the logs or roks.

木插座與石插座

這裡所顯示的「木插座」與「石插座」套件是真實的圓木與岩石的精選玻璃強化聚酯纖維偽裝。它們被用以隱藏半自主性或非自主性移動式生活容器的插座。它們將無法自現實物體中被辨認出來，因此可引入高度的支援至任何環境中，而不破壞自然美景（這意味著，當無硬體設備插接時，此村落即不存在）。所有套件均供應嵌入的芽孢潤飾，以適應任何地點，加速青苔、地衣或菌類的覆蓋。

此圖示說明了典型的偽裝圓木的運作。圓木與岩石的固著接合填料為標準化且可替換的。1. 出入口蓋，2. 冷水設施，3. 纜線傳輸：交流電與直流電、電話、國際資訊轉播、教育轉播，4. 操作信用卡與插孔，5. 插座連結，6. 設施量錶與控制，7. 可移除式表蓋，8. 插座供應原始來源，9. 補給纜線。

「木插座」與「石插座」的操作過程——打開出入口蓋 1。從移動式單元體插入標準插頭至連結插座 5。關上閉鎖裝置。將信用卡置入插孔。必須利用插孔邊的轉盤選擇服務項目。接通啟動開關。所有費用將依您的信用卡號碼扣除；這些費用藉由按下黃色按鈕即可顯示於您的圓木供應裝置上。

假設所有的廢棄物將以靜電方式處理，而後灰燼將隨風飄散，或存入圓木或岩石內的袋子裡。

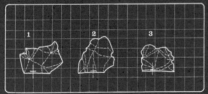

Holographic Scene Setter, Ron Herron
雷射光立體攝影佈景調節器，朗‧赫倫

Four US students shot dead by National Guardsmen during anti-war demonstrations at Kent State University, Ohio — Nobel Prize for Literature for Russian dissident writer Alexander Solzhenitsyn — De Gaulle dies — Race riots in Georgia — Aswan Dam in Egypt is completed — Radioactivity leak at Windscale power station — Terrorists blow up three hi-jacked planes at Dawson's Field in Jordan' — Riots at Gdansk shipyard — Police and Blacks clash in Notting Hill, London — UK age of majority reduced from 21 to 18 — The philosopher and peace campaigner Bertrand Russell dies at 97 — Eastern mysticism and Transcendental Meditation are the trend — Janis Joplin and Jimi Hendrix die of drug overdoses — FASHION — Flowers — Beads — Kaftans — Sandals — THE ARTS — Young Vic Theatre company formed in London — Play - 'Vivat Vivat Regina' — Film - 'Butch Cassidy and the Sundance Kid' — BOOK — 'Papillon'.

四名美國學生於俄亥俄州肯特州立大學舉行的反戰示威中遭國民兵射殺身亡－蘇俄反共作家亞歷山大‧索忍尼辛獲頒諾貝爾文學獎－戴高樂辭世－喬治亞州種族暴動－埃及亞斯文水壩完工－溫史凱爾發電廠輻射外洩－恐怖分子於約旦道森草場劫持引爆三架飛機－波蘭格但斯克造船廠暴動－倫敦諾丁丘發生警察與黑人對立衝突－英國將成年年紀自21歲降至18歲－哲學家伯特藍‧羅素於97歲與世長辭－「東方神秘主義」與「超覺靜坐」成為趨勢‧珍妮絲‧喬普林與吉米‧罕醉克斯於嗑藥過量－時尚－嬉痞－珠飾－「卡夫坦」－涼鞋－藝術－少年維克劇院於倫敦成立－戲劇－《女王萬歲》－電影－《虎豹小霸王》－出版－《惡魔島》。

1970

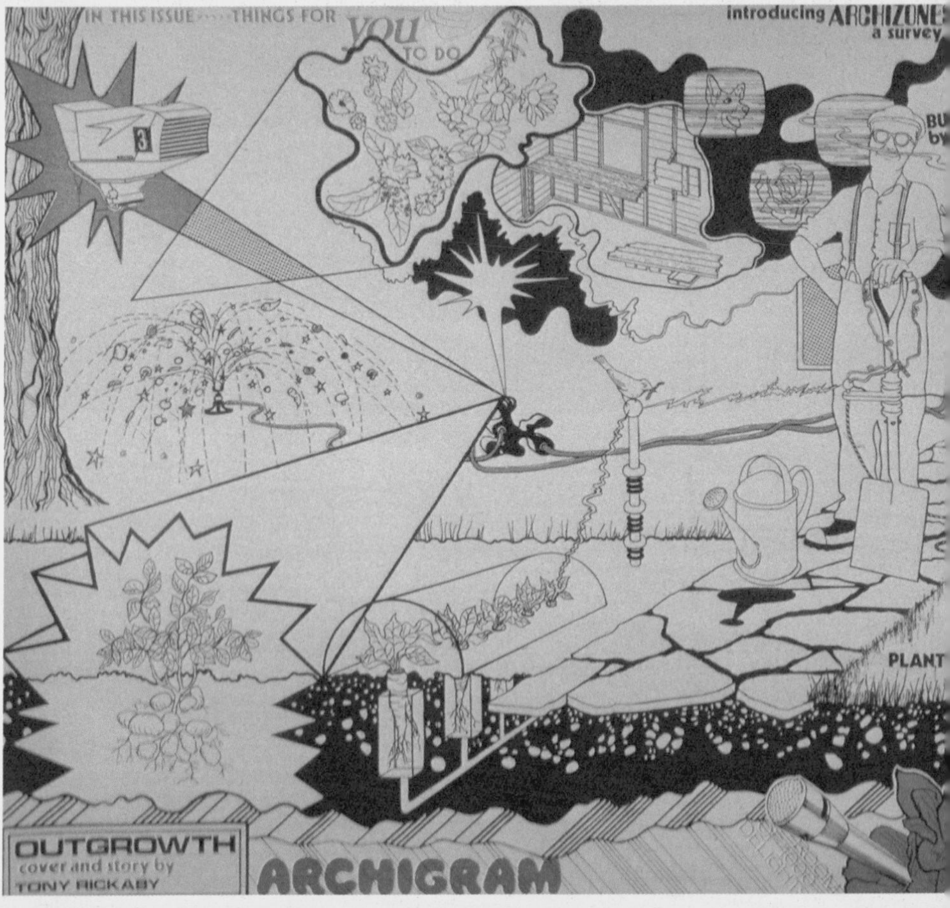

302

IN THIS ISSUE>>>>THINGS FOR *YOU* TO DO

introducing ARCHIZONE® a survey

OUTGROWTH
cover and story by
TONY RICKABY

ARCHIGRAM

PLANT

Gardener's Notebook

L.A.W.U.N. PROJECT

NUMBER ONE

CONTENTS

An Experimental Bottery

「即時機器」	**THE BOT**
景觀中	Machine Transient
短暫佇留的機器	in the Landscape
別帶著它團團轉	Don't carry it all around with you
到了再撥個號碼	Dial it up when you arrive

First published in *ARCHITECTURAL DESIGN*, September 1969
首度出版於1969年9月《建築設計》雜誌

GARDENER'S NOTEBOOK 園丁備忘錄

David Greene

大衛・葛林

Get LAWUN onto your lawn –

**替您的草坪弄個
「地區性可利用之世界不可見聯絡網」吧!**

Could the whole world be an all-green-grass-sphere?

If you had a quiet chuckle over Electronic Tomato or Manzak then take a fast look under your bed or your better-than-real-leather Naugahyde chair and check that MOWBOT isn't sleeping there, purring like some overloved kitten waiting to chew up your carpet when you go out the door. This is the mower that sleeps in the shed, that mows the lawn, that goes back to the shed. You groove away in the rose-bed while the lawn-mower-with-the-brain makes out in the grass of your own back door great yonder.

Mowboat has no appetite for flowers, plants, shrubs, etc.; while it completes its grass-cutting chores you may now potter in the garden with no concern for the safety of your flower beds – any time of the day or night. The real point is it's available, it's on the market; mow now pay later.

Nowhere is safe from unseen signals and like all your enemies it is far better to embrace them as your friend and learn to live rather than cry morality or history. Get your LA to electrify their park and give the gardeners time to tend the blossoms and cover the cities with geraniums. Take a look at mowbot, is it a freak?.....another natty gadget? Can you be sure a

L	ocally	地區性
A	vailable	可利用
W	orld	世界
U	nseen	不可見
N	etworks	聯絡網

整個世界可能是個完全綠色草皮的球體嗎?

倘若您低聲竊笑著「電子蕃茄」或「寵物機器人」,那麼趕快瞧瞧您的床底,或是那張比真皮還優的諾加海德人造皮椅,確定一下割草器沒有睡在那兒,像個寵壞了的小貓,等著當您出門時咬一咬您的地毯般地嗚嗚叫。這是睡在屋裡,割著草,又回到屋裡的割草器。當這有智慧的割草器在您自家後門遠處的草皮幹活時,您正在玫瑰花圃上鬆土。

割草器對花、小樹、灌木……等不感興趣;當它完成了割草雜務之後,您就可以在花園裡散步,勿須擔心您花床的安全——不論是白天或夜晚的任何時刻。真正的重點在於它是可取得的,它就在市場上販售;先割草後付款。

在不可見信號的面前,沒有任何地方是安全的,且就像您所有的敵人一樣,最好欣然地接受他們為朋友並學習和平共存,而非哭求著道德或過往。要求您的有關當局將公園電氣化,給園丁一些時間去照料盛開的繁花,並將城市覆滿天竺

Fridgebot won't be marketed tomorrow or a bed-bot, housebot, all ready and responsive to Lawun, and everyone knowing about Lawun and it being all over and calling up your bots from some kind of a scene in the forest glades and setting up your village without moving. Don't move, it'll come to you.

Typical yard layout shows how border wire goes down to limit mower travel and keep it crisscrossing.

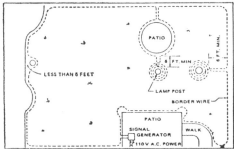

這個典型的庭院配置，顯示出鐵絲圍籬如何圈限割草器的行動自由，並保持它縱橫交織。

葵。瞧瞧這割草器，它是個怪物嗎？……另一種整潔的新玩意兒嗎？您真能確定「冰箱器」明天不會上市，亦或是「床器」、「房器」，全都準備好可感應到「地區性可利用之全球不可見聯絡網」，而大家也都認識「地區性可利用之全球不可見聯絡網」，且到處都有它的足跡，自某處林間的空地裡為您的「即時機器」訂貨，接著組合您的村落而不再移動。不需要移動的，因為它將自己朝您而來！

LAWUN means the striving after basic objectives – doing your own thing without disturbing the events of the existing scene and in a way which is invisible because it involves no formal statement, and because it is related to time, may or may not be there at any given point in time.

World's Last Hardware Event
and
Gardening Series

DEFINITION:
A Bottery is a fully serviced natural landscape.

CONTENTS:

1. The picture of this man by the river collects together most of the images and influences that produced

---

「**地區性可利用之全球不可見聯絡網**」意味著為了基本目標而努力——自己動手做而不干擾現有場景中的事件，並以一種不可見的方式進行，因為它並不涉及形式的陳述，且因為它與時間有關，不一定可能於任何特定的時間點出現於該處。

世界上最後的硬體事件
與
園藝系列

定義：
「設施景觀」是一種設施完善的自然景觀。

內容：

1. 這張河邊男人的圖片聚集了這個設計案所產生的大部份影像與影響。此瞬時性非專門化環境因複雜精巧之攜帶式硬體設備的發展而可能實現。圖中他坐在電視機與冷藏箱旁邊，汽車就在他身後，一切井然有序，構成適合他自己的場景，然而全部又都可以被移走，而當被移走之後又不會留下曾出現於此的線索，除了少量被壓扁的草皮之外，或許還有些輪胎痕跡與腳印吧！所以就某種意義而言一切均不可見，這個臨時性場所，也

this project – the transient non-specialised environment made possible by the development of sophisticated portable hardware.

Here he is sitting with his TV, ice box, car behind him, all neat, got his own scene going for him, and yet it can all be taken away, and when it's gone there's nothing to show that it was there at all, except a small amount of crushed grass and perhaps a tyre track, a footprint. So it's all invisible in a way. The temporary place, retained perhaps permanently in the memory. An architecture that exists only with reference to time.

It's funny that for some years now time has been an important influence in the 'arts', that is except in architecture. (Apart from nominal and superficial concessions to 'movement' and 'communications'.) Perhaps architects knew all along that if they came to grips with time they would be right out of a job.

2 *I have a desire for*
   The built environment
   To allow me to do
   My own thing.

More and more people want to determine their own parameters of behaviour. They want to decide how they shall behave, whether it's playing, working, loving, etc. People are less and less prepared to accept imposed rules and patterns of behaviour. Doing your own thing is important.

. . . . *people are becoming more interested in people and reality, rather than in feeding mythical systems.*

Warren Chalk

Unfortunately, however, in terms of doing your own thing, architecture is clearly not working.

許會永遠地留存於記憶裡。一種存在性只與時間有關的建築。

有趣的是經過這些年之後，時間目前對於「文理學科」具有重要的影響，更正確地說應該是，除了建築以外（除了對「運動」與「通訊」之些微與表面上的讓步以外）。或許建築師打從一開始就知道，如果他們醒悟而開始認真對待時間的問題的話，他們即將立刻失業。

SEED SPECIAL

2. 我希望
    構築的環境
    能允許我去完成
    我自己想要的東西

愈來愈多的人希望決定他們自己的行為參數。他們希望決定自己的舉止該如何表現，不管是遊樂、工作、戀愛……等。人們愈來愈不準備接受強制性的規則與行為模式。自己動手做十分重要。

……人們變得對人與現實愈來愈感興趣，而非對於維持神話的體系。

華倫・裘克

It is important to note that all the trends in society and technology are searching for flexibility and versatility. Specialisation is dead. In the building world the idea of the multi-purpose shed pays lip-service to this observation, the idea of non-specialised systems and architecture begin to interact, the place that jumps, the boat that walks, the tie that is a pen.

The idea of rooms for specific purposes is not viable any more – that's obvious, even before you ask whether rooms are viable any more. Everything is all mixed up, it's all fragmented.

That is except for architects, who still seem to think that building types exist and that it's useful to give 'rooms' specific purposes on their drawings.

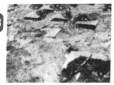 

3. . . . . *I have a desire for the environment to be invisible in order that I may be free from the pornography known as buildings. . . .*

One of the most interesting observables for the architect about some recent 'sculpture' (if it exists) is that it takes great care not to disturb the existing environment and in fact draws from its situation and feeds on all the on-going events and processes that any particular site contains.

. . . . using the untapped energy and information network of the day-to-day environment.

Jack Burnham

然而不幸地，就自己動手做的這個觀點而言，建築無疑地毫無成效。

察覺到社會與科技中的所有趨勢都正追求著彈性與多元性是很重要的。專門化已經窮途末路了。在建築的世界裡，多用途遮蔽所表面上支持了這項觀察的結果，非專門化系統與建築的構想開始互相地影響：會跳的飛機、會走的船、可以當筆寫的領帶。

特殊用途房間的想法已經不再可行了，這是很明顯的，而此現象甚至浮現在您問及房間是否還可行之前。所有東西都是彼此混合牽連的，也都是斷簡殘篇的。

也就是說，只有建築師似乎仍認為存在著建築物的類型，並認為賦予他們建築圖裡的「房間」特殊目的是有用的。

3. ……*我希望環境是不可見的，如此我才可能擺脫名叫建築的色情*……

有關最近的一些「雕塑」（若真存在的話），最有趣且值得建築注意的一點就是它很小心地不去干擾到既有的環境，事實上它自情境中汲取所需，並以任何特定基地裡所有進行中的事件與過程為養分。

……*利用日常環境中尚未開發的能源與資訊網路。*

傑克‧伯恩翰

The common threads that exist between the fisherman and his Sony and the project above. Robert Smithson's 'Incidents of mirror travel in the Yucatan' are important.

Both involve the temporary placing of bits of hardware in the natural scene and their ultimate removal; about this project Smithson writes: 'It is the dimension of absence that is to be found.' So maybe you might say that the development of portable hardware produces an architecture of absence. You've got to know about when it's not there as well as when it's there.

4. Cowboy international nomad hero. It used to seem a nice idea to carry your environment around with you (spaceman, cushicle, suitaloon etc.), but it can be as much of a drag as having it stuck in one place. Cowboy was probably one of the most successful carriers of his own environment because his hardware needs were low (mug, saddle, bedroll, matches) and because his prime mover, horse, selected its own fuel, and was a fairly efficient animal robot. The ranch was his oasis, his base. Modern nomad needs sophisticated servicing, Howard Johnson understands this; and in the bottery this is achieved by the technique of calling it up wherever you are, it's delivered by robots. It's anarchy – and it's hardware – supported until it's under the skin or in the mind.

ALONE, WITH AN ALONENESS THAT SEEMED UNBEARABLE, PEL TOBIN DRESSED, PACKED A BED ROLE AND SADDLED HIS HORSE/

共同脈絡就存在於漁夫與他的新力牌電視機以及以上所提之設計案間。羅伯特・史密斯森的「猶加敦半島上的鏡射傳導」極為重要。

二者均涉及到硬體設備零件臨時安置於自然背景中與它們最終的撤除；關於這個設計案史密斯森寫道；「它是將被發掘的不存在次元。」因此也許您可能說攜帶式硬體設備的發展產生了一種不存在的建築。您必須知道它何時不存在且何時存在。

4. 牛仔就像是個跨國性游牧英雄。帶著您的環境四處走（太空人、「氣墊車」、「家衣」……）曾經似乎是個不錯的點子，但是想將它安置於一個地方也可夠煩人的。牛仔也許可算是最成功地攜帶他自己的環境者之一，因為他硬體設備的需求極低（馬克杯、馬鞍、舖蓋捲、火柴以及他的牽引機，馬匹——它會自己選擇燃料並且是一個相當有效率的動物自動裝置）。牧場是他的綠洲，他的根據地。現代游牧使需求設施變得複雜而精巧，霍華德・強森瞭解這一點；在「設施景觀」中這方面是藉由無論身處何地的召集技術而達成，它將由自動裝置遞送。它是無政府狀態的——而且它是硬體裝置——將維持直到它深入人心為止。

5. Marshall McLuhan has said that the planet earth can be understood now as a piece of sculpture in the galaxies.

The Bottery is part of the idea of the Spacepark Earth (write to Sierra Club Foundation, Mill Tower, San Francisco, California 94104 for further information).

6. Keymatic (purchasable), is a familiar piece of hard-ware, part of a long line of crude domestic robots, dishwasher, mixer, central heating, etc. The thing about keymatic that's nice is the system of program-ming which is done by a plastic plate. It is interesting to compare the image of keymatic to much recent cooker design which has a jet-fighter cockpit aesthet-ic. The kitchen robot has become, in keymatic, not a vast piece of technical iconery, but an anonymous box and slot into which you place your programme. Every house now contains crude robots. Everybody wants a house full of robots but no-one wants to look like a house full of robots, so why not forget about the house and have a garden, and a collection of robots.

The one with the Keyplate

5. 馬歇爾・麥克魯漢曾說過地球目前可被視為銀河系裡的一件雕塑。

「設施景觀」是「太空－公園地球」構想的一部份（詳細資料請函洽希勒社團基金會，加州舊金山密爾塔樓　94104）。

6. 「按鍵式裝置」（可購得的）是一種很普通的硬體設備，就像其它簡陋的家庭自動裝置、洗碗機、攪拌機、中央暖氣……一樣。按鍵式裝置不錯之處在於由一片塑膠面板所完成之程式系統。將按鍵式裝置的形象與許多最近具有噴射戰鬥機駕駛艙美學的炊具做比較是件有趣的事。廚房的自動裝置，在按鍵式裝置裡，已經變成不再是一大件的科技標誌，而是您可設定自己的程式之不具特徵的盒子與溝槽。每棟房子現在都具有簡陋的自動裝置。每個人都希望擁有一棟充滿自動裝置的房子，但卻沒有人希望它看起來像是一棟充滿了自動裝置的房子。因此何不忘掉房子並擁有一座庭院並收集一群自動裝置呢？

7. This is the diagram of LAWUN. This project is about calling it all up wherever you are. (Environmental anarchy.) A bottery is a robot-serviced landscape. This project is about the setting up of an experimental bottery used solely by pedestrians for the purposes of (a) studying the nature and operation of the botman relationship (b) the development of reliable and efficient bot system.

The selected site is a UK area of heathland between the B3351 and Poole Harbour. A little-used area of considerable natural beauty. Included in the bottery are Arne Heath, Grep Heath, Slepe Heath, Wytch Heath, Rempstone Heath, Round Island, Newton Heath and Botham Plantation.

8. For hardware lovers: a selection of available electric aids to natural growth to help the gardener in the world park. Also a diagram of a cross section of a skinbot. The basic bot consists of a primary frame, a power module and an exchange unit. On to this are

7. 這是「地區性可利用之全球不可見聯絡網」一覽圖。這個設計案是有關不論身處何地的訂貨設計（環境的無政府狀態）。「設施景觀」是一種自動裝置操作的景觀。這個設計案是有關設立一個僅供行人使用的實驗性「設施景觀」，其目的為 (a) 研究「即時機器－人」關係的特質與運作；(b) 發展可靠且有效率的即時機器系統。

選定之區域位於英國B3351與普勒港間一處石南叢生的荒野地區。一處擁有不少自然美景但並未善加利用的區域。「設施景觀」中還包括有亞內荒地、葛列普荒地、史列普荒地、維奇荒地、藍普史東荒地、圓島、紐頓荒地，以及鮑翰林地。

8. 提供給硬體設備的愛好者：精選可購得且有助於世界公園園丁的自然栽培電子輔助器。此外還有一張殼板器的橫切面圖解。基本的即時機器包含一個主要的骨架、一個動力基

clipped combinations of modules for various performance requirements. Compatibility is assured by the exchange unit which rejects any mismatched modules

9. Mowbot (purchasable), like Keymatic, is easy, no sweat, set the grass cutting height on the dial and it will sense when the grass is needing a trim, you don't need to worry. And it's anonymous, and it's invisible, it's not a piece of permanent lawn furniture. It's still a fairly crude robot however, because you will still need a hard network of wires embedded under the ground at the perimeter of its territory. It has to be a very short step from having just mowbot to having a shed full of bots and then all you would need would be a shed, and a lawn.

10. Firebot is a piece of experimental hardware, a heat-sensitive bot, homing on to do its own thing. Developed by Professor Thring at Sheffield. (Who said sleepbot, the deliverer of sluberatic comforts to the needy body and mind, was an absurd idea?)

本單位與一個交換機單元體。上面夾著多性能要求的基本單元組合。藉由排拒任何不相配單元體的交換機單元體以確保其相容性。

9. 「割草器」（可購得的），如同按鍵式裝置一樣，簡單而不費力，在儀器面板上設定割草高度，然後它將自動感應是否草皮需要修剪，您毋需操心。而且它是不具特徵的，它是不可見的，它不是一件永久性草坪固定設備。然而它仍舊是一種相當簡陋的自動裝置，因為您仍需要一個埋於它的領域周圍地下的電線硬體網路。從只擁有割草器到擁有一個充滿自動裝置的遮蔽所必定只是一蹴而幾，而後您所需要的將只是一處遮蔽所與一片草坪而已。

10. 「消防器」是一種實驗性的硬體設備，一種熱感應器，自動追蹤完成它的使命。由雪菲爾大學的施瑞教授所發明。（誰說「睡眠器」，遞送睡眠舒適給拮据身心的救助器，是一個荒謬的點子呢？）

11. Bot base module for maintenance, storage, etc. They are contained within prefabricated plastic shells designed to blend in with the local scene. The one shown here is from the cottage range and is delivered flat. Net weight 1,543 kg.

11. 供維修、貯藏等用途的即時機器基礎模矩。它們裝在被設計以融合至地方場景裡的預製塑膠殼中。本圖所示來自一列茅舍且呈現平坦狀態。淨重1543公斤。

12. Picnic Groove (dressed) some-where in the world park. Skinbot delivers 18 cu. metres of air-conditioned deformable space, enclosed by a Sunfilta gossamer membrane that can glow at night by voice command and whose opacity is infinitely variable to choice.

Combot brings to your side out of the bluebells a way into your own secret mind, or selects out of the world's transmitted invisible pictures and sounds your own pattern of information and shows it on your shirt or on a screen.

314

12. 野餐樹叢（裝飾）於世界公園的某處。殼板器釋放出18立方米備有空調設備的可變形空間，圍著晚上可藉由聲控而發光且其不透明度具有無數可變選擇性的陽光過濾薄膜。
「多用途人型自動裝置」從風信子叢裡帶給您一種進入您自己神秘心靈的方法，或者從全世界所傳送之不可見的畫面中選取，發出您自己的資訊模式，並將其顯示於您的襯衫或螢幕上。

This is a brief community of people gathered together in the world park. They have called up their bots. The gathering is only related to time. Tomorrow, in half an hour, next week, it will all have changed, there'll be nothing remaining to indicate that it was there. The natural scene will remain unchanged. This small instant village will only exist in the memories of the people that were there and in the information memory of the robot. An invisible village. An architecture existing only in time.

這是一個人們齊聚於世界公園裡的短暫社區。他們召集了他們的即時機器。聚集只與時間有關。明天、半小時後、下星期，它都將會改變，將不會有任何的殘留顯示它曾經出現過那裡。自然的現場將維持不變。小型的「即時村落」將只存在於曾經在場的人們的記憶裡與自動裝置的資訊記憶體裡。只存在於時間裡的建築。

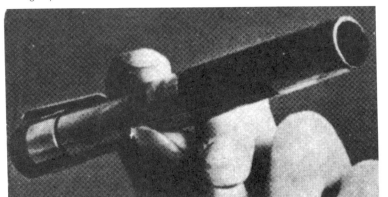

13. Bot call-up device. The type of service required is selected on a dial and the homing button pressed. Time to elapse before arrival is displayed on the end. If more than one Bot is required the multi-selection switch is activated. This is the only piece of hardware you need to carry with you in a bottery.

13. 訂貨器裝置。所需服務類型可由操控面板與自動導引按鈕選擇。到貨需要一些時間。若需要一件以上的即時機器，多重選擇開關可加速其反應。這是您在「設施景觀」中唯一必須攜帶的硬體設備。

| 4. DIAGRAM – 圖表

THE OPERATION OF SYSTEM EIGHT DEFINES AND ACTIVATES MOST BOTTIC ACTIVITY
系統8的操作定義且活化了大部份的即時機器活動

NO 編號	SYSTEM 系統	PRESENT FORM. 呈現形式	BOT-FORM. 即時機械形式
1.	Access to food silos 糧食穀倉入口	Shop, automat, market, etc... 商店、自動販賣機、市場……	Eatbot 飲食器
2.	Access to information 資訊入口	Books, schools, records, TV, universities, mags., etc... 書、學校、唱片、電視、 大學、雜誌……	Combot 多用途人型自 動裝置
3.	Access to communication systems 溝通系統入口 Bodymoving. 身體移動 Nonbodymoving. 非身體移動	Car, boat, cycle, plane, train, etc... 汽車、船、機踏車、飛機、火車…… Radio, TV, phone, semaphor, writing, etc... 收音機、電視、電話、信號機、著作……	Combot 多用途人型自 動裝置
4.	Access to personal shelter. 個人住所入口	House, flat, tent, palace, caravan, etc 房屋、公寓、帳蓬、華廈、拖車式住宅……	Skinbot 殼板器
5.	Access to play and escape. 玩樂與放鬆入口	TV, sport, cinema, etc... 電視、運動、電影……	
6.	Access to systems that give reward known as money with which one buys 1, 2, 3, 4, 5, 7 & 8 提供購買1、2、3、4、5、6、7與8 的獎勵金系統入口	Work. 工作	
7.	Maintenance service, and repair. 維修服務	Hospital, fire rescue, 999, etc... 醫院、消防隊、緊急救護……	
8.	Access to other people. 與其他人接觸的入口	Society, etc. 社會……	

15. This couple still living in their nice house turn on with combot in the evenings. However they are already wondering why they need any furniture and have got combot networked into their office in town and don't need to commute any more. Maybe next year they can move to a soft grass field somewhere. One of the questions often asked about this kind of project is 'how do you make this happen?' As well as the experimental landscape venture it can also happen through the marketing of robots, and their gradual absorption into our everyday life, just as frozen food has made a cooker less necessary, less useful and yet even more necessary as a tool for creativity in the 'kitchen', so increasingly sophisticated and efficient domestic robots will make the permanent living box or house less useful, less needed and yet even more useful as a tool to the creative extensions of our new lives, as a medium for building a truly responsive environment and for bringing about a reduction in the architectural hardware now filling up our forests.

15. 這對仍居住在他們舒適的家裡的情侶，傍晚時打開了多用途人型自動裝置。然而他們早已開始懷疑自己為何需要任何家具，並將多用途人型自動裝置網接於他們鎮上的辦公室而不需再替換。或許明年他們可以搬進某處的草原裡。關於這類設計案經常會被問到的問題之一就是「如何實現呢？」在這個設計案與實驗景觀的冒險中，可藉由自動裝置的製造銷售與它們逐漸融入我們日常生活之中而實現。就某種意義而言，就像冷凍食品使炊具變得更不必要、更無用處，而卻實際上更適合成為廚房裡的創造性工具，因此愈來愈複雜精巧與有效率的家庭自動裝置將使永久性生活據點（或者房屋）變得更無用處與必要性，然而對於我們新生活的創意延伸、建造一種真正感應式的環境，以及縮減目前填滿我們森林的建築硬體而言，卻是更有用的工具與媒介。

DREAMS COME TRUE

Mike Webb

DREAMS COME TRUE is the idea of an organization which offers wonderful new ways of living, not only the hardware (gadgetry, enclosures, vehicles, etc.) necessary, but also non-physical things like what work you do. So DREAMS COME TRUE churns out a big catalogue, and the resulting environment is a compo of what everyone has chosen . . . you may say 'How do people know what to choose and would they anyway plump for what they're used to?' This is where the soap opera comes in – daily

on CBS TV you can see the passion and loves of people living in the world that DREAMS COME TRUE has made possible. So folks know what they're choosing and the environments or 'scenarios' are anyway test pieces . . . DREAMS COME TRUE is really a co-ordinating group with industry and finance to make possible that wonderful new world we all dream about . . .

love from Spid . . .

P.S. The fan-shaped thing and the oil painting show. what oerndaspeodic living can be like . . . and are both sides of the sendout.

DREAMS COME TRUE INC
EXPLANATORY SHEET C9 13

PREPARED BY DREAMS COME TRUE
COPY WRITING DEPARTMENT 28G

美夢成真 麥克・威柏

「美夢成真」是一個提供美好新生活方式之組織體的構想，不只是必要的硬體設備（精巧的設備、圍蔽物、交通工具……），還有非實體的東西，例如您做的事情。因此「美夢成真」不斷地推出大型目錄，而最終的環境則是每個人的選擇的混合體……您可能會說：「人們怎麼知道如何選

擇而且他們是否會一股腦兒地選擇過去所習慣的東西呢？」這正是連續劇的切入點——在美國哥倫比亞廣播公司的電視頻道上，您每天都可以看到生活在「美夢成真」所創造的世界裡的人們的愛恨糾葛。所以人們知道自己在選擇什麼東西，而環境或「劇情腳本」正是試驗的例子……「美夢成真」確實是一個可利用工業與財力來實現我們大家所夢想的美好新世界的協調性團體……誠摯的問候，史派德……附記：扇形物件與油畫呈現出雲端之上歡樂生活的可能情景……兩側是摺疊鐵條。

ROOM OF 1000 DELIGHTS
follow a dream
UNTIL YOU
MAKE IT HAPPEN
01
03
07 08 09 10 11 12 13 15
ELECTRIC DANCE
mechanised hand
hands
hands
arms and hands
arms and hands

WHAT IS A ROOM

WHAT DOES IT DO?

THE "CONTAINER" WAS A CENTRAL DEFINING DEVICE IN THE PAST
WHAT CAN IT DO FOR YOU? IT CAN ACT AS HOST TO THE PROBLEMS AND DEVICES THAT DREAM USE SOME OF OUR DREAMS
NOW OUR DREAMS HAPPEN THROUGH WIRES AND WAVES AND PICTURES
THE INTERFACE IS BETWEEN THE PICTURE
AND THE UNKNOWN THE REAL AND
THE UNREAL

FREE

FREE

OWER OF THE MIND HAS ALWAYS RANGED
FURTHER THAN
THE LIMITS OF
ENVIRONMENT

AND THEN?

PETER COOK ⓕ ARCHIGRAM ⓕ 1970

First published in *ARCHITECTURAL DESIGN*, January 1970

TRYING TO FIND OUT IS ONE OF MY CONSTANT DOINGS

Warren Chalk

Horror stories of man systematically destroying his environment are still snowballing, but by now, all too familiar, fatalistic, and dull, the boom is about to go bust. Give a bloke a bulldozer and what can you expect? It depends where you look and whose gang you belong to. Man's resistance to change, desire for stability and permanence, and need for static identification are overemphasised. Survival is easy – let's get stoned. What we really need is increased environmental stimulus. Because the environmental stimulus is weak, man is inventing novelties like wife-swapping and Unisex dressing. He is bored.

Work on the threshold of specialisation reveals a skilful but spiritless existence; people with enormous fatigue trying to cope with the banalities of not-too-well-serviced environments.

The future need is for environmental super-stimulus, interfacing, and soul-engineering. Current revolts against 'reason' are a strange, deliberate confusion mechanism – a kind of mental anarchism that could produce good vibes. The irrational, the new unreason, are distinct, ignorance-surmounting ploys towards a greater communications sensitivity. Super-stimuli, like sit-ins, drug-taking, or voyeurism, are not accidental. This is man the inventor, playing for all he is worth, in a quick turn-over field. Desperate attempts to communicate with something or someone or to discover himself – when 'normal' communications break – produce super-stimulus pressure devices. This is the dawning of the age of Aquarius, and 'What sign are you?' is a good opening gambit at any chance meeting of kindred souls. Watch how many people succumb to exposure they would not normally allow, through the mind-shift device of the horoscope. See those who hide behind the traditional disbelief guise shaken into response, recognising some vague character trait, good news, or astrological prospects of love and good fortune. Apart from the obvious horoscope page in the women's fashion glossies, there is a sharply increasing interest in tarot cards, numerology, teacup reading, palmistry and even the psychic powers of candle wax drippings. Currently the occult is moving into the computer field with up-to-the-minute knock-out personality analysis. United Industries Electronics Division have Anavac, which gives a semi-computerised electrographic analysis of your handwriting, while Time Pattern Research Institute have a computerised in-depth personalised horoscope. Twenty-five million bits of astrological data are stored in an IBM/360 computer memory bank; you just feed in your date of birth, place of birth, time of birth, name, address and Bank Americard number for a 15,000-word personal horoscope printout.

Anyway, why should the human animal control inferior present satisfaction on the grounds of being too intelli-

首度發表於1970年1月《建築設計》雜誌

試著找出答案是我一直在做的事情之一

華倫・裘克

人類有系統地摧毀自己的環境這樣恐怖的情節依舊持續地增加，但截至目前，一切都太熟悉、太宿命且無趣，然而此景就快改變了。給個傢伙一部推土機後您能有何期待呢？這端視您的企盼與您所屬的派別。人們過分強調人類的抗拒改變、渴望穩定與永恆，以及需要不變的歸屬感。生存是容易的……讓我們喝個酩酊大醉吧。我們真正需要的是增加的環境刺激。因為環境的刺激是脆弱的，人們創造出像換妻與男女共用衣著這類新玩意兒。他們很無聊。專門化開端的努力透露出一股熟練與無生氣；疲憊的人們試圖對付那維修不佳的平庸環境。

對環境的「極度刺激」而言，其未來的需求是「介面形成」與「心靈工程」。現今對於「理性」的反抗是個怪異且刻意的混亂結構……某種可產生良好共鳴的精神無政府主義狀態。非理性不同於新非理智，是超越無知，邁向更高度的溝通敏感性的手段。極度刺激，就像靜坐抗議、吸毒，或窺淫癖一樣，並非偶發性的。這是身為發明者的人類在急速變化的領域裡的全力以赴。極度渴望與某件事或某些人溝通，或是自我發現——當「正常」溝通中斷時——引發了極度刺激壓力裝置的設計。這是水瓶座年代的開端，「您是哪個星座」對志同道合者的偶遇而言，是個絕佳的開場白。透過占星這種改變意識的工具，看看多少人因此成了屈從的受害者。看看那些躲在傳統的無信仰偽裝下的人們，若能辨識出好消息或愛情與好運的占星機運的某些曖昧含糊特質的話，當能醒悟。除了女性時尚雜誌中顯而易見的占星專欄之外，尚有對於塔羅紙牌、命理學、茶杯預卜、手相術，甚至蠟燭滴蠟的靈異力量的興趣激增。最近這種秘術正轉移至電腦領域中的最新式個性分析。「聯合工業電子局」有「阿納法克」設備，可提供筆跡的半數位化電子圖像分析，而「時間模式研究協會」則有數位化深入個人占星術。2500萬元的占星術資料貯藏於一部IBM/360的電腦記憶庫裡；您只需要輸入您的出生日期、出生地點、出生時間、姓名、地址與信用卡號碼，即可印出一份1萬5000字的占星報告。

然而，為何人類這種動物只因據稱太聰明，就必須放棄其卑微的當下滿足呢？是否可能一旦人類有了更具深度的理解性與感受性的精神力量後，便對於文明產生了歸屬感的模糊記憶呢？

gent for all that kind of stuff? Could it be possible that individual man has dim recollections of belonging to a civilisation that once had mental powers with greater depths of understanding and sensibility?

Those cosmic religious ground patterns discovered in the area of Glastonbury Ring (see *Gandalph's Garden* published by Gandalph's Garden, World's End, London SW10 and *Glastonbury* published by Research into Lost Knowledge Organisation, 36 College Court, London W6) indicated a mental source run dry. This kind of soul-engineering, dealing with alignments of sacred sites and routes across countries and continents, implies some lost system of prehistoric magic, difficult to comprehend. But don't laugh – it's not that easily dismissed. This is not something of mere archaeological interest: more important is the notion of, in Professor Mary Williams' words, 'the archaeology of ideas'.

The secret Zodiac of Glastonbury　格拉斯頓伯里的神秘黃道12宮圖案

Reaching even greater heights of speculative extravagance, we could ask if this is the equivalent to today's UFOs? Or are there some Rip van Winkles in our midst? Science fiction based on science fact mirrors the power and the enigmas of scientific thought. The paradoxes and consequences drawn out to their extreme, with absurd hypotheses, scandalising common sense, are usually the result of harsh mind-searching and a more ambitious logic. Is magic more ambitious logic, and more ambitious logic synectics? We are accustomed to judge by images and the limited significance we attach to words. If we try to discover where it's really at, irrespective of preconceived notions, the bewildered imagination may come up with an idea. To make the familiar strange, stand thoughts on their head or put them out of focus, then you have that anxious insecure creative bit. Try-it-and-see, make the familiar unfamiliar, the invisible visible, cast new light on old problems to drag out fresh solutions. Now try it to music. Russian scientists are working with a team of physicists and electronics engineers to develop a system in which machines can be controlled by the simple act of thinking about them. A research team is investigating this fantastic use of the human mind. Before it moves the muscles of the body, the human will is no more

華倫 • 裘克的筆跡電子圖像分析

在格拉斯頓伯里環區所發現的那些宇宙宗教性地面圖案（詳見「干達夫花園」所出版的《干達夫花園》，世界盡頭，倫敦SW10，以及「失落知識研究協會」所出版的《格拉斯頓伯里》，學院天井36號，倫敦W6）暗示了某種精神源泉的枯竭。這種心靈工程，涉及了跨越國界與洲界之神聖的地點與路程的密切合作，暗示著某種史前魔法的失落體系，令人難以理解。但別發笑——這可不能等閒視之。這並非僅為某種考古學上的興趣：更重要的是那個概念，用瑪莉•威廉斯教授的話來說，亦即「構想的考古學」。

倘若我們延及更高度的怪誕臆測，可否問道這等同於今日的幽浮嗎？或者我們之中存有幾個瑞普•凡•文寇斯？以科學事實為基礎的科幻小說，反映了科學思考的力量與謎團。使人類「正常的」理解力為之愕然的似非而是議論，與其達到極致所引出的歸結，以及荒謬的假設，通常是嚴苛的心智探索與更具野心的邏輯。魔法是否為更具野心的邏輯，而此更具野心的邏輯是否為創意性的解決之道呢？我們習慣於根據影像與我們附加於字面上的偏狹意義進行判斷。若我們試圖找出它真正的所在，不顧慮先入之見，則困惑的想像力或可孕育出某種構想。為了使熟悉的事物變得陌生，將想法怪異化或模糊其焦點，而後您將焦慮不安地進行創作。試試看會如何，當熟悉變得陌生，不可見變得可見，且老問題有了新的認識以誘發新的解決之道？現在試試看音樂。俄國科學家正與一幫物理學家及電子工程師合力發展一套系統，於其中，機器可藉由單純的思考行為進行控制。一個研究小組正對這種出色的人類心智運用展開調查。在牽動身體肌肉之前，人類的意志不過

than an electric signal conducted along a nerve path. These electric signals can be intercepted and transferred into electric circuitry, switched through a special control panel and straight into the works of a machine. Refinement and improvement of this system could enable man to operate machine controls without even twitching a finger, simply by thinking about it – real soul-engineering.

The Russians also claim to have two women who have already mastered this wish-control system. One of them, a female demonstrator at the Polytechnic Museum in Moscow, by clenching and unclenching her fists and with ESP, creates nerve signals that are picked up by a toy train radio control unit. From a distance of several feet the girl makes the train start, stop or go backwards. Another woman directs her thought impulses into controlling an electric clock, making it go faster, slower, or stop.

The permutations are endless and impressive: produce your own scene machine today. EAT (Experiments with Art and Technology Inc.) have been at it for some time now. Based at 235, Park Avenue South, New York, NY 10003, and headed by pop artist Robert Rauschenberg, Billy Kluver of Bell Telephone Laboratories, Walter Allner, Art Director of *Fortune* magazine, Gyorgy Kepes, Professor of Visual Design, MIT, John Cage, the composer, and Buckminster Fuller, etc., EAT is evolving a network of artists, technicians, and other nuts in professions exploring the possibilities of the new technology. The collaboration between

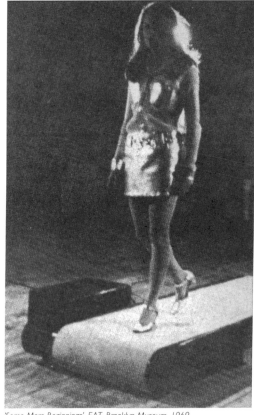

'Some More Beginnings', EAT, Brooklyn Museum, 1969
「更多些開端」，藝術科技實驗有限公司，布魯克林博物館，
1969年

是沿著神經路徑傳導的電子信號。這些電子信號可被攔截與轉換成電路，透過特殊控制面板的開關而直接轉變為一部機械。這種系統的精煉與進步可使人類於操控機器時，甚至無須牽動手指，而僅須藉由思考——名符其實的「心靈工程」。俄國人亦宣稱有兩名女性已經精通這種「願望控制」系統。其中一位是一名莫斯科工藝博物館的女性示教員，藉由緊握與鬆開拳頭與「超感知覺」，創造出可以玩具火車無線電控制裝置接收的神經信號。那位女士於數呎距離之外讓火車啟動、停止或後退。另一位女士則指揮其思想以刺激控制一部電子鐘，讓它走得更快、更慢或停止。

變化是無窮盡且令人印象深刻的：現在就創造您自己的場景機器吧！「藝術科技實驗有限公司」已從事這方面的研究一段時日了。設立於紐約南公園大道235號，紐約10003，並由普普藝術家羅伯特·勞玄柏格、「貝爾電話實驗室」的比利·克魯佛、華特·艾爾納、《財富雜誌》藝術總監喬治·凱普斯、麻省理工學院的視覺設計教授與作曲家村翰·凱吉，以及布克敏斯特·富勒……等人領軍，「藝術科技實驗有限公司」發展出一套藝術家、工程師及其他各類專業怪傑的網路，探索著新科技的可能性。藝術家與電子工程師間的合作已創造出一套各式各樣的視聽計劃，包括數位影片、動態藝術、流體雕塑、迷幻環境、抗引力機器、數位控制視聽轉換……等。「藝術科技實驗有限公司」於布魯克林博物館的「更多些開端」展覽，證明了結合藝術家的腦力激盪與電子工程師的紮實知識技術的重要性。某些瘋狂構想的介面形成因而產生。但想符合湯姆·伍爾夫的觀點並不困難——詳見1969年7月號《建築設計》雜誌——例如梅爾文·柴佛格早已做到了——在我們提出環境極度刺激與脫離極度保守的工作室情勢之前，仍有許多進度得趕上。

胡士托音樂節與才子賽卓克·普萊斯的「非計畫」構想（詳見1969年5月號《建築設計》雜誌）具有相同的特質。胡士托，一塊600英畝的農地，來自美國各地的年輕人，「血汗淚樂團」樂團、「罐裝熱氣」樂團、克里登斯·克利爾華特、「感激死亡」樂團、吉米·罕醉克斯、珍妮絲·喬普林與「誰」樂團。

一片接通開關的曠野，一座3天的城市，50萬年輕人，摩肩擦踵，處於最不舒適的情境中，只有唯一的硬體設備睡袋與擴大的亢奮情緒，但沒有暴力，不似拳擊賽般。這就是您的電子環境、即時城市與（三天後即恢復為農地）具備電力插座的非計畫生態循環。

這是「極度刺激」、「介面形成」與「心靈工程」的合而為一，就像童話故事一樣，將魔法視為理所當然。雖然這則童話故事的「極度刺激」特質就如同新色情文學，而人們被誘使將格林兄弟、漢斯·克里斯提安·安徒生與休·海夫納聯想為同類傢伙。儘管如此，孩子們的仙境依舊十分穩定，因為，

artists and electronics engineers has produced a range of varied audio-visual programmes, including computer-generated films, kinetic art, liquid sculpture, psychedelic environments, anti-gravity machines, computer-controlled audio-visual conversion, etc. EAT's exhibition 'Some More Beginnings', at the Brooklyn Museum, demonstrated the importance of matching artists' brain-storming with electronics engineers' hard know-how. Some crazy-headed interfacing resulted. But it isn't hard to go along with the Tom Wolfe outlook – See AD 7/69 – like Melvin Zeitvogel already did it – and there is a lot of catching up to do before we make with the environmental super-stimulus and get out of the uptight studio workshop scene.

Woodstock Music Festival shares common characteristics with whiz king Cedric Price's Non-plan ideas (AD 5/69). Woodstock, a 600-acre farm, young people from all over the United States, Blood Sweat and Tears, Canned Heat, Creedence Clearwater, Grateful Dead, Jimi Hendrix, Janis Joplin and The Who.

A field turned on, a three-day city, half a million young people, elbow-to-elbow, in the most uncomfortable kind of situation, the only hardware sleeping bags and mind-blowing amplification, but no violence, not so much as a fist-fight. Here is your electronic environment, instant city and (it reverted to farmland after the three days) a non-plan ecological cycle with power points.

This is a super-stimulation, interfacing, and soul-engineering in one, it's like a fairy story, enchantment taken for granted and magic as the rule. Although the super-stimulation qualities of the fairy story are equatable with neo-pornography, and one is tempted to suggest that the brothers Grimm, Hans Christian Andersen and Hugh Heffner are the same bloke. Nevertheless the children's fairyland world is remarkably stable, because they tend to create their own environmental stimulus, regardless.

And this environment is never sufficiently established for stress to occur. Children seem to adapt themselves easily, and create their own never-never situation, with natural penetrating insight into evading the absurdities of the adult world. How about this for expediency? A geography test paper for nine-year-olds asked for observations on Canada. Two super replies: 'I am not sure how many provinces there are in the altogether part of Canada but trying to find out is one of my constant doings.'

and

> Lake Winnipeg is in Manitoba
> Maybe it is in North Manitoba
> Maybe it is in South Manitoba
> I do not know
> It takes me all my knowing
> To know that Lake Winnipeg is in Manitoba.

無論如何，他們總會創造出他們自己的環境刺激。

然而這個環境從未充分地建立，因此壓力不至於產生。孩子們似乎極容易適應，並創造他們自己的私密情境，以天生敏銳的洞察力迴避成人世界的荒謬。多棒的權宜之策啊！9歲兒童的地理課考題問及對於加拿大的評論。兩個極佳的回答：「我不確定加拿大究竟一共由多少個省份所組成，不過試著找出答案是我一直在做的事情之一。」

以及

> 溫尼裴湖位於曼尼托巴省
> 也許是在北曼尼托巴
> 或者是在南曼尼托巴
> 我不曉得
> 竭盡我所知
> 方能知曉溫尼裴湖就位於曼尼托巴省

OSAKA WORLD EXPO 70

Our exhibit for Osaka is basically a corridor, through which thousands of people an hour will pass. The message has to be simple. The audience participation is a 'yes' or 'no' push-button response to five simple questions about 'Cities'. The form of the thing is that a curious 'growth' object hanging from the ceiling changes from formal to informal, structured to free, mechanistic to symbiotic as you move through the corridor. We hope that this will be a simple thing to understand (in any language), but that the implication of the questions might linger.

330

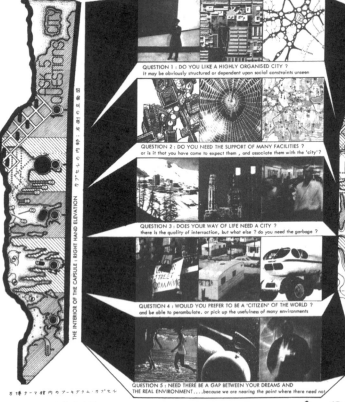

QUESTION 1 : DO YOU LIKE A HIGHLY ORGANISED CITY ?
it may be obviously structured or dependent upon social constraints unseen

QUESTION 2 : DO YOU NEED THE SUPPORT OF MANY FACILITIES ?
or is it that you have come to expect them , and associate them with the 'city' ?

QUESTION 3 : DOES YOUR WAY OF LIFE NEED A CITY ?
there is the quality of interraction, but what else ? do you need the garbage ?

QUESTION 4 : WOULD YOU PREFER TO BE A 'CITIZEN' OF THE WORLD ?
and be able to perambulate, or pick up the usefulness of many environments

QUESTION 5 : NEED THERE BE A GAP BETWEEN YOUR DREAMS AND
THE REAL ENVIRONMENT....because we are nearing the point where there need not

万博テーマ館内のアーキグラム・カプセル
都市の重要性の崩壊を意味する
都市に関する五つの質問

アーキグラム

大阪

1970年大阪世界博覽會

我們在大阪的展覽基本上是個通廊，每小時約有幾千人經過。訊息必須簡單明瞭。觀眾的參與是對於5個有關「城市」的簡單問題的「是」與「否」按鍵回答。物體的形式是個懸於天花板的怪異「生長」物件，當您穿越通廊時，它自形式性轉為非形式性，自結構性轉為自由性，自機械性轉為共生性。我們希望這會是件簡單易懂的東西（以任何語言），但問題的暗示卻可縈繞耳際。

關於城市的五個問題
大阪電訊
暗示著城市的意義崩解

MON REPOS STRIP

Peter Cook

The typical English suburban avenue could evolve into quite a different environment by the introduction of simple elements of a very wide range. They could be bought over the counter as components, and allow for a high degree of 'do-it-yourself' involvement. The styling is wide open: it can be bolted-in, and 'Gothic', 'Bauhaus', 'Pop-Art' – or off-the-cuff, aesthetics are interchangeable.

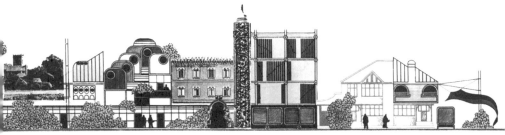

特別型 典型的英國郊區街道可藉由引入各式各樣的簡單元件而發展成相當不同的環
彼得・庫克 境。它們是在櫃檯上買得到的組件,並且必須極高程度地參與自己動手做。樣
式極為廣泛:它可能是「關在屋內的」、也可能是「哥德式的」、「包浩斯式
的」、「普普藝術的」──或是可替換之即興式美學。

NORTH KENSINGTON CORNER 1

NORTH KENSINGTON CORNER 2

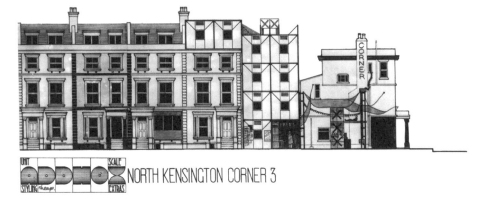

NORTH KENSINGTON CORNER 3

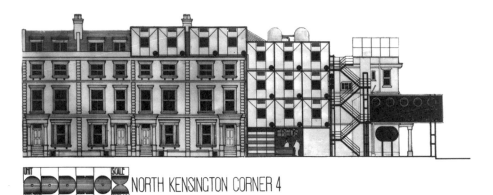

NORTH KENSINGTON CORNER 4

BOURNEMOUTH STEPS

The Bournemouth Project carries on a dialogue with that of Monte Carlo: the culture of rich and well-heeled seaside with entertainments as a main function. A surrounding of cliffs or mountain with trees. gardens and rockeries and cream-painted hotels and villas, Bournemouth served as a blistering out of several expressionist games that we had purged from the Monte Carlo Scheme.

It extends an already existing pattern of shopping arcades that network the centre of Bournemouth. Through the scheme these develop into piers and decks and into the seafront scene. The seaside is traditionally the place where our notions of a flexible and 'responsive' environment are carried out: as the seasons and the weather change so do the functions and the architecture. The 'Steps' are formed by the piling-up of the shops and sheds and capsules that emanate from the arcades. The stepping is covered by undergrowth and extends the lawns and rockeries that are already there. The whole thing was designed very quickly, with several hands at work, and proved to be exhilarating, if some what undisciplined. It throws up a characteristic of Archigram: the need for exuberance and freewheel designing as well as the demonstration of a thesis.

336

SOLENT CLIFFS   HOTELS AND PARKING   WEST BEACH PAVILION   BOURNEMOUTH PIER
                       DAY HOTEL

波茅斯梯階

「波茅斯設計案」持續著與蒙地卡羅設計案的對話：豪門文化與主要功能為娛樂設施的富人海濱。四周環境圍繞著懸崖或佈滿綠樹、花園與岩石庭園的山岳、乳白色的飯店與別墅，波茅斯可視為我們自「蒙地卡羅計畫」中所淨化出的某些表現派。

它擴展了與波茅斯市中心建立關係網之購物連環拱廊的樣式。透過此一計畫，這些都將發展成碼頭與甲板，以及濱海風景區。傳統上海濱是我們的「彈性式」與「感應式」環境概念實現的場所：因為季節與氣候會改變，且機能與建築也會變化。「梯階」由來自連環拱廊的商店、遮篷與艙室的堆疊所構成。梯階被矮樹叢所覆蓋，並擴展了原先已經存在的草坪與岩石庭園。整個設計十分地快速，許多人同時進行，整個過程十分愉快，縱使稍有些紀律不足之處。它揚棄了「建築電訊」的某種特質：精力旺盛之需求與隨心所欲的設計，以及一個論題的證明。

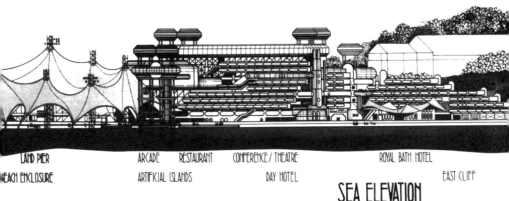

SEA ELEVATION

LAND PIER   ARCADE   RESTAURANT   CONFERENCE / THEATRE   ROYAL BATH HOTEL

BEACH ENCLOSURE   ARTIFICIAL ISLANDS   DAY HOTEL   EAST CLIFF

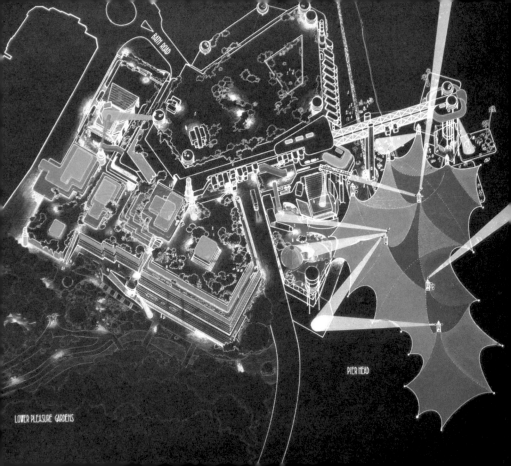

BATH ROAD

PIER HEAD

LOWER PLEASURE GARDENS

Apollo 14 lands on the Moon — Kurt Waldheim elected UN Secretary General — UK brings in decimal currency — Soviet spacecraft docks with space station — Italy – Mount Etna erupts — USSR – three cosmonauts die on return trip from space — Internment introduced in Northern Ireland — US – comedian Harold Lloyd dies — Haitian dictator 'Papa Doc' Duvalier dies — Nikita Kruschev dies — Driving on the Moon: David Scott and James Urwin become the first astronauts to drive on the surface of the Moon. The Apollo 15 team drove their lightweight battery-controlled Lunar Roving Vehicle on the rear wheels only, as the front wheels failed to work — UK – Fleet of 100 fishing trawlers from the south and east coasts sail up the River Thames to the Houses of Parliament in fishing limit protest — Lone UK yachtsman Chay Blyth sails round the world — Andy Warhol exhibition at the Tate Gallery, London — FILMS – 'A Clockwork Orange', 'Death in Venice' — Louis Armstrong dies — Igor Stravinsky dies.

阿波羅14號登陸月球－科特・華德翰當選聯合國秘書長－英國引進十進位貨幣－蘇俄太空船與太空站會合－義大利－埃特納火山爆發－蘇聯－3名太空人死於返回地球的途中－北愛爾蘭成立俘虜營－美國－喜劇演員哈洛・洛伊德辭世－海地獨裁者杜瓦利辭世－蘇聯總理尼奇塔・赫魯雪夫辭世－月球駕駛：大衛・史考特與詹姆斯・爾文成為首次於月球表面駕駛的太空人，因輕型電池控制之漫遊車前輪無法運作，阿波羅15號小組僅能以後輪行駛於月球表面－英國－百艘拖網漁船自南岸及東岸沿泰晤士河航至英國國會以抗議漁獲量限制政策－孤獨的英國遊艇愛好者裘伊・布萊斯爵士繞航世界一周－安迪・沃荷於倫敦泰特美術館展出作品－**電影**－《發條橘子》－《威尼斯之死》－路易斯・阿姆斯壯辭世－伊格爾・史特拉文斯基辭世。

1971

THE CHAMELEON AND THE PALM TREE

Bournemouth Steps was a developer's competition and the Summer Casino projects were also designed in competition both external and internal. Archigram made two projects for this facility, which had to include gambling rooms, a night club, a restaurant and an events space known as the Gala Hall. The present building contains such a space which is really a trelliswork able to absorb a quick change of surface styling and event. The whole thing is very much open to the air and the sea.

We designed the two versions, one with the symbol of the chameleon and one with the symbol of the palm tree. The chameleon representing the notion of frequent change of atmosphere and the palm tree calling attention to the slightly unreal atmosphere of a select club out on a flat promontory in the Mediterranean. In both schemes the mounding and softening of natural landscape and designed elements and mechanised elements was at once obvious and – on second glance – ambiguous. These schemes represent a continuation of the Bournemouth Steps thinking but are perhaps simpler and more gentle.

SPORTING D'ETE MONTE CARLO
夏日運動 蒙地卡羅
變色龍與棕櫚樹

「波茅斯梯階」是開發商的競圖案,而「夏日賭場」設計案亦是為了一項國內外競圖所設計。「建築電訊」為這個必須包含賭博室、夜總會、餐廳與一個做為娛樂廳之活動空間的設備完成了兩個設計案。目前的建築物包含了這樣的空間,實際上它是一個能夠吸收外表型式與活動之快速變化的格架構造。整個物體充分地對戶外與海洋開放。

我們設計了兩種版本,一個具有變色龍的象徵,另一個具有棕櫚樹的象徵。變色龍代表頻繁之氣氛改變的概念,而棕櫚樹則引人注意到地中海中升起的平坦岬角上突起的一座上流社會俱樂部的些許虛幻氣氛。在這兩個計劃中,自然景觀均呈現小丘化與軟化,且設計性元素與機械性元素乍看之下十分明顯,然而第二眼望去卻又十分模稜兩可。這些方案代表了「波茅斯梯階」想法的延續,但也許更簡單些且更溫和些。

SALLE

UX AMBIANCE GENERALE. PLAN N° 31

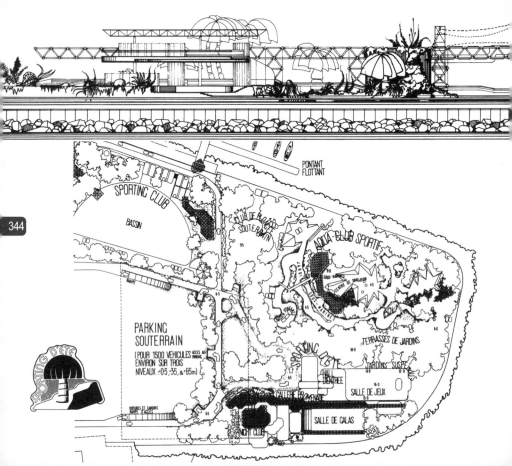

SPORTING CLUB

BASSIN

PONTANT FLOTTANT

CLUB DE PLONGÉ SOUTERRAIN

AQUA-CLUB SPORTIF

SOUS-MARINS
CENTRE DE SIMULATION

PARKING
SOUTERRAIN

(POUR 1500 VEHICULES ACCÈS AU
ENVIRON SUR TROIS
NIVEAUX : -0.5 , -3.5 , & -6.5m)

SPORTING D'ÉTÉ

TERRASSES DE JARDINS

JARDINS SUSPE

HAL
D'ENTRÉE

SALLE DE JEUX

VOITURES ET CAMIONS
RAMPE D'ACCÈS

GALERIE PROMENADE

NIGHT CLUB

SALLE DE GALAS

SPORTING D'ÉTÉ

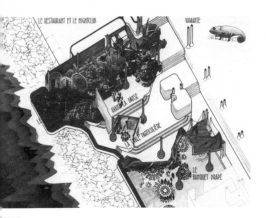

LE RESTAURANT ET LE NIGHTCLUB

VARIANTE

AVANT LA DANSE

ISOLE PARTICULIÈRE

LE BANQUET DRAPÉ

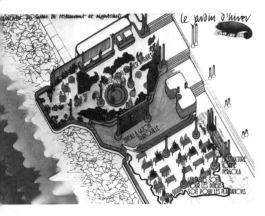

le jardin d'hiver

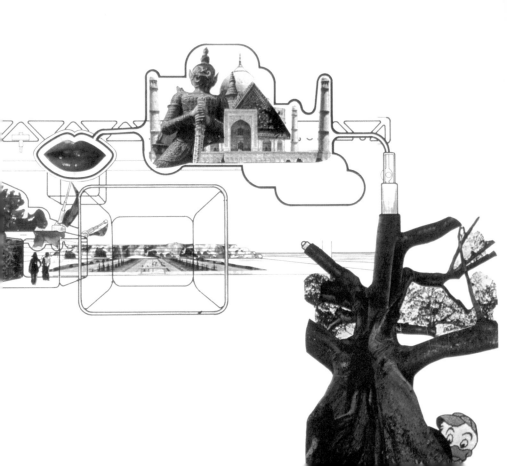

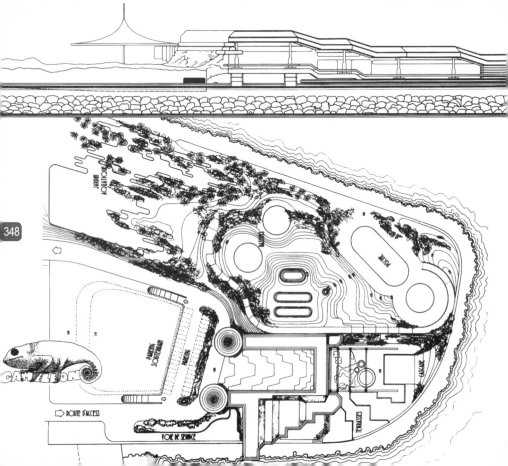

348

towards a **Q**uietly **T**echnologised **F**olk **S**uburbia

CRATER CITY AND HEDGEROW VILLAGE
KRATERSTADT UND HECKENDORF

Peter Cook

邁向一個寂靜科技化庶民郊區
坑洞城市與樹籬村落

彼得・庫克

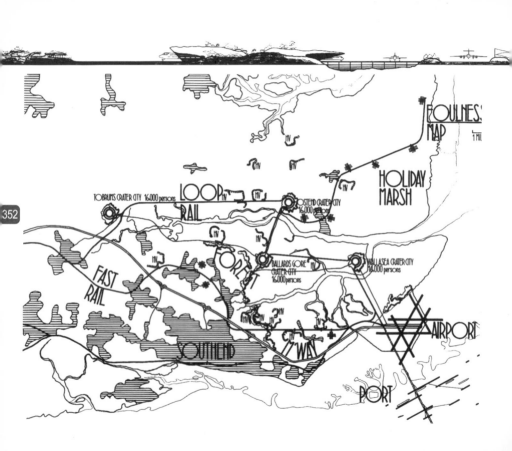

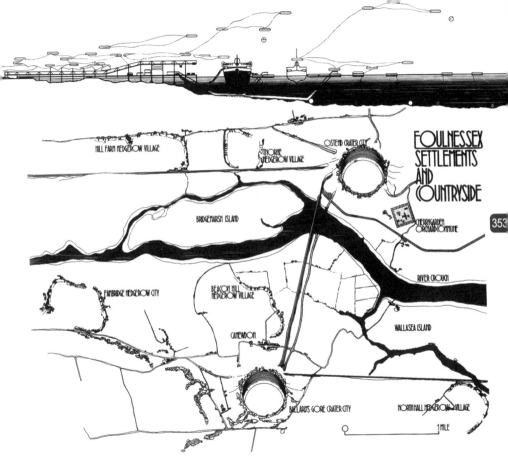

FOULNESSEX
SETTLEMENTS
AND
COUNTRYSIDE

HILL FARM HEDGEROW VILLAGE

THORNE HEDGEROW VILLAGE

OSTEND CRATER CITY

CHERRY GARDEN ORCHARD COMMUNE

BRIDGEMARSH ISLAND

RIVER CROUCH

FAMBRIDGE HEDGEROW CITY

BEACON HILL HEDGEROW VILLAGE

CANEWDON

WALLASEA ISLAND

BALLARD'S GORE CRATER CITY

NORTH HALL HEDGEROW VILLAGE

1 MILE

353

The **CRATER CITY** and the **HEDGEROW VILLAGE** are two parts of a strategy for the hinterland to the new Foulness Airport. Instead of building an 'airport city' we propose to provide either of two extreme suburb types. The 'crater city' would be virtually a hotel for 16,000 people, with carpeted corridors, a very high level of servicing, and air-conditioned apartments. It would have an outer wall which is a conservatory so that in summer the apartments would become one-third bigger and in winter the two skins that sandwich the conservatory would insulate the apartments. The

WHAT IS HAPPENING BEHIND THE HEDGEROWS?

'crater city' looks inward onto a large, impeccably mown lawn a third of a mile across. This whole city is a circular crater and the outside of the circle is earth-banked up like a prehistoric mound with a ring of trees planted on the top. Nothing would be seen except this hill with trees.

The 'hedgerow village', by contrast, is a surreptitious development which is progressively fed into narrow strips alongside large fields. Each village would be imperceptible from the country lane. Each village would permit the implanting of a very wide range of dwelling types from 'architected' houses to wayfarers with sleeping bags and spanning through lean-tos, inflatable tents, caravans, etc. – a deliberately relaxed and ramshackle combination/conglomeration.

Some ADDHOX elements

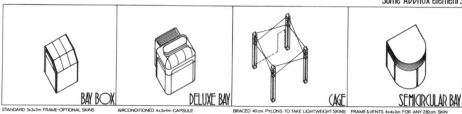

BAY BOX — STANDARD 3x3x3m FRAME-OPTIONAL SKINS

DELUXE BAY — AIRCONDITIONED 4x3x4m CAPSULE

CAGE — BRACED 40cm PYLONS TO TAKE LIGHTWEIGHT SKINS

SEMICIRCULAR BAY — FRAME & VENTS 4x4x3m FOR ANY 230cm SKIN

THE POSSIBILITY OF CASUAL DWELLINGS

SOFTER   OR   HARDER

「坑洞城市」與「樹籬村落」是新浮爾尼斯機場腹地策略中的兩個主要部份。我們並不打算建造一座「機場城市」，而是建議提供兩種極端郊區類型的其中之一。「坑洞城市」實際上是一座可容納1萬6000人的旅館，備有鋪設地毯的廊道、極高水準的服務設施與裝有空調設備的公寓。它有一道可構成一間溫室的外牆，因此夏天時公寓將增大三分之一，而冬天時夾住溫室的兩層殼板將可隔絕公寓。「坑洞城市」的內部面向一大片橫越三分之一哩長由乾草堆積的完美草坪。整座城市是一個環狀的坑洞，且環形的外部是土堆堤，就像過去頂端種著一圈樹木的小土墩。除了這座植樹的小丘之外什麼也看不到。

「樹籬村落」，相反地，是一個秘密式的發展結果，沿著一大片曠野漸漸地融入狹長的基地。每座村落都無法自鄉間小道上察覺到。每座村落都允許植入包羅廣泛的居住類型，自「建築師型」房屋至攜著睡袋的旅者，一直到單斜面屋頂小屋、充氣式帳篷、拖車屋……等，一種刻意的鬆懈與搖搖欲墜的組合體／複合體。

PEEPING FROM THE TREES. CONCEALED UNDERGROUND. OR EXPLKIT !

no dividing line between home in a paper sleeping bag and the sophistication of the Farnsworth House : between one night and ten years : give the edge of a field service lines....under discreet outlets....and let it happen

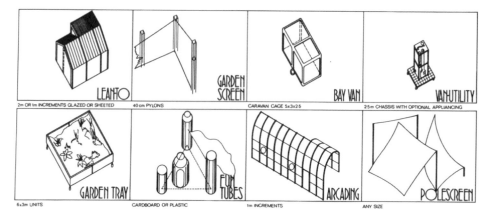

356

LEANTO — 2m OR 1m INCREMENTS GLAZED OR SHEETED

GARDEN SCREEN — 40 cm PYLONS

BAY VAN — CARAVAN CAGE 5x3x2.5

VANUTILITY — 2.5m CHASSIS WITH OPTIONAL APPLIANCING

GARDEN TRAY — 6x3m UNITS

FUM TUBES — CARDBOARD OR PLASTIC

ARCADING — 1m INCREMENTS

POLESCREEN — ANY SIZE

THE ANATOMY OF THE "HEDGEROW VILLAGE" CAN BE DETERMINED

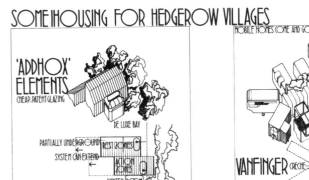

Left panel:

SPRINKLES BEACON
HARDER HOUSING
LANE
OUTLETS
DISCREET OUTLETS SUCH AS
MORE PLUG-OLES
'STUMP PLUGS'
TENTS, SHACKS.
OR WHATEVER
'FROG PLUGS'
NESTLES AGAINST THE HEDGEROW
FIELD
'ROK PLUGS'

Right panel:

FORMAL
CASUAL

AND INTERPRETED IN A RELAXED WAY

SOME HOUSING FOR HEDGEROW VILLAGES

Left panel:

'ADDHOX' ELEMENTS
CHEAP, PATENT GLAZING
DE LUXE BAY
PARTIALLY UNDERGROUND
SYSTEM CAN EXTEND
REST ZONES
ACTION ZONES
WINTER ROOM
○ 10 M. PLAN

Right panel:

MOBILE HOMES COME AND GO
FINGER FACILITIES MAKE FOR THAT *EXTRA* COMFORT
VANFINGER
VENDORS
CRECHE
KITCHEN
BATHS
PLAN ○ 10 M.

TOUCH NOT *the shoulder of the knight*

who passes. He would turn and it would be night, a night without stars, without arc or clouds. What then would become of all that makes the sky, the moon in its passage and the sound of the sun? You would have to wait until a second knight as powerful as the first consented to pass. On such an expectancy rests a large part of the fantasy in science fiction. The co-existence of interlinked and separate notions, and the hazard, the improbable hazard of passing from one notion, from one set of ideas, to another and back again along the protracted time scale of the now.

To the silent awareness the skinny cat is all cat, the very essence of cat. Its sneaky feline motions are of a piece, speaking directly to the consciousness in soundless tones of all that cat means, of cat in past, present, future. The eternal cat. And even buildings, they have less to say than cats, but they communicate. They almost turn themselves inside out in their eagerness to share secrets. They tell of the men that made them, the beings that dwell in them. They portray a whole history of architecture, but without words, without discourse.

358

We seem to have found the art of suspended time. What we said ten years ago we are saying today, repeating the same recurrent episode, the same series of events as a stylus caught in the groove. What we must look for now is the linkage of the simultaneous and not the vista of the successive. A self-scan display system reveals a discreet trauma, the glow on each side of the cathode transfers itself to the understanding that life systems are important, that they really matter. The seed packet in *Archigram 9* is available. Great. The problem is discovering some fertile ground in which to plant these seeds. And beware of the creeping slugs. Apparently the path of events has been deflected from its original direction. We have discovered something – technological backlash. And bargain-hunters for tomorrow are reluctantly tuning down their electronic cycle environmental equipment of events. The electric last minute no longer thrills. But dare we face the source of our own negation? Could it be technocratic society? Everyone is too giddy to notice. Everyone? Well, not quite. The very sense men have of reality, the wisdom of insecurity, the search for the miraculous is still there.

Ecology – there, I've said that word – is a social problem. We have been told so by *Time, Life, Newsweek, Look* and the Nixon administration. Pollution is insidiously growing. Either the environment goes or we go. And you all know what will happen if the environment goes. We have produced a society with production for the sake of production. The city has become a market place, every human being a commodity. Nature is a resource. Human beings are a resource. Well. Our very survival depends on an ecological utopia, otherwise we will be destroyed.

This technological backlash we are experiencing must be fought with a more sophisticated technology, a more sophisticated science. Present beautiful chemistry has turned out as not so beautiful biology. But if we are to prevent eco-catastrophe it can only be done by more sophisticated environmental systems, not by dropping out. Nor the hippy type philosophy. Did you see Drop City in 'Easy Rider'? Every man his own tree, an acre to till. Let's face it, total dispersal won't work economically any more than total centralisation. Apart from being a head-in-the-sand attitude we need to fight technology, to produce David Greene's cybernetic forest. Too simplistic translations of technology average out people's lives. What we look for is technological play, so that individuals can create an even greater environmental stimulation. A person switched on to the Electronic Tomato, or the proud possessor of the personalised robot like Manzak, can extend an existing situation, and a new man/machine relationship be established getting people, through their extension with a machine, into action.

Experiments such as these could achieve a people-oriented technology of human liberation, directed towards pleasure, enjoyment, experimentation: a try-it-and-see attitude.

Synthetic environments are something different. Synthetic experience is not better or worse, just different, than that from the natural environment. But let's have it all. At Woodstock Music Festival you got both – a field turned on, a three-day city, half a million young people: the only hardware, mind-blowing amplification. Beautiful. On the brink of the 70s a whole new era can be seen to be opening up. Man has jumped up and down on the moon and in the streets. Students have laid down at Woodstock and Hyde Park and on campus. Some, unfortunately, for the last time. Among all the conflicting ideas, all these divergent opinions, none seems more important at this time than creating a humane environment Life systems, trees, plants, flowers, animals, birds and man himself, are fantastically responsive mechanisms. Mechanical systems, including the goop and ticky-tacky with which we construct the man-made environment, have always been less so: with little ability to respond. But our search for adaptive systems should have a prime objective, to produce an environment to which the ordinary individual at any level of intensity can reconcile himself without the intolerable effort and stress of his own mental and physical adaptation. We must continue to try to establish appropriate systems for a natural relationship between life systems and mechanical systems. Hopefully some environmental magic will then prevail and we will again think up the impossible in order to be realistic.

* A packet of seeds was inserted in each copy of *Archigram 9*.

70年暑期由華倫・裴克提出，發表於1971年4月號《建築設計》雜誌

別碰

經過騎士的肩膀。他會一個轉身然後就變成一個沒有星星、沒有天宇或雲朵的夜晚。那構成蒼穹的一切，如月亮的運行與旭日的東昇，將會變得如何呢？您將必須等候與第一位騎士一樣強而有力的第二位騎士答應經過這裡時才知道。如此之期待裡的大部分奇想寄託於科幻小說之中。同時存在有相互連結與單獨之念頭，以及偶然性，某種允許自一種念頭與一連串構想轉移至其它想法且反之亦可之不大可能的偶然性。

概念上來說，瘦削的貓兒終究還是隻貓兒，不折不扣的貓兒。它鬼祟的貓科動物動作就像是同一個模子裡出來的一樣，以過去、現在與未來的貓兒們慣有之沉默聲調直接與意識進行交談。不朽的貓兒。而建築物也會說話，或許比貓兒話少，但它們懂得溝通。在分享秘密的渴望中，它們幾乎已徹底地開誠佈公了。它們道出了建造者、居住者。它們描寫了整段建築史，但不利用文字、不利用推論。

360

我們似乎找到了懸滯時間的巧術。我們正說著我們十年前曾說過的事，重複相同的周期性插曲，相同的連續性事件，如同唱片跳針一般。我們現在必須追尋的是同時性的連結而非連續性的設想。當自我診斷系統察覺出隱藏的創傷，陰極兩端的閃光自我轉換以領悟生命體系價值的重要性，知悉它們的確收關緊要。《建築電訊》第9期裡的種子包裹可以利用。*太棒了。問題正發現一些可以播撒這些種子的肥沃土地。要謹防那些葡匐潛行的行動遲緩無力者。似乎事件的軌道已經偏離了原來的方向。我們發現了一些事——科技的反動。而未來的冒險家逐步不情願地移走他們的事件電子循環環境設備。電子產品不再是最時髦的了。但我們敢正視我們自己突然不安的原因嗎？它可能是科技專家政治的社會嗎？每個人都太暈頭轉向而注意不到。每個人嗎？嗯，不盡然。極端理性者對於現實具有不安全感的睿智，對於驚奇的追尋仍依舊持續。

生態環境——瞧！我曾提過這個字眼——是個社會性問題。《時代雜誌》、《生活雜誌》、《新聞週刊》、《看雜誌》與尼克森政府全都如此地告訴我們。污染正暗中地增加。不是環境完蛋就是我們完蛋。而您們都知道若環境完蛋將會發生什麼事。我們創造了一個為了生產而生產的社會。城市成了市集廣場，每個人都是商品。自然是一種資源。總之，我們的生存仰賴一個生態環境的烏托邦，否則我們將被毀滅。

集廣場，每個人都是商品。自然是一種資源。總之，我們的生存仰賴一個生態環境的烏托邦，否則我們將被摧毀。

這種我們正經歷的科技反動必須以一種更複雜的科技與一種更精密的科學與之對抗。當前美好的化學已經變成不怎麼美好的生物學。但若我們想避免生態災難的話，唯有藉由更複雜精密的環境系統才能達成，而非放棄退出，抑或仰賴嬉痞式哲學。您看過《逍遙騎士》電影中的「滴城」嗎？每個人有自己的一株喬樹與一英畝耕地。面對現實吧，全然分散不再比完全集中更能經濟地運作。除開迴避現實的態度，我們必須與科技對抗，必須創造大衛 • 葛林的人工智慧森林。科技的過分簡化轉換使人們的生活達到一般水準。我們所追尋的是科技遊戲，如此一來個人可以創造一種更佳的環境刺激。連接至「電子蕃茄」的人，或是如「寵物機器人」之個人化自動裝置的驕傲擁有者，均可延伸目前的情境，而一種新的人／機器的關係得以建立，透過機器產生的延伸而使人開始行動。

像這樣的實驗，可以完成人類解放之人類導向性科技，邁向歡愉、享樂與實驗：一種「試試看會如何」的態度。

人造環境是不一樣的東西。人造經驗不特別好或特別差，只是不一樣，與自然環境的經驗不一樣。但，同時擁有二者如何！？在胡士托音樂節裡您二者皆有—— 一片接通開關的曠野、一座3天的城市、50萬年輕人；唯一的硬體設備，就是令人迷醉興奮的擴音器。太完美了。在70年代的邊緣，可見一個全新的時代正被開啓。人類在月球上與大街裡一上一下地跳躍。學生們躺在胡士托與海德公園以及校園裡。很不幸地，對有些人而言這是最後一次了。在所有的衝突性構想中，所有的這些分歧意見裡，此時似乎沒有任何一個想法比創造一個人性的環境更為重要。生命的體系、花、草、樹木、動物、鳥類與人類自己，都是出色的感應式機械裝置。機械系統，包括我們用以構築人造環境的黏糊接著劑與廉價次等建材，始終不具太大的回應能力。但我們對於具適應性之系統的探索應該具有一個首要的目標，即創造出一個任何強度水平之一般個體均能毫無心理或身體適應上無法承受的努力與壓力而得到滿足的環境。我們必須持續嘗試建立一個生命體系與機械體系間之自然關係的適當系統。順利的話，某種環境的魔力屆時將普及而我們將再度想出難以實現之藉口以切合實際。

★ *每份《建築電訊》第9期裡都附有一袋種子。*

NOTES intended 1. to encourage a closer relationship between man; electronics and nature (as electronics gets more and more sophisticated, maybe man can become more and more primitive) and 2. to make illegal the construction of any new building – a declared moratorium on building, a search for

備忘錄：意圖1，鼓勵人與電子學及自然間更緊密的關係（當電子學變得愈來愈精密複雜，或許人就可以變得愈來愈原始）；意圖2，使任何新建築物的興建變成非法——宣佈暫停建築物，追求

LAWUN Project No. 2,

THE INVISIBLE UNIVERSITY
不可見大學，「地區性可利用之全球不可見聯絡網」設計案2號

Photograph 1　　　　　　　　　　　照片 1

The symbiosis between man and nature is well known. The symbiosis has been extended in this picture to include electronics, which could be any group in concert.

There is a circuit:
conceive
play
response

The relationship established by the 'musicians' with the gear is symbiotic. This could equally be a picture of an intensive learning situation – the output from the gear dependent on how it is 'played' and the 'progress' related to the responses of the 'player' (and the class). The concert and the class are the same, only the messages change.

人與大自然間的共生關係眾所皆知。此共生關係在這張圖片中被延伸包含了電子學，可能是任何正在舉辦音樂會的樂團。

有一個電路：
構思
演奏
回應

「音樂家」與樂器所建立的關係是共生的。這可能與密集學習的情況一樣——樂器的輸出端賴它如何被「演奏」以及與「演奏者」（和班級學生）之反應有關的「進步」。音樂會與上課其實是一樣的，只是訊息改變了。

Out of the building and into the field – concert in a field or university in a field, the building behind could be a hardware store. Like a discarded automobile, rusting and weed-grown, the formal relationship between hardware and landscape is not designed. Learning and 'playing' your gear in the grass.

Photograph 2

照片 2

走出建築物步入田野——野地裡的音樂會或野地裡的大學，其背後的建築物可能是個硬體倉庫。就像被拋棄的汽車，鏽蝕且雜草叢生，硬體與景觀的形式關係並未被設計。在草地裡學習並「演奏」你的樂器。

The juxtaposition of this fridge against the landscape has nice aesthetic overtones – it might be a grocery store in a bush, a service point eliminating the building – it's just lying about, no fuss, no 'landscaping', no grids or megastructures. It's waiting to be used.

這座冰箱置於景觀中具有極佳的美學弦外之音——可能是間灌木叢裡的雜貨店，一個除去了建築物的服務據點——它就擱置著，沒有焦躁，沒有「造景」，沒有格柵或超大型結構。它等著被使用。

Photograph 4

A servicing frame in a field waiting to be used or built upon. Very concentrated. The nearest thing to a village or town or building that should be allowed.

照片 4

野地裡的服務性構架等著被使用或搭建。十分集中。最靠近村落、城鎮或建築物所該考慮到的東西。

Photograph 5

These marks on the ground are the building or traces of the visible university. They mark out the territory. They could be seen as catalysts for the symbiosis. This is where the writer is not sure what is going on. We obviously need hardware at the moment, but we obviously confine its uses by pre-electric life-styles and constraints. This picture might have something to do with what it could be – how the development of electronics will displace the building.

照片5

這些地上的記號是不可見大學的建築物或痕跡。它們劃出領域。它們可視為共生的觸媒。這正是作者所不確定是怎麼回事之處。此刻我們顯然需要硬體設備，但顯然地我們因先前的電力生活型態與約束而限制了它的使用。這張照片或許與其可能的結果——電子學的發展如何取代建築物——有關。

The artist: Sally Hodgson

The artist's intention: Unknown to the author

The author's intention: To suggest to the reader that this picture contains information relevant to the architect, and to show to the reader this borrowed picture because it seems to have certain areas of correspondence to certain dreams of the author. The author's dreams that seemingly correspond to the artist's photograph can be described in quotation format....... 'I was looking at some photographs of the work of Richard Long – mowed marks in large areas of grass – and they appeared as works of architecture although I had previously been informed that they were intended to be read as works of art. I was interested as to why they seemed to be works of architecture.

'I was similarly puzzled by the photograph. What are these lines? Are they the residue of some departed building, are they the plotted routes in space of a temperature gradient, are they the territorial limits (like the lines marking out a football pitch) of some environment yet to take place? What information exists within these lines, how far does it extend beyond them and in what direction and is it available for my use? I can see in my mind a picture of a nomad and within the pocket of his long-haired coat rests a television device, his life previously only interwoven with the electronic environment, but both exist together, one does not replace the other, both together produce a new environment, an electronic aborigine. Perhaps this long-haired-coat man understands these lines and also the marks of Richard Long. He has learned to weave his life almost chameleon-like into his environments.

'Like the guerrilla he makes a lot out of his minimal hardware. The development of electronics has allowed him to be a well-serviced primitive – a ridiculous thought maybe, but it is equally ridiculous to continually use electronics as a device for supporting industrial revolution life-styles (and hence an "architecture' to service these life-styles).'

366

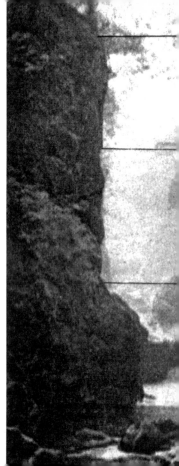

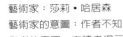

照片6

藝術家：莎莉・哈居森
藝術家的意圖：作者不知
作者的意圖：向讀者提示這張圖片包含了與建築師有關的資訊，並將這張
借用的圖片呈現給讀者因為它似乎有某些地方與作者的某些夢想吻合。作
者的夢想中似乎與藝術家的照片相吻合之處可以引語的方式描述出來：
「……我看著理察・隆作品中的一些照片——一大片草皮上的收割痕跡—
—它們看起來有如建築的作品，雖然之前有人曾告訴過我它們應該以藝術
作品的角度被閱讀。我對於為何它們看起來像是建築作品十分感興趣。」
「我同樣地對於照片感到些許困惑。這些線條是什麼呢？它們是某些過去建
築物的殘餘嗎？它們是溫度變化曲線在空間裡的標定路線嗎？它們是某些
尚未發生之環境的區域範圍（就像足球的罰球線嗎）？這些線條之中存在
了什麼訊息呢？它們可以延伸至多遠並朝向何方呢？而且，我可以利用它
們嗎？我可以在心裡看見一幅流浪者的畫面，在他的嬉痞式外套裡放著一
台電視裝置，他過去只與自然環境交錯一起的生活現在也必須與電子環境
交織在一起，但是兩者同時存在，彼此無法取代，二者一起共同創造了一
個新的環境，一個電子土著。」
「就像游擊隊隊員一樣，他將最少的硬體設備做了最充分的利用。電子的發
展允許他成為一個配備完整的原始人——也許是個荒謬的想法，但是繼續
將電子學運用於維持工業革命時期之生活型態的裝置上亦同樣地可笑（因
此需要某種「建築」以滿足這些生活型態的需求）。」

Arab terrorists kill eleven Israeli athletes at Olympic Games in Munich — Israeli commandos rescue 92 hi-jack victims at Entebbe — Rome Michelangelo's Pietà damaged by maniac — UK – Miners strike for seven weeks — US – FBI Director J. Edgar Hoover dies — Duke of Windsor dies in Paris — 350 Soviet Jews emigrate to Israel — UK – Poet Cecil Day Lewis dies — US – Watergate scandal — Ex-President Perón returns to Argentina after 17 years — Vietnam War nears its end — John Betjeman becomes new Poet Laureate — Chi-Chi the Giant Panda dies at London Zoo — Britain joins the European Community — World's first pocket calculator designed and manufactured in Britain by Clive Sinclair — THEATRE – Lloyd Webber's musical 'Jesus Christ Superstar' — FILM – 'The Godfather'

阿拉伯恐怖份子於慕尼黑奧運殺害11名以色列運動員－以色列突擊隊於恩特比解救92名遭劫持人質－羅馬米開朗基羅作品《聖母慟子》遭瘋漢破壞－英國－礦工罷工7週－美國－聯邦調查局局長艾得格‧胡佛辭世－溫莎公爵於巴黎辭世－350名蘇俄猶太人移民以色列－英國－詩人瑟希‧戴‧路易斯辭世－美國－水門事件醜聞－阿根廷前總統裴隆結束17年的流亡生涯返回祖國－越戰接近尾聲－英國約翰‧班傑明成為新桂冠詩人－倫敦動物園大貓熊奇奇死亡－英國加入歐洲經濟共同體－克里夫‧辛克萊於英國設計製造全球首部口袋型計算機－**戲劇**－洛伊‧韋伯的音樂劇《萬世巨星》－**電影**－《教父》。

URBAN MARK

A Study in Disintegration and Metamorphosis

Peter Cook

都市地標 「分解」與「變形」的研究

彼得・庫克

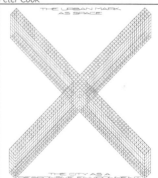

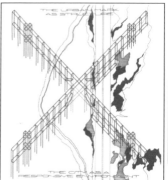

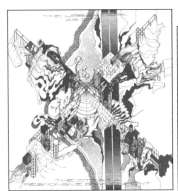

towards a **Q**uietly **T**echnologised **F**olk **S**uburbia 邁向一個安靜科技化庶民郊區
ORCHARD PLACE 果園廣場

Peter Cook 彼得・庫克

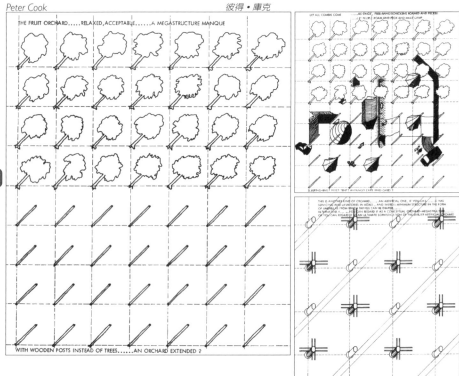

THE FRUIT ORCHARD.....RELAXED, ACCEPTABLE.....A MEGASTRUCTURE MANQUE

WITH WOODEN POSTS INSTEAD OF TREES.....AN ORCHARD EXTENDED ?

LET ALL COMERS COME.....................AS ONCE, FREE-RANGING CHICKENS ROAMED AND PECKED
.....SO PEOPLE ROAM AND PECK AND MAKE CAMP

SLEEPING-BAG? RIDGE TENT? AWNING? EASY CAMP WHO CARES ?

THIS IS ANOTHER KIND OF ORCHARD.....AN ARTIFICIAL ONE, IF YOU LIKE.....IT HAS SERVICING AND LAVATORIES IN ROWS.....AND SHELTERS: MINIMUM STRUCTURE IN THE FORM OF UMBRELLAS FROM WHICH THINGS CAN BE DRAPED.....
ALTERNATIVELY YOU CAN REGARD IT AS A CONCEPTUAL ORCHARD-MEGASTRUCTURE.....
OR YOU CAN REGARD IT AS AN ULTIMATE SOPHISTICATION OF THE EARLIER ARTIFICIAL ORCHARD

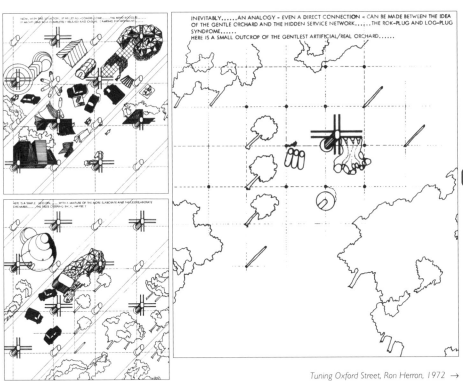

Tuning Oxford Street, Ron Herron, 1972 →

調頻牛津街，朗・赫倫，1972年 →

TUNING LONDON
Ron Herron

調頻倫敦
朗·赫倫

It's a . . .

Ron Herron

SHIT – The label's come off. The sign's down. What is it – it was a conference arena last May / a tuned-for-sound concert happened for three days in August / September it was full of guys and their birds cooking, eating, sleeping, fooling around, and generally living the good life / last week it was full of people, cars and the painful scream of stripduster, hounddog and the Chrysler rail as they belted down the quarter mile straight-burn out for grabs / tomorrow it's a . . .

Let's leave the label off for Christsake – let the sheep back in – the grass needs cutting.

Hang on though – we don't want to upset the sheep – let's put the old label up – for today it's a meadow . . . what's in a label anyway? The action comes and goes. The servicing goes too, on your back, in your car, on your truck. In your trailer, in your minds. The architecture of the invisible. What's in a label anyway? It's a . . .

Take the label off a can of beans and what have you got – a can of beans. Take the label off a can of soup and put the beans label on it, and what have you got – a can of beans? No . . . a can of soup. Space and time and servicing condition use and activity – labels condition nothing but your mind.

'"It's a poor sort of memory that only works backwards," the Queen remarked' (*Through the Looking Glass*). 'The Failure of the Modern Movement to establish an architectural language for public buildings is a reflection of a much wider confusion of what public life is about.' (Quote from *RIBA Journal*)

FLASH !

A select committee will be set up to study the potential architectural language for . . . public baths – public houses – public conveniences, etc., etc. . . . yeah, I'm widely confused – what is public life about anyway, and what's architectural language? . . . You can always put a label on a building . . . you can have a label so that when people arrive they know what they are in for, you could do even better that, you could have a typed description – like they have in front of the cages in the zoo . . . but then the animals don't know what they are in for.

'The Metropolis today is a classroom: the ads are its teachers.' 'The traditional classroom is an obsolete detention home, a feudal dungeon.' (Marshall McLuhan, *Counterblast*)

It's not a university – it can't be . . . show me, where's the building. Where's the label? I have to sit in the comfort of my own home with the telly or radio on to be a part of it, with an occasional chat with my tutor in the local drill hall. That's not a university, a university is a lot of buildings and a lot of people milling around on bicycles . . . come on. The Open University asks that you are 21 (pity, why not 16?) or over and have the energy to fill in the application form. Of course there is a mandatory one-week resi-

它是﹒﹒﹒﹒﹒﹒

朗‧赫倫

該死——標籤掉下來了。標誌掉了。那是什麼——那是去年5月的一場研討會／一場在8月舉行了3天的演奏會／9月裡擠滿了一群嬉痞與他們的甜心在做菜、吃飯、睡覺、鬼混，大體上過得還不錯／上個星期擠滿了一堆人、汽車，以及四分之一哩追逐賽跑車呼嘯而過時所產生之震耳欲聾的刺耳聲音／明天它是……

看在老天的份上我們就別再管標籤了吧——讓羊群回來吧——草也該鋤一鋤了！

不過不要放棄——我們不想叨擾羊群——我們還是把舊標籤貼上吧——因為今天它是一片牧場……標籤到底是什麼呀？活動來來去去變化不定。設施也會跑到您的背上、您的車子裡、您的卡車上、您的拖車屋裡、您的心裡。不可見的建築。標籤裡到底是什麼呀？它是……

撕掉豆子罐頭的標籤之後您還有什麼呢——一罐豆子。撕掉一罐湯的標籤之後再把豆子標籤貼上去，之後您還有什麼呢——一罐豆子嗎？不……是一罐湯才對。空間與時間以及設施決定了使用方式與活動——而標籤所能決定的不過是您的想法罷了！

「『只能延遲運作是極差的記憶力。』女王說」（透過魔鏡）（譯註）

「現代運動為公共建築建立一種建築語彙的失敗，是對於何謂公共生活之更偏離的混淆之反映。」（引述自英國《皇家建築師協會學報》）

靈機一動！

將成立一個傑出精選的委員會以研究……公共浴室－國民住宅－公共設施……等的可能性建築語彙……是的，我十分地混淆不清——到底什麼是公共生活，什麼是建築語彙呢？……您隨時可以在一棟建築物上貼上標籤……您可以有一個標籤，如此一來，當人們抵達之後他們就會知道他們究竟來這裡做什麼，更棒的是，您甚至可

ITS ALL ROTHEROE'S ARCHIGRAM JAMSAI

以貼上說明——就像動物園獸籠前的那種……只不過……動物們始終不知道，它們究竟在這裡做什麼。

「今日的大都會是一間教室；廣告是它的老師。」

「傳統的教室是過時的拘留所，是封建時期的地牢。」（馬歇爾•麥克魯漢於《強烈反駁》中指出）

它不是一所大學——它不可能是……告訴我，建築物在那兒，標籤在那兒？我必須舒適地坐在自己的家裡打開電視或收音機，並偶而前往地方的講堂與我的指導老師討論。那不是一所大學，一所大學是一堆建築物與一堆人騎著自行車四處兜著圈子……得了吧。空中大學要求您得年齡超過21歲（真可惜，為何不是16歲呢？）並有能力填寫申請表格。當然會有個為期一週的義務性暑期校內實習提供給2萬5000名大學部的學生——而這當然會在某種圍蔽物裡舉行並呈現，至少為期一週，某種大學的形體化。但倘若某些怪人將它置於帆布、紙睡袋、野營氣墊或其它類似東西之下呢……它是？

「藉由避開校內設施的龐大花費，英國人設法將空中大學前5年營運的資金預算控制為只有1440萬美元——其中大部份將投入位於倫敦市郊50哩處的白金漢郡大學中心建設」（《新聞週刊》，1971年1月25日）

又來了，我知道這會有某種大學的形體化，一棟我們可以貼上標籤——大學——的結構物。不過，等等，它是一個行政中心——沒有學生、沒有大學服、沒有學生會、沒有社團與學生宿舍。我們無法貼上標籤……而且就空中大學、不可見大學……程式／輸入／控制／貯藏／處理／輸出……之觀點而言的行政中心的建築語彙呢……它是？

人們促進活動——活動決定使用——設施回應活動＋使用——時間決定一切——今天還在那兒明天就離開了。

「在『依莉莎白女王2世郵輪』上您可能完全無法與外界取得聯繫。抑或是，倘若您喜歡的話，船上的電傳打字機、電話、電報與圖片傳送機設

dential summer school session for the 25,000 undergraduates – surely this will take place in an enclosure of some description and give, for a week at least. some physical manifestation of university. But supposing some nut puts it under canvas, paper sleeping bags, PNU's or the like . . . It's a?

'By side-stepping the mammoth cost of establishing a residential program, the British have managed to hold the capital budget for Open U's first five years of operation to only $14.4 million – most of which will be devoted to the construction of the University Center in Buckinghamshire, 50 miles outside London' (*Newsweek*, Jan. 25 1971).

There we go, I knew there would be some physical manifestation of university, a piece of architecture on to which we can hang the label – university. Hold on, though, it's an administrative centre – no students, no caps and gowns, no student's union, no colleges and no halls of residence. We can't attach the label . . . and what about the architectural language. What is an administrative centre in terms of the Open U, the invisible university . . . program / input / control / storage / processing / output . . . It's a?

People promote activity – activity conditions use – servicing responds to activity + use – time conditions all – here today, gone tomorrow.

'On the QE2 you can be totally inaccessible to the rest of the world. Or, if you prefer, the ship's telex, telephone, telegram and picture transmission service are at your disposal 24 hours a day. Lift the phone, and shorthand typists, dictaphones, conference rooms, recording facilities, film and slide projectors, screens, blackboards and printers, are all yours. Let us know and we'll even arrange simultaneous translation equipment for you.'

Is it an administrative centre? A university? Government centre? . . . A ship? . . . It's a?

'After work – or instead of it – QE2 offers you a West End-sized cinema, with three performances a day. Plus night clubs, the theatre bar, card rooms, libraries and four swimming pools. Not to mention sports decks, a turkish bath, sauna and gambling casino.'

Is it an entertainment centre? Soho? The Strip? . . . A ship? . . . It's a?

Sit and play cards – it's a cardroom? Call up a projector – it's a cinema? Drink with your friends – it's a bar? Sit at a typewriter – it's an office? Soak up information – it's education ? . . . Or wrap these up and it's an enclosure . . . Label the monument and it's architecture?

Goodyear has put eye-popping colour and cartoons in the sky and they call it 'Super Skytacular' night sign Columbia – more than 7,000 lights are mounted on the side of the company's airship, the Columbia. The lights spell out messages and animated cartoons in colour. The sign screen, on either side of the ship, is 105 feet long by 24.5 feet high. A typical six-minute tape consists of 40 million bits of 'on-off' information which, when run through electronic readers aboard the ship, control lamp and colour selection and the speed at which messages are run. It's an airship? It's an educational tool? It's entertaining, it's that, it's instant information . . . **It's a?**

施一天24小時全天候供您使用。只要拿起電話、速記打字機、口述錄音機、會議廳、影音攝錄裝備、影片與幻燈片放映機、銀幕、黑板與印表機，全都是您的。通知我們一聲即為您安排同步翻譯的設備。」

它是行政中心嗎？大學嗎？政府中樞機構嗎？……船嗎？……它是？

「下班後──或不上班時──『依莉莎白女王2世郵輪』提供您一座倫敦西區規模的電影院，每天播放3部影片。再加上夜總會、劇院酒吧、玩牌室、圖書館與4座游泳池。更別提還有郵輪休閒娛樂甲板、土耳其浴、三溫暖室與賭場了。」

它是娛樂中心嗎？蘇活區嗎？日落大道嗎？……船嗎？……它是？

坐下來玩牌－－它就是間玩牌室？用放映機播映──它就是間電影院？和您的朋友喝一杯──它就是間酒吧？坐在打字機前──它就是間辦公室？吸收資訊──它就是教育？……或者，將這些包裹好它就是個圍蔽物……將紀念性遺蹟貼上標籤它就是建築？

固特異公司將大眾流行色彩與卡通擺在天上然後他們就稱它為「超級空中奇觀」夜間信號哥倫比亞號──超過7000個發光體安裝在公司的飛船的側面。發光體詳細地傳達出訊息與彩色卡通影片。信號螢幕位於船的兩側，有105呎長、24.5呎高。典型的6分鐘錄影帶包含了4千萬位元的雙位資訊，當通過船上的電子讀數器時，控制著燈與色彩選擇以及訊息傳送的速度。它是一艘飛船嗎？它是一種教育的工具嗎？它是娛樂嗎──它是，它是即時資訊……**它是？**

譯註：摘錄自路易斯‧卡洛(Lewis Carroll)所著之《透過鏡子》
(Through the Looking Glass)。書中主角艾莉絲(Alice)對女王提到自己的記憶力不能雙向運作，無法於事情發生之前就記得它，於是女王回答：「只能追溯運作是極差的記憶力。」艾莉絲接著問道：「那麼您記得最清楚的是哪類事情呢？」女王漫不經心地回說：「噢！下下星期發生的事吧！」

Vietnam peace treaty signed in Paris — Ex US President Lyndon B. Johnson dies — Archbishop Makarios re-elected President of Cyprus — Native Americans take hostages at Wounded Knee — Greek Republic proclaimed with Papadopolous as President — 5,000 evacuated in Iceland after long-dormant volcano erupts — Last US troops quit Vietnam — US Skylab put into orbit — Watergate hearings begin — Oil billionaire Paul Getty's grandson kidnapped — London – cars bombed by IRA — Arab terrorists hijack US jet, killing 31 — Spanish Prime Minister Carrero Blanco assassinated — Yom Kippur War: Egypt and Syria attack Israel — Student riots in Athens — British writer JPR Tolkien dies — Pablo Picasso dies — Austrian scientist Konrad Lorenz wins Nobel Prize for Medicine — Noel Coward dies in Jamaica — FILM – 'The Sting' — Pulitzer Prize for Watergate journalists — THEATER – Peter Schaffer's 'Equus'.

越戰和平協議於巴黎簽訂－前美國總統林頓・班納斯・詹森辭世－大主教馬卡里歐斯當選塞浦路斯首任總統－美國印地安人於傷膝谷挾持人質－希臘共和國宣佈帕帕多普洛斯為總統－冰島蟄伏已久的火山爆發，5000人撤離－最後一批美軍撤出越南－美國太空實驗室被送入軌道－水門事件聽證會開始－石油鉅子保羅・蓋堤之孫遭綁架－倫敦－北愛爾蘭共和軍製造汽車炸彈－阿拉伯恐怖份子劫持美國噴射機並殺害31人－西班牙總理卡列羅・布蘭可遭暗殺－贖罪日戰爭：埃及與敘利亞攻擊以色列－雅典學生暴動－英國作家托爾金辭世－帕布羅・畢卡索辭世－奧地利科學家康拉德・羅倫茲獲頒諾貝爾醫學獎－全才藝人諾爾・科沃德於牙買加辭世－電影－《刺激》－普立茲獎頒與揭發水門事件記者－戲劇－彼得・謝弗的《戀馬狂》。

1973

INSTANT MALAYSIA

EXHIBITION, Commonwealth Institute
Dennis Crompton, Ron Herron

瞬間馬來西亞

展覽，大英國協會館

丹尼斯・克藍普頓、朗・赫倫

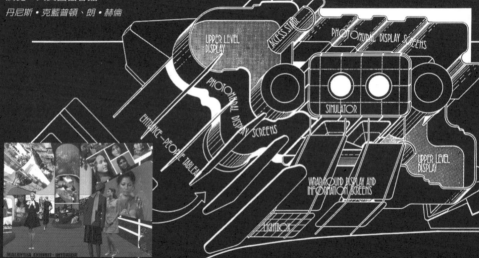

UPPER LEVEL DISPLAY

ACCESS STAIR

PHOTO-MURAL DISPLAY SCREENS

PHOTO-MURAL DISPLAY SCREENS

SIMULATOR

ENTRANCE – PEOPLE TABLEAU

WRAPAROUND DISPLAY AND INFORMATION SCREENS

UPPER LEVEL DISPLAY

LIGHTBOX

MALAYSIA EXHIBIT-INTERIOR

AXONOMETRIC

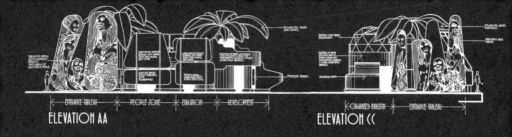

ELEVATION AA

ENTRANCE TABLEAU · PEOPLE ZONE · EDUCATION · DEVELOPMENT

ELEVATION CC

ORGANISED INDUSTRY · ENTRANCE TABLEAU

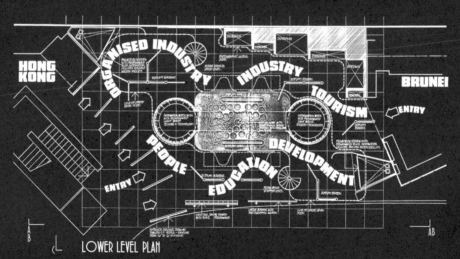

HONG KONG

ORGANISED INDUSTRY

INDUSTRY

TOURISM

BRUNEI

ENTRY

PEOPLE

DEVELOPMENT

ENTRY

EDUCATION

LOWER LEVEL PLAN

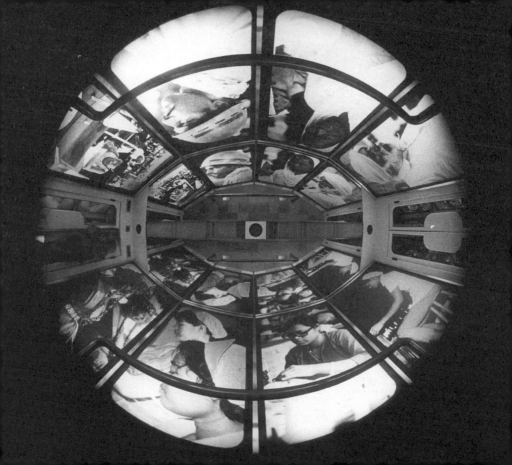

First published in *ARCHITECTURAL DESIGN*, September 1969

OWING TO LACK OF INTEREST, TOMORROW HAS BEEN CANCELLED

Warren Chalk

All animals have a strong exploratory urge, but for some it is more crucial than others. It depends largely on how specialised they have become during the course of evolution. If they have put their effort into the perfection of one survival trick, they do not bother so much with the general complexities of the world around them. So long as the ant eater has its ants and the Koala bear its gum leaves, then they are well satisfied and the living is easy. The non-specialists, however, the opportunists of the animal world, can never afford to relax. They are never sure where their next meal is coming from, and they have to know every nook and cranny, test every possibility and keep a sharp lookout for the lucky chance. They must explore and keep on exploring. They must investigate and keep on rechecking. They must have a constantly high level of curiosity.

The Naked Ape, *Desmond Morris*

Do we know with Len Lye the 'absolute Truth of the happiness acid'? How do we possibly find out where it's at? Do we try to listen to the now to discover the sound of yesterday? Is the Lennon-Yoko nude-in where it's at? A liberation through fame and power celebrating man as animal, and the newfound permissiveness – is this key image for the future? I suspect that yes it is.

People are becoming more interested in people and reality than in feeding mythical systems.

Doing your own thing has spread, from California to all over. Even today's culture heroes like Steve McQueen take the cult of doing your own thing into the jaws of Hollywood. And it's actually him up there on the wide screen, no stunt man rides the motorcycle, or handles the Mustang so superbly through downtown San Francisco, in that fantastic car chase sequence. But what is he trying to prove? Simply that we all have to run faster in order to stay in the same spot. It's called survival, and relates to the special world that surrounds us. And what is this world? How is it discovered or defined? Is it, as Calvin Tomkins has suggested (referring to Andy Warhol's paintings) 'the archetypal 20th-century nightmare – up and down narrow aisles between high walls of brand name uniformity, with the lights glaring down, and

由於興趣缺缺，明天已遭取消

華倫・裘克

> 所有動物都有一股強烈的探究衝動，但對於不同動物而言其重要性並不相同。它絕
> 大部份取決於演化過程當中它們變得多特殊化。倘若它們已努力熟練完備一項生存
> 訣竅，它們就不必太費神周圍世界的全面錯綜複雜性。只要食蟻獸有它的螞蟻且無
> 尾熊有它的尤迦利樹葉，它們便心滿意足且生活愜意。然而，非特殊化者、那些動
> 物界裡的機會主義者，則無法如此輕鬆度日。它們永遠不確定下一餐是否有著落，
> 而且它們必須對四處瞭若指掌，嘗試各種可能性並留心注意著每個良好時機。它們
> 必須探險且持續地探險下去。它們必須勘查且持續地再核查。它們必須保持一股持
> 續的高度好奇心。

> 「裸猿」，戴斯蒙得・莫里斯

我們瞭解實驗電影藝術家連恩・雷的「核酸幸福的絕對真理」嗎？我們如何知道它在那兒呢？我們曾
試圖聆聽現在以覺察昨日的意義嗎？可以在藍儂與洋子的裸照裡找得到嗎？自名氣與權力中解放，稱
頌人類身為動物的一份子，以及新發現的性解放——這是未來的主要形像嗎？我想是的。人們變得對
人與現實愈來愈感興趣，而非針對於維持神話的體系。

自己動手做的風氣已經蔓延開來，自加州至各處。甚至今日的文化界知名人士史帝夫・麥昆亦將自己
動手做的熱潮帶入好萊塢。大銀幕上驚險的飛車追逐場面中，出現騎著摩托車或駕馭著野馬瀟灑地穿
越舊金山城裡的正是他本人，而非替身。但，他想證明什麼呢？簡單地說，不過是我們都必須跑快一
點才能夠維持於原點。這就叫做生存，而且它與我們周遭的特殊世界有關係。那這個世界又是什麼
呢？它如何被覺察與定義呢？它是否誠如卡文・湯姆金斯所暗示的（請參照安迪・沃荷的繪畫），
「典型的20世紀夢魘——上下千篇一律的商標產品牆之間的狹窄通道，刺目的強光毫不留情地照射，
預錄的音樂令人厭煩地入耳，正當您極度渴望尋找一罐蘑菇醬然而每張標籤上卻都寫著蕃茄？」或許
不是。

canned music boring in, as we search desperately for one can of Cream of Mushroom where every label reads Tomato'? Possibly not.

It isn't necessary to be dreary to make a point, or to be profound to have something to say; some of the greatest insights in the world accompany a joke. And many of the mind-blowing ideas about futures in never-never-lands have originated off the pages of comic books and science fiction picture backs. Cartoons help us to discover the hidden realities of life, where straighter communications may fail.

From Krazy Kat to the Yellow Submarine or Egbert Nosh is just the passage of time. Any one of us opportunists trying to create a dreamland in the sky quickly turns to the funnies for reassurance that we can do our own thing, without fear of reprisals.

Bugs Bunny makes a fool of himself, but he does so with élan, and always survives in the iris-shuttered end. He has perfected more than one survival trick and spreads his resources, turning a changing situation to advantage. Egbert Nosh has this house that follows him around along with the garage and the dustbin, protesting their rights. Eventually he relents and agrees to take them for a walk in the park on Sundays providing they promise to stay home the rest of the week. Absurd? I think not. If this is the way we treat our children, why not a budding nomadic house?

To understand one must possess a love of the absurd, which is a love of life. I have this thirst for clowns who, out of mental voids, ask the sublime questions, or make the devastating statement.

'Owing to lack of interest tomorrow has been cancelled.'

At the 'This is Tomorrow exhibition' Richard Hamilton, the daddy of Pop in the UK, showed a montage entitled 'Just what is it that makes today's homes so different, so appealing?'

It was a key image then and nostalgically still is; it led to a whole revolution in attitudes, and up on the back wall is, if not a space comic, something pretty close: 'Young Romance' – 'True Love' with Superman-type figures breathing heavily over a Lois Lane cutie.

Here is a total mythical environment that incorporates everything we have been playing with ever since, and if it moved like Egbert Nosh's nomadic (9 Acacia Avenue) the thread would be complete.

And it's a thin thread, a stocking top operation, and the operators have to be as deft as Bugs Bunny.

Of all prototypes for the new man, that technological opportunist, the inventor, comes closest. Barnes Wallis, inventor of airships, bouncing bombs, fling-

不一定得枯燥無味地主張些什麼，或深奧地說出一番大道理；一些全世界最敏銳的洞察都伴隨著詼諧。而且在香格里拉中許多有關未來令人興奮的構想都源自於漫畫書與科幻小說。卡通幫助我們發現生命中隱藏的事實，直接的訊息傳遞可能並不管用。

自「瘋狂貓」至「黃色潛水艇」或「艾格伯特・諾胥先生」只不過是時間的變遷罷了。我們每個試圖創造雲端上夢土的機會主義者迅速地求助於連環圖畫，確信我們可以自己動手做而無需擔心遭報復。卡通裡的兔寶寶鬧笑話了，但他可鬧得生氣蓬勃，且在引起一陣騷動之後總能全身而退。他已練就一種以上的生存訣竅並延伸他的應變能力，能扭轉多變的處境為優勢。故事書《艾格伯特・諾胥先生》裡的主角諾胥先生有棟隨時隨地跟著他且連同車庫與垃圾桶的房子，向他抗議爭取它們應有的權利。最後他終於心軟並同意星期天帶它們到公園散步，假如它們答應其它時間乖乖待在家裡的話。荒謬嗎？我不認為。倘若這是我們對待自己孩子的方式，為何對於剛萌芽的游牧式房屋不能如法炮製呢？想理解的話，您必須擁有一股對於荒謬性的熱愛，而這正是對於生命的熱愛。對於小丑我有種熱望，其空洞的智能總能有大哉問或驚人的註解。

「由於興趣缺缺，明天已遭取消。」

在「這是明日展覽」中，理察・漢彌爾頓，英國普普藝術之父，展示了一件名為「究竟是什麼使得現今的家屋如此與眾不同、如此扣人心弦呢？」的蒙太奇作品。

這是當時的主要形像且始終仍維持著某種懷舊的方式；它導致了態度上的全然革命，而牆後貼的則是某種類似科幻漫畫的東西：「稚戀」－「真愛」，一旁則是超人型肖像站在美人兒洛蕙絲・蓮恩邊深呼吸的模樣。

這是一個結合所有長久以來我們自娛東西的全然虛構環境，且倘若它像艾格伯特・諾胥的流浪式房屋（刺槐大道9號）一樣可以移動的話，脈絡就更完整了。

然而這是條纖細的脈絡，長襪內衣的操作，而操作者必須像兔寶寶般機靈。

wing aircraft and all that stuff is just such an animal. A breaker of boundaries. Breaking boundaries is a hazardous occupation, a stocking top operation.

The design of pantihose seemed a logical inventive step towards an evolutionary fashion future, but occasionally we get the slightly perverse but very real and necessary reversal that gives added momentum to the headlong pursuit of idea into the future.

Pantihose somewhere along the line missed out on the stimulus factor; so in order to reassess the direction of evolution, the suspender top is brought back to bridge the gap – a reassessment, necessary to maintain vitality. It is something we have to learn in whatever field we are engaged.

The whole question of connection, the glue that binds one idea to another or one course of action to the next, is becoming less and less a physical solution problem.

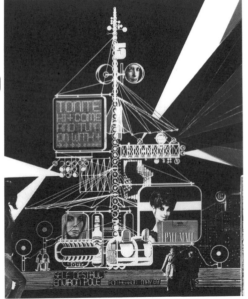

The sonar beacons stabilising any locational shift of the Delos platform is a 'non-physical' solution, free from any structural device.

This points up the current desire goal of doing less with nothing, and the soft think.

Like the freedom riders, five nuns in perfect echelon, held together by faith, likemindedness and bending the Highway code. A soft solution, a regulating link by association. The interrelation, sequence and event, is an extension of the personalities involved; it is a question of relationships and of connection. The comic strip has sometimes reassured me that outside my own wisdom and understanding lies a future different from that which we already predict. The disintegrated gesture of the Cybernetic Forest, Environmental Pole, or the Self-Destructing Happiness Bath are exercises in getting the message into a lot of heads and, as important, increasing the amazement brain.

We are really only at the beginning of 'the absolute Truth of the happiness acid'.

The Freedom Riders

在新人類的所有典型中，技術性機會主義者與發明家最接近。巴尼斯・沃立斯，這位飛船、跳躍式炸彈、螺旋翼飛機……等東西的發明者，正是最佳的例子。一位界限的突破者。突破界限是件冒險的事，是種長襪內衣的操作。連襪褲的設計似乎是邁向革命性時尚之未來的合理發明進展，偶而我們會變得有些執拗但卻是十分真實且必要的根本轉變，卯足全力躁急地追逐接軌未來的構想。

連襪褲某些方面忽略了刺激性的因素，因此為了重新評估演化的方向，不得不再次求助於吊褲帶內衣──重新評估，是維持生命力所必要的。這是不論我們投身任何領域皆須學習的事。

連接的整體問題，亦即連結構想間或連續行為間的黏著劑，已變得愈來愈不是解決實體的問題了。

穩定狄洛斯小島平台位置之任何移動的聲納信號是一種「非實體性」的解決方法，不需依賴任何結構裝置。

這點出了當前對於不藉外力而能減少干預與軟性思考之目標的嚮往。

就像自由騎士一般，5位騎著摩托車排列成完美梯隊的修女，藉由信仰、志同道合與對於公路交通規則的曲解而結合在一起。一種軟性的解決方法，一種藉由聯合之規範性聯繫。這種相互關係、連續與事件，是相關之獨特氛圍的外延；這是個關係與聯繫的問題。連環圖畫有時候能令我感到放心，知道在我自己的智慧與領會之外存有一個迥異的未來，而這點我們早已預料到了。「人工智慧森林」、「環境桅杆」，或「自毀式快樂浴室」的分解式表現都是令眾人得以理解並同時處於驚訝狀態的某種練習。

我們真的只是處於「核酸幸福的絕對真理」的開端而已。

SIMULATION No. 136 HE.28.CD.560, Ron Herron

模擬136號，HE.28.CD.560，朗・赫倫

EXPRO I – Olympia

Peter Cook, Ron Herron

博覽會 I──奧林匹亞

彼得・庫克、朗・赫倫

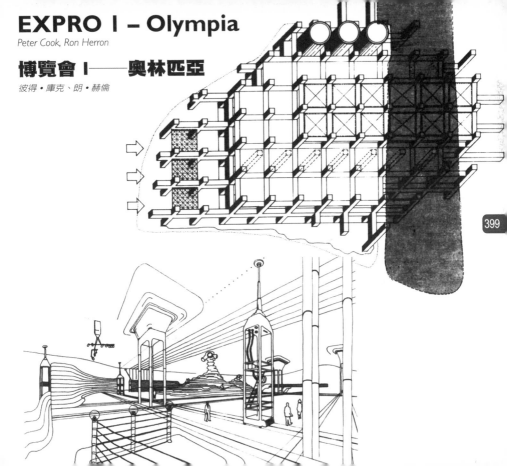

Watergate scandal – Nixon resigns as US President and is replaced by Gerald Ford — US Mariner spacecraft photographs planet Mercury — Makarios ousted by military coup in Cyprus — Turkey invades Cyprus — West German terrorist leader Ulrike Meinhof is jailed — More IRA bombings in London — IRA outlawed in U.K. — Greece votes to abolish monarchy — Georges Pompidou dies; new French President is Valéry Giscard d'Estaing — Jazz musician Duke Ellington dies — Willi Brandt resigns – Helmut Schmidt becomes new West German Chancellor — American newspaper heiress Patty Hearst –supposedly kidnapped by revolutionary group– is seen taking part in bank raid — Coup in Ethiopia deposes Emperor Haile Selassie — Russian dissident writer Alexander Solzenitsyn is exiled from the Soviet Union — Tom Stoppard's play 'Travesties' — David Hockney exhibition in Paris.

水門事件演成政治醜聞－美國總統尼克森下台並由副總統傑拉德・福特接任－美國水手號太空船拍攝到水星－馬卡里歐斯大主教因軍事政變遭逐出塞浦路斯－土耳其入侵塞浦路斯－西德恐怖份子領袖烏爾里克・邁因霍夫入獄－北愛爾蘭共和軍於倫敦製造多起爆炸事件－英國宣佈北愛爾蘭共和軍為非法組織－希臘投票廢止君主制度－喬治・龐畢度辭世；新任法國總統為法雷立・季斯卡・戴斯旦－爵士音樂家艾靈頓公爵辭世－西德總理威利・布藍特辭職－黑爾穆特・施密特繼任西德總理－美國報業鉅子之孫派蒂・赫斯特-據悉遭激進團體綁架洗腦-被目擊參與銀行搶劫－衣索比亞政變罷黜皇帝黑勒・瑟雷西－反共作家亞歷山大・索忍尼辛自蘇俄流亡海外－湯姆・史托普的戲劇《滑稽》－大衛・哈克尼於巴黎展出作品。

1974

PREPARED LANDSCAPE

Peter Cook

預備景觀

彼得・庫克

A NORMAL LANDSCAPE

THE EVENT OF THREE TREES
occurring in a re-iterated way:
hitherto commonplace: is now
perhaps a clue to some further
place or thing or intention OUR
ANTENNAE HAVE BEEN ACTIVATED

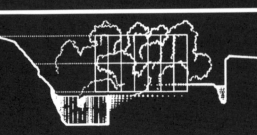

THE EDGE
is sudden, alien?
certainly anticipatory

THE MATRIX
is delightfully
heedless of old
concepts, like
ground or datum

NATURAL ELEMENTS:
trees, bushes, streams:
intermingle with the
matricised space

LUMP 隆起

Peter Cook
彼得・庫克

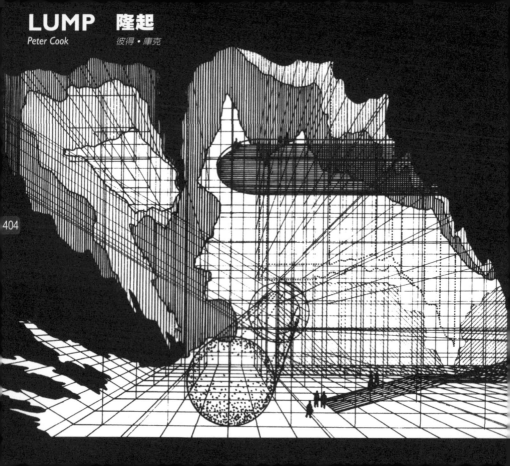

Mound 3 Side 1
3號小丘，第1側

Mound 3 Side 2
3號小丘，第2側

Mound Interior　小丘內部

Mound 3 Side 2

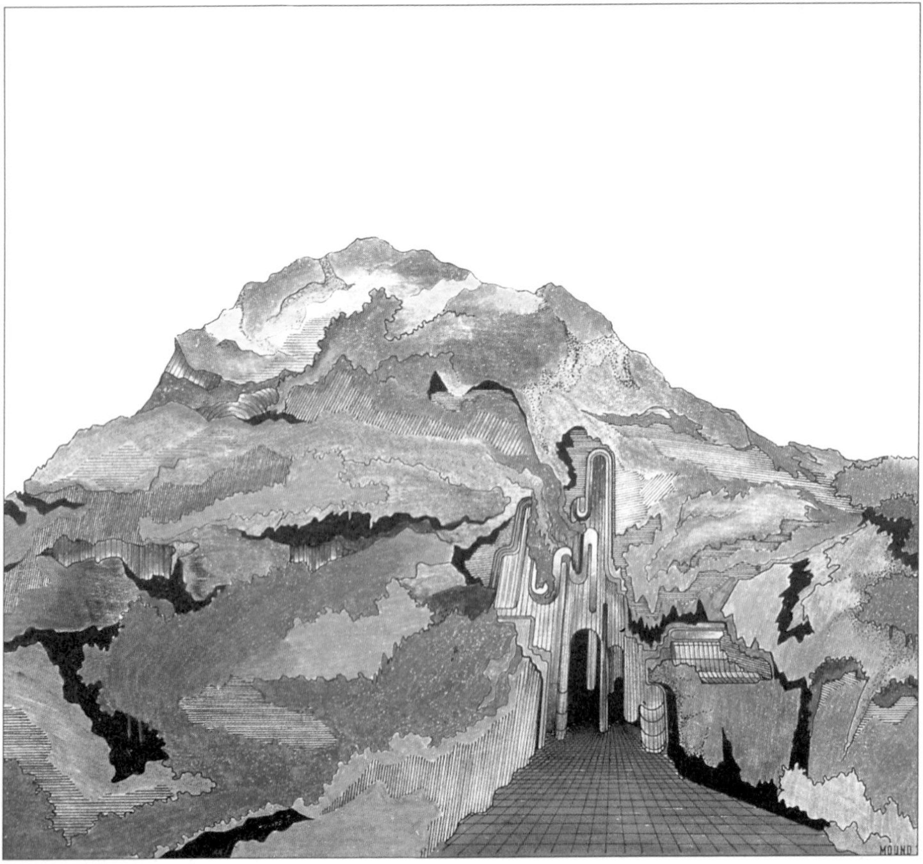
MOUND

SLEEK, Peter Cook　　光滑，彼得・庫克

HOUSE OF THE SEVEN VEILS

Peter Cook

7層面紗住宅

彼得・庫克

house of the seven veils section version'b' (lump exterior)
「7層面紗住宅」b版本剖面圖（「隆起」外部）

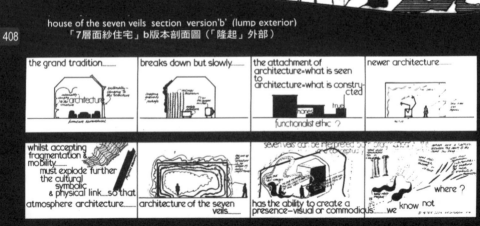

the grand tradition.........

breaks down but slowly.........

the attachment of architecture=what is seen to architecture=what is constructed

honest   true

functionalist ethic ?

newer architecture.........

whilst accepting fragmentation & mobility......... must explode further the cultural symbolic & physical link...so that

atmosphere architecture.........

architecture of the seven veils.........

seven veils can be interpreted

has the ability to create a presence—visual or commodious......we know not

where ?

SORIA MORIA Competition for University Building, Trondheim

Peter Cook, Dennis Crompton, Ron Herron with Toby Dugdale, Per Kartvedt, Cedric Price

「索里亞墨里亞」 大學建築物競圖·挪威特倫翰

彼得·庫克·丹尼斯·克藍普頓·朗·赫倫·以及湯貝·道格戴爾·波·卡爾特維·賽卓克·普萊斯

DRIVE-IN KINO/PARK.   PARKERING

TOT. 350

DAG HJEM

SORIA MORIA

409

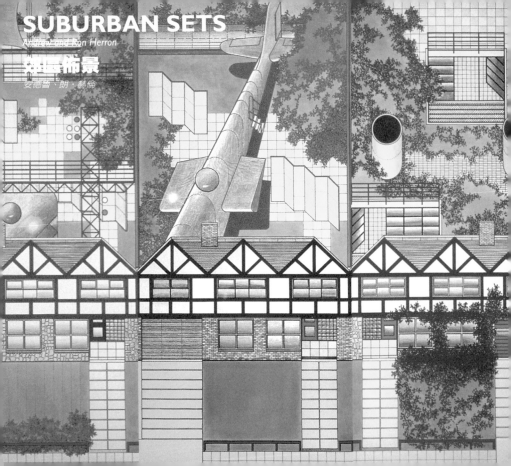

SUBURBAN SETS
Andrew and Ron Herron

郊區佈景

安德魯‧朗‧赫倫

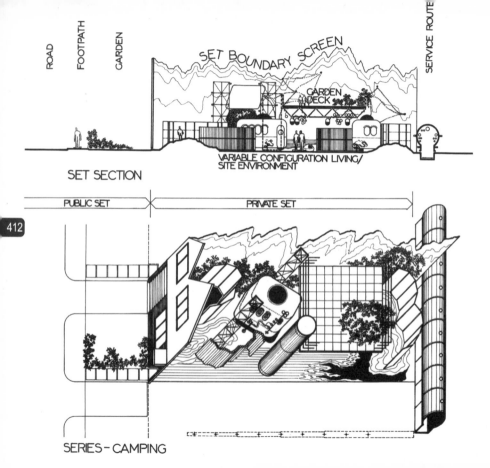

ROAD

FOOTPATH

GARDEN

SET BOUNDARY SCREEN

SERVICE ROUTE

GARDEN DECK

SET SECTION

VARIABLE CONFIGURATION LIVING/
SITE ENVIRONMENT

PUBLIC SET

PRIVATE SET

SERIES – CAMPING

Appendix:

A GUIDE TO ARCHIGRAM EXHIBITION

附錄：

建築電訊參展作品

Archigram Diagram showing the progress of the Magazine and related projects
Cook 1970 : Felt-tip pen on light card

建築電訊雜誌及相關計劃案的圖面
庫克 1970：簽字筆、亮光卡

Archigram Number 1 published in 1961 with just these two sheets. Litho printing on copy paper with colour potato hand-print.

1961年發行只有2頁的《建築電訊》第1期
石版印刷、彩色馬鈴薯手印

Archigram Number 3 published in 1963. The Expendability issue. Front cover : litho printing on coloured paper

1963年發行的《建築電訊》第3期：消費性
封面：石版印刷、色紙

Archigram Number 2 published in 1962.
Front cover : litho printing. Text pages inside were typeset for the first and last time!

1962年發行的《建築電訊》第2期
封面石版印刷：內頁則首次、也是最後一次採用排版印刷

Archigram Number 4 published in 1964. Zoom Issue.
Litho printing on board with silk-screen overprint in two colours

1964年發行的《建築電訊》第4期：變焦
石版印刷、絹版雙色套印

Archigram Number 5 published in 1964. Metropolis issue.
Litho print on gloss paper with silk-screen overprint

1964年發行的《建築電訊》第5期：大都會
石版印刷、絹版套印、光面紙

Archigram Number 6 published in 1966 included a survey of the 40s.
Front cover silk-screen on colour paper, back cover litho printed.

1966年發行的《建築電訊》第6期，包括了四〇年代的研究
封面：絹版、色紙；封底：石版印刷

Archigram Number 7 published in 1967. A collection of printed sheets loose in a plastic bag
Cover sheet ; litho printed

1967年發行的《建築電訊》第7期，未裝訂的內頁裝於塑膠袋內
封套：石版印刷

Archigram Number 9 published in 1970 - the "Gardners" issue included a packet of seeds
Front and back wrap : two-colour litho on coloured paper

1970年發行的《建築電訊》第9期：園丁，隨雜誌贈送一袋種子
封面／底：雙色石版印刷、色紙

"ARCHIGRAM" the book, published by Studio Vista, London in 1972
Wrap and covers printed four-colour litho

《建築電訊》一書之封面，1972年由遠望工作室於倫敦發行
封面／底：四色石版印刷

Archigram Number 8 published in 1968 to coincide with the Archigram section at the Milan Triennale
Litho print on both sides of card, folded to form pocket with magazine pages inserted

1968年發行的《建築電訊》第8期，配合「米蘭三年展」的「建築電訊」展區
卡紙雙面石版印刷、摺成袋狀內附雜誌頁面

Archigram Number 9 and a half published in 1974. Not a real issue, just a news sheet on Archigram's activities
Front page, litho print

《建築電訊》第9期一半於1974年印行，並非是一份刊物，而是「建築電訊」活動的新聞頁
封面：石版印刷

PRE- ARCHIGRAM :
A selection of
work by members
of the Group
before 1961

前－建築電訊：
1961年之前團體成
員的部分作品

Mosque Project - section DD
Greene 1958 : Red ink drawing
on pink board

清真寺計畫－DD剖面圖
葛林 1958：紅色墨水、粉彩紙版

Mosque Project - elevation
Greene 1958 : Cut-out red ink
drawing on pink mounted on
black

清真寺計畫－立面圖
葛林 1958：紅墨水、粉彩紙裁
剪、裱黑色紙

Furniture   Manufacturers
Association Headquarters - End
and front elevations
Webb 1958 : 2 Photographic
prints

家具製造商協會總部－前後立面
圖
威柏 1958：2件相片版畫

Mosque Project - sketches, plan,
section and elevation
Greene 1958 : Reversed photographic print

清真寺計畫－草圖，平、立、剖
面圖
葛林 1958：圖片翻拍

Mosque Project - plan
Greene 1958 : Red ink drawing
on pink board

清真寺計畫－平面圖
葛林 1958：紅色墨水、粉彩紙版

Furniture   Manufacturers
Association Headquarters - Plan
in two parts
Webb 1958 : Ink drawing on tracing paper mounted on board

家具製造商協會總部－二個部分
的平面圖
威柏 1958：墨水、描圖紙、裱紙
版

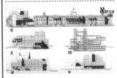

National Gallery Competition -
Elevations and sections
Chalk + Herron 1959 : Ink on
tracing paper

國家美術館擴建競圖－立、剖面
圖
裴克＋赫倫 1959：墨水、描圖紙

National Gallery Competition -
Site plans
Chalk + Herron 1959 : Ink on
tracing paper

國家美術館擴建競圖－基地配置
圖
裘克＋赫倫 1959：墨水、描圖紙

Highfield Housing Competition -
Site plan and section
Chalk + Herron 1960 : Dyeline
print mounted and laminated

海菲爾德住宅競圖－基地配置及
剖面圖
裘克＋赫倫 1960：重氮氨基版
畫、薄版裝裱

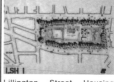

Lillington Street Housing
Competition - Site plan
Chalk + Crompton + Herron 1961
: Ink on tracing paper

李寧頓街住宅競圖－基地配置圖
裘克＋克藍普頓＋赫倫 1961：墨
水、描圖紙

420

WORK BY THE
ARCHIGRAM
GROUP
1961-1975

建築電訊作品
1961-1975

Metal House Project - elevation
and plan ; terrace plan and elev.
Cook 1961 : Ink on tracing ; photographic collage

金屬牆住宅案－平、立面圖；連
續梯狀的平、立面圖
庫克 1961：墨水、描圖紙；相片
拼貼

National Gallery Competition -
Axonometric
Chalk + Herron 1959 : Ink on
tracing paper

國家美術館擴建競圖－立體圖
裘克＋赫倫 1959：墨水、描圖紙

Seaside Entertainment Building -
model photo
Greene 1961 : photographic print

濱海樂園建築－模型
葛林1961：相片版畫

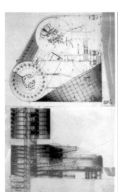

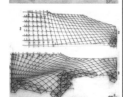

Sin Centre - Wire-frame details of ramps
Webb 1961-63 : Ink on Mylar

罪惡中心－鋼架坡道細部
威柏 1961-63：墨水、聚脂薄膜

Gas House - Plans, sections and elevations
Cook 1961 : Ink on tracing paper

煤氣廠－平、剖、立面圖
庫克 1961：墨水、描圖紙

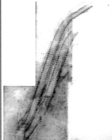

Sin Centre - Plan, elevation and detail of roof net structure
Webb 1961-63 : Ink drawing on film and 3 photographic prints

罪惡中心－平、立面圖及屋頂網狀結構細部
威柏 1961-63：墨水、軟片，及3幅相片版畫

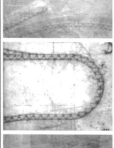

Sin Centre - Details studies of escalators
Webb 1961-63 : Ink and colour on film ; pencil on tracing paper

罪惡中心－升降梯細部草圖
威柏 1961-63：墨水、軟片；鉛筆、描圖紙

Spray Plastic House - Plans and sections of three phases
Greene 1961 : Photographic print

枝狀塑膠屋－三個階段的平、剖面圖
葛林1961：相片版畫

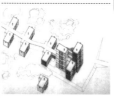

Gas House - Axonometric
Cook 1961 : Ink on tracing paper

煤氣廠－立體圖
庫克 1961：墨水、描圖紙

Liverpool University Halls of Residence Competition - Site plan
Chalk + Herron 1962 : Print off ink and pencil drawing

利物浦大學學生宿舍競圖－基地配置圖
裘克＋赫倫 1962：墨水、鉛筆畫列印

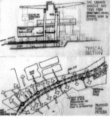

Nottingham Shopping Centre - Four sketch studies
Cook + Greene 1962 : Felt-tip pen on paper

諾丁罕購物中心－四張草圖
庫克＋葛林 1962：簽字筆、紙

Nottingham Shopping Centre - Elevation
Cook + Greene 1962 : Ink on tracing paper

諾丁罕購物中心－立面圖
庫克＋葛林 1962：墨水、描圖紙

Living City Exhibition - Drawn diary
Cook 1963 : Ink and film on tracing paper

生活城市展覽－繪圖記事簿
庫克 1963：墨水、軟片、描圖紙

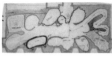

Living City Exhibition - Plan and two sections
Chalk + Cook + Crompton + Greene + Herron + Webb 1963 : Ink, crayon and felt-tip pen on tracing paper

生活城市展覽－一張平面圖及二張剖面圖
裘克＋庫克＋克藍普頓＋葛林＋赫倫＋威柏 1963：墨水、蠟筆、簽字筆、描圖紙

Living City Exhibition - Three illustrations drawn for the exhibition catalogue - Come Go / Place / Communication
Chalk + Cook + Crompton + Greene + Herron + Webb 1963 : Photographic prints

生活城市展覽－展覽手冊的三張插圖：來去／場所／溝通
裘克＋庫克＋克藍普頓＋葛林＋赫倫＋威柏 1963：相片版畫

Living City Exhibition - Photographs of the installation : Manikin / Tick Tick / Sick
Chalk + Cook + Crompton + Greene + Herron + Webb 1963 : Photographic prints

生活城市展覽－展覽裝置相片：模特兒模型／滴答／不適
裘克＋庫克＋克藍普頓＋葛林＋赫倫＋威柏 1963：相片版畫

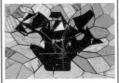

City Synthesis - Photograph of model ; Collage
Crompton 1963 : Photographic prints ; newspaper cuttings

城市綜合體－模型相片；拼貼
克藍普頓 1963：相片版畫；剪報

City Interchange Project - Two sketches
Chalk + Herron 1963 : Prints from ink on tracing paper sketches

城市替換計畫－二張草圖
裘克＋赫倫 1963：墨水、描圖紙草圖的版畫

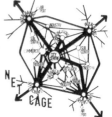

423

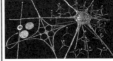

City Interchange Project - Plan, elevation and detail
Chalk + Herron 1963 : Prints from ink on tracing paper drawings

城市替換計畫－平、立面及細部圖
裘克＋赫倫 1963：墨水、描圖紙草圖的版畫

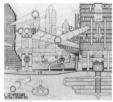

City Interchange Project - Photograph of Exhibition Model
Chalk + Herron 1963/1994

城市替換計畫－展出模型相片
裘克＋赫倫 1963/1994

House Project - Reverse photo-print of Perspective with annotation
Greene 1964 : Photographic print

（機械化鎮形）住宅計畫－附註解之透視圖翻拍
葛林 1964：相片版畫

Dream City Project/Story of The Thing
Greene + Webb 1963 : Photographic collage and original model photo

夢中之城計畫／一件物體的故事
葛林＋威柏 1963：相片拼貼及原始模型照

Plug-in City Study - Europa Lons 50, elevation/section in 3 parts
Cook 1964 : Ink, colour film and felt-tip pen on board

插接城市－三個部分的立、剖面圖
庫克 1964：墨水、彩色軟片、簽字筆、紙版

Plug-in City Study - Hover vehicle; City section; Business components; Sustenance components
Cook 1964 : 4 drawings each ink on tracing paper

插接城市－氣墊式交通工具；城市剖面圖；商業組件；維生組件
庫克 1964：墨水、描圖紙共四張圖

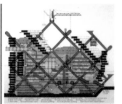

Plug-in City Study - Typical section
Cook 1964 : Print off ink on tracing drawing with added colour film

插接城市－典型的剖面圖
庫克 1964：墨水、描圖紙原作、軟片上色印出

Plug-in City Study - Overhead view
Cook 1964 : Print off ink on tracing drawing with added colour film

插接城市－空中景
庫克 1964：墨水、描圖紙原作、軟片上色印出

Plug-in City Study - Max Pressure Area
Cook 1964 : Print off ink on tracing drawing with added colour film

插接城市－最繁忙區域
庫克 1964：墨水、描圖紙原作、軟片上色印出

Plug-in City Study - Photograph of Exhibition Model
Cook 1964-7/94 : Archigram Number 7 contained two sheets of cut-out components which when assembled made a model of the Plug-in City

插接城市－展出模型相片
庫克 1964-7/1994：包含二張裁剪頁的《建築電訊》第7期組合起來後就成了插接城市的模型

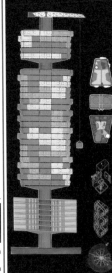

Plug-in-City Capsule Tower - Tower elevation and plans, elevation and details of capsules
Chalk 1964 : 7 Prints with added film mounted on black board

插接城市艙室塔樓－塔樓平、立面圖，及艙室立面、細部圖
裘克 1964：7張上色軟片，裱黑紙版

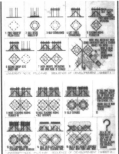

Plug-in City University Node - 2 drawings of developing sequence
Cook 1965 : Ink on tracing paper

插接城市大學節點－發展階段的二張圖
庫克 1965：墨水、描圖紙

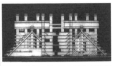

Plug-in City University Node - Elevation and plan
Cook 1965 : Ink and coloured film on tracing paper

插接城市大學節點－平、立面圖
庫克 1965：墨水、彩色軟片、描圖紙

Plug-in City University Node - Elevation
Cook 1965 : Print off ink drawing with added colour film

插接城市大學節點－立面圖
庫克 1965：墨水畫作、軟片上色印出

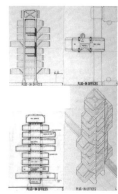

Plug-in Offices Project - Elevation, plan, section and axonometric
Cook 1964 : Ink on paper; 2 ink on tracing paper; ink on paper

插接辦公室計畫－平、立、剖及立體圖
庫克 1964：墨水、紙張、描圖紙

Montreal Tower - Plan and elevation
Cook 1963 : Black line print on silver background mounted on black

蒙特婁塔－平、立面圖
庫克 1963：銀底、黑線作品、裱黑紙

City Mound Project - Section
Cook 1964 : Ink on tracing paper

城市小丘計畫－剖面圖
庫克 1964：墨水、描圖紙

Plug-in-City Planning Studies - Map of UK + detail from animation sequence
Crompton 1965 : Geographic map with added colour film; ink and felt-tip pen on tracing paper cut out and mounted on colour paper

插接城市設計稿－英國地圖及動態過程的細部
克藍普頓 1965：彩色軟片地形圖；墨水、簽字筆、描圖紙作品裁剪裱色紙

Plug-in City Study - Stage 3, Central London
Cook 1963 : Route map with added collage

插接城市－階段3，倫敦市中心
庫克 1963：路線圖拼貼

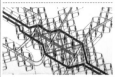

Computer City Project - Axonometric
Crompton 1964 : Photoprint from ink drawing with added colour film

電腦城市計畫－立體圖
克藍普頓 1964：墨水畫原作、軟片上色印出

Plug-in City: Paddington East,
Expendable Place Pads - Typical
Infill
Cook 1966 : Photoprint from ink
drawing with added colour film

插接城市：派丁敦東區，可消耗
場所填塞－典型的填入
庫克 1966：墨水畫原作、軟片上
色印出

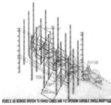

Hornsey Housing Study -
Axonometric of frame and routes
Cook 1966 : Ink on tracing paper

霍恩西檔室－架構及路線立體圖
庫克 1966：墨水、描圖紙

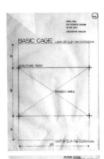

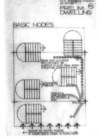

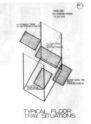

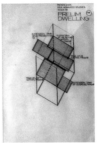

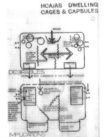

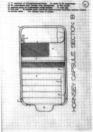

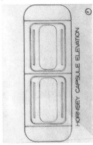

Hornsey Housing Study - 8
pages of diagrams
Cook 1966 : Ink on tracing
paper ; 1 ink on graph
paper

霍恩西檔室－8頁圖面
庫克 1966：墨水、描圖
紙；方格紙

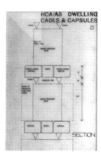

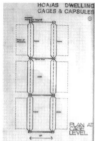

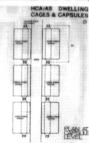

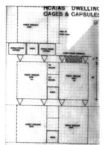

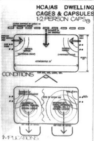

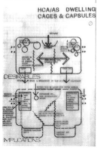

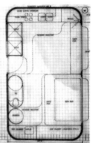

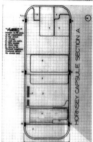

Hornsey Housing Study - 8 pages of diagrams
Cook 1966 : Ink on graph paper

霍恩西續室－8頁圖面
庫克 1966：墨水、方格紙

Plug'n Clip House Project - Mews House Interior Perspective
Cook 1965 : Print from ink drawing with added colour film

插／夾住宅計畫－公寓住宅室內透視圖
庫克 1965：墨水畫原作、軟片上色版畫

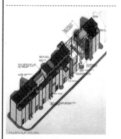

Plug'n Clip House Project - Axonometric of mews block
Cook 1965 : Print from ink drawing with added colour film

插／夾住宅計畫－集合公寓透視圖
庫克 1965：墨水畫原作、軟片上色版畫

428

Plug'n Clip House Project - Interior perspective ; Planning diagram
Cook 1965 : Print from ink drawings with added colour film; Ink and felt-tip pen on card

插／夾住宅計畫－室內透視圖及設計圖
庫克 1965：墨水畫原作、軟片上色版畫；墨水、簽字筆、卡紙

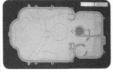

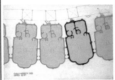

Gasket House - Detail Plan + Terrace plan
Chalk + Herron 1965 : Prints cut out and mounted with added colour

接合住宅－平面細部及梯狀平面
裘克＋赫倫 1965：圖片裁剪、上色、裝裱

Gasket House - Gasket plan + Section of capsule
Chalk + Herron 1965 : Prints of ink drawing on tracing paper

接合住宅－接合住宅平面及艙室剖面
裘克＋赫倫 1965：墨水、描圖紙原作的版畫

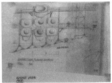

Gasket House - Sketch Plan; Montage axonometric; Sketch Elevation
Chalk + Herron 1965 : Print of plan and elevation on tracing paper; copy of montage mounted on board

接合住宅－平面草圖、蒙太奇式立體圖、立面草圖
裘克＋赫倫 1965：平、立面描圖紙原作的版畫；裱於紙版的蒙太奇作品複本

Leisure Study: Inflatable Units Sea/Land/Air - Elevation + Sketch
Herron 1966 : Prints of ink drawings on tracing paper

休閒研究：海中、陸上與空中之充氣式單元－立面圖、草圖
赫倫1966：墨水、描圖紙原作的版畫

Living Pod - Concept sketch
Greene 1966 : Pencil and wax crayon on drawing paper

生活莢－概念草圖
葛林 1966：鉛筆、粉蠟筆、圖畫紙

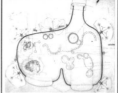

Living Pod - Lower Level Plan
Greene 1966 : Print on tracing paper with collage elements

生活莢－下層平面圖
葛林 1966：描圖紙拼貼原作的版畫

Living Pod - 4 Sketches of Satellites
Greene 1966 : Pencil and ink on tracing paper

生活莢－4張衛星草圖
葛林 1966：鉛筆、墨水、描圖紙

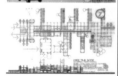

Free Time Node - Elevation and Plan
Herron 1967 : Colour print of collage ; Print on tracing paper

休閒節點－平、立面圖
赫倫 1967：彩色拼貼版畫；描圖紙

Living Pod - Section + Elevation
Greene 1966 : Pencil drawing with collaged figure; Print with collage

生活莢－剖、立面圖
葛林 1966：拼貼式鉛筆畫；拼貼版畫

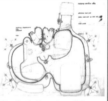

Living Pod - Upper Level Plan
Greene 1966 : Print on tracing paper with collage elements

生活莢－上層平面圖
葛林 1966：描圖紙拼貼原作的版畫

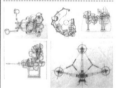

Living Pod - 5 Drawings of Satellites
Greene 1966 : Ink on tracing paper

生活莢－5張衛星草圖
葛林 1966：墨水、描圖紙

Living Pod : Model Photograph
Greene 1966 : Ink Jet print

生活莢-模型相片
葛林 1966：噴墨版畫

Pod in Piraneziesque Landscape
Greene 1979 : photocopies of
etching with added collage

皮藍內西景觀中的莢
葛林 1979：拼貼蝕刻畫相片

Pod Muerto Diptych
Greene 1998 : Acrylic paint on
ply wood

「火山莢」版本
葛林 1998：樹脂畫、膠合版

Bathamatic - Perspective with
annotation
Chalk 1969 : Print with colour collage mounted on card

自動沐浴鬆弛裝置-透視圖附標
註
裘克 1969：彩色拼貼、裱卡紙之
版畫

431

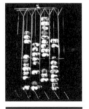

Living Pod - Net Structure -
Photograph of Model + Plan
Greene 1966 : Photographic
prints

生活莢-網狀結構-模型相片及
平面圖
葛林 1966：相片版畫

Pod in Housing
Greene 1979 : Silk screen print
from collage

住宅中的莢
葛林 1979：拼貼絹版畫

Pod Vivo Diptych
Greene 1998 : Acrylic paint on
ply wood

「活力莢」版本
葛林 1998：樹脂畫、膠合版

432

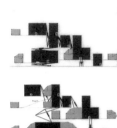

Auto-Environment - Hydraulic Lifting Mechanism in 3 Phases
Webb 1964 : Ink on tracing paper with added colour film

汽車環境－水壓升降操作裝置的3個階段
威柏 1964：墨水、描圖紙、上色軟片

Auto-Environment - Overhead Perspective + Plan
Webb 1964 : Pencil and colour crayon on card; Ink and colour crayon on tracing paper

汽車環境－空中透視圖及平面圖
威柏 1964：鉛筆、色筆、卡紙；墨水、色筆、描圖紙

Rent-a-Wall - Collage + Version Revisited in 1997
Webb 1966/1997 : Collages on card

出租牆－拼貼及1997再訪版本
威柏 1966/1997：拼貼、卡紙

Auto Environment - Photograph of Exhibition Model
Webb 1966/1994

汽車環境－展出模型相片
威柏 1966/1994

Room of 1000 Delights - Collage in 2 parts
Cook 1970 : Collage mounted on boards

千椿嘉悅之室－二個部分的拼貼
庫克 1970：拼貼裱紙版

Oasis - Collage + 2 sketches
Herron 1968 : Colour print of
Collage + 2 colour copies of
sketches

綠洲－拼貼及二張草圖
赫倫 1968：彩色拼貼相片，及二
張草圖的彩色影本

Cheek by Jowl - High Street -
Time sequence as four strip elevations
Cook 1970 : Mounted print of line
drawing with added felt-tip pen
colour

頻貼著頰－高度開發的街道－4
幅時間序列的連環圖
庫克 1970：線圖、色簽字筆、裱
版畫

Addhox - Typical Suburban Add-
Types Sheet 1
Cook 1970 : Mounted print of line
drawing with added felt-tip pen
colour

特別型－典型的社區加入型
庫克 1970：線圖、色簽字筆、裱
版畫

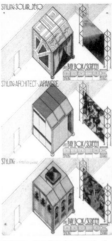

Addhox - Bay Box Screens 3 - 5
Cook 1970 : Mounted print of line
drawing with added felt-tip pen
colour

特別型－灣盒，階段3-5
庫克 1970：線圖、色簽字筆、裱
版畫

Addhox - North Kensington
Corner Phases 1 & 2
Cook 1970 : Mounted print of line
drawing with added felt-tip pen
colour

特別型－北坎辛頓街角，階段1-2
庫克 1970：線圖、色簽字筆、裱
版畫

433

Addhox - North Kensington
Corner Phases 3 & 4
Cook 1970 : Mounted print of line
drawing with added felt-tip pen
colour

特別型－北坎辛頓街角，階段3-4
庫克 1970：線圖、色簽字筆、裱
版畫

Control and Choice - A Series of Paradoxes
Cook 1967 : Mounted print of line drawing with added colour film

控制與選擇－ 一系列的矛盾
庫克 1967：線圖、軟片上色、裱版畫

Control and Choice - Part Section
Herron 1967 : Print on tracing paper of ink line drawing

控制與選擇－ 一系列的矛盾
庫克 1967：描圖紙、墨水線圖版畫

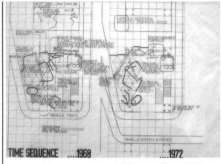

TIME SEQUENCE 1968 1972

Control and Choice - Part Section
Chalk + Herron 1967 : Montage of prints with added ink line drawing

控制與選擇－ 部分剖面圖
裘克＋赫倫 1967：蒙太奇圖片加上墨水線圖

Control and Choice - Axonometric of Time Sequence
Cook 1967 : Print of ink line drawing hand coloured

控制與選擇－ 時間序列立體圖
庫克 1967：手繪彩色線圖版畫

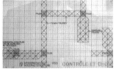

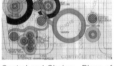

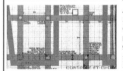

Control and Choice - Plans of Time sequence 1968-72 + 76-82, 4 diagrams, Plan, Route, Structure, Event Interface
Cook 1967 : Ink on tracing paper; Ink and colour film on graph paper

控制與選擇－ 1968-72時間序列平面圖、4張圖表、平面、路線、結構、活動介面
庫克 1967：墨水、描圖紙；墨水、彩色軟片、方格紙

Control and Choice - Plans of Time Sequence 1988-90; Axonometric Metamorphosis
Cook 1967 : Ink and coloured film on tracing paper; Ink on tracing paper

控制與選擇－ 1988-90時間序列平面圖；立體變形圖
庫克 1967：墨水、上色軟片、描圖紙；墨水、描圖紙

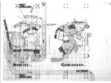

Control and Choice - Plans B-level and C-level
Cook 1967 : Ink on tracing paper with added red arrows

控制與選擇－ B層及C層平面圖
庫克 1967：墨水、描圖紙、紅色箭號

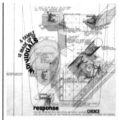

Control and Choice - Axonometric, A Family is Made Up of Individuals
Cook 1967 : Print of ink drawing mounted with collage and colour film

控制與選擇－ 立體圖，由個體組成的家庭
庫克 1967：墨水畫、拼貼、彩色軟片的版畫

Control & Choice : Model Photograph
Chalk + Cook + Crompton + Herron 1967 : Ink Jet Print

控制與選擇－ 模型照
裘克＋庫克＋克藍普頓＋赫倫 1967：噴墨列印

St Katherin's Dock - Section/Elevation + Overhead view
Cook + Crompton + Herron 1967 : 2 Colour photographic prints

聖凱薩琳船塢－剖、立面圖及空中景
庫克＋克藍普頓＋赫倫 1967：2 幅彩色相片版畫

House 1990 - Location Plan + Exhibition Floor Plan
Cook + Crompton + Herron 1967 : Ink on tracing paper

住宅1990－基地配置圖＋展覽樓層平面圖
庫克＋克藍普頓＋赫倫 1967：墨水、描圖紙

House 1990 - 2 Interior perspectives
Cook 1967 : Ink on Tracing with added felt-tip pen and colour film

住宅1990－2幅室內透視圖
庫克 1967：墨水、描圖紙、簽字筆、彩色軟片

House 1990 - Weekend Telegraph Colour Supplement 1967 : News print mounted on board

住宅1990－週末訊報彩色增刊 1967：報紙裱版

House 1990 - Exhibition Installation
Chalk + Cook + Crompton + Herron 1967 : Colour photographic print

住宅1990－展覽裝置
裴克＋庫克＋克藍普頓＋赫倫 1967：彩色相片版畫

House 1990 - Exhibition Installation
Chalk + Cook + Crompton + Herron 1967 : Colour photographic print

住宅1990－展覽裝置
裴克＋庫克＋克藍普頓＋赫倫 1967：彩色相片版畫

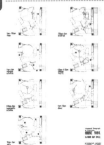

House 1990 - Plans of 24 Hour Day Cycle
Chalk 1967 : 8 drawings ink on tracing paper

住宅1990－ 一天24小時的平面圖
裴克 1967：墨水、描圖紙

House 1990 - Exhibition Installation
Chalk + Cook + Crompton + Herron 1967 : Colour photographic print

住宅1990－展覽裝置
裴克＋庫克＋克藍普頓＋赫倫 1967：彩色相片版畫

House 1990 - Exhibition Installation
Chalk + Cook + Crompton + Herron 1967 : Colour photographic print

住宅1990－展覽裝置
裴克＋庫克＋克藍普頓＋赫倫 1967：彩色相片版畫

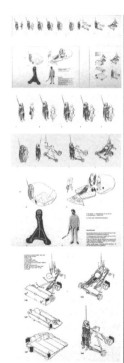

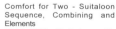

Comfort for Two - Suitaloon
Sequence, Combining and
Elements
Webb 1968 : 3 photographic
prints

兩人世界－家衣系列及其組件與
元件
威柏 1968：3幅相片版畫

Comfort for Two - Suitaloon
Merging Sequence
Webb 1968 : Photographic print

兩人世界－家衣系列的組合
威柏 1968：相片版畫

Cushicle - Opening Sequence
Webb 1966 : Ink line and air
brush colour on card

氣墊車－展開順序
威柏 1966：墨線、噴槍上色、卡
紙

Suitaloon in Milan - Six stages to
inflation of prototype suit
Cook + Crompton + Greene +
Herron 1967-68 : Colour prints
from slides mounted on board

家衣（米蘭）－充氣成標準家衣
的6個步驟

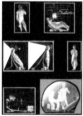

Cushicle - Dave + Pat + 5 Stages
of Transformation
Webb 1966 : 6 Photoprints cut
out and mounted on blue board
with added colour film

氣墊車－戴夫、派特，和5種不
同的變化
威柏 1966：6幅彩色軟片裁剪裱
藍版畫

Cushicle - Exhibition Model
Webb 1966/94

氣墊車-展覽模型
威柏 1966/94

437

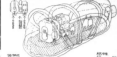

438

Air-Hab - Photo Collage + 5 sketches
Herron 1967 : Photoprint; copy on tracing paper; 4 colour copies

充氣式住所－相片拼貼＋5張草圖
赫倫1967：相片版畫；描圖紙複本；4張彩色複本

Air-Hab - Elevation with Car, Girl and Cow; Mobile Home Site Collage;
Air-Hab Nomad Collage
Herron 1967 : 3 colour copies mounted on board and laminated

充氣式住所－汽車、女孩及牛隻＋流動式居家基地＋充氣式住所：游牧拼貼
赫倫 1967：彩色薄版裱裝

Manzak - Exhibition Model
Herron 1967/94

寵物機器人－展覽模型
赫倫 1967/94

Manzak - Optional Extras; Out for
a Walk; On Beach; Seat
Herron 1967 : 4 colour copies
mounted on board and laminated

寵物機器人－超選擇；外出散
步；海灘；座椅
赫倫 1967：彩色薄版裱裝

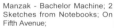

Manzak - Bachelor Machine; 2
Sketches from Notebooks; On
Fifth Avenue;
2 Collages from Notebooks; In
Griffen Park
Herron 1967 : 7 colour copies
mounted on board and laminated

寵物機器人－學士機器；2張草
圖；第五大道；2張拼貼；葛瑞
芬公園
赫倫 1967：彩色薄版裱裝

Electric Tomato - Collage
Chalk + Greene 1969 : Ink, tape,
newsprint and felt-tip pen

電子蕃茄－拼貼
裘克＋葛林 1969：墨汁、膠帶、
報紙、簽字筆

Walking City - Collage, Fantasy and Reality; Sketch Mobile Capital City
Herron 1964 : Colour print mounted on board and laminated; colour print on tracing paper

步行城市－想像與真實之拼貼；流動式首都
赫倫1964：彩印薄版裱裝版畫；描圖紙彩印

Walking City - New York at Night + At Rest / Night
Herron 1964 : Colour photoprints

步行城市－紐約夜晚；夜晚歇息
赫倫1964：彩色相片版畫

Walking City - In the Desert
Herron 1964 : Colour photoprint

步行城市－沙漠
赫倫1964：彩色相片版畫

440

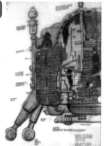

Walking City - Sketches 2 Plans and 1 Detail Section
Herron 1964 : Prints of ink and colour drawings on tracing paper

步行城市－2張平面圖及1張細部剖面圖
赫倫1964：墨水、彩圖、描圖紙原作版畫

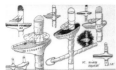

Walking City - 12 Sketches from Notebooks
Herron 1964 : Colour laser prints

步行城市－12幅草圖
赫倫 1964：電射彩印版畫

Walking City - Elevation of Vehicle
Herron 1964 : Print hand coloured in crayon and signed by author

步行城市－交通工具正立面
赫倫 1964：蠟筆上色、作者親簽版畫

Walking City New York - Collage
Herron 1964 : Colour photoprint

步行城市－拼貼
赫倫 1964：彩色相片版畫

Blow-out Village - Three Stages of Inflation
Cook 1966 : Three inkjet prints from ink on tracing paper drawings with added colour

爆裂村落－膨脹的3個階段
庫克 1966：噴墨列印，原作為墨水、描圖紙

Milanogram - First Display Section, Elevation and Two Plans
Cook + Crompton + Greene + Herron 1967-68 : Print from ink on tracing paper drawing with added colour film and marker

米蘭電訊－第一展示區，立面圖及平面圖
庫克＋克藍普頓＋葛林＋赫倫 1967-68：墨水、描圖紙原作、彩色軟片、麥克筆

441

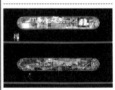

Milanogram, Bag - Elevations of Either Side (in four parts joined)
Cook + Crompton + Greene + Herron 1967-68 : Collaged on mounted prints with newsprint, marker and colour film

米蘭電訊，囊袋－各邊立面
庫克＋克藍普頓＋葛林＋赫倫 1967-68：報紙、麥克筆、彩色軟片拼貼裝裱

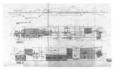

Milanogram, Bag - Plan and Elevation
Cook + Crompton + Greene + Herron 1967-68 : Mounted print taken from ink on tracing paper working drawing

米蘭電訊，囊袋－平、立面
庫克＋克藍普頓＋葛林＋赫倫
1967-68：墨水、描圖紙原作、裝裱版畫

Milanogram, Bag - Key to contents
Cook + Crompton + Greene + Herron 1967-68 : Mounted print with annotation and collage newsprint and photographs

米蘭電訊，囊袋－關鍵內容
庫克＋克藍普頓＋葛林＋赫倫
1967-68：註記、報紙、相片拼貼原作、裝裱版畫

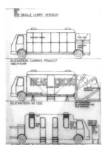

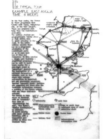

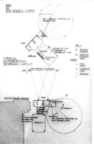

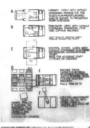

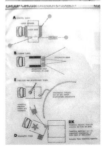

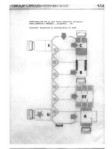

Ideas Circus - 8 Diagrams
Cook 1969 : 7 Ink and type on tracing paper with added symbols; 1 colour collage newsprint, cut-out drawing and Lettraset

構想集會場－8幅畫作
庫克 1969：描圖紙上墨色、打字；彩色拼貼、報紙、圖畫裁切

Ideas Circus - Exhibition Model
Cook 1969/94

構想集會場 - 展覽模型
庫克 1969/94

Instant City - 10 sketches from
notebooks
Herron 1968 : Colour copies of
ink and wax pencil drawings with
some collage

即時城市－10幅塗鴉
赫倫 1968：墨水、蠟筆畫作、拼
貼原作之彩印

Instant City - Glamour +
Response Unit
Cook 1968 : 2 Colour photo-
graphic prints of collages

即時城市－魅力：回應單元
庫克 1968：2幅拼貼作品的彩色
相片版畫

443

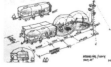

Instant City - Urban Action Tune
Up
Herron 1969 : Collage with photo-
print, newsprint and colour film

即時城市－都市行為的調整
赫倫 1969：彩印、報紙及彩色軟
片拼貼

Instant City - In a field Elevation
Cook 1968 : Print from line drawing mounted on blue board and coloured with film and collage, in two halves butt jointed

即時城市－整個場地的立面
庫克 1968：線稿、藍版、彩色軟片、拼貼原作之版畫

Instant City - In a field - Exhibition Model
Cook 1968/94

即時城市－整個場地的展覽模型
庫克 1968/94

Instant City - Santa Monica & San Diego Freeway Intersection
Herron 1969 : Colour laser prints off collages

即時城市－聖塔蒙尼卡及聖地牙哥公路交叉口
赫倫 1969：雷射彩印拼貼作品

Instant City - Monaco Simultaneous Event Facility; In Death Valley
Herron 1969 : 4 Colour laser prints off collages

即時城市－摩納哥同時性事件設施；死亡谷
赫倫 1969：雷射彩印拼貼作品

Instant City - In a field Plan
Cook 1968 : Print from line drawing mounted on green board and coloured with film and felt-tip pen, in two halves butt jointed

即時城市－整個場地的配置
庫克 1968：線稿、綠版、彩色軟片、簽字筆
原作之版畫

Instant City - At Bournemouth - Exhibition Model
Cook + Crompton 1968/94

即時城市－波茅斯－展覽模型
庫克＋克藍普頓 1968/94

444

Instant City - At the Intersection of the Santa Monica & San Diego Freeways - Exhibition Model
Herron 1968/94

即時城市－聖塔蒙尼卡及聖地牙哥公路交叉口－展示模型
赫倫 1968/94

Instant City - Giant Sky Hook + Rupert IC2
Cook 1968 : Colour laser copy of collage; Colour photograph of collage

即時城市－巨大天鉤；魯伯特 IC2
庫克 1968：雷射彩印拼貼作品；彩色相片拼貼

Instant City - Airship M3
Cook 1968 : Collage of photographs and newsprint, over-drawn

即時城市－飛船 M3
庫克 1968：相片、報紙拼貼

Instant City - Airship Visits Sleeping Town, Phases 1 - 6
Cook 1968 : 3 Reversed photo-prints from ink line drawings

即時城市－飛船拜訪沈睡中的城鎮，階段1-6
庫克 1968：墨線圖翻拍

Instant City - At Night
Herron 1970 : Colour inkjet print of collage mounted on board

即時城市－夜晚
赫倫 1970：彩色噴墨列印拼貼作品、裱版

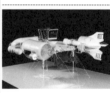

Instant City : AirShip Model Photograph
Cook Crompton Herron 1968/94 : Ink Jet print

即時城市－飛船模型照
庫克 + 克藍普頓 + 赫倫 1968/94：噴墨列印

446

Self Destruct Environ Pole - Day
+ Night versions
Herron 1969 : 2 Colour prints off
collages

自毀式圍繞桿－白天及晚上的版
本
赫倫 1969：2張彩色相片拼貼

Enviro-Pill - It's My Choice + It's
In The Mind + Holographic Set
Herron 1969 : 3 Colour Laser
prints mounted and laminated

環境－迷藥－這是我的選擇；這
是我的意志；綜合衍射圖
赫倫 1969：3幅雷射列印、薄版
裱裝版畫

Holographic Scene Setter -
Versions 1 + 2
Herron 1969 : 2 Colour Laser
prints mounted and laminated

綜合衍射圖安裝者－二種版本
赫倫 1969：2幅雷射列印、薄版
裱裝版

Info-Gonks - Collage & Portrait
(Gonks Modelled by Cook)
Cook 1968 : Collage with
newsprint, tracing paper and ink
drawing; colour photographic
print

資訊小丑－拼貼及肖像（小丑為
庫克所扮）
庫克 1968：報紙拼貼、描圖紙、
墨畫；彩照

Soft Scene Monitor: MK1 - Isometric
Crompton 1968 : Cut-out print from line drawing mounted on black card and coloured with film and collage

軟體場景顯示器：MK1－等體積
克藍普頓 1938：線圖剪裁、裱黑卡紙、軟片拼貼上色

Daily Express - Instant City and Monte Carlo
1969 : Newsprint mounted and laminated

《每日快報》－即時城市及蒙地卡羅
1969：報紙裱裝薄版

Features Monte Carlo - Hendrix Interior + Surface of Mound
Herron 1969 : Ink drawing with added collage ; Collage with newsprint , ink drawing colour film and felt-tip pen on mounting board

特色：蒙地卡羅－罕醉克斯室內表演；小丘外貌
赫倫 1969：墨水、拼貼畫；報紙拼貼、墨水畫、彩色軟片、簽字筆、裱版

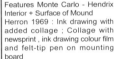

Tuned Suburb
Herron 1968 : Inkjet print from colour transparency

調頻郊區
赫倫 1968：彩色幻燈片噴墨列印

Features Monte Carlo - Site Photographs, Before and After Construction
Cook + Crompton + Herron 1969 : 1 colour print ; 3 B&W photographs with airbursh

特色：蒙地卡羅－基地照，施工前及施工後
庫克＋克藍普頓＋赫倫 1969：1張彩色版畫；3張噴槍黑白版畫

Features Monte Carlo : Land Pier
Cook + Crompton + Herron 1969
: Collage of cut-out printed material with colour film and Lettraset

特色：蒙地卡羅－陸上月台
庫克＋克藍普頓＋赫倫 1969：圖片裁剪拼貼、彩色軟片

Features Monte Carlo - Plan of Interior
Cook + Crompton + Herron 1969

特色：蒙地卡羅－室內平面圖
庫克＋克藍普頓＋赫倫 1969

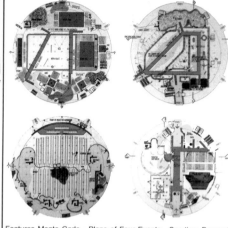

Features Monte Carlo - Plans of Four Events - Sporting, Banquet, Expo, Cultural
Cook + Crompton + Herron 1969 : 4 B&W photographic prints with applied colour film

特色：蒙地卡羅－四個事件的平面圖－運動、宴會、展覽、文化
庫克＋克藍普頓＋赫倫 1969：4幅應用彩色軟片的黑白相片版畫

Features Monte Carlo - Plage Jardin
Cook + Crompton + Herron 1969
: B&W photographic print in four parts

特色：蒙地卡羅－海濱浴場
庫克＋克藍普頓＋赫倫 1969：黑白相片版畫

Features Monte Carlo - Tables des Elements
Cook + Crompton + Herron 1969
: Ink on tracing paper

特色：蒙地卡羅－設備裝置
庫克＋克藍普頓＋赫倫 1969：墨水、描圖紙

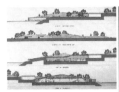

Features Monte Carlo - Two Elevations + two sections
Cook + Crompton + Herron 1969 : B&W photographic print in four parts

特色：蒙地卡羅－立面圖、剖面圖
庫克＋克藍普頓＋赫倫 1969：黑白相片版畫

Features Monte Carlo - Coupe Transverse AA + BB
Cook + Crompton + Herron 1969 : Print cut out and mounted with added collage and colour film

特色：蒙地卡羅－雙房橫向並置
庫克＋克藍普頓＋赫倫 1969：裁剪、拼貼、彩色軟片之裱裝版畫

Features Monte Carlo - Elevations Cote Mer + Princess Grace
Cook + Crompton + Herron 1969 : 4 Prints cut out and mounted with added collage, colour film, felt-tip marker and air-brush colour

特色：蒙地卡羅－海洋之棚及葛麗思王妃大道立面圖
庫克＋克藍普頓＋赫倫 1969：4 幅裁剪、拼貼、彩色軟片、簽字麥克筆、噴槍著色、裱裝的版畫

Features Monte Carlo - Exhibition Model
Cook + Crompton + Herron 1969/94

特色：蒙地卡羅－展出模型
庫克＋克藍普頓＋赫倫 1969/94

449

Features Monte Carlo - Three Events - Sporting, Expo, Banquet
Cook + Crompton + Herron 1969 : Three inkjet prints from colour transparencies

特色：蒙地卡羅－3項事件：運動、展覽、宴會
庫克＋克藍普頓＋赫倫 1969：彩色幻燈片噴墨列印版畫

Features Monte Carlo - Section through Dome
Cook + Crompton + Herron 1969 : Print cut out and mounted with added collage and colour film

特色：蒙地卡羅－圓頂剖面
庫克＋克藍普頓＋赫倫 1969：裁剪、拼貼、彩色軟片之裱裝版畫

Features Monte Carlo - Axonometric of Loby and part Interior of Dome
Cook + Crompton + Herron 1969 : Print cut out and mounted with added collage, film and air-brush colour

特色：蒙地卡羅－大廳及半球形建築物的室內部分透視圖
庫克＋克藍普頓＋赫倫 1969：裁剪、拼貼、軟片、噴槍著色、裱裝的版畫

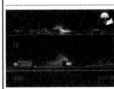

New Summer Sporting - Monte Carlo Palm Tree - Elevations
Cook + Crompton + Herron 1971 : Reversed print mounted with added collage, felt-tip marker and air-brush colour

新潮夏日活動中心－蒙地卡羅棕櫚樹－立面
庫克＋克藍普頓＋赫倫 1971：裱裝、拼貼、簽字麥克筆、噴槍著色作品之翻印

New Summer Sporting - Monte Carlo Palm Tree - Variantes La Salle Galas

Crompton + Herron : 6 Reversed prints mounted with added collage, felt-tip marker and air-brush colour

新夏日運動－蒙地卡羅棕櫚樹－宴會大廳各式變體
克藍普頓＋赫倫：裱裝、拼貼、簽字麥克筆、噴槍著色作品之翻印

New Summer Sporting - Monte Carlo Palm Tree - Salle de Jeux

Chalk + Crompton + Herron 1971 : Collage on board with newsprint, felt-tip marker and air-brush colour

新夏日運動－蒙地卡羅棕櫚樹－娛樂廳
裝克＋克藍普頓＋赫倫 1971：報紙拼貼、紙版、簽字麥克筆、噴槍著色

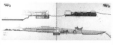

New Summer Sporting - Monte Carlo Chameleon - Coupe A-A + B-B

Cook 1971 : 4 Prints mounted on board with added felt-tip marker and air-brush colour

新夏日運動－蒙地卡羅變色龍－雙房：AA＋BB
庫克 1971：圖片裱紙版、簽字麥克筆、噴槍著色

Moment Village - Plan 'For an Instant'

Cook 1968 : Collage on board with cut-out prints, Lettraset, felt-tip marker and colour film

瞬間村落－「即時」平面圖
庫克 1968：剪裁圖片拼貼、紙版、單字、簽字麥克筆、彩色軟片

450

New Summer Sporting - Monte Carlo Palm Tree - Gala : Ambiance 29

Chalk + Crompton + Herron 1971 : Collage on board with newsprint, felt-tip marker and air-brush colour

新夏日運動－蒙地卡羅棕櫚樹－節慶：氛圍29
庫克＋克藍普頓＋赫倫 1971：報紙拼貼、紙版、簽字麥克筆、噴槍著色

New Summer Sporting - Monte Carlo Palm Tree - Gala : Ambiance 30

Chalk + Crompton + Herron 1971 : Collage on board with newsprint, felt-tip marker and air-brush colour

新夏日運動－蒙地卡羅棕櫚樹－節慶：氛圍30
裝克＋克藍普頓＋赫倫 1971：報紙拼貼、紙版、簽字麥克筆、噴槍著色

Instant Country - Makes Adelaide House

Cook 1968 : Collage of newsprint and Lettraset with annotation

即時國家－艾德蕾德住宅
庫克 1968：報紙拼貼、單字標註

Instant Village - Model photographs
Cook 1968 : 5 colour prints made from slides of model

即時村落－模型相片
庫克 1968：5幅模型彩色版畫

Nomad - Sequence
Cook 1968 : 4 colour prints made from slides of model

游牧－過程
庫克 1968：4幅模型彩色版畫

Foulness (Q.T.F.S) - Location Map
Cook 1971 : Print of map mounted on board drawn over and with added annotation and colour

「污穢」的研究－位置圖
庫克 1971：地圖加註上色裱版之版畫

Foulness (Q.T.F.S) - Settlements and Countryside
Cook 1971 : Ink drawing on tracing paper

「污穢」的研究－村落及鄉下
庫克 1971：墨水畫、描圖紙

451

155 → p452

Foulness (Q.T.F.S) - Hedgerow
Village : 8 drawings
Cook 1971 : 6 prints mounted on
card with added felt-tip pen
colour; 1 print cut out and mounted with felt-tip pen and colour
film; 1 collage with newsprint, cut-
out drawings, felt-tip pen and
colour film

「污穢」的研究－樹籬村落：8幅
畫
庫克 1971：6幅裱版、彩色簽字
筆版畫；1幅裁剪裱裝、簽字
筆、彩色軟片版畫；1張報紙拼
貼、圖片裁剪、簽字筆、彩色軟
片

452

Foulness (Q.T.F.S) - Crater City
Plan
Cook 1971 : Ink on tracing paper

「污穢」的研究－坑洞城市配置圖
庫克 1971：墨水、描圖紙

Foulness (Q.T.F.S) - Typical
Section of Crater City
Cook 1971 : Collage of drawing
and colour paper mounted on
card

「污穢」的研究－典型的坑洞城市
剖面
庫克 1971：圖畫拼貼、色紙裱卡
紙

Foulness (Q.T.F.S.) - Crater City :
Elevation/Section
Cook 1971 : 2 Prints from ink line
drawings coloured with airbrush
and felt-tip pens

「污穢」的研究－坑洞城市：立面
／剖面
庫克 1971：2幅墨線圖噴槍上
色、簽字筆之版畫

Prepared Landscape -
Axonometric
Cook 1973 : Colour laser print of
air-brushed drawing

精製景觀－立體圖
庫克 1973：雷射彩印、噴槍版畫

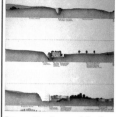

Prepared Landscape - 3 Sections
A-C
Cook 1973 : 3 Air brush and
hand coloured True To Scale
prints

精製景觀－剖面圖A-C
庫克 1973：3幅噴槍、塗手上
色、原寸版畫

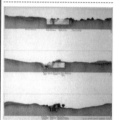

Prepared Landscape- 3 Sections
D-I
Cook 1973 : 3 Air brush and
hand coloured True To Scale
prints

精製景觀－剖面圖D-I
庫克 1973：3幅噴槍、塗手上
色、原寸版畫

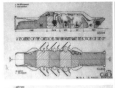

Osaka - Section BB & Ceiling Plan + Section AA & Floor Plan
Cook 1968 : 2 sheets, ink on tracing paper

大阪－BB剖面及頂篷平面；AA剖面及樓版平面
庫克 1968：墨水、描圖紙

Osaka - Ask 5 Questions
Cook 1968 : Collage, cut-out print from ink drawing with added film and felt-tip pen colour

大阪－問5個問題
庫克 1968：拼貼、墨筆畫圖片裁剪、軟片、簽字色筆

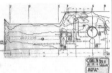

Osaka - Capsule section at Entry End + Section B-B Entry End
Cook 1968 : Collage with cut-out drawing, newsprint and added colour

大阪－艙室入口端剖面；BB入口端剖面
庫克 1968：圖片裁剪、報紙拼貼著色

Malaysia Exhibition - Axonometric
Crompton + Herron 1972 : Print of drawing with collage and colour film

馬來西亞展覽－立體圖
克藍普頓＋赫倫 1972：拼貼、彩色軟片版畫

453

Malaysia Exhibition - Cross Section + Upper Level Plan
Crompton + Herron 1972 : 2 Blue prints of drawings

馬來西亞展覽－橫剖面；上層平面圖
克藍普頓＋赫倫 1972：藍圖

Bournemouth Steps : Site Plan
Cook + Crompton + Herron 1970
: Print from original ink-line drawing with added colour film

波茅斯梯階－基地配置圖
庫克＋克藍普頓＋赫倫 1970：墨
線圖、彩色軟片

Bournemouth Development -
West Beach Pavilion Area
Cook + Crompton + Herron 1970
: Collage with cut-out drawing, segments, newsprint, colour felt-tip pen and film, and airbrush

波茅斯開發案－西向海濱大帳蓬
區
庫克＋克藍普頓＋赫倫 1970：拼
貼、裁切圖片、報紙、簽字色
筆、軟片、噴槍

Bournemouth Development -
Exhibition Models
Cook + Crompton + Herron 1970

波茅斯開發案－展示模型
庫克＋克藍普頓＋赫倫 1970

Malaysia Exhibition - Elevation
AA + Elevation CC
Crompton + Herron 1972 : 2 Blue
prints of drawings

馬來西亞展覽－立體圖
克藍普頓＋赫倫 1972：藍圖

454

Bournemouth Development -
Preliminary Sketch Plan of
Centre Area
Cook + Crompton + Herron 1970
: Ink and colour felt-tip pen on
board

波茅斯開發案－市中心初步平面
圖草圖
庫克＋克藍普頓＋赫倫 1970：上
墨、簽字色筆、紙版

Bournemouth Development - Sea
+ Pleasure Gardens Elevations
Cook + Crompton + Herron 1970
: Ink on tracing paper

波茅斯開發案－海邊：娛樂花園
立面
庫克＋克藍普頓＋赫倫 1970：描
圖紙上墨色

Bournemouth Development -
Artificial Beach
Cook + Crompton + Herron 1970
: Collage with cut-out drawing
segments, newsprint, colour felt-
tip pen and film, and airbrush

波茅斯開發案－人工海灘
庫克＋克藍普頓＋赫倫 1970：拼
貼、裁切圖片、報紙、簽字色
筆、軟片、噴槍

It's A... - Marylebone Road
Herron 1971 : Collage with cut-
out drawing, newsprint, colour
felt-tip pen and film, and airbrush

它是……－馬里波恩路
赫倫 1971：拼貼、裁切圖片、報
紙、簽字色筆、軟片、噴槍

It's A.....- Beach
Herron 1971 : Collage with cut-out drawing, newsprint, colour felt-tip pen and film, and airbrush

它是……－ 海灘
赫倫 1971：拼貼、裁切圖片、報紙、簽字色筆、軟片、噴槍

Tuning London - Sections through London Features 1
Herron 1972 : Sketches + Route Map, with text + Collage with cut-out drawing, newsprint, colour felt-tip pen and film, and airbrush

調頻倫敦－剖面圖：倫敦特色 1
赫倫 1972：素描及路線圖、文章、拼貼、裁切圖片、報紙、簽字色筆、軟片、噴槍

Tuning London - Sections through London Features 3
Herron 1972 : 3 Collages with cut-out drawing, newsprint, colour felt-tip pen and film, and airbrush

調頻倫敦－剖面圖：倫敦特色 3
赫倫 1972：素描、拼貼、裁切圖片、報紙、簽字色筆、軟片、噴槍

Soria Moria, Trondcomp - Plan + Section
Cook + Crompton + Herron 1974 : 2 sheets of ink on tracing with felt pen onerlays drawn by Cedric Price

夢之城－平、剖面圖
庫克＋克藍普頓＋赫倫 1974：描圖紙著墨、簽字筆，普萊斯繪圖

Tuning London - Oxford Street
Herron 1972 : Collage with cut-out drawing, newsprint, colour felt-tip pen and film, and airbrush; 4 mounted drawings butted as one

調頻倫敦－牛津街
赫倫 1972：拼貼、裁切圖片、報紙、簽字色筆、軟片、噴槍；4 幅裱畫接合

Tuning London - Sections through London Features 2
Herron 1972 : 3 Collages with cut-out drawing, newsprint, colour felt-tip pen and film, and airbrush

調頻倫敦－剖面圖：倫敦特色 2
赫倫 1972：拼貼、裁切圖片、報紙、簽字色筆、軟片、噴槍

Soria Moira, Trondcomp - View from Car Park
Cook + Crompton + Herron 1974 : Photomontage of ink drawing onto landscape photo with added colour

夢之城－停車場一景
庫克＋克藍普頓＋赫倫 1974：合成相片、墨水著色

Soria Moira, Trondcomp - Elevation
Cook + Crompton + Herron 1974 : print of ink on tracing drawing mounted on board and coloured with air brush and colour pens, with collage elements

夢之城－立面圖
庫克＋克藍普頓＋赫倫 1974：描圖紙、墨水、噴槍、色筆、拼貼之版畫

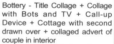

Bottery - Title Collage + Collage with Bots and TV + Call-up Device + Cottage with second drawn over + collaged advert of couple in interior
Greene 1969 : Photo collage + Newsprint with collage and drawn elements + Altered newsprint + 2 postcards with drawing + newsprint collage

設施景觀－主題拼貼；電視畫面拼貼；號令器；畫面重覆拼貼；一對在室內的夫婦拼貼作品
葛林 1969：相片拼貼；新聞畫面拼貼圖；新聞畫面變造；明信片繪圖；新聞畫面拼貼

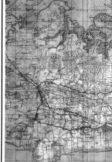

Bottery - Map of Test Area +
Collage of Sources + Landscape
collage + People on lawn
Greene 1969 : 4 items in frame :
Map with annotation + Collage of
newsprint + Landscape photo-
graph with collage items +
Photograph detail of previous

設施景觀－測試區地圖；拼貼；
景觀拼貼；草地上的人們
葛林 1969：地圖加標註；新聞畫
面拼貼；景觀照拼貼；相片

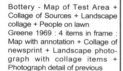

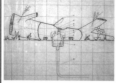

Log-Plug & Roc-Plug - Section
through Logplug
Greene 1969 : Ink on tracing
paper

石插座及木插座－石插座剖面
葛林 1969：墨水、描圖紙

Mobot - Detail Section
Greene 1969 : Print of ink on
tracing drawing

割草機－剖面細部
葛林 1969：墨水、描圖紙版畫

Log-Plug & Roc-Plug - Elevations
of Log-Plug and Details of Roc-
Plug + 3 Photographs of installations in landscapes
Greene 1969 : Ink on tracing
paper ; 3 photographic prints

石插座及木插座－石插座立面、
木插座細部；裝置於地景中的相
片
葛林 1969：墨水、描圖紙；3幅
相片版畫

Gold poster
Greene 1969 : Silk-screen print
on Gold mylar

金色的海報
葛林 1969：印在金色聚脂薄膜上
的絹版畫

457

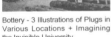

D.G. Plugs - Post card, front and back + Collage + Routcity + Memory Mindcity
Greene 1969 : 2 Photographic prints; Photo collage; 2 prints of ink line drawings on tracing film

D.G. 插座－明信片正面及背面；拼貼；驛動城市：記憶心情城市
葛林 1969：2張相片版畫；相片拼貼；2幅描圖紙著墨線版畫

Bottery - 3 Illustrations of Plugs in Various Locations + Imagining the Invisible University
Greene 1969 : 3 Photographic collages; Reversed photoprint overdrawn

設施景觀－3張設在不同地點的插座圖片；想像不可見大學
葛林 1969：3張相片拼貼；相片轉印

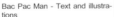

Bac Pac Man - Text and illustrations
Greene 1969 : 6 magazine pages describing project mounted on board

背箱人－文字及圖片
葛林 1969；6頁描述該設計的雜誌內頁裱裝於版上

Searching for a Perfect Location for an Architectural Suicide- 3 Photo Collages
Greene 1973/94 : 3 colour photoprints with collage

為建築自毀尋找完美的地點－3張相片拼貼
葛林 1973/94：3張彩色拼貼相片版畫

Temple Island - Section of Folly
Webb 1984 : Black and white ink and pencil on board

廟島-剖面
威柏 1984：黑白畫作、墨汁、鉛筆、紙版

459

Naked David
Greene 1973 : Xerox prints mounted on board

裸體的大衛
葛林 1973：全錄影印圖片裱版

Temple Island - Perspective Foreshortening
Webb 1984 : Air brush and Lettracolor on board

廟島-透視法縮短
威柏 1984：噴槍、紙版

Temple Island - Twenty Phases
Webb 1984 : 2 strips of photo-graphic prints

廟島-20個階段
威柏 1984：2列圖片

Resurgam - Elevation
Webb 1984 : Lettraset and air brush on board

復甦器-立面
威柏 1984：噴槍、紙版

Temple Island - Trace of course 1 + 2
Webb 1984 : Oil paint on canvas

廟島－過程追蹤1,2
威柏 1984：油畫

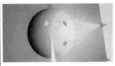

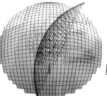

Temple Island - 3 Study sketches
Webb 1984 : Ink, pencil and air brush on board

廟島－3張草圖
威柏 1984：墨水、鉛筆、噴槍、紙版

Temple Island - Isometric of Cone of Vision
Webb 1984 : Ink wash and Pantone on mounted tracing paper

廟島－等軸錐體觀察
威柏 1984：水墨、色卡、描圖紙裝裱

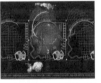

Studio Strip - Spacial Variations + Planar Shift
Herron 1986 : 2 ink jet prints

單身套房－空間變體；平行移轉
赫倫 1986：噴墨印版畫

Studio Strip - Spacially Indeterminate + Spacially Responsive
Herron 1986 : 2 ink jet prints

單身套房－空間未定性；空間回應
赫倫 1986：噴墨印版畫

Studio Strip - Variable Containment + Expand/Contract
Herron 1986 : 2 ink jet prints

單身套房－不同的涵體：擴大／收縮
赫倫 1986：噴墨印版畫

Studio Strip - Interior Collage + Computer Model
Herron 1986 : 2 ink jet prints

單身套房－室內拼貼；電腦模型
赫倫 1986：噴墨印版畫

Suburban Sets - Exhibition Model
Herron 1974/94

郊區套房－展示模型
赫倫 1974/94

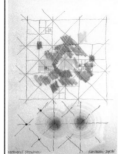

Kawasaki - Six Sketches from Notebooks
Crompton + Herron 1986 : 6 Laser prints of ink drawings with wax crayon colour and collage

川崎－6張草圖
克藍普頓＋赫倫 1986：墨筆畫、彩色蠟筆、拼貼原作之電射版畫

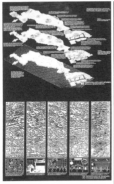

Kawasaki - Intensity Levels + Networks
Crompton + Herron 1986 : 2 Reverse photoprints of line drawings and high contrast prints with collage on mount board

川崎-密度等級及網絡
克藍普頓＋赫倫 1986：2幅墨筆畫、高反差列印、拼貼之相片翻拍版畫

Kawasaki - Outdoor Plaza
Crompton + Herron 1986 : Xerox print, ink, collage with newsprint and text on tracing paper

川崎-戶外廣場
克藍普頓＋赫倫 1986：全錄影印、墨汁、報紙文章拼貼、描圖紙

Kawasaki - Campus Festival
Crompton + Herron 1986 : Xerox print, ink, collage with newsprint and text on tracing paper

川崎-校園慶典
克藍普頓＋赫倫 1986：全錄影印、墨汁、報紙文章拼貼、描圖紙

A Genuinely Useful Arrangement - Layout of Containers in Asphalt and Sodium Light Field
CASAVERDE Greene + Holmes 1988 : Xerox print on cartridge paper with mounted Polaroid prints

真實有用的配置-柏油路及鈉光燈下的場地外觀
卡薩維吉．葛林＋福爾摩斯 1988：全錄影印、膠紙、拍立得圖片裝裱

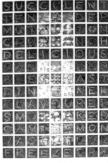

A Genuinely Useful Arrangement - Succulent Tender
CASAVERDE Greene + Holmes 1988 : Xerox print on cartridge paper with mounted Polaroid prints

真實有用的配置-多汁植栽
卡薩維吉．葛林＋福爾摩斯 1988：全錄影印、膠紙、拍立得圖片裝裱

A Genuinely Useful Arrangement - Additives Fatten
CASAVERDE Greene + Holmes
1988 : Xerox print on cartridge paper with mounted Polaroid prints

真實有用的配置－變得肥美
卡薩維吉‧葛林＋福爾摩斯
1988：全錄影印、膠紙、拍立得圖片裝裱

A Genuinely Useful Arrangement - Ice Ewe Fat
CASAVERDE Greene + Holmes
1988 : Xerox print on cartridge paper with mounted Polaroid prints

真實有用的配置－冰／母羊／肥
卡薩維吉‧葛林＋福爾摩斯
1988：全錄影印、膠紙、拍立得圖片裝裱

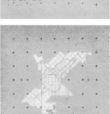

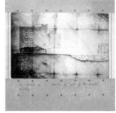

Trondheim Housing - Photograph of Model + 5 sheets of collage
Greene + Heigel 1987 : 1 Colour photoprint; 5 beige coloured boards with ink line drawings and worked over photographs

托溫翰住宅計畫－模型照；5張拼貼
葛林＋黑格爾 1977：彩色圖片；5幅灰棕色版、墨線畫、相片

463

Trondheim Library - Plan
Cook + Hawley 1977 : Print of ink line drawing mounted and hand coloured

托溫翰圖書館－配置
庫克＋賀威 1977：墨線畫版畫、手工上色

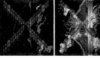

Urban Mark - As Structure + As City 1
Cook 1972 : 2 Laser prints, mounted and hand coloured with crayons

都市地標－結構：城市
庫克 1972：2張雷射版畫、蠟筆上色

Urban Mark - As City 4 + As City 5
Cook 1972 : 2 Laser prints, mounted and hand coloured with crayons

都市地標－城市4, 5
庫克 1972：2張雷射版畫、蠟筆上色

255 Solar City - Axonometric
Cook 1981 : True to Scale print, mounted and hand coloured with air brush and markers

太陽能之城－立體圖
庫克 1981：原寸版畫、噴槍、麥克筆上色

464

Trondheim Library - Elevation and Section
Cook + Hawley 1977 : Print of ink line drawing mounted and hand coloured

托溫翰圖書館－立、剖面圖
庫克＋賀威 1977：墨線畫版畫、手工上色

Urban Mark - As City 2 + As City 3
Cook 1972 : 2 Laser prints, mounted and hand coloured with crayons

都市地標－城市2, 3
庫克 1972：2張雷射版畫、蠟筆上色

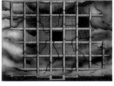

Arcadia D - Elevation and Plan
Cook 1978 : True to Scale print, mounted and hand coloured with air brush and markers

「阿卡迪亞城」D計畫－平、立面圖
庫克 1978：原寸版畫、噴槍、麥克筆上色

Oslo Towers - Daytime Elevation
Cook 1984 : Print, mounted and hand coloured with air brush and markers

奧斯陸燈塔－白天時的立面
庫克 1984：版畫、噴槍、麥克筆上色

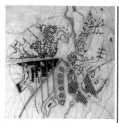

Arcadia City - City Plan
Cook 1978 : Black and red ink on tracing paper

阿卡迪亞城－城市配置圖
庫克 1978：描圖紙著黑、紅墨色

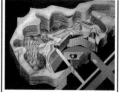

Arcadia C - Axonometric
Cook 1978 : True to Scale print, mounted and hand coloured with air brush and markers

「阿卡迪亞城」C計畫－立體圖
庫克 1978：原寸版畫、噴槍、麥克筆上色

House of Two Studios - Elevation
Cook 1981 : Pencil, ink and watercolour on art board

二個工作室的房子－立面
庫克 1981：鉛筆、墨水、水彩、銅版紙

Layer City - Various Ideas
Cook 1982 : True to Scale print, mounted and hand coloured with air brush and markers

千層市－各種構想
庫克 1982：原寸版畫、噴槍、麥克筆上色

Arcadia Town - Axonometric
Cook 1978 : True to Scale print, mounted and hand coloured with air brush and markers

阿卡迪亞城－立體圖
庫克 1978：原寸版畫、噴槍、麥克筆上色

Arcadia Town - Mesh March and Trickling Towers : Elevation
Cook 1978 : True to Scale print, mounted and hand coloured with air brush and markers

阿卡迪亞城－網狀結構發展、裝飾複雜的塔樓：立面
庫克 1978：原寸版畫、噴槍、麥克筆上色

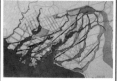

Layer City - Structure Plane
Cook 1982 : True to Scale print, mounted and hand coloured with air brush and markers

千層市－整個配置圖
庫克 1982：原寸版畫、噴槍、麥克筆上色

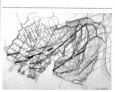

Layer City - Layer Strategy
Cook 1982 : True to Scale print, mounted and hand coloured with air brush and markers

千層市－千層策略
庫克 1982：原寸版畫、噴槍、麥克筆上色

Layer City - Outriders of the
Layer City : Elevation
Cook 1981 : True to Scale print,
mounted and hand coloured with
air brush and markers

千層市－千層市的前哨站：立面
庫克 1981：原寸版畫、噴槍、麥
克筆上色

Real City Frankfurt - Elevation
Cook 1984 : Hand coloured in ink
and water colours on art board

真實城市：法蘭克福－立面
庫克 1984：墨水、水彩、銅版紙

Real City Frankfurt - Hulk With
Slivers
Cook 1986 : True to Scale print,
mounted and hand coloured with
air brush and markers

真實城市：法蘭克福－廢墟計畫
庫克 1986：原寸版畫、、噴槍、
麥克筆上色

Real City Frankfurt -
Oberrath/Offenbach Map
Cook 1986 : True to Scale print,
mounted on board

真實城市：法蘭克福－奧伯瑞茲
／奧芬巴克地圖
庫克 1986：原寸版畫、裱版

Layer City - South East from the
Shadow House : Plan and
Elevation
Cook 1981 : Hand drawn on art
board with ink and air brush

千層市－影屋的東南向：平、立
面
庫克 1981：手繪圖、銅版紙、墨
水、噴槍

Real City Frankfurt - Flip-Flop
Skin Varient
Cook 1986 : True to Scale print,
mounted and hand coloured with
air brush and markers

真實城市：法蘭克福－變色計畫
庫克 1986：原寸版畫、、噴槍、
麥克筆上色

Real City Frankfurt - Perspective
of Out Building
Cook 1986 : Ink on tracing paper

真實城市：法蘭克福－建築外觀
庫克 1986：描圖紙、墨水

Real City Frankfurt - The Avenue
Oberrath Sud
Cook 1986 : True to Scale print,
mounted and hand coloured with
air brush and markers

真實城市：法蘭克福－南奧伯瑞
茲大道
庫克 1986：原寸版畫、裱版、噴
槍、麥克筆

Real City Frankfurt - Skyglade
Westhafen : Elevation Strik (left)
Cook 1986 : True to Scale print,
mounted on board

真實城市：法蘭克福－立面（左）
庫克 1986：原寸版畫、裱版

Real City Frankfurt - Skyglade
Westhafen : Section
Cook 1986 : True to Scale print,
mounted on board and hand
coloured with air brush and markers

真實城市：法蘭克福－剖面
庫克 1986：原寸版畫、裱版、噴
槍、麥克筆

Real City Frankfurt - Skyglade
Westhafen : Elevation Strik (right)
Cook 1986 : True to Scale print,
mounted on board

真實城市：法蘭克福－立面（右）
庫克 1986：原寸版畫、裱版

Real City Frankfurt - Skyglade
Westhafen : Plan
Cook 1986 : True to Scale print,
mounted on board

真實城市：法蘭克福－平面
庫克 1986：原寸版畫、裱版

Way Out West Berlin - Strategy
Plan + Plan Stage E
Cook 1988 : True to Scale print
hand coloured with air brush and
markers; Ink drawing on tracing
paper, colour added with crayon
and felt-tip markers

出走西柏林－策略配置圖；階段
E配置圖
庫克 1988：原寸版畫、噴槍、麥
克筆；描圖紙、墨水、蠟筆、簽
字麥克筆

Way Out West Berlin - Plans
Stages C + D
Cook 1988 : 2 ink drawings on
tracing paper, colour added with
crayon and felt-tip markers

出走西柏林－階段 C、E配置圖
庫克 1988：描圖紙、墨水、蠟
筆、簽字麥克筆

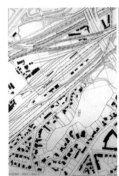

Way Out West Berlin - Section
BB at Stage F
Cook 1988 : True to Scale print
hand coloured with water colour,
air brush and markers

出走西柏林－階段F剖面
庫克 1988：原寸版畫、水彩、噴
槍、麥克筆

Way Out West Berlin - Detailed
Section at K (Early Stage)
Cook 1988 : True to Scale print
hand coloured with water colour,
air brush and markers

出走西柏林－階段K前期剖面細
部
庫克 1988：原寸版畫、水彩、噴
槍、麥克筆

Way Out West Berlin - Elevation
of Skyscraper at Stage E
Cook 1988 : True to Scale print
hand coloured with water colour,
air brush and markers

出走西柏林－階段E摩天大樓立
面
庫克 1988：原寸版畫、水彩、噴
槍、麥克筆

Way Out West Berlin - Plans
Stages A + B
Cook 1988 : 2 ink drawings on
tracing paper, colour added with
crayon and felt-tip markers

出走西柏林－階段 A、B配置圖
庫克 1988：描圖紙、墨水、蠟
筆、簽字麥克筆

Way Out West Berlin - Detailed
Section at K (Later Stage)
Cook 1988 : True to Scale print
hand coloured with water colour,
air brush and markers

出走西柏林－階段K後期剖面細
部
庫克 1988：原寸版畫、水彩、噴
槍、麥克筆

Dampstead Housing - Elevation
Cook 1992 : True to Scale print
hand coloured with pencil, crayon, water colour, air brush and
markers

丹普斯德住宅－立面
庫克 1992：原寸版畫、鉛筆、蠟
筆、水彩、噴槍、麥克筆

Art Park - Site Plan
Cook 1999 : Hand coloured negative print from original ink-line drawing

藝術公園－基地配置圖
庫克 1999：墨水畫原作、負片上色

Kunsthaus Graz - Cross Section + Plan at Street Level
Cook + Fournier 2000 - White line on black print of computer drawing

葛拉茲美術館－橫向剖面圖；街道層平面圖
庫克＋傅尼葉 2000：電腦繪圖的黑色版畫、線條為白色

Kunsthaus Graz - First floor and Gallery Level Plans
Cook + Fournier 2000 - White line on black print of computer drawing

葛拉茲美術館－第一層樓及美術館樓層平面
庫克＋傅尼葉 2000：電腦繪圖的黑色版畫、線條為白色

Kunsthaus Graz - Perspective and detail drawings
Cook + Fournier 2000 : Ink Jet print of collage of digital presentation drawings

葛拉茲美術館－長向剖面；遠景及細部圖
庫克＋傅尼葉 2000：數位圖像拼貼、噴墨列印

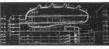

Kunsthaus Graz - Long Section + Plan at Parking Level
Cook + Fournier 2000 - White line on black print of computer drawing

葛拉茲美術館－長向剖面圖；停車場樓層平面圖
庫克＋傅尼葉 2000：電腦繪圖的黑色版畫、線條為白色

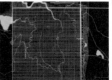

Super Houston - City Grid
Cook 2000 : Hand coloured negative print from original ink line drawing

超級休斯頓－城市網格
庫克 2000：墨水線圖原作、負片上色

Super Houston - 3 Blocks x 4 Blocks
Cook 2000 : Hand coloured negative print from original ink line drawing

超級休斯頓－3塊區塊×4塊區塊
庫克 2000：墨線圖彩色負片

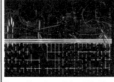

Super Houston - Edge Strip Plan 1 of 4
Cook 2000 : Hand coloured negative print from original ink line drawing

超級休斯頓－邊緣地帶平面圖1
庫克 2000：墨線圖彩色負片

Super Houston - Edge Strip Plan 3 of 4
Cook 2000 : Hand coloured negative print from original ink line drawing

超級休斯頓－邊緣地帶平面圖3
庫克 2000：墨線圖彩色負片

Super Houston - Neighbourhood Plan
Cook 2000 : Hand coloured negative print from original ink line drawing

超級休斯頓－鄰近區域配置圖
庫克 2000：墨線圖彩色負片

Super Houston - Super Block plan
Cook 2000 : Hand coloured negative print from original ink line drawing

超級休斯頓－超級區域平面圖
庫克 2000：墨線圖彩色負片

Super Houston - Edge Strip Plan 2 of 4
Cook 2000 : Hand coloured negative print from original ink line drawing

超級休斯頓－邊緣地帶平面圖2
庫克 2000：墨線圖彩色負片

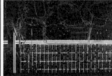

Super Houston - Edge Strip Plan 4 of 4
Cook 2000 : Hand coloured negative print from original ink line drawing

超級休斯頓－邊緣地帶平面圖4
庫克 2000：墨線圖彩色負片

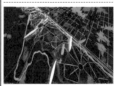

Super Houston - Aerial View
Cook 2000 : Hand coloured negative print from original ink line drawing

超級休斯頓－鳥瞰
庫克 2000：墨線圖彩色負片

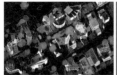

Super Houston - Houses
Cook 2000 : Hand coloured negative print from original ink line
drawing

超級休斯頓－住宅
庫克 2000：墨線圖彩色負片

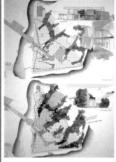

Veg-House - Stages 1 + 2
Cook 2001 : Copy of hand
coloured print off original ink-line
drawing

蔬菜屋－階段1、2
庫克 2001：墨線圖上色作品複本

Veg-House - Stages 3 + 4
Cook 2001 : Copy of hand
coloured print off original ink-line
drawing

蔬菜屋－階段3、4
庫克 2001：墨線圖上色作品複本

Veg-House - Stages 5 + 6
Cook 2001 : Copy of hand
coloured print off original ink-line
drawing

蔬菜屋－階段5、6
庫克 2001：墨線圖上色作品複本

471

The Final Avant-Garde of an Ageing Modernism?

ARCHIGRAM

Herbert Lachmayer

Philosophy can never be free of architecture. The impossibility of pure freedom, of pure positivity and thus of a radical and absolute break entails that what is at stake here is, as a consequence, precisely philosophy and architecture themselves.[1]

Andrew Benjamin

Just what was it that made Archigram so radical?

If we answer this question without nostalgia, we will be able to determine the group's place in history – and, in the process, rediscover the relevance of their architecture today.

When Archigram formed in the early 1960s, architecture was constrained not only by post-war office practices but by a Functionalism that had become dependent on the forms of the pre-war International Style. Against this, Archigram set not just a political and programmatic critique of society, but a utopian vision of an aesthetic that would permeate everyday life. Their radicalism was an explosive spawning of innovations based on the dream of a technologically accelerated industrial and consumer society. The group used subversive charm, futuristic élan, and an unbounded delight in experimentation and technical mega-fantasies to challenge national architectural conventions and wage a campaign against the tedium of the International Style. In an article entitled 'An Unaccustomed Dream', Warren Chalk wrote:

Not to worry, the artist, designer, architect, may have no relevant role in society in any accepted form, but leaping about stimulates hide-bound mentalities. Cartoons and clowns are more meaningful than the Nixons, Heaths, Germaine Greers or Frosts of this world – hollow pretentiousness for humane humility. Only more sophisticated humanity, only more sophisticated technology, working together in harmony, will help our children's children's children.[2]

Archigram tuned into the broad innovative impulses of the 1960s – advanced technology and space travel, science fiction and comics, pop culture, hallucinatory drugs and other avant-garde sub-cultures – and fused them into an architectural vision that swept aside the vocabulary of classic Modernism. They saw no sense in trying to perpetuate the 'stylistic tradition' of Modernism, no point in using it to legitimate their utopian schemes.

Our document is the Space-Comic; its reality is in the gesture, design and natural styling of hardware new to our decade – the capsule, the rocket, the bathyscope, the Zidpark, the handy-pak.

was how Peter Cook characterised the mood of the group in 'Zoom and "Real" Architecture'.[3]

The work of the time, he said, *shared much of its expression with those dim, neurotic, enthusiastic days of the Ring,*

Der Sturm, and the Futurist Manifesto – the architectural weirdies of the time feeding the infant Modern Movement.[4]

By making a clean break with tradition, Archigram proved to be a *modern* avant-garde. Unlike the later Post-Modernists, they did not distance themselves aesthetically from Modernism. In Post-Modernism, innovation came to mean simply quoting architectural styles. The whole of architectural history could be turned into an ironic game, and the full spectrum of styles and symbolic forms homogenised into a single style. Archigram's critique of Modernism, on the other hand, was a splintered gesture – reflecting the patchwork of society itself.

The spectacular innovations in technology during the 1960s were for Archigram not just a means to realise projects, but one of their most potent sources of inspiration. Their anticipation of future technology was both serious and fantastical. They wanted the technological utopias of a 'Second Machine Age' (Reyner Banham) to enrich the architecture of the future:

Is it possible for the space comic's future to relate once again to buildings-as-built? Can the near-reality of the rocket-object and hovercraft-object, which are virtually ceasing to be cartoons, carry the dynamic (but also non-cartoon) building with them into life as it is? [5]

Archigram envisaged a society in which technology would allow the harmonious integration of all facets of life – work, consumerism, opportunities for pleasure and happiness. Rather than fetishise technology, however, they transformed it into fictions. Archigram was a *profane* avant-garde movement.

Today, when we have moved beyond the 'First Machine Age' into an Information Society, that faith in the power of technology to bring progress seems at best naive. We have become aware of the threats posed by technology to both the environment and our jobs. As technology has become more of an end in itself, it has tended to make people passive, dependent as individuals on the apparatus of anonymous organisational structures. This can be seen in the massive bureaucratisation of the working environment and of people's private lives. The primary role of technology in everyday culture has become questionable, as people still seem to yearn for traditional symbols of individual and collective values. Social progress has not kept pace with technological progress. There have been no sweeping advances to give meaning to the new forms of communication and interaction between people, but at best partial reforms and the kind of increased awareness we see in some 'alternative' groups. Whereas we are cautious or pessimistic, a whole generation of young people in the 1960s were decidedly optimistic, buoyed by pop art and a pleasure-oriented, anti-authoritarian counter-culture. Cornelius Costariadis' escapist vision, 'My boots are made for walking, why shouldn't my cities be too', could have been the slogan for all the media-generated sub-cultures of the time – as well as the starting point for any number of Archigram projects.

For the student movements of the 1960s, anti-authoritarianism meant 'dropping out' and destructive critiques of state capitalism and the social and cultural establishment. For Archigram, provocation was second nature (in the great British tradition of the 'Goons' and, later, pop culture), and their critique of society was practical yet radical. They proposed a 'democratic emancipated capitalism', directed towards a humane working environment, pleasure-oriented consumption, and the pursuit of individual happiness. Henri Lefebvre's 'Critique of Everyday Life' was given a coating of pop culture. The editorial of Archigram 8 read:

The history of the last 100 years has been one of continued emancipation, irrevocably moving forwards despite the immense obvious setbacks of war and poverty, and the more hidden ones sustained by facets of culture and tradition that seek to preserve as much as possible in the face of social change. We are nearing the time when we can all realise our aspirations. It is too simple to see this merely as the amassing of objects, but they represent pretty accurately the direction outwards that our mental environment can reach: to the furthest imaginable limits. This is the crux of the matter: in the past the indulgence of the mind and intellect (as applied to artefacts) was the privilege of the rich.

If architecture laid claims for human sustenance, it should surely have responded as human experience expanded. For architects the question is: do buildings help towards emancipation of people within? Or do they hinder because they solidify the way of life preferred by the architect? It is now reasonable to treat buildings as consumer products, and the real justification of consumer products is that they are the direct expression of a freedom to choose.[6]

In Archigram's vision of an evolving world, social progress went hand in hand with an enthusiasm for the wonders of technology. There was no conflict between technology and the right of every individual – or society – to pursue happiness. Together, consumerism and technology could help to satisfy desires and needs, giving people the means to act on their imagination and shape their own lives. Some critics charged that Archigram's schemes ignored the needs of the people who were supposed to live in them. Warren Chalk replied:

One of the most flagrant misconceptions held about us is that we are not ultimately concerned with people. This probably arises directly from the type of imagery we use. A section through, say, something like City Interchange, appears to predict some automated wasteland inhabited only by computers and robots. How much this is justified is difficult to assess, but if our work is studied closely there will be found traces of a very real concern for people and the way in which they might be liberated from the restrictions imposed on them by the existing chaotic situation, in the home, at work, and in the total built environment.[7]

Chalk's article defined the new freedom that technology could bring:

In a technological society more people will play an active part in determining their own individual environment, in self-determining a way of life. We cannot expect to take this fundamental right out of their hands and go on treating them as cultural and creative morons.[8]

He continued:

The techniques of mass-production and automation are a reality, yet we see the research that goes into, and the products that come out of, today's building and are dis-mayed. The Plug-in Capsule attempts to set new standards and find an appropriate image for an assembly-line prod-uct.[9]

Archigram's capsules were shells for the people or social organisms that inhabited them – in contrast to the Austrian avant-garde architects of the time, who defined architec-ture as an artificial second skin, a literal and metaphorical extension of the human body, reflecting its authenticity, sen-sitivity, vulnerablility. (See the early projects of Hans Hollein, Walter Pichler, Raimund Abraham, 'Haus-Rucker-Co', Coop Himmelblau and Günther Domenig.)[10] These ideas ulti-mately concealed a *static* conception of architectural space. Archigram, on the other hand, thought in terms of flexible and dynamic structures which were designed to be inter-changeable and mobile. Their capsules were 'machines for living in' for individuals in a state of *acceleration*.

Like the Futurists, the members of Archigram were fasci-nated by the aesthetic potential of technology. Their imagi-nations were stimulated by the fantasies of science fiction and comics, as described by Peter Cook, in the editorial to Archigram 4:

One of the greatest weaknesses of our immediate urban architecture is the inability to contain the fast-moving object as part of the total aesthetic – but the comic imagery has always been strongest here. The representa-tion of movement-objects and movement-containers is con-sistent with the rest, and not only because 'speed' is the main gesture.

The positive quality that the rocket (both actual and repre-sented), the Futurist scribble and the space-city share is their ultimateness – which has most significance as a coun-terweight to so-called 'real' architecture. We connect this

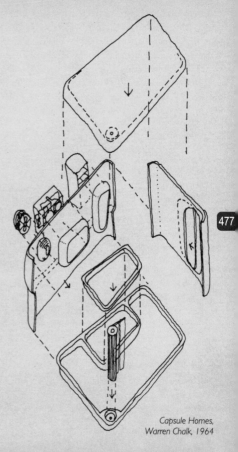

Capsule Homes,
Warren Chalk, 1964

material with serious projects for making living space, entertainment space – and the city, in the context of the near future.[11]

However it would be misleading to say that Archigram idealised or fetishised technology. The article on hardware and software in Archigram 8 reveals a tempered view:

Systems are not a panacea. They have a necessary place in the evolution of intelligence. They will take short cuts towards solving problems. The Plug-in City needed the Computer City as its shadow, otherwise it could not function. The Control-and-Choice discussion revolved around the potential of the unseen microswitches and sensors, but more than this: these devices would need the intelligence of a computed relay of information so that they came into your service at the moment when you needed them.[12]

Archigram's designs combined the abstract rationality of technological systems with the sensuous of symbolic images. But during this time, the relationship between technology and architecture looked increasingly fraught. Reyner Banham described the situation in this way:

It may well be that what we have hitherto understood as architecture, and what we are beginning to understand of technology are incompatible disciplines. The architect who proposes to run with technology knows now that he will be in fast company, and that, in order to keep up, he may have to emulate the Futurists and discard his whole cultural load, including the professional garments by which he is recognised as an architect. If, on the other hand, he decides not to do this, he may find that a technological culture has decided to go on without him.[13]

In rejecting the principles of the Futurists, the International Style had driven itself into a dead-end. Its desire for perfection and prestige had given rise to a closed ideology – and the endless repetition of standard 'quasi-rationalist' formulae, as Reyner Banham made clear:

In cutting themselves off from the philosophical aspects of Futurism, though hoping to retain its prestige as Machine Age art, theorists and designers of the waning Twenties cut themselves off not only from their own historical beginnings, but also from their foothold in the world of technology, whose character Fuller defined, and rightly, as an

. . . unhaltable trend to constantly accelerating change

a trend that the Futurists had fully appreciated before him. But the mainstream of the Modern Movement had begun to lose sight of this aspect of technology very early in the Twenties, as can be seen (a) from their choice of symbolic forms and symbolic mental processes, and (b) their use of the theory of types. The apparent appositeness of the Phileban solids as symbols of mechanistic appropriateness depended in part on an historical coincidence affecting vehicle technology that was fully, though superficially, exploited by Le Corbusier in Vers une Architecture, and partly on a mystique of mathematics. In picking on mathematics as a source of technological

Villa Rosa, Coop Himmelblau, 1968

prestige for their own mental operations, men like Le Corbusier and Mondrian contrived to pick on the only important part of scientific and technological methodology that was not new, but had been equally current in the pre-machine epoch.[14]

Archigram was not prepared to consign Modernism to history, as a ritualised aesthetic (that would be the preserve of the Post-Modernists). But equally, they were not prepared to perpetuate its totalitarian aspirations to uniformity. Modernism's unrelenting desire for innovation had led it to dismiss all traditional values, giving rise to a new form of compulsion – the belief that it represented the only valid course for architecture. Functionalist premises pushed out all alternatives – Futurism, Expressionism and Constructivism. No deviation was allowed to pass unpunished. In the words of the German cultural philosopher Wolfgang Welsch, 'Functionalism became the uniform style of modern civilisation all the world over.'[15] Welsch has pointed out the paradox of the inherent conservatism of this would-be radical movement:

The dilemma lies in the fact that the primacy of function is bound to lead to diminished responsibility. One has either to permit a higher degree of freedom, with more possibilities for variation, as was Mies's way. Or else one is to be a consistent Functionalist, working on the premise that there is a mechanism not just behind the processes of work but the processes of life itself. In this case, whenever the premises turn out to be unworkable – which is practically all the time – there is no alternative but to plan the processes exactly; in other words, to programme them. The architect is tailoring suits for new men. The coda of this Functionalism is no longer 'form follows function' but 'life follows architecture.'[16]

Julius Posener also wrote about the rigidity of Functionalism:

Sullivan spoke of the high-rise's 'magnificence' as a function – of an 'unmistakable voice of feeling'. This was not 'function' as Häring understood it. Häring's Functionalism of 1925 went too far in claiming that form did not need to be invented, but merely found – that form was determined by function. We need only look at Häring's famous cowshed in Garkau (his own model example of this theory) to see that this was not the case.[17]

Of Le Corbusier, Posener said: *Anyone who builds for the people of tomorrow is building for no-one.*[18] This was how emancipators turned into dictators, as people in Europe realised even before the war. The Berlin critic Adolf Behne said it all in 1930:

The advocates of row housing would like to make it the cure for all ailments, and no doubt they have people's best interests at heart. But the fact is that to them 'people' are merely a concept. They think people only have to live in their houses in order to become well and they dictate how they should live down to every last detail.[19]

After the International Style became established in the US, American experts, including Frank Lloyd Wright, also spoke of the 'totalitarianism' of the new style. Functionalism's aspirations to autocracy contained the seeds of formalism. The German architect Hannes Meyer recognised this danger in 1929, when he said: *We despise any form which prostitutes itself as a formula.*[20]

For Wolfgang Welsch, the essential merit of Post-Modernism is that it did away with the uniformity of Functionalism. He wrote:

Jacques Derrida took one of the oldest stories in architecture, the one about the Tower of Babel, as a metaphor for the current conflict between hegemony and pluralism, i.e. between Modernism and Post-Modernism.[21] *Modernism set about rebuilding the Tower, trying to establish a single uniform language that would dominate everything. Its dream was to abolish diversity. But the dream has been shattered; the variety of languages has reasserted itself. Now we see that truth lies in diversity – which only a blinkered striving for uniformity could dismiss as 'confusion'. It is not just that diversity cannot be controlled – it is the urge to control that is wrong. The dream of uniformity is hubris, less to the gods than to humanity in its myriad forms. But – and here I would go further than Derrida – the real problem is dismissing this obsession with uniformity, and recognising that what looks like medicine is in fact poison.*[22]

In Welsch's view, Post-Modernism should be recognised as the movement which deposed the elite absolutism of Modernism and, through its diversity, gave populist levellers the opportunity to build. Of course, had Archigram been in charge, the Tower would have been a walkway – all on one level.

Were Archigram the representatives of a 'trans-Futurism', with their all-out quest for universalism, their utopian schemes for architecture and life? Or was Post-Modernism already crystallising in the richness of their symbolism and architectural language, and in their space comic populism? In other words, were Archigram the apotheosis of a technology-obsessed 'trans- or ultra-Modernism', or were they the start of Post-Modernism?

I think it is important, at this point, to remember that Archigram did not see themselves primarily as a new style or approach to construction within the mainstream of architectural history.

Up to the period of Archigram 3 (1963) the experiments discussed in the magazine and designed by the group made direct conversation with the tradition of modern architecture. This conversation took the form of either suggesting replacements for earlier models of useful building, or of deliberately flying in the face of a known position by suggesting its inefficiencies. During the period of Archigram 3 the range of these conversations widened so that the throwaway architecture and the plug-in kits would be added to the rest of the vocabulary.

Gradually the Archigram party began to set up its own motion and generated further departures from mainstream vocabulary. What is much more important is the way in which the middle period experiments of the Plug-in City, the capsules and the Walking City created values that replaced almost a total range of modern architectural values. From 1965 onwards, the discussions were sufficiently removed to gain a certain freedom and coolness. It began to be less necessary for the criteria of a project to respond to any architectural morality and the projects themselves began to form a natural generic series.[23]

What was avant-garde about Archigram was their experimental approach to complex problems. They did not necessarily look for an architectural solution in the accepted sense of the word. Peter Cook and Ron Herron's maxim to their students at the Architectural Association was: *When you are looking for a solution to what you are told is an architectural problem – remember it may not be a building.*[24] Rather than develop a system to be applied across the board, they would keep all opportunity for experiment open, and first make a transitory change that allowed them to look more closely at the complex issues to be resolved. Ron Herron described this process in a text on the 'Walking City':

This is the value of the half-step in relation to any near absolute that is being thought of. Once one has an open-ended system with one experiment at one scale and with one degree of technology or organisational anticipation, it can be seen as affecting the whole range of other experiments. The half-step living capsule can be seen as the prototype for a generation of capsules gradually evolving until the term and definition of capsule is irrelevant to the developed hybrid. At the same time this can be seen in relation to an urban philosophy (at a practical, infill level as well as at a problem-solving level) and this urban development is only part of a continuing process in which the urban model itself will disappear into something else.[25]

The emphasis was on designing for urban life as an organised whole, but there was no prevailing architectural style or principle of construction. Instead, the complexity of life in a technology-dominated society was reflected in architectural forms and solutions that remained symbolically ambiguous.

A hybrid that is sometimes machine, sometimes architecture, sometimes animal-like growth, sometimes electrical circuitry, sometimes part of a mathematical progression and sometimes completely random.[26]

Archigram's pluralistic forms ranged from the collaged symbolism of the advertising world to spaceship-like cities, robot metaphors and quasi-organic urban landscapes. These were not eclectic, decorative design elements, but rather attempts to find symbolic forms of expression appropriate to the times, reflecting an understanding of individual (human) and collective (social) issues. In insisting on experimentation, the group increasingly became a kind of creative channel through which ideas 'flowed' and manifested themselves in an outpouring of design and thought.

The gesture of translating events from a formal limitation to a mechanised liberation began to be symbolic more than directly necessary. Perhaps some necessary conflict between gestures and the great desire to manifest : to build : to experiment.

The experiments were beginning to burst the seams of architectural response but at the same time the examples began to fall into two categories: the ultimate stage and the half-step. In a way it was very useful to play the two against each other, and later we began to find that the continuing process of metamorphosis brings both together again as merely stages in a continually evolving state of parts and functions.

Physically, too, the objects seemed to be bursting their seams. In the Living Pod, what is basically a capsule has satellite parts working inside it, but these themselves can also travel outside. In the Mobile Village, an organism is at once building and vehicle, small and large, tightly-knit and extended. The Auto-Environment develops from an organisation of panels and surfaces into a continuous system of parts of very varied kinds, the only link being the intention to widen the performance of the home. The discussion of house and car as interrelated is a necessary response to the planning problem of what to do with cars, but at the same time it questions the need for fixed places at all. And parallel to this burst is all the time a feeling, backed up by the newspapers and one's own observations, that the world is beginning to evolve quite complex environments without the need for architects or respect for architectural interaction. One feels carried along by history.[27]

Here Archigram seemed to be paraphrasing Heidegger's reading of Hölderlin: 'Man lives poetically'.

Quite apart from their innovative and visionary conception of architecture, what makes Archigram important even today is that they revolutionised the design process and presentation of architectural ideas: they also had the ability to pass on their creative inspiration to others. The sweep of their imagination allowed them to do away with conventional working methods. They took their inspiration not only from the art world but from the so-called 'trivial' art of comics, advertising images, the aesthetics of everyday consumer goods and space travel, futuristic urban utopias and experimental engineering – to reiterate only the most important themes. Their aim was not to make an original mix of diverse elements, but to change architectural thinking, to challenge accepted judgements and values in general.

Most cultured designers have been bred to regard one state of organisation against another in terms of prefer-ence. Even non-formally, there are arrangements that are 'good' and 'bad'. Religion, formula, idea, thesis, antithesis – all force one towards stating a fixed preference: a stated state. If we really believe in change, it will be a change in what we believe in, rather than a change in the means towards a different ideal. Growth itself has a dynamic and becomes a useful objective because it is the natural analogue of change. Now the analogy must be widened so that all parts are in an evolutionary state.

This business of widening range has taken us through some weird territory; it means that most of the projects we make are hybrid in content as well as notion. They themselves are in a constant change of state, assembly, and value.[28]

There were some parallels, both conscious and unconscious, in the art world, as the same ideas developed around the same time – from the Land Art of Robert Smithson, to the work of Eduardo Paolozzi, or Richard Hamilton, or the Art & Language group, amongst others.

Archigram's anarchistic, inter-disciplinary approach produced a synergy of the different stimuli fuelling their imaginations and drove their creativity towards a universal vision for survival.

Architecture is probably a hoax, a fantasy world brought about through a desire to locate, absorb and integrate into an overall obsession a self-interpretation of the everyday world around us. An impossible attempt to rationalise the irrational. It is difficult to be exact about influences, but those influences that enter our unconscious consciousness are what I call 'ghosts'.

We are confronted with a dynamic shifting pattern of events at both popular and intellectual levels, both simulating and confusing. In this ever-changing climate, old ghosts may be cast out and replaced by new; it is right that influences should last only as long as they are useful to us, and our architecture should reflect this. At a general level it is becoming increasingly apparent that due to historical circumstances the more tangible ghosts of the past — those grim, humourless, static, literary or visual images — will succumb to the onslaught of the invisible media, the psychedelic vision; the insight accompanying a joke; the phantoms of the future.[29]

The result of this approach was the highly suggestive imagery of projects such as 'Walking City', 'Living Pod', 'Blow-Out Village' and 'Plug-in City'. To progressive architects all over the world during the 1960s, Archigram acted like a beacon, reaffirming the purpose of their own work and giving them the strength to 'stay the course'. They sent out a signal which spoke of a revolutionary vision, a utopian atmosphere and an uncompromising, pleasure-seeking approach to life.

Also revolutionary was the group's cooperative method of working, which ran against the traditional hierarchical division of labour within architectural practices and left no room for ego-trips by isolated heroic 'geniuses'. Together, this group of highly individualistic people of varying educational backgrounds and experience (see the biographies at the back of this catalogue) turned their backs on the idea of a career in a conventional London practice and used their collective imagination on projects which rebelled against the monotony of office life and standard architecture.

These distinct individuals developed a dynamic 'communal sense' of productivity; their combined talents gave new meaning to collective imagination and creativity. They were what the Maoist Lyotard, a decade later, would have called 'a patchwork of minorities'. Amazed by the fact that their communal 'mega-fantasies' worked so well, they saw the clear benefits of not competing with each other as individual 'creative egos' (in keeping with the general mood of the 1960s). Instead, they worked together to achieve a kind of 'utopian transcendence of the self'. In this, Archigram embodied one of the traits of the 'old' Modernist avant-garde. Their sensitivity and ability to communicate and cooperate also made them committed teachers. As a group, they trained a number of world-class architects at the Architectural Association and elsewhere.

Archigram's work represented a 'total existential experiment' against established architectural conventions; they were not looking for some group-dynamic recipe to improve the efficiency of market-oriented offices. Their irrepressible collective imagination allowed them to maintain a vision in face of the world, and to assert a utopia that would find confirmation in history itself. The impact of Archigram's projects on like-minded people stemmed, to a great extent, from the precision with which they brought the 'phantom' of the future into the present. As an avant-garde movement, they generated a creative acceleration, which hot-wired a present bound by tradition and convention into the future. In their work also, there was an area of interplay between the concept and the obsession, between dream and reality:

There then emerges a stage where the notions themselves can be taken outside the description of a single design or proposition, and read against several. They can be detected in some ideas, and come through fiercely in others. We have eight notions that are still unanswered by any complete set of experiments though we have begun the series. They are dreams because we keep returning to them. They are dreams because they may never be completely satisfied by what a designer or a strategist or any operator can do. They are open-ended, and, whatever we are doing by the time that you are reading this, may in some way have sprung out of a dream or two.[30]

What is characteristic – and perhaps peculiarly English – about Archigram's utopias is that the individual always holds sway over the anonymous 'superstructure': the individual's rights to freedom and personal happiness are paramount. Archigram's futuristic cities are stripped of all vernacular cultural traditions, in order to create an internationalism that would transcend all boundaries.

Another Archigram idea reminiscent of Futurism was 'nomadism':

This could be the most upsetting idea since it is close to the instincts of many people who like to be thought of as steady guys: those who rely upon being able to plug into a known network, who demand of life a continuity. It is these who are nearest the edge of escaping from it all. The car is useful for the game of freedom. The implication that the whole surface of the world can give equal service is possibly pointing to the time when we can all be nomads if we wish. At the same time the network of support (even if 'soft' – like radio) is still there to be escaped from.

At the moment the situation is open-ended. This is the attraction of the car-as-satellite-of-the-pad. Next the car becomes its own pad. Next the pad itself takes on the role of car. It divides and regroups. So too could larger combinations of environment. The status of the family and its direct connotation with a preferred, static house, cannot last. What about the evidence of the Teenybopper family-within-the-family? Multiplication and proliferation (and a dynamic use of mass availables) could lead to breakaway and re-group as naturally as the traditional strict hierarchies. Time is a factor. Coming together and independence are compatible if we use time.

The moment-village is a project suggested by this development out of nomadism. Its group-regroup-shift impli-

NeoBabylone, Constant Niewenhuis, 1962-63

cation suggests that its ultimate might be an anarchy-city or that the concept of 'place' exists only in the mind.[31]

The idea of nomadism can also be linked – obliquely – to the theory of the *dérive* formulated by the Situationist International in the late 1950s. The Situationist Guy Debord described the experience of metropolitan architecture in these terms:

Among the various situationist methods is the dérive [literally: 'drifting'], a technique of transient passage through varied ambiances. The dérive entails playful-constructive behavior and awareness of psycho-geographical effects, which completely distinguishes it from the classical notions of the journey and the stroll ... The element of chance is less determinant than one might think: from the dérive point of view cities have a psychogeographical relief, with constant currents, fixed points and vortexes which strongly discourage entry into or exit from certain zones... Today the different unities of atmosphere and of dwellings are not precisely marked off, but are surrounded by more or less extended and indistinct bordering regions. The most general change that the dérive leads to proposing is the constant diminution of these border regions, up to the point of their com-

plete suppression. Within architecture itself, the taste for dériving tends to promote all sorts of new forms of labyrinths made possible by modern techniques of construction.[32]

The idea of the dérive combines a breaking away from the conventional constraints on life with an unleashing of the imagination. The desired result is a 'natural' (anarchistic) community of free individuals; the means to achieve it, flexible structures designed using the most advanced technology of the time. In a text entitled 'Another City for Another Life', the Situationist Constant wrote:

The crisis of urbanism is becoming worse all the time. The buildings in old and new districts no longer correspond to traditional patterns of behaviour, even less to the new forms of living that we are seeking. This is the root cause of the clouded and unfruitful atmosphere of our surroundings ... We are on the way to finding a new technology; we are examining the possibilities offered by existing cities in order to produce models and plans for future cities. We are aware of the need to use all technological innovations and we know that the structures we propose for the future will have to be flexible to fit in with a dynamic attitude towards life ... Though the project we have outlined might be condemned by some as a fantastic dream, we would like to emphasise that it is feasible from a technical point of view, desirable from a human point of view, and inevitable from a social point of view.[33]

Coming back, finally, to the question of whether Archigram were Modernists or the precursors of Post-Modernism, we can say that as a group, they showed some of the unmistakable characteristics of a classic avant-garde – a radical approach, and a utopian vision relatively untainted by the ironic, aesthetic distancing from Modernism that became characteristic of Post-Modernism. As one of the last avant-garde groups, Archigram laid claim to the true spirit of Modernism, as opposed to the imitation of it that prevailed at the time. This was not an historicist gesture but a sovereign act of self-definition which proclaimed: *from now on* – in other words, *since we came into being*. This might be seen as naive – Modernism, as it aged and became melancholic, reflected with irony and scepticism on the historical process (as Post-Modernism later proved). Archigram, however, had not yet recognised this 'ageing Modernism' as part of an historical continuum, but had insisted on an avant-garde 'discontinuity'. By daring to go against the 'self-styled' formal conventions of Functionalist Modernism, Archigram managed to synthesise and synchronise divergent architectural periods and cultures, and infuse their projects with a populist everyday aesthetics and advanced technology that captured the essence of their time. Their authentic relationship to Modernism is invoked, unequivocally, in a poem by David Greene:

A new generation of architecture must arise with forms and spaces which seems to reject the precepts of 'Modern' yet in fact retains these precepts.

WE HAVE CHOSEN TO BYPASS THE DECAYING BAUHAUS IMAGE WHICH IS AN INSULT TO FUNCTIONALISM.[34]

NOTES

1 Andrew Benjamin, 'Art, Mimesis and the Avant-Garde', London 1991, p. 107.

2 Warren Chalk, 'An Unaccustomed Dream', Archigram 4, 1964.

3 In Archigram 4, 1964.

4 ibid.

5 ibid.

6 In Archigram 8, 1968.

7 Warren Chalk, 'Housing as a Consumer Product', formed part of the editorial of Archigram 3, 1963. It was first published in Arena, the Journal of the Architectural Association.

8 ibid.

9 ibid.

10 This interpretation arose from a discussion between the author and Georg Schoelhammer.

11 In Archigram 4, 1964.

12 In Archigram 8, 1968.

13 Reyner Banham, Theory and Design in the First Machine Age, London, 1960, pp. 329-30

14 ibid., p. 327-8

15 Wolfgang Welsch, Unsere postmoderne Moderne, Weinheim, 1991, p. 93. Cf. also in this respect Rosalind Krauss, The Originality of the Avant-Garde and other Modernist Myths, Cambridge, Mass., 1986.

16 Wolfgang Welsch, op. cit. p. 95.

17 Julius Posener, 'Die moderne Architektur – eine lange Geschichte', in Vision der Moderne, Heinrich Klotz (ed.), Munich, 1986, p. 30.

18 Julius Posener, foreword to Otto Wagner – Möbel und Innenräume, Salzburg, 1984, p. 4.

19 Wolfgang Welsch, op. cit. p. 96.

20 Rainer Wick, Bauhaus-Pädagogik, Cologne, 1982, p. 46.

21 Jacques Derrida and Eva Meyer, 'Labyrinth und Archi/Textur', in Das Abenteuer der Ideen – Architektur und Philosophie seit der industriellen Revolution, catalogue, Berlin, 1984, p. 95ff.

22 Wolfgang Welsch, op. cit. p. 114.

23 Ron Herron, 'Walking City', in Archigram, (edited by the members of Archigram), London, 1972, p. 50f.

24 As reported in Vision der Moderne, op. cit. p. 316.

25 Ron Herron, op. cit. pp. 50-1.

26 ibid., p. 51.

27 ibid., p. 50.

28 In Archigram 8, 1968.

29 Warren Chalk, ''Letter to David Greene: Ghosts', 1966, in Archigram, op. cit. note 23, p. 85.

30 In Archigram 8, 1968

31 ibid.

32 Guy Debord, 'Theory of the Dérive' in the Situationist International Anthology (edited and translated by Ken Knabb), Berkeley, Ca. 1981, pp. 50 and 53. The author is grateful to Andreas Puff-Trojan for pointing out this connection.

33 Constant, 'Another City for Another Life', published in German in Situationistische Internationale 1959-1969, Hamburg, 1976, pp. 112-5.

34 David Greene, poem published in Archigram 1, 1961.